Regulatory Autonomy in International Economic Law

ELGAR INTERNATIONAL INVESTMENT LAW

Series Editors: Andrea K. Bjorklund, *McGill University, Montreal, Quebec, Canada* and August Reinisch, *University of Vienna, Austria*

This monograph series provides a point of convergence for authoritative, original works focused specifically on international investment law in all its forms. Works will be single or co-authored, theoretically rigorous and analytically precise, often considering the intersection of investment law with other fields of law such as trade, intellectual property, environment or public international law. The series will comprise works from established authors as well as from younger scholars whose work is genuinely innovative and challenging. Proposals are encouraged that primarily engage with new and previously underdeveloped themes in the field, draw on other disciplines in order to further thinking in the field, or alternatively attempt to offer a definitive statement on areas of uncertainty in the existing law.

The development of original thinking in international investment law and research of the highest quality is the main emphasis of the series. Both international and comparative in its approach, it aims to include some of the best theoretical and empirical work from both well-established researchers and the next generation of scholars.

Titles in this series include:

International Investment Law and the Environment
Saverio Di Benedetto

Intellectual Property Rights as Foreign Direct Investments
From Collision to Collaboration
Lukas Vanhonnaeker

Performance Requirements and Investment Incentives Under International Economic Law
David Collins

The ASEAN Comprehensive Investment Agreement
The Regionalisation of Laws and Policy on Foreign Investment
Julien Chaisse and Sufian Jusoh

Non-Discrimination and the Role of Regulatory Purpose in International Trade and Investment Law
Andrew D. Mitchell, David Heaton and Caroline Henckels

Regulatory Autonomy in International Economic Law
The Evolution of Australian Policy on Trade and Investment
Andrew D. Mitchell, Elizabeth Sheargold and Tania Voon

Regulatory Autonomy in International Economic Law

The Evolution of Australian Policy on Trade and Investment

Andrew D. Mitchell

Melbourne Law School, University of Melbourne, Australia

Elizabeth Sheargold

Melbourne Law School, University of Melbourne, Australia

Tania Voon

Melbourne Law School, University of Melbourne, Australia

ELGAR INTERNATIONAL INVESTMENT LAW

Edward Elgar PUBLISHING

Cheltenham, UK • Northampton, MA, USA

Published by
Edward Elgar Publishing Limited
The Lypiatts
15 Lansdown Road
Cheltenham
Glos GL50 2JA
UK

Edward Elgar Publishing, Inc.
William Pratt House
9 Dewey Court
Northampton
Massachusetts 01060
USA

A catalogue record for this book
is available from the British Library

Library of Congress Control Number: 2017947089

This book is available electronically in the **Elgar**online
Law subject collection
DOI 10.4337/9781785368172

FSC www.fsc.org MIX Paper from responsible sources FSC® C013056

ISBN 978 1 78536 816 5 (cased)
ISBN 978 1 78536 817 2 (eBook)

Typeset by Columns Design XML Ltd, Reading
Printed and bound in Great Britain by TJ International Ltd, Padstow

For our parents: Sandy and Wayne, Chris and Marie,
Betsy and Chester

Contents

Tables

About the Authors

Andrew D. Mitchell is Professor at Melbourne Law School, Australian Research Council Future Fellow, and Director of the Global Economic Law Network. He has previously practised law with Allens Arthur Robinson (now Allens Linklaters) and consults for States, international organisations and the private sector. Andrew has taught law in Australia, Canada, Singapore, and the US and is the recipient of four major grants from the Australian Research Council and the Australian National Preventive Health Agency. He has published over 130 academic books and journal articles and is an Editorial Board Member of the *Journal of International Economic Law* and a General Editor of the *Journal of International Dispute Settlement.* He has held visiting positions at the British Institute of International and Comparative Law, the Lauterpacht Research Centre for International Law at the University of Cambridge, the Jean Monnet Center at NYU School of Law, the Institute of International Economic Law at Georgetown University, and PluriCourts at the University of Oslo. Andrew has law degrees from Melbourne, Harvard and Cambridge and is a Barrister and Solicitor of the Supreme Court of Victoria.

Elizabeth Sheargold is PhD candidate with the Global Economic Law Network at Melbourne Law School, Australia and a Legal Adviser at the Iran–United States Claims Tribunal in The Hague, the Netherlands. Her PhD research considers the relationship between international trade and investment agreements and domestic regulation for public purposes, such as the protection of human health or the environment. Previously, she worked in the Melbourne office of law firm Allens Arthur Robinson (now Allens Linklaters), as Associate Director of the Center for Climate Change Law at Columbia University in New York, and as a research fellow and sessional lecturer at Melbourne Law School. She completed her undergraduate studies at the University of Melbourne, and her Master of Laws at Columbia University.

Tania Voon is Professor at Melbourne Law School and was Associate Dean (Research) from 2012 to 2014. She is a former Legal Officer of the WTO Appellate Body Secretariat and has previously practised law with

Mallesons Stephen Jaques (now King & Wood Mallesons) and the Australian Government Solicitor and taught law at the National University of Singapore, Georgetown University, the University of Western Ontario, the University of British Columbia, and several Australian universities. Tania undertook her Master of Laws at Harvard Law School and her PhD in law at the University of Cambridge. She is the author of *Cultural Products and the World Trade Organization* (Cambridge University Press, 2007), editor of *Trade Liberalisation and International Co-operation: A Legal Analysis of the Trans-Pacific Partnership Agreement* (Edward Elgar, 2013), and co-editor of the *International Economic Law Series* of Oxford University Press. Tania is a member of the Roster of Panelists for the Energy Charter Treaty and of the Indicative List of Governmental and Non-Governmental Panelists for resolving WTO disputes.

Acknowledgments

This book was written with generous funding from the Australian Research Council pursuant to the Discovery Project scheme for the project *Revisiting Australia's preferential trade agreements and bilateral investment treaties to safeguard regulatory autonomy* (DP130100838). Much of the work was conducted at the University of Cambridge, where Andrew and Tania were hosted in 2016 by the Lauterpacht Centre for International Law and Clare Hall. The Faculty of Law at the University of Cambridge also provided assistance to Tania through the Herbert Smith Freehills Visitor Scheme. Melbourne Law School at the University of Melbourne fully supported this project, including through the Office for Research, the Academic Research Service, the Law Library, the Melbourne Collaborative Project Fund, and the Research Support Funds available to higher degree research candidates.

By way of disclosure, Andrew is a member of the Australian government's Expert Advisory Group for Plain Packaging of Tobacco Products (an honorary position). He and Tania are also the recipients of two major grants (from the Australian Research Council and the Australian National Preventive Health Agency) to conduct independent research in collaboration with the McCabe Centre for Law and Cancer (a joint initiative of Cancer Council Victoria and the Union for International Cancer Control) on the interaction of international economic law with the regulation of common risk factors for non-communicable diseases including tobacco, alcohol and unhealthy diet.

For helpful comments on our research leading to this volume we thank the participants in events at which we presented parts of this research, including at the Attorney-General's Department of the Commonwealth of Australia (Office of International Law, November 2013), the Finance Canada Legal Retreat (Ottawa, July 2014), the Joint Asian International Economic Law Conference (Bali, July 2015), Sydney Law School (Australian and New Zealand Society of International Law and Korean Society of International Law, December 2015), the University of Oslo (PluriCourts, September 2015 and August 2016), Melbourne Law School (Global Economic Law Network, November 2015 and May 2016), Clayton Utz (Brisbane, March 2016), the Chinese University of Hong

Kong (May 2016 and November 2016), the University of New South Wales (China International Business and Economic Law, June 2016 and April 2017), the Australian National University (Australian and New Zealand Society of International Law Annual Conference, June 2016), the University of Witwatersrand, Johannesburg (Society of International Economic Law, July 2016), and Georgetown University (International Economic Law Interest Group, American Society of International Law, September 2016).

Parts of Chapter 3 first appeared as Tania Voon, 'Balancing Regulatory Autonomy with Liberalisation of Trade in Services: An Analytical Assessment of Australia's Obligations under Preferential Trade Agreements' (2017) 18(2) *Melbourne Journal of International Law*.

We are grateful to the many experts who kindly read drafts of our work and shared their insights, including Rudolf Adlung, Andrew Christie, Peter Gallagher, Jarrod Hepburn, James Munro, Luke Nottage, Sam Ricketson, and Matthew Rimmer. We also benefited from valuable research and editorial assistance from Luisa Borg, Philip Hainbach, Ridhi Kabra, Pei Xuan Liu, Neha Mishra, and Ana María Palacio Valencia. Any views expressed here are our own and do not necessarily represent those of any employer or other entity. Any errors are also ours.

Finally, we thank our families for their ongoing caring and patience.

Andrew D. Mitchell
Elizabeth Sheargold
Tania Voon
18 April 2017

Abbreviations

ALRC	Australian Law Reform Commission
ASEAN	Association of Southeast Asian Nations
BIT	bilateral investment treaty
CSL	CSL Ltd (formerly Commonwealth Serum Laboratories)
DFAT	Department of Foreign Affairs and Trade, Commonwealth of Australia
DSB	Dispute Settlement Body of the WTO
EGA	Environmental Goods Agreement
EPA	Environmental Protection Agency
EU	European Union
FDI	foreign direct investment
FET	fair and equitable treatment
FIRB	Foreign Investment Review Board of Australia
FTA	free trade agreement
ICSID	International Centre for Settlement of Investment Disputes
ICSID Additional Facility Rules	Rules governing the Additional Facility for the Administration of Proceedings by the Secretariat of the International Centre for Settlement of Investment Disputes, effective 10 April 2006
IIA	international investment agreement
IMF	International Monetary Fund
IP	intellectual property
ISDS	investor–State dispute settlement
JSCOT	Joint Standing Committee on Treaties of the Parliament of the Commonwealth of Australia
MAI	multilateral agreement on investment
MEA	multilateral environmental agreement

MFN	most-favoured nation
MTBE	methyl tertiary butyl ether
NCM	non-conforming measure
NGO	non-governmental organisation
OECD	Organisation for Economic Co-operation and Development
PBS	Pharmaceutical Benefits Scheme
PCB	polychlorinated biphenyl
PTA	preferential trade agreement
RCEP	Regional Comprehensive Economic Partnership Agreement
SPS	sanitary and phytosanitary
TBT	technical barriers to trade
TiSA	Trade in Services Agreement
TPM	technological protection measure
TPP	Trans-Pacific Partnership
TTIP	Transatlantic Trade and Investment Partnership
UK	United Kingdom
UN	United Nations
UNCITRAL	United Nations Commission on International Trade Law
UNCITRAL Arbitration Rules	UNCITRAL Arbitration Rules adopted in 1976, revised in 2010, and further revised in 2013
UNCITRAL Transparency Rules	UNCITRAL Rules on Transparency in Treaty-based Investor-State Arbitration, incorporated in the UNCITRAL Arbitration Rules as adopted in 2013
UNCTAD	United Nations Conference on Trade and Development
US	United States of America
USTR	United States Trade Representative
WIPO	World Intellectual Property Organization
WTO	World Trade Organization

Table of Cases

INVESTOR–STATE ARBITRATIONS

WTO CASES

Short title	**Full citation**
Appellate Body Report, *Argentina – Financial Services*	Appellate Body Report, *Argentina – Measures Relating to Trade in Goods and Services*, WTO Doc WT/DS453/AB/R (circulated 14 April 2016, adopted 9 May 2016) … 113, 207
Appellate Body Report, *Australia – Apples*	Appellate Body Report, *Australia – Measures Affecting the Importation of Apples from New Zealand*, WTO Doc WT/DS367/AB/R (circulated 29 November 2010, adopted 17 December 2010) … 142, 200, 201
Panel Report, *Australia – Automotive Leather II*	Panel Report, *Australia – Subsidies Provided to Producers and Exporters of Automotive Leather*, WTO Doc WT/DS126/R (circulated 25 May 1999, adopted 16 June 1999) … 141
Appellate Body Report, *Australia – Salmon*	Appellate Body Report, *Australia – Measures Affecting Importation of Salmon*, WTO Doc WT/DS18/AB/R (circulated 20 October 1998, adopted 6 November 1998) … 141, 20
Panel Report, *Brazil – Retreaded Tyres*	Panel Report, *Brazil – Measures Affecting Imports of Retreaded Tyres*, WTO Doc WT/DS332/AB/R (circulated 12 June 2007, adopted 17 December 2007) … 229
Appellate Body Report, *Brazil – Retreaded Tyres*	Appellate Body Report, *Brazil – Measures Affecting Imports of Retreaded Tyres*, WTO Doc WT/DS332/AB/R (circulated 3 December 2007, adopted 17 December 2007) … 158, 160, 200, 228, 234
Panel Report, *Canada – Pharmaceutical Patents*	Panel Report, *Canada – Patent Protection of Pharmaceutical Products*, WTO Doc WT/DS114/R (circulated 17 March 2000, adopted 7 April 2000) … 72
Appellate Body Report, *China – Publications and Audiovisual Products*	Appellate Body Report, *China – Measures Affecting Trading Rights and Distribution Services for Certain Publications and Audiovisual Entertainment Products*, WTO Doc WT/DS363/AB/R (circulated 21 December 2009, adopted 19 January 2010) … 93
Panel Reports, *China – Rare Earths*	Panel Reports, *China – Measures Related to the Exportation of Rare Earths, Tungsten, and Molybdenum*, WTO Docs WT/DS431/R, WT/DS432/R, WT/DS433/R (circulated 26 March 2014, adopted 29 August 2014) … 230

Appellate Body Report, *US – Carbon Steel*	Appellate Body Report, *United States – Countervailing Duties on Certain Corrosion-Resistant Carbon Steel Flat Products from Germany*, WTO Doc WT/DS213/AB/R (circulated 28 November 2002, adopted 19 December 2002) ... 41
Appellate Body Report, *US – Clove Cigarettes*	Appellate Body Report, *United States – Measures Affecting the Production and Sale of Clove Cigarettes*, WTO Doc WT/DS406/AB/R (circulated 4 April 2012, adopted 24 April 2012) ... 32, 113, 207
Appellate Body Report, *US – COOL (Article 21.5 – Canada and Mexico)*	Appellate Body Reports, *United States – Certain Country of Origin Labelling (COOL) Requirements – Recourse to Article 21.5 of the DSU by Canada and Mexico*, WTO Docs WT/DS384/AB/RW, WT/DS386/AB/RW (circulated 18 May 2015, adopted 29 May 2015) ... 159
Appellate Body Report, *US – Gambling*	Appellate Body Report, *United States – Measures Affecting the Cross-Border Supply of Gambling and Betting Services*, WTO Doc WT/DS285/AB/R (circulated 7 April 2005, adopted 20 April 2005) ... 160
Panel Report, *US – Gasoline*	Panel Report, *United States – Standards for Reformulated and Conventional Gasoline*, WTO Doc WT/DS2/R (circulated 29 January 1996, adopted 20 May 1996) ... 230
Appellate Body Report, *US – Gasoline*	Appellate Body Report, *United States – Standards for Reformulated and Conventional Gasoline*, WTO Doc WT/DS2/AB/R (circulated 29 April 1996, adopted 20 May 1996) ... 41, 200, 228, 230, 234
Panel Report, *US – Section 110(5) Copyright Act*	Panel Report, *United States – Section 110(5) of the US Copyright Act*, WTO Doc WT/DS160/R (circulated 15 June 2000, adopted 27 July 2000) ... 50
Appellate Body Report, *US – Shrimp*	Appellate Body Report, *United States – Import Prohibition of Certain Shrimp and Shrimp Products*, WTO Doc WT/DS58/AB/R (circulated 12 October 1998, adopted 6 November 1998) ... 158, 200, 231, 234
Appellate Body Report, *US – Tuna II (Mexico)*	Appellate Body Report, *United States – Measures Concerning the Importation, Marketing and Sale of Tuna and Tuna Products*, WTO Doc WT/DS381/AB/R (circulated 16 May 2012, adopted 13 June 2012) ... 32, 200

Table of Treaties

PREFERENTIAL TRADE AGREEMENTS

Short title	Full citation
AANZFTA	*Agreement Establishing the ASEAN–Australia–New Zealand Free Trade Area*, signed 27 February 2009 (entered into force 1 January 2010), as amended by the *First Protocol to Amend the Agreement Establishing the ASEAN–Australia–New Zealand Free Trade Area*, signed 26 August 2014 (entered into force 1 October 2015) … 8, 27, 29, 41, 42, 45, 56, 57, 69, 84, 85, 87, 88, 89, 91, 92, 95, 96, 97, 98, 99, 103, 104, 111, 112, 114, 115, 116, 118, 127, 129, 132, 142, 144, 145, 146, 147, 148, 150, 153, 156, 157, 162, 169, 171, 172, 175, 176, 182, 183, 184, 185, 189, 197, 201, 206, 228, 231, 232, 233
ACIFTA	*Australia–Chile Free Trade Agreement*, signed 30 July 2008 (entered into force 6 March 2009) … 8, 27, 28, 30, 40, 45, 47, 56, 65, 66, 69, 75, 84, 85, 87, 88, 89, 92, 96, 97, 98, 99, 105, 107, 109, 110, 111, 114, 115, 123, 126, 127, 129, 132, 142, 144, 145, 146, 147, 150, 153, 154, 157, 158, 165, 172, 175, 176, 182, 183, 184, 185, 189, 193, 201, 206, 228, 229, 231, 232, 233, 246, 251
ANZCERTA	*Australia–New Zealand Closer Economic Relations Trade Agreement*, signed 28 March 1983 (entered into force 1 January 1983) … 3, 14, 15, 16, 17–22, 35, 38, 45, 65, 69, 83, 89, 145, 171, 172, 201, 228
ANZCERTA Investment Protocol	*Protocol on Investment to the Australia–New Zealand Closer Economic Relations Trade Agreement*, signed 16 February 2011 (entered into force 3 January 2013) … 19, 35, 126, 127, 129, 141, 142, 145, 146, 150, 153, 154, 157, 158, 159, 172, 173, 197, 206, 229, 230, 231, 233, 234, 235, 236
ANZCERTA Protocol on Acceleration of Free Trade in Goods	*Protocol to the Australia–New Zealand Closer Economic Relations Trade Agreement on Acceleration of Free Trade in Goods,* signed 18 August 1988 (entered into force 18 August 1988) … 19

KAFTA — *Korea-Australia Free Trade Agreement*, signed 8 April 2014 (entered into force 12 December 2014) … 8, 35, 40, 45, 47, 55, 58, 65, 66, 69, 75, 84, 85, 87, 88, 89, 92, 96, 97, 98, 99, 105, 107, 108, 109, 110, 111, 114, 115, 126, 127, 128, 129, 130, 132, 142, 144, 145, 146, 147, 148, 150, 151, 153, 154, 155, 157, 158, 161, 172, 177, 178, 182, 183, 184, 185, 188, 190, 191, 193, 197, 201, 202, 206, 228, 229, 231, 232, 233, 237, 238, 239, 240, 246

MAFTA — *Malaysia–Australia Free Trade Agreement*, signed 22 May 2012 (entered into force 1 January 2013) … 8, 35, 45, 56, 57, 66, 69, 75, 84, 85, 87, 88, 89, 91, 92, 95, 96, 97, 98, 99, 103, 104, 110, 111, 114, 115, 116, 126, 127, 129, 132, 142, 144, 145, 146, 147, 148, 159, 153, 154, 156, 157, 162, 172, 177, 201, 206, 228, 230, 231, 232, 233, 238

NAFTA — *North American Free Trade Agreement*, signed 17 December 1992 (entered into force 1 January 1994) … 29, 31, 39, 87, 131–6, 201, 203–27, 236, 243, 244, 251, 256, 257

SAFTA — *Singapore–Australia Free Trade Agreement*, signed 17 February 2003 (entered into force 28 July 2003), as amended from 24 February 2006, 13 February 2007, 11 October 2007 and 2 September 2011 and (not yet in force) 13 October 2016 … 3, 8, 26, 27, 28, 29, 30, 35, 36, 45, 47, 55, 68, 69, 83, 84, 85, 87, 88, 89, 91, 92, 96, 97, 98, 99, 100, 104, 105, 107, 108, 109, 110, 111, 113, 114, 115, 117, 122, 127, 128, 129, 130, 131, 132, 138, 139, 142, 143, 144, 145, 146, 147, 148, 149, 150, 151, 152, 153, 154, 155, 156, 157, 159, 162, 172, 173, 174, 175, 176, 178, 182, 183, 184, 185, 189, 191, 193, 194, 195, 196, 201, 205, 206, 207, 226, 228, 229, 231, 232, 233, 234, 251

TAFTA — *Australia–Thailand Free Trade Agreement*, signed 5 July 2004 (entered into force 1 January 2005) … 8, 27, 28, 41, 45, 68, 69, 84, 85, 87, 88, 89, 92, 95, 96, 97, 98, 99, 103, 104, 110, 111, 113, 114, 126, 127, 129, 132, 142, 143, 153, 154, 156, 157, 172, 175, 176, 182, 183, 184, 185, 189, 201, 205, 206, 228, 231, 232, 233

TPP — *Trans-Pacific Partnership*, text released following legal review 26 January 2016, signed 4 February 2016 (not in force) … 1, 6, 8, 13, 34, 35, 36, 37, 38, 40, 41, 42, 43, 44, 45, 46, 47, 48, 49, 50, 51, 54, 55, 56, 65, 66, 68, 69–75, 77, 79, 80, 83, 84, 85, 87, 88, 89, 91, 92, 96, 97, 98, 99, 100, 104, 105, 107, 108, 109, 110, 111, 113, 114, 115, 116, 117, 120, 122, 126, 127, 128, 129, 130, 132, 138, 139, 142, 143, 144, 145, 146, 147, 148, 149, 150, 151, 152, 153, 154, 155, 157, 158, 159, 163, 170, 171, 173, 180, 181, 182, 183, 184, 185, 189, 191, 193, 194, 195, 197, 198, 201, 202, 206, 207, 226, 228, 229, 231, 232, 233, 234, 237, 238, 239, 240, 245, 246, 247, 251, 252, 254, 255

BILATERAL INVESTMENT TREATIES

Australia–Hong Kong BIT	*Agreement between the Government of Hong Kong and the Government of Australia for the Promotion and Protection of Investments*, 15 September 1993 (entered into force 15 October 1993) … 17, 32, 63, 123, 131, 137, 164, 206
Australia–Hungary BIT	*Agreement between Australia and the Republic of Hungary on the Reciprocal Promotion and Protection of Investments*, signed 15 August 1991 (entered into force 10 May 1992) … 17, 131, 205
Australia–India BIT	*Agreement between the Government of Australia and the Government of the Republic of India on the Promotion and Protection of Investments*, signed 26 February 1999 (entered into force 4 May 2000, unilaterally terminated by India as of 23 March 2017) … 17, 123, 131, 155, 165, 170, 171, 228
Australia–Indonesia BIT	*Agreement between the Government of Australia and the Government of the Republic of Indonesia concerning the Promotion and Protection of Investments*, signed 17 November 1992 (entered into force 29 July 1993) … 17, 131, 165, 167, 168, 169, 170, 205
Australia–Lao PDR BIT	*Agreement between Australia and the Lao People's Democratic Republic on the Reciprocal Promotion and Protection of Investments*, signed 6 April 1994 (entered into force 8 April 1995) … 16, 17, 205
Australia–Lithuania BIT	*Agreement between the Government of the Republic of Lithuania and the Government of Australia on the Promotion and Protection of Investments*, signed 24 November 1998 (entered into force 10 May 2002 … 17, 205
Australia-Mexico BIT	*Agreement between the Government of Australia and the Government of the United Mexican States on the Promotion and Reciprocal Protection of Investments*, signed 23 August 2005 (entered into force 21 July 2007) … 10, 27, 125, 132, 206
Australia-Pakistan BIT	*Agreement between the Islamic Republic of Pakistan and Australia on the Promotion and Protection of Investments*, signed 7 February 1998 (entered into force 14 October 1998) … 16, 17, 170, 205
Australia-Papua New Guinea BIT	*Agreement between the Government of Australia and the Government of the Independent State of Papua New Guinea for the Promotion and Protection of Investments*, signed 3 September 1990 (entered into force 20 October 1991) … 17, 124, 131, 135, 205
Australia-Peru BIT	*Agreement between Australia and the Government of the Republic of Peru on the Promotion and Protection of Investments* signed 7 December 1995 (entered into force 2 February 1997) … 17, 206

Australia-Philippines BIT	*Agreement between the Government of Australia and the Government of the Republic of the Philippines on the Promotion and Protection of Investments, and Protocol*, signed 25 January 1995 (entered into force 8 December 1995) … 17, 131, 205
Australia-Poland BIT	*Agreement between Australia and the Republic of Poland on the Reciprocal Promotion and Protection of Investments*, signed 7 May 1991 (entered into force 27 March 1992) … 17, 131, 135, 137, 205
Australia-Romania BIT	*Agreement between the Government of Australia and the Government of Romania on the Reciprocal Promotion and Protection of Investments*, signed 21 June 1993 (entered into force 22 April 1994) … 17, 205
Australia-Sri Lanka BIT	*Agreement between the Government of Australia and the Government of the Democratic Socialist Republic of Sri Lanka for the Promotion and Protection of Investments*, signed 12 November 2002 (entered into force 14 March 2007) … 17, 132, 206
Australia-Turkey BIT	*Agreement between the Republic of Turkey and Australia on the Reciprocal Promotion and Protection of Investments*, signed 16 June 2005 (29 June 2009) … 27, 125, 126, 132, 206
Australia-Uruguay BIT	*Agreement between Australia and Uruguay on the Promotion and Protection of Investments*, signed 3 September 2001 (entered into force 12 December 2002) … 17, 205
Australia-Viet Nam BIT	*Agreement between Australia and the Socialist Republic of Vietnam on the Reciprocal Promotion and Protection of Investments*, signed 5 March 1991 (entered into force 11 September 1991) … 17, 123, 131, 205
Chile-Spain BIT	*Agreement between Chile and Spain for the Promotion and Reciprocal Protection of Investments*, signed 2 October 1991 (entered into force 28 March 1994) … 127
France Model BIT (2006)	Draft Agreement between the Government of the Republic of France and the Government of the Republic of ___ on the Reciprocal Promotion and Protection of Investments … 136
Germany–Pakistan BIT	*Treaty between the Federal Republic of Germany and Pakistan for the Promotion and Protection of Investments*, signed 25 November 1959 (entered into force 28 April 1962) … 22
India Model BIT (2015)	Model Text for the Indian Bilateral Investment Treaty: Bilateral Investment Treaty between the Government of the Republic of India and ___ (December 2015) … 140, 150, 155, 164, 256

GATT/WTO AGREEMENTS

TBT Agreement	*Marrakesh Agreement Establishing the World Trade Organization*, opened for signature 15 April 1994, 1867 UNTS 3 (entered into force 1 January 1995) annex 1A ('*Agreement on Technical Barriers to Trade*') ... 99, 100, 101, 112, 113, 159, 200, 207, 232, 250
TRIMS Agreement	*Marrakesh Agreement Establishing the World Trade Organization*, opened for signature 15 April 1994, 1867 UNTS 3 (entered into force 1 January 1995) annex 1A ('*Agreement on Trade-Related Investment Measures*') ... 90, 91
TRIPS Agreement	*Marrakesh Agreement Establishing the World Trade Organization*, opened for signature 15 April 1994, 1867 UNTS 3 (entered into force 1 January 1995) annex 1C ('*Agreement on Trade-Related Aspects of Intellectual Property Rights*') ... 40, 41, 42, 43, 44, 45, 46, 47, 50, 51–5, 60, 61, 62, 65, 66–75, 76, 77, 79, 80, 142, 143, 144, 145, 154, 250

OTHER TREATIES

Short title	**Full citation**
Aarhus Protocol	*Protocol to the 1979 Convention on Long-Range Transboundary Air Pollution on Persistent Organic Pollutants*, opened for signature 24 June 1998, 2230 UNTS 79 (entered into force 23 October 2003) ... 214
Berne Convention (1971)	*Paris Act Relating to the Berne Convention for the Protection of Literary and Artistic Works*, opened for signature 24 July 1971, 1161 UNTS 30 (entered into force 10 October 1974) ... 45, 46, 54
CITES	*Convention on International Trade in Endangered Species of Wild Fauna and Flora*, opened for signature 3 March 1973, 993 UNTS 243 (entered into force 1 July 1975) ... 240
ICSID Convention	*Convention on the Settlement of Investment Disputes between States and Nationals of Other States*, opened for signature 18 March 1965, 575 UNTS 159 (entered into force 14 October 1966) ... 2, 12, 165, 166, 167, 169, 170, 171, 172, 173, 242
MARPOL	*International Convention for the Prevention of Pollution from Ships*, opened for signature 2 November 1973, 1340 UNTS 184 (entered into force 2 October 1983) ... 240
Mauritius Convention	*United Nations Convention on Transparency in Treaty-Based Investor-State Arbitration*, opened for signature 17 March 2015 (entry into force 18 October 2017) ... 148, 186, 187, 188, 197, 248

Montreal Protocol	*Montreal Protocol on Substances that Deplete the Ozone Layer*, opened for signature 16 September 1987, 1522 UNTS 28 (entered into force 1 January 1989) … 240
Stockholm Convention	*Stockholm Convention on Persistent Organic Pollutants*, opened for signature 22 May 2001, 2256 UNTS 119 (entered into force 17 May 2004) … 214
VCLT	*Vienna Convention on the Law of Treaties*, opened for signature 22 May 1969, 1155 UNTS 331 (entered into force 27 January 1980) … 41, 53, 55, 159, 161, 168, 179, 249, 250
WHO FCTC	*WHO Framework Convention on Tobacco Control*, opened for signature 16 June 2003, 2302 UNTS 166 (entered into force 27 February 2005) … 59

1. Regulatory Autonomy and the Evolution of Australia's Participation in PTAs and BITs

I INTRODUCTION

In just over 30 years, from 1983 through to 2015, Australia entered into 21 BITs and 10 PTAs.[1] The enthusiasm of successive Australian governments for these bilateral and regional economic agreements continues, with the TPP having been signed by 12 Pacific-rim countries including the US, Japan, Chile and Malaysia in February 2016 (although the US has now withdrawn from that agreement)[2] and more PTAs under negotiation. These include: the RCEP being negotiated among the ten ASEAN member States and those countries with PTAs with ASEAN (Australia, China, India, Japan, the Republic of Korea, and New Zealand); separate bilateral PTAs with India, Indonesia and the EU; the TiSA being negotiated outside the WTO to enhance liberalisation of trade in services among 23 WTO Members including the EU representing its 28 Member States (with negotiations led by the US, the EU and Australia); and the EGA being negotiated by representatives of 43 WTO Members to reduce tariffs on environmentally friendly goods.[3] Yet both concluded agreements and ongoing negotiations have met with varying levels of controversy in Australia. Apart from the fear that bilateral and regional negotiations may distract from multilateral efforts to liberalise trade, one

[1] See Tables 1.1, 1.2 and 1.3 below.

[2] Letter from Maria L Pagan, Acting USTR, to the Trans-Pacific Partnership Depositary (30 January 2017).

[3] See generally DFAT, *Status of FTA Negotiations* <http://dfat.gov.au/trade/agreements/Pages/status-of-fta-negotiations.aspx> (last visited 7 April 2017). DFAT announced on 24 April 2017 the commencement of negotiations with Hong Kong towards a PTA.

of the major sources of concern has been the perceived threat posed by PTAs and BITs to Australia's sovereignty and 'regulatory autonomy'.[4]

In the context of international economic law, regulatory autonomy and policy space refer to the ability of a State to determine its regulatory goals (such as the protection of public health or the conservation of natural resources) and to adopt and implement policies to pursue those goals. Growing concerns about regulatory autonomy reflect a shift in the focus of international economic law, from overt barriers to trade (such as quotas on the importation of particular products, tariffs or customs duties imposed on imports as they cross the border, and trade remedies such as anti-dumping duties), to more subtle 'behind the border' measures that may reduce competitive opportunities for imports or infringe the rights of foreign investors. These measures may include registration or licensing requirements for service suppliers, health and safety standards for products, environmental standards applied to investments, and a vast range of other regulatory measures. For example, the PTA concluded between Australia and the US in 2004 (the AUSFTA) faced considerable backlash within the Australian community, centred on fears that the agreement could require significant changes to Australia's intellectual property laws,[5] undermine public health initiatives (particularly access to affordable medicines through Australia's established system for subsidising pharmaceuticals: the PBS),[6] and threaten policies promoting local media content.[7]

This book provides the first extended legal analysis of how Australia's current framework of PTAs and BITs affects Australia's regulatory autonomy. This analysis offers lessons for not only Australia but also other countries engaged in international trade and investment and attempting to improve the legal framework for these activities, including the 164 Members of the WTO and the 153 contracting States of the ICSID Convention. Investigating one country's treaties allows us to examine in depth the causes and implications of particular national

---

[4] The concept of 'regulatory autonomy' is defined more fully below in part II.

[5] Robert Burrell and Kimberlee Weatherall, 'Exporting Controversy? Reactions to the Copyright Provisions of the US–Australia Free Trade Agreement: Lessons for US Trade Policy' [2008] *University of Illinois Journal of Law, Technology and Policy* 259.

[6] Evidence to JSCOT, Canberra (3 May 2004) (Dr Mukesh Haikerwal, Vice-President of the Australian Medical Association).

[7] Ann Capling, *All the Way with the USA: Australia, the US and Free Trade* (University of New South Wales Press, 2005).

strategies in trade and investment rather than drawing broad generalisations from the experiences of a wider range of countries. We focus on four key disciplines within Australia's PTAs and BITs—intellectual property rights, trade in services, standards for the protection of foreign investors, and their enforcement through ISDS—and then examine the impact of these agreements on regulating to protect the environment as a case study of a specific policy area. Before moving into this discussion, however, we need to locate Australia's PTAs and BITs in their political, social and economic context. This chapter provides this context.

In part II of this chapter we seek to define regulatory autonomy and its relationship with international economic law for the purposes of this book, turning in part III to offer further relevant background and details about the scope of agreements addressed and terminology used in this volume. We go on in parts IV to VI to analyse Australia's modern international economic agreements, which we group into three generations. The first and longest of these generations spans from the early 1980s through to the early 2000s, including almost all of Australia's BITs and its most deeply integrated PTA: the 1983 ANZCERTA. The second generation begins in 2003 with the conclusion of the SAFTA and includes many of Australia's PTAs and a few remaining BITs. The third generation of agreements are those concluded after 2010. In November 2010, the Australian Government's Productivity Commission issued an influential report evaluating the benefits of Australia's bilateral and regional trade agreements, covering both trade liberalisation and investment protection. Despite the reservations of the Productivity Commission about the benefits of PTAs, the conclusion of several significant PTAs after 2010 demonstrates the Australian government's continued interest in these agreements, although the content of these most recent treaties reflects greater public scrutiny and concern about the impact of international economic agreements on regulatory autonomy. Concluding in part VII of this chapter, we elaborate on the purpose and structure of the rest of the book.

II DEFINING 'REGULATORY AUTONOMY' AND ITS CONSTRAINTS

A The Development of International Economic Law as a Constraint on Autonomy

Traditionally, the regulation of domestic industry and economic activity has been the prerogative of the State, governed primarily by domestic rather than international law. At its broadest level, regulatory autonomy may refer to the whole universe of areas in which a government might choose to act, whether for economic or non-economic objectives. Deciding to nationalise an industry, impose tariffs on particular imports, ban a carcinogenic substance, or impose environmental labelling standards would all fall within this broad notion of regulatory autonomy. Until the mid-20th century, the regulatory space available to States was 'almost unlimited'.[8]

However, the very purpose of agreements regulating international trade or foreign investment, particularly as they began to emerge more prominently after World War II, was to constrain States' use of certain regulatory and policy tools, in order to pursue broader welfare objectives at national and international levels. The GATT 1947 restricted the use of various trade-related measures, including tariffs and non-tariff barriers such as 'quantitative restrictions' on imports.[9] In addition to these rules targeting import restrictions, the GATT 1947 included more general obligations not to discriminate against imported products. These obligations extended to the use of internal taxes or charges, or any other 'laws, regulations and requirements affecting their internal sale, offering for sale, purchase, transportation, distribution or use'.[10] In this way, the multilateral trade disciplines of the GATT regime began to impose constraints on States' use of measures that may not have appeared to be directly related to trade. Similarly, the BITs and other agreements relating to international investment that began to proliferate in the 1950s and 1960s imposed requirements on governments regarding a wide range of domestic regulatory and administrative actions. Given their historical context, in which capital-exporting States were seeking protection for their nationals investing in developing countries, these agreements were often designed to 'avoid under-inclusiveness' through the use of broadly framed obligations.[11]

To say that international economic law—as contained especially in the multilateral rules of the WTO (which entered into being in 1995 as the successor to the GATT 1947), and bilateral or regional PTAs and BITs—imposes limitations or constraints on regulatory autonomy is

---

8 Markus Wagner, 'Regulatory Space in International Trade Law and International Investment Law' (2014) 36(1) *University of Pennsylvania Journal of International Law* 1, 4.

9 See, eg, GATT 1947 arts II, XI.

10 GATT 1947 arts III:2, III:4. See also GATT 1947 art I:1.

11 Caroline Henckels, 'Protecting Regulatory Autonomy through Greater Precision in Investment Treaties: The TPP, CETA, and TTIP' (2016) 19(1) *Journal of International Economic Law* 27, 31–32.

neither profound nor necessarily a criticism. It could be said that the very purpose of these agreements is to constrain regulatory autonomy, in order to prevent governments from acting in a 'protectionist' manner (that is, to protect their domestic industries) or infringing on the rights of foreign investors. As Natens says of multilateral or preferential agreements to liberalise trade:

> As with all international obligations, this necessarily implies a loss of regulatory autonomy: by agreeing to be bound by certain obligations, a domestic regulator may no longer adopt regulations which violate these international obligations.[12]

Nevertheless, as the scope of domestic measures that may be subject to trade and investment rules has expanded, questions about the encroachment of international economic law into States' regulatory space have become both more frequent and more intense. Community concerns about these agreements have been particularly strong in relation to regulations that are not, on their face, concerned with international trade or foreign investment, instead pursuing some other public purpose.

In the early years of the GATT 1947, the GATT contracting parties retained significant regulatory autonomy, particularly with regard to elements of public welfare such as health, safety, and the natural environment.[13] But with the gradual reduction of tariffs and quantitative restrictions on trade, focus shifted to measures enacted behind the border that affect the competitiveness of imports. Regulatory measures could be classified as 'non-tariff barriers' to trade on the basis of various criteria, such as their intent, their usual effect, or their legality under WTO rules.[14] The difficulty with which international economic law has wrestled, particularly in more recent years (when explicit discrimination has become less commonplace), is distinguishing between legitimate regulatory measures and disguised acts of protectionism. Writing in the context of the WTO, Mattoo and Subramanian have noted:

> The difficulty lies in distinguishing between two types of situations. In one situation, a non-protectionist government cannot prevent certain domestic policies from incidentally discriminating against foreign competitors; in the

---

[12] Bregt Natens, *Regulatory Autonomy and International Trade in Services* (Edward Elgar, 2016) 4.

[13] Wagner, above n 8, 4.

[14] Roy Santana and Lee Ann Jackson, 'Identifying Non-Tariff Barriers: Evolution of Multilateral Instruments and Evidence from the Disputes (1948–2011)' (2012) 11(3) *World Trade Review* 462, 465.

> other, a protectionist government uses a legitimate objective as an excuse to design domestic policies which inhibit foreign competition. The challenge is to devise rules which are sensitive to the difference between these two situations, exonerating the former while preventing the latter.[15]

Although this passage was directed at the multilateral trading regime, its sentiment applies equally to the rules of PTAs and BITs. Discussing the impact of ISDS on regulatory autonomy, Broude, Haftel and Thompson have described the regulatory space available to States as a sort of continuum where:

> at one extreme states have a great deal of flexibility to pursue policies they see fit, and are thus insulated from external pressure or influence attempts … At the other extreme, governments have little room to maneuver and are highly constrained by the ability of foreign investors to challenge their policies under BITs and ISDS …[16]

In referring in this book to 'regulatory autonomy' (which may also be called regulatory space, policy space, or perhaps even the 'right' to regulate), the aspect of that freedom with which we are primarily concerned is the ability of governments to take action for *bona fide*, non-economic public welfare purposes. To this extent, we view regulatory autonomy as a public good, which should be safeguarded in the design and implementation of PTAs and BITs. However, we note from the outset that absolute regulatory autonomy—allowing States virtually unfettered discretion to implement policies as they see fit—may be unhelpful in the international economic law context. Trade and investment agreements discipline domestic regulations, even those with an ostensible public purpose, due to 'concern that some useful forms of regulation may be viewed as discriminatory, or as unduly burdensome, or as effective barriers to market access'.[17] As the Australian Parliamentary committee JSCOT noted in its report on the TPP, the ISDS mechanism

---

15 Aaditya Mattoo and Arvind Subramanian, 'Regulatory Autonomy and Multilateral Disciplines: The Dilemma and a Possible Resolution' (1998) 1 *Journal of International Economic Law* 303, 303.

16 Tomer Broude, Alexander Thompson and Yoram Z Haftel, 'Who Cares About Regulatory Space in BITs? A Comparative International Approach' (SSRN Scholarly Paper ID 2773686, Social Science Research Network, 2 May 2016) 7, forthcoming in Anthea Roberts et al (eds), *Comparative International Law* (Oxford University Press).

17 Andrew TF Lang, 'The GATS and Regulatory Autonomy: A Case Study of Social Regulation of the Water Industry' (2004) 7(4) *Journal of International Economic Law* 801, 802.

may open Australian regulatory measures to challenge, but if the Australian government fails in its defence of a measure, either the ISDS provisions are not functioning correctly or the measure is 'poor policy'.[18] In this latter situation, JSCOT suggested that an investor should be entitled to compensation.[19]

B International Economic Law: Impacts and Rationales

When we discuss the potential for Australia's PTAs and BITs to constrain Australia's regulatory autonomy, we do not mean that they prevent the enactment or implementation of legislation or regulations, or the taking of certain administrative decisions. For Australia, PTAs, BITs and other treaties do not have direct effect in domestic law. Some legislation is usually necessary to comply with new trade obligations, for example to implement international commitments relating to tariffs, customs, intellectual property or other standards.[20] However, the general obligations contained in the treaty do not automatically become part of domestic law.

The obligations contained in PTAs and BITs may nevertheless influence and limit Australia's policy choices as a result of domestic implementation of these norms and international compliance and enforcement mechanisms. Australia is also keen to be seen as a reliable economic partner in the international community, which affects how it applies laws and responds to even informal concerns raised about its compliance with international obligations. If an Australian measure is found inconsistent with WTO law in the WTO dispute settlement system, Australia needs to bring that measure into conformity with its WTO obligations, either immediately or within a 'reasonable period of time',[21] or risk prospective retaliation in the form of 'suspension of concessions' (that is, non-compliance with WTO obligations) by the successful complainant WTO Member.[22] Similarly, the State-to-State

---

[18] JSCOT, *Report 165: Trans-Pacific Partnership Agreement* (November 2016) [6.46].

[19] Ibid [6.47].

[20] See, eg, *US Free Trade Agreement Implementation Act 2004* (Cth).

[21] DSU arts 21.1, 21.3.

[22] DSU art 22.2. See generally Chad Bown and Joost Pauwelyn (eds), *The Law, Economics and Politics of Retaliation in WTO Dispute Settlement* (Cambridge University Press, 2010).

dispute settlement mechanisms in Australia's PTAs and BITs[23] could also require regulatory change, although in practice those mechanisms are not operative at present and are relatively rare in the broader international context as well.[24]

ISDS offers a more forceful means of enforcing investment obligations in many of Australia's PTAs and BITs,[25] in which an investor may bring an investment treaty claim directly against the host State (whether that be Australia or Australia's treaty partner). In many contemporary investment agreements, the remedies available in ISDS proceedings are limited to monetary awards or restitution of property.[26] Although claimants using provisions of older BITs may request an order that the host State withdraw the measures at issue,[27] or seek specific performance or other satisfaction, such remedies are rarely awarded in ISDS.[28] But it is not only a finding of liability and award of monetary compensation that may impact upon a State's regulatory decision-making. ISDS may be extremely costly for a host State in terms of both human resources and financial cost, even if the host State successfully defends its challenged measure. ISDS in particular may also create 'regulatory chill', causing a host State to hesitate before imposing more restrictive, intrusive or progressive regulatory measures 'even if not challenged in practice, or even if actual challenges are ultimately unsuccessful'.[29]

To some extent, such hesitation may be appropriate. As noted above, PTAs and BITs, as well as international economic law more generally, are intended to prevent protectionist or discriminatory measures in order to pursue broader welfare goals. For example, the objectives of the WTO are recognised in the preamble to the Marrakesh Agreement that established the organisation:

---

[23] See SAFTA ch 16; TAFTA ch 18; AUSFTA ch 21; ACIFTA ch 21; AANZFTA ch 17; MAFTA ch 20; KAFTA ch 20; JAEPA ch 19; ChAFTA ch 15; TPP ch 28.

[24] But see Anthea Roberts, 'State-to-State Investment Treaty Arbitration: A Hybrid Theory of Interdependent Rights and Shared Interpretive Authority' (2014) 55(1) *Harvard International Law Journal* 1.

[25] For a more detailed discussion of ISDS mechanisms included in Australia's PTAs and BITs, see Chapter 5.

[26] See, eg, KAFTA art 11.26.1.

[27] See, eg, *Philip Morris v Australia*, Jurisdictional Decision, [89].

[28] Rudolf Dolzer and Christoph Schreuer, *Principles of International Investment Law* (Oxford University Press, 2nd ed, 2012) 293–294.

[29] Broude et al, above n 16, 7. Cf JSCOT, *Report 165*, above n 18, [6.61].

> *Recognizing* that their relations in the field of trade and economic endeavour should be conducted with a view to raising standards of living, ensuring full employment and a large and steadily growing volume of real income and effective demand, and expanding the production of and trade in goods and services, while allowing for the optimal use of the world's resources in accordance with the objective of sustainable development, seeking both to protect and preserve the environment and to enhance the means for doing so in a manner consistent with their respective needs and concerns at different levels of economic development ...[30]

Trade liberalisation (through 'the substantial reduction of tariffs and other barriers to trade and ... the elimination of discriminatory treatment in international trade relations')[31] is a means towards these ends, as further noted in the preamble.

The causal connection between international trade liberalisation and national and global welfare gains[32] is explained by the theory of comparative advantage, which is widely accepted in mainstream economics[33] and supported by empirical evidence of the impact of trade on poverty reduction in developing countries.[34] However, the implementation of the theory in practice can be problematic, for example as regards the allowance of significant agricultural subsidies by WTO Members,[35] the limitations of 'special and differential treatment' provided to developing countries,[36] the inclusion of intellectual property as a

---

[30] Marrakesh Agreement, preamble (italics in original; underlining added).

[31] Marrakesh Agreement, preamble.

[32] See, eg, Kym Anderson, 'Contributions of the GATT/WTO to Global Economic Welfare: Empirical Evidence' (2016) 30(1) *Journal of Economic Surveys* 56.

[33] See, eg, Alan Sykes, 'Comparative Advantage and the Normative Economics of International Trade Policy' (1998) 1 *Journal of International Economic Law* 49.

[34] See, eg, IMF, World Bank and WTO, *Making Trade an Engine of Growth for All: The Case for Trade and for Policies to Facilitate Adjustment* (2017) [84]; World Bank and WTO, *The Role of Trade in Ending Poverty* (2015).

[35] See, eg, Kym Anderson and Will Martin, 'Agricultural Trade Reform and the Doha Development Agenda' (2005) 28(9) *The World Economy* 1301.

[36] See, eg, Alexander Keck and Patrick Low, 'Special and Differential Treatment in the WTO: Why, When, and How?' in Simon Evenett and Bernard Hoekman (eds), *Economic Development and Multilateral Trade Cooperation* (World Bank, Palgrave Macmillan, 2006) 147.

topic of international trade agreements at all,[37] and, indeed, the impact of PTAs on the multilateral trading system.[38]

In addition to these challenges at the international level, domestically, countries need to deal with the 'adjustment costs' of trade liberalisation by providing financial or other forms of support such as retraining for industries and workers whose jobs may be lost as a result of trade.[39] International trade agreements such as the WTO agreements and PTAs do not usually contain prescriptions regarding such matters, instead allowing each party to determine how best to redistribute the gains from trade in accordance with its own circumstances. A 2017 report by the WTO, IMF and World Bank notes that '[m]itigating adjustment costs' through domestic policies 'can help to alleviate resulting negative attitudes toward trade … and make trade openness more socially sustainable'.[40] The WTO Director-General Roberto Azevêdo has also noted that 'innovation, automation and new technologies are responsible for roughly 80% of the manufacturing jobs that have been lost'.[41]

The purpose of IIAs is typically understood as promoting or encouraging the flow of foreign direct investment into host States, by providing high standards of legal protection for the interests of investors, accompanied by an effective means of enforcement. For example, the preamble to the Australia–Mexico BIT states that the parties entered into the agreement:

> Recognising the need to *promote and protect foreign investments* with the aim to foster their economic prosperity; …

---

[37] See, eg, Jayashree Watal, *Intellectual Property Rights in the WTO and Developing Countries* (Kluwer Law International, 2001).

[38] See, eg, Richard Baldwin, 'Preferential Trading Arrangements' in Martin Daunton, Amrita Narlikar and Robert Stern, *The Oxford Handbook on the World Trade Organization* (Oxford University Press, 2012) 632; M Rafiqul Islam, 'The Australian Policy and Practice of Preferential Bilateral Trade: A Benign or Malign Alternative to the WTO Multilateral Free Trading System?' (2003) 2(2) *Journal of International Trade Law & Policy* 43.

[39] See, eg, Greg Thompson, Tim Murray and Patrick Jomini, 'Trade, Employment and Structural Change: The Australian Experience' in Douglas Lippoldt (ed), *Policy Priorities for International Trade and Jobs* (OECD, 2012) 113. See also Alan Winters, 'International Trade Regulation and Job Creation' (September 2014) *World of Labor* (online).

[40] IMF, World Bank and WTO, above n 34, [44].

[41] WTO, 'Trade Recovery Expected in 2017 and 2018, Amid Policy Uncertainty', Press/793. Trade Statistics and Outlook (12 April 2017).

> Intending to create and maintain favourable conditions for investments by Investors of one Contracting Party in the territory of the other Contracting Party; and
>
> Recognising that pursuit of these objectives would be facilitated by a clear statement of principles relating to the protection of investments, combined with rules designed to render more effective the application of these principles within the territories of the Contracting Parties;[42]

Providing legal protections for foreign investors is beneficial to host States, at least in theory, as they receive the benefits of increased foreign investment.[43] However, debate exists as to whether the conclusion of IIAs or the availability of ISDS under those treaties does, in fact, promote or encourage foreign investment.[44]

From the perspective of capital-exporting States, BITs provide their nationals with greater protection when investing in foreign countries, and ISDS mechanisms allow the enforcement of these protections without the need for the home State to exercise any rights of diplomatic protection.[45] In this way, BITs have also been described as a means of depoliticising investment disputes and avoiding so-called 'gunboat diplomacy'.[46] The availability of a formal means of resolving investment disputes may be particularly important for investment in countries with unstable political systems or under-developed judicial systems.

---

42 Emphasis added.

43 On the impact of foreign investment on the economic development of recipient states, see: Olivier de Schutter et al (eds), *Foreign Direct Investment and Human Development* (Routledge, 2013); Jonathan Bonnitcha, 'Foreign Investment, Development and Governance: What International Investment Law Can Learn from the Empirical Literature on Investment' (2016) 7 *Journal of International Dispute Settlement* 31.

44 See generally Karl Sauvant and Lisa Sachs (eds), *The Effect of Treaties on Foreign Direct Investment* (Oxford University Press, 2009); Jason Webb Yackee, 'Do BITs "Work"? Empirical Evidence from France' (2016) 7 *Journal of International Dispute Settlement* 55; Thomas Schultz and Cédric Dupont, 'Investment Arbitration: Promoting the Rule of Law or Over-Empowering Investors? A Quantitative Empirical Study' (2014) 25 *European Journal of International Law* 1147.

45 On the difficulties of diplomatic protection or 'espousal' as a means of enforcing investor rights, see Kenneth J Vandevelde, 'A Brief History of International Investment Agreements' (2005) 12 *UC Davis Journal of International Law & Policy* 157, 160.

46 Stephen M Schwebel, 'In Defense of Bilateral Investment Treaties' (2015) 31 *Arbitration International* 181, 182.

However, IIAs generally contain reciprocal obligations and benefits, protecting both inward and outward investment with respect to each State party. Developed and developing countries alike have increasingly realised that ISDS represents a potentially intrusive form of dispute settlement that may be used by an investor of either party. Concerns about international investment law in general and ISDS in particular have mounted in more recent years especially because of factors such as the absence of a centralised appellate mechanism, the unpredictability of the reasoning and outcomes of investment treaty arbitrations, the potential for conflicts of interest in the overlap between arbitrators and counsel, the targeting of regulatory measures with a range of policy goals, and the size of monetary awards.[47] These kinds of concerns have led to some States terminating BITs, withdrawing from the ICSID Convention[48] (which provides the framework for many ISDS proceedings), or re-evaluating their approaches to ISDS, as in the case of Australia as discussed further below.

In discussing Pakistan's BITs as an example of developing country approaches to international investment law, Poulsen writes:

> BITs had merely been considered a diplomatic token of goodwill. There was an expectation that the treaties would lead to increased inflows of foreign investment, something Pakistan desperately needed, but they were not thought to have any liabilities or regulatory constraints ... It was ... not until Pakistan was hit by a multimillion-dollar arbitration claim that officials realized the implications of treaties signed by shifting governments since 1959.[49]

From a behavioural perspective, Poulsen explains the acceptance by many developing countries of the 'modern investment treaty regime' as arising from 'bounded rationality': 'policy-makers are subject to cognitive constraints and often prone to make mistakes', suffering from

---

[47] See, eg, Gus van Harten, 'Perceived Bias in Investment Treaty Arbitration' in Michael Waibel et al (eds), *The Backlash Against Investment Arbitration* (Kluwer Law International, 2010) 433; M Sornarajah, 'The Case Against a Regime on International Investment Law' in Leon E Trakman and Nicola W Ranieri (eds), *Regionalism in International Investment Law* (Oxford University Press, 2013) 475; UNCTAD, *Investor–State Dispute Settlement: Review of Developments in 2014* (IIA Issues Note No 2, May 2015) 5.

[48] See the examples of termination and withdrawal in Tania Voon and Andrew D Mitchell, 'Denunciation, Termination and Survival: The Interplay of Treaty Law and International Investment Law' (2016) 31(2) *ICSID Review* 413.

[49] Lauge N Skovgaard Poulsen, *Bounded Rationality and Economic Diplomacy: The Politics of Investment Treaties in Developing Countries* (Cambridge University Press, 2015) xv.

'systematic information processing biases' rather than engaging in 'sophisticated cost-benefit calculations'.[50] He suggests that a preference for the status quo may also explain why the growing awareness among developing countries of the unexpected costs of ISDS has not led to wholesale reform and renegotiation of their investment treaties.[51] On the contrary, the 'motivated optimism that resulted in a rush to sign BITs during the 1990s seems to be repeating itself with investment chapters in PTAs'.[52]

Poulsen also notes that developed countries that have themselves been challenged under ISDS may be more open to pursuing major reforms in international investment law.[53] Australia falls in that category, having now successfully defended its first ISDS claim (brought by Philip Morris Asia Ltd against Australia's world-first 'plain' tobacco packaging scheme, as elaborated in Chapter 2). As Australia awaits the outcome of multiple complaints against the same scheme in the WTO (also addressed in Chapter 2), and in view of the US withdrawal from the TPP and ongoing changes to the landscape of international economic law flowing from the election of President Donald Trump, now is an appropriate time to reflect on Australia's engagement with international economic law through its PTAs and BITs. With full understanding of the potential for international trade and investment disputes to constrain regulatory decision-making, and of the possibility that unexpected developments such as Brexit and the US election will have lasting impacts on international institutions and the global economy, Australia has the opportunity to evaluate its past treaty practice and make improvements for the future.

III IDENTIFYING AUSTRALIA'S PTAs AND BITs: HISTORY, SCOPE AND TERMINOLOGY

Australia's PTAs and BITs may pursue public policy objectives beyond narrow goals of liberalising trade and promoting inward and outward investment, which may explain why Australia's approaches to these agreements have changed over time. The intention of this chapter is not to provide a comprehensive history of Australia's trade and investment

50 Ibid 17.
51 Ibid 200, 203.
52 Ibid 197.
53 Ibid 200.

policies, or of the nation's participation in international economic agreements.[54] Instead, we are concerned with exploring the origins and context of the PTAs and BITs that currently influence Australia's regulatory autonomy, laying the foundation for the discussion of specific disciplines contained in these treaties in the chapters that follow. For this reason, our detailed examination begins with ANZCERTA, the PTA concluded between Australia and New Zealand in 1983 (which, as discussed below, has evolved considerably over time).

However, ANZCERTA was not Australia's first bilateral economic agreement. Australia had entered several earlier bilateral agreements,[55] the most significant being with the United Kingdom[56] and Japan.[57] These agreements were, however, quite different from the more modern PTAs discussed in this book. Many of these agreements, including 11 treaties that Australia concluded rapidly between 1972 and 1975, were intended to 'provide a peg for governmental discussion and development of

---

[54] For more detailed accounts of this history, see John Crawford, Nancy Anderson and Margery GN Morris, *Australian Trade Policy, 1942–1966: A Documentary History* (Australian National University Press, 1968); Richard H Snape, Lisa Gropp and Tas Luttrell, *Australian Trade Policy, 1965–1997: A Documentary History* (Allen & Unwin, 1998); Richard WT Pomfret (ed), *Australia's Trade Policies* (Oxford University Press, 1995); David Meredith and Barrie Dyster, *Australia in the Global Economy: Continuity and Change* (Cambridge University Press, 2nd ed, 2012); Ann Capling, *Australia and the Global Trade System: From Havana to Seattle* (Cambridge University Press, 2001).

[55] See, eg, *Trade Agreement between Australia and Canada*, signed 8 July 1931, [1931] ATS 1 (entered into force 3 August 1931); *Trade Agreement between the Governments of the Commonwealth of Australia and the Federation of Rhodesia and Nyasaland*, signed 30 June 1955, [1955] ATS 10 (entered into force 6 July 1955); *Trade Agreement between the Government of the Commonwealth of Australia and the Government of the Republic of the Philippines, and Agreed Minutes*, signed 16 June 1965, [1965] ATS 7 (entered into force 16 June 1965).

[56] See, eg, *Trade Agreement between Australia and the United Kingdom of Great Britain and Northern Ireland*, signed 20 August 1932, [1932] ATS 16 (entered into force 20 August 1932); *United Kingdom–Australia Trade Agreement*, signed 26 February 1957, [1957] ATS 2 (entered into force 9 November 1956).

[57] See, eg, *Agreement on Commerce between the Commonwealth of Australia and Japan, and Four Exchanges of Notes*, signed 6 July 1957, [1957] ATS 15 (entered into force 4 December 1957); *Basic Treaty of Friendship and Co-operation between Australia and Japan, and Protocol*, signed 16 June 1976, [1977] ATS 19 (entered into force 20 August 1977). See also Meredith and Dyster, above n 54, 225.

commercial relations'.[58] In other words, these agreements were intended to provide a starting point for the deepening of trade and economic relations, without making much substantive progress towards that goal. The coverage and scope of trade liberalisation commitments and investor protections in Australia's early bilateral trade agreements was very limited. For example, the 1957 trade agreement with the United Kingdom focussed on tariff preferences for only a small range of scheduled products, rendering its coverage far narrower than modern PTAs.[59] Similarly, in 1976 Australia concluded a general economic treaty with Japan that included investor protections, but these were limited in scope, covering only full protection and security, FET and MFN treatment obligations, and with no mechanism for enforcement.[60] Although this treaty was the 'first of its kind that Australia had concluded with any country',[61] it bears little resemblance to the more comprehensive BITs that Australia began to conclude from 1988 onwards.

Australia's first modern PTA (ANZCERTA) came in the 1980s, reflecting broader reforms in economic policy and trends towards liberalisation. For the first half of the 20th century, through to the 1970s, Australia had maintained a relatively high degree of protection of its domestic industry, particularly in manufacturing.[62] Protectionist policies were seen as necessary for nation-building in Australia—which was still economically developing and highly reliant on commodities/agriculture—and to provide employment for a growing population.[63] Although Australia was a party to the GATT from 1947 and involved in multilateral trade negotiations, it did not 'participate to any significant extent' in the negotiated tariff reductions of the Kennedy and Tokyo

---

[58] R Burnett, 'Australia's Bilateral Trade Treaties—Developments 1972–1975' (1974) 6 *Australian Yearbook of International Law* 153, 157.

[59] *United Kingdom–Australia Trade Agreement*, signed 26 February 1957, [1957] ATS 2 (entered into force 9 November 1956) sch A.

[60] *Basic Treaty of Friendship and Co-operation between Australia and Japan, and Protocol*, signed 16 June 1976, [1977] ATS 19 (entered into force 20 August 1977) arts IX.1, IX.2.

[61] Moreen Dee, *Friendship and Co-operation: The 1976 Basic Treaty between Australia and Japan* (DFAT, 2006) 44.

[62] Jonathan Pincus, 'Evolution and Political Economy of Australian Trade Policies' in Pomfret, *Trade Policies*, above n 54, 53.

[63] These Australian policies can be compared to the Canadian approach to international trade relations, given that country's relatively similar economic profile. See Richard Pomfret, 'Trade Policy in Canada and Australia in the Twentieth Century' (2000) 40 *Australian Economic History Review* 114.

Rounds of GATT negotiations.[64] Australia did not make international commitments for significant tariff cuts until the Uruguay Round of GATT negotiations, and, at that same time, it began to engage in unilateral trade liberalisation, such as phased cuts announced in 1988.[65]

After the conclusion of ANZCERTA in 1983, Australia continued to enter into trade agreements that we do not classify as PTAs for the purposes of this book.[66] Like many of the earlier trade agreements, these bilateral treaties were often aspirational agreements to explore future opportunities to promote trade, rather than comprehensive agreements to lower barriers to trade.[67] Although these agreements vary significantly, the PTAs we examine in this book are detailed and relatively comprehensive trade agreements, covering a range of disciplines relating to trade in both goods and services.[68] The BITs that we examine include the core obligations that have become synonymous with modern international investment law, such as provisions on expropriation and FET (see Chapter 4); most also provide for enforcement through ISDS (see Chapter 5). We use the term BIT to refer to bilateral agreements that relate exclusively to investment, regardless of the nomenclature used in the official title of the agreement.[69] In addition to BITs, investment obligations are also included as a specific chapter of some PTAs. We use the term international investment agreement or IIA to refer collectively to BITs and PTAs containing investment obligations.

---

[64] Snape, Gropp and Luttrell, above n 54, 363.

[65] Ibid.

[66] See, eg, *Trade Agreement between the Government of Australia and the Government of the Federal Republic of Nigeria*, signed 6 August 1989, [1989] ATS 20 (entered into force 6 August 1989); *Trade Agreement between the Government of Australia and the Government of the Islamic Republic of Pakistan*, signed 12 July 1990, [1990] ATS 24 (entered into force 12 July 1990).

[67] See, eg, *Agreement on Economic Cooperation between the Government of Australia and the Government of the Kingdom of Thailand*, signed 6 August 1990, [1990] ATS 29 (entered into force 6 August 1990) arts II, III.

[68] Essentially, these agreements would at least purport to be consistent with the requirements for PTAs established by GATT 1994 art XXIV(8)(b) and GATS art V(1), meaning that they eliminate duties or other restrictions on substantially all trade between the constituent territories of the free trade area. In Chapters 2 and 3 we offer some thoughts on these requirements in the context of intellectual property and services respectively.

[69] Most of Australia's BITs are titled agreements 'for the Promotion and Protection of Investments'. See, eg, Australia–Pakistan BIT; Australia–Lao PDR BIT; Australia–Czech Republic BIT.

IV FIRST GENERATION: ANZCERTA AND BITs

The first generation of Australia's PTAs and BITs, as defined in this book, includes the largest number of agreements, as set out in Table 1.1.

Table 1.1 Australia's 'First Generation' BITs and PTAs in Order of Signature

Year of signature	Agreement
1983	ANZCERTA
1988	Australia–China BIT
1990	Australia–Papua New Guinea BIT
1991	Australia–Viet Nam BIT
1991	Australia–Poland BIT
1991	Australia–Hungary BIT
1992	Australia–Indonesia BIT
1993	Australia–Romania BIT
1993	Australia–Hong Kong BIT
1993	Australia–Czech Republic BIT
1994	Australia–Lao PDR BIT
1995	Australia–Argentina BIT
1995	Australia–Peru BIT
1995	Australia–Philippines BIT
1996	Australia–Chile BIT
1998	Australia–Pakistan BIT
1998	Australia–Lithuania BIT
1999	Australia–India BIT
2001	Australia–Egypt BIT
2001	Australia–Uruguay BIT
2002	Australia–Sri Lanka BIT

As this table illustrates, all of the agreements in this 'first generation' are BITs, with the exception of ANZCERTA. Given the unique timing and content of ANZCERTA we consider it first, before turning to discuss Australia's program of negotiating BITs.

A International Trade Agreements: ANZCERTA as an Exception to the Multilateral Focus

ANZCERTA was the first of Australia's modern bilateral trade agreements, but its predecessors date back to the 1920s.[70] ANZCERTA replaced the 1965 *New Zealand–Australia Free Trade Agreement*, which had removed 80 per cent of the tariffs on trade between the two countries by the late 1970s,[71] leaving some significant barriers still in place. Tariff reductions applied only to scheduled goods, and the agreement lacked any mechanism for compulsorily removing the remaining restrictions.[72] Other barriers to trade that were not removed by the 1965 agreement included significant quantitative restrictions (such as Australia's unwillingness to open much of its dairy market to products from New Zealand) and export incentives.[73] Agreement to promote further growth in trade between the two countries provided the impetus for negotiation of a new agreement to create a 'closer economic relationship'.[74]

What has made the ANZCERTA so significant, beyond it simply being Australia's first modern PTA, was the depth of integration that the parties have achieved through the evolution of the agreement. ANZCERTA did not immediately liberalise or remove all barriers to trade between Australia and New Zealand: '[i]n its initial form … ANZCERTA was a cautious, even timid agreement.'[75] In the late 1970s and early 1980s, politicians from the two countries discussed a range of models for promoting wider economic cooperation, including an extension of the

---

[70] These included: *Trade Agreement between Australia and New Zealand*, signed 11 April 1922, [1922] ATS 5 (entered into force 1 September 1922); *Trade Agreement between the Commonwealth of Australia and the Dominion of New Zealand*, signed 5 September 1933, [1933] ATS 14 (entered into force 1 December 1933); *New Zealand–Australia Free Trade Agreement*, signed 31 August 1965, [1966] ATS 1 (entered into force 1 January 1966).

[71] DFAT, *Closer Economic Relations: Background Guide to the Australia New Zealand Economic Relationship* (DFAT, February 1997) 6.

[72] Ibid.

[73] Meredith Kolsky Lewis, 'The Politics and Indirect Effects of Asymmetrical Bargaining Power in Free Trade Agreements' in Tomer Broude, Marc L Busch and Amelia Porges (eds), *The Politics of International Economic Law* (Cambridge University Press, 2011) 19, 26.

[74] See communiqué issued by Prime Ministers Fraser and Muldoon, Wellington, New Zealand (21 March 1980).

[75] Robert Scollay, Christopher C Findlay and Uwe Kaufmann, *Australia New Zealand Closer Economic Relations Trade Agreement (ANZCERTA) and Regional Integration* (Institute of Southeast Asian Studies, 2011) 22.

limited free trade area set up by the 1965 agreement, a full free trade area, a customs union, an economic community, or a monetary union.[76] The decision not to pursue a customs union or other closer form of integration was in part due to significant differences in the tariff structures of the two countries at the time,[77] as well as Australian concerns that the adoption of a common external tariff would necessitate an increase over current Australian levels, in turn 'encourag[ing] the expansion of industries which are inefficient by world standards'.[78]

Despite these limitations of the original ANZCERTA, this treaty has provided the framework for what is now a highly integrated Trans-Tasman market. By mid-1990, all tariffs and quantitative restrictions had been lifted on trade between Australia and New Zealand, as a result of the 1988 ANZCERTA Protocol on Acceleration of Free Trade in Goods: five years ahead of the schedule originally agreed in 1983.[79] Although the initial treaty did not include trade in services or protection of foreign investment, disciplines on these topics were added through subsequent protocols agreed in 1988 and 2011 respectively.[80] Another significant feature of the current ANZCERTA relationship is the mutual recognition arrangements that have been created for many product standards, food standards, and qualifications in professional services, which remain unrivalled in any of Australia's other PTAs.[81] ANZCERTA has also

---

[76] Lusaka Agreement, 'Prime Minister's Meeting with Mr Muldoon' (6 August 1979) [7], document 20 in Pamela Andre, Stephen Payton and John Mills (eds), *The Negotiation of the Australia New Zealand Closer Economic Relations Trade Agreement 1983* (DFAT and New Zealand Minister of Foreign Affairs and Trade, 2003).

[77] Scollay, Findlay and Kaufmann, above n 75, 23.

[78] See Department of the Treasury, Commonwealth of Australia, 'Closer Economic Integration between Australia and New Zealand—Possible Impact on the Australian Economy' (October 1979), document 34 in Andre, Payton and Mills, above n 76.

[79] ANZCERTA Protocol on Acceleration of Free Trade in Goods. See also DFAT, above n 71, 6.

[80] ANZCERTA Services Protocol; ANZCERTA Investment Protocol.

[81] See generally Council of Australian Governments, *The Trans-Tasman Mutual Recognition Arrangement,* <https://www.coag.gov.au/about-coag/agreements/trans-tasman-mutual-recognition-arrangement-arrangement-between-australian> (last visited 7 April 2017); Food Standards Australia and New Zealand, *About FSANZ*, <http://www.foodstandards.gov.au> (last visited 7 April 2017); Lewis, above n 73, 26; Debra P Steger, 'Institutions for Regulatory Cooperation in "New Generation" Economic and Trade Agreements' (2012) 39 *Legal Issues of Economic Integration* 109, 115.

facilitated cooperation in other fields, including harmonisation of business law and reducing discrimination in government procurement.[82]

At the time of ANZCERTA, Australian politicians had little desire to seek similarly deep or comprehensive economic agreements with other trading partners. In a statement to the GATT Ministerial Meeting in 1982, then Deputy Prime Minister and Minister for Trade and Resources, Doug Anthony, linked bilateral trade agreements with protectionism, arguing:

> This resort to solving one's problems at the expense of one's trading partners or of seeking bilateral solutions outside the multilateral framework put very great pressure on all of us, especially the smaller trading nations.[83]

Many of Australia's key aims in international trade diplomacy at the time centred around improving access to markets in major industrialised countries for its agricultural exports and commodities—difficult goals that most expected would be more achievable through multilateral negotiations.[84] As Frederick Abbott and others have argued, relatively small or weak nations have greater power in multilateral negotiations, as they can band together to resist pressure from major economic powers such as the US or the EU.[85] In 1986, the Department of Trade and Economic Planning Advisory Council considered whether or not Australia should pursue a bilateral trade agreement with the US, but concluded that it would be preferable for Australia to lower its tariff barriers unilaterally, and that multilateral or large regional efforts to liberalise were preferable to bilateral initiatives.[86]

Thus, the ANZCERTA was something of an anomaly, and the parties sought to ensure that it would 'be designed to enhance relationships with

---

[82] See Memorandum of Understanding Between the Government of New Zealand and the Government of Australia on the Coordination of Business Law (2010); Australian and New Zealand Government Procurement Agreement (revised September 2013).

[83] 'Australia's Opening Statement to the GATT Ministerial Meeting', document 9:15 in Snape, Gropp and Luttrell, above n 54, 406.

[84] See generally Richard H Snape, Jan Adams and David Morgan, *Regional Trade Agreements: Implications and Options for Australia* (Australian Government Printing Service, 1993).

[85] Frederick M Abbott, 'A New Dominant Trade Species Emerges: Is Bilateralism a Threat?' (2007) 10 *Journal of International Economic Law* 571.

[86] 'Should Australia Seek US Trade Preferences', document 10:1 in Snape, Gropp and Luttrell, above n 54, 471.

third countries', rather than being inward-looking.[87] The conclusion and evolution of ANZCERTA reflects the close political relationship between Australia and New Zealand, as much as their economic connection. Neither country has been 'the most important trading partner of the other', particularly since historically both States have had a similar focus on commodity exports and agricultural production.[88] The Australian negotiators in the early stages of talks noted that the economic gains on offer from an agreement were likely to be small.[89] In many respects, ANZCERTA has been driven by the unique 'deep ties of common origin and shared ideals and institutions which give a sound basis for the closest co-operation'.[90]

Unsurprisingly given the close historical relationship of Australia and New Zealand, as well as their economic and cultural similarities, we have found no evidence that the conclusion of ANZCERTA was seen as a threat to regulatory autonomy. During the 1980s, international trade law was still largely concerned with tariffs and more obvious non-tariff barriers to trade, rather than regulatory measures.[91] As a result, concerns about regulatory autonomy were not widespread at this time. Moreover, to the extent that harmonisation of standards was discussed in the ANZCERTA negotiations, Australia was unlikely to be concerned that this would threaten its regulatory space. As the larger economy, Australia may have presumed that any harmonised standards would likely be based on existing Australian approaches.[92] As explained below, this presumption did not hold for later PTAs, such as the AUSFTA.[93]

---

[87] Statement of Understanding, 'Australian—New Zealand Economic Co-operation—Statement of Understanding between Permanent Heads', Canberra (3 November 1979), document 52 in Andre, Payton and Mills, above n 76.

[88] Ian McLean, 'Trans-Tasman Trade Relations: Decline and Rise' in Pomfret, *Trade Policies*, above n 54, 171, 171.

[89] See Department of the Treasury, Commonwealth of Australia, 'Closer Economic Integration between Australia and New Zealand—Possible Impact on the Australian Economy' (October 1979), document 34 in Andre, Payton and Mills, above n 76.

[90] Nareen Statement, 'Joint Statement of the Prime Minister of Australia Malcolm Fraser and the Deputy Prime Minister of New Zealand Brian Talboys' (20 March 1978), document 1 in Andre, Payton and Mills, above n 76.

[91] This concern began to emerge more prominently in the late 1990s, as discussed in part V below.

[92] Lewis, above n 73, 27.

[93] See part V below.

B International Investment Agreements: Australia as a Relative Latecomer

It was not until the late 1980s, several years after ANZCERTA was signed, that Australia began concluding BITs and other IIAs. The first of these agreements was with China in 1988,[94] as part of an ongoing process of encouraging bilateral trade and economic relations.[95] Australia was a rather late arrival to the world of BITs, compared to other highly industrialised nations. Many European countries had begun to seek specific agreements for the protection of their foreign investors in the 1950s and 1960s, with the 1959 Germany–Pakistan BIT often cited as the first modern BIT. The US started entering BITs from the early 1980s,[96] although it had concluded 20 Friendship, Commerce and Navigation treaties that included at least some protections for foreign investors between 1945 and 1966.[97] Canada, which had similar economic interests and priorities to Australia throughout much of the 20th century,[98] did not begin negotiating BITs until 1989.[99] Once Australia had begun its program of entering into BITs, it did so enthusiastically, concluding 19 agreements between 1988 and 2002.[100] Australia's embrace of BITs in the 1990s mirrored a wider international trend: during this decade up to 200 such agreements were concluded globally each year.[101] The increasing acceptance of investment protection norms in bilateral treaties sparked efforts to create a multilateral framework through the OECD in the mid-late 1990s. Consistent with its approach to international trade policy, Australia was an active participant in the OECD's efforts to create

---

[94] Australia–China BIT.

[95] Snape, Gropp and Luttrell, above n 54, 466.

[96] See, eg, *Treaty Between the United States of America and the Republic of Panama Concerning the Treatment and Protection of Investments,* signed 27 October 1982 (entered into force 30 May 1991); *Treaty Between the United States of America and the Republic of Senegal Concerning the Reciprocal Encouragement and Protection of Investment*, signed 6 December 1983 (entered into force 25 October 1990).

[97] Vandevelde, above n 45, 162.

[98] See generally Pomfret, above n 54.

[99] *Agreement between the Government of Canada and the Government of the Union of Soviet Socialist Republics for the Promotion and Reciprocal Protection of Investments*, signed 20 November 1989 (entered into force 27 June 1991).

[100] See Table 1.1.

[101] UNCTAD, 'Recent Trends in IIAs and ISDS', *IIA Issues Note No 1* (February 2015) 2.

a multilateral agreement on investment (MAI),[102] although these efforts ultimately failed.[103]

Unfortunately, few publicly available documents directly explain why Australia began to seek out BITs in the late 1980s and throughout the 1990s. A joint communiqué issued by federal, state and territory governments in Australia in 1991 called for 'coordinated action programs to pursue bilateral trade and investment strategies for priority interests',[104] without explicitly mentioning treaty negotiation. The welcoming of foreign investment in the late 1980s and 1990s was in sharp contrast to investment policy espoused by Australia in the 1970s, which could almost have been described as an environment of overt hostility: 'political opinion in Australia was running strongly in favour of curbing the role of foreign direct investment'.[105] The enactment of the *Companies (Foreign Take-overs) Act of 1972* (Cth) was the first legislative step taken by the Australian government to enable regulation of foreign investment (beyond the use of foreign exchange controls)[106] and a precursor to the *Foreign Acquisitions and Takeovers Act 1975* (Cth), which regulated take-overs of companies as well as certain purchases of real assets.[107] Australia resisted pressure throughout the 1970s from some members of ASEAN to enter into agreements for the protection and promotion of investment.[108]

The conclusion of BITs—reciprocal agreements designed to encourage and protect foreign investments—in the late 1980s and 1990s represented a major shift towards liberalisation in Australia's policy, although controls on and oversight of inbound foreign investment remained. A major factor behind Australia's move towards BITs in the late 1980s is likely to have been the increase in outward foreign investment from Australia. For

---

102 See JSCOT, *Report 18: Multilateral Agreement on Investment: Final Report* (March 1999).

103 See Rainer Geiger, 'Multilateral Approaches to Investment: The Way Forward' in José E Alvarez et al (eds), *The Evolving International Investment Regime* (Oxford University Press, 2011) 153, 157–160.

104 *Towards a National Trade Strategy*, Joint communiqué by Commonwealth, state and territory ministers with responsibilities for international trade and business development (28 November 1991).

105 Meredith and Dyster, above n 54, 214.

106 See Snape, Gropp and Luttrell, above n 54, 666–667.

107 At the time of writing, this Act is still in force and continues to provide the legislative framework for Australia's foreign investment policy, although it has been amended several times since 1975.

108 Palitha TB Kohona, 'Investment Protection Agreements: An Australian Perspective' (1987) 21 *Journal of World Trade* 79, 87.

most of the 20th century, Australia was largely a recipient of foreign capital and investment.[109] By the 1980s, however, more Australian companies were investing in other countries, particularly in Asia, creating an incentive for the government to negotiate treaties to ensure protection of their rights.[110] In addition, the general liberalisation of the Australian economy in the 1970s and 1980s, which included relaxing controls on foreign investment, diminished concerns that entering into BITs would undermine the ability of the Australian government to regulate the entry of foreign investment.[111]

The countries with which Australia entered BITs during this period did not follow any obvious geographic pattern. Several Eastern European countries were included in the program, such as Hungary, Poland, Romania, and the Czech Republic.[112] Negotiating with these States was part of a broader strategy of seeking access to markets and economic opportunities in formerly Communist countries, particularly following the collapse of the Eastern Bloc.[113] These historic events were viewed as opening up 'potentially significant opportunities' for Australian companies to invest in Eastern Europe.[114] Australia also entered BITs with neighbours in Asia—including China, Indonesia, Laos, the Philippines, and Viet Nam—and with a number of South American countries, including Argentina, Uruguay, and Peru.[115] Although Australia had recognised the importance of markets in Asia for some time, the country was only beginning to recognise the potential for investment and trade with Latin American States by the 1990s.[116] In particular, investment by major mining companies in Latin America was cited as a basis for entering into these BITs.[117] Thus, while possible motivations for entering

---

[109] Ibid 67.

[110] Ibid 87.

[111] See, eg, Statement by the Treasurer (Paul Keating), 'Further Foreign Investment Liberalisation' (28 July 1986), document 15:31 in Snape, Gropp and Luttrell, above n 54, 724; Statement by the Minister Assisting the Treasurer (C Hurford), 'Foreign Investment Guidelines Eased' (29 October 1985), document 15:30 in Snape, Gropp and Luttrell, above n 54, 722.

[112] See Table 1.1 above.

[113] Snape, Gropp and Luttrell, above n 54, 456.

[114] Address by the Minister for Foreign Affairs and Trade (Senator Evans) (7 February 1990), document 10:24 in Snape, Gropp and Luttrell, above n 54.

[115] See Table 1.1 above.

[116] See generally Standing Committee on Foreign Affairs, Defence and Trade, Senate, Parliament of Australia, *Australia and Latin America* (June 1992).

[117] See JSCOT, *Report 4: Treaties Tabled on 15 and 29 October 1996* (November 1996) [1.56], [1.65].

into treaties with particular partners can be identified, no single public narrative explains the range of new BIT partners during this period. In the mid-1990s Australia also entered negotiations with major emerging economies including Russia, India, Brazil, and South Africa, without concluding BITs with those countries.[118]

Australia's BITs were generally seen as protecting its outbound investors when they entered foreign markets, particularly developing countries or economies in transition. Negotiators appear to give only limited consideration to the possibility that these agreements could be used by foreign investors entering Australia to challenge regulatory actions. For example, in its report on the Chile and Peru BITs, JSCOT found 'little evidence' of Chilean or Peruvian investment in Australia at the time.[119] Thus, although the obligations contained in the BITs are reciprocal and almost all contain ISDS mechanisms,[120] Australia thought it 'highly unlikely' that it would ever be required to pay compensation for expropriation or other harm to a foreign investor.[121] Moreover, these BITs closely followed the Australian model agreement, hence reflecting its interests and agenda.[122] As a result, these BITs were generally signed and ratified with no serious concerns being raised.

This apparently limited foresight about the potentially far-reaching implications of investment obligations, particularly through ISDS (as we discuss in Chapters 2 and 5), mirrors the experiences identified in other countries, both developed and developing, as noted above. In Australia, the negotiations for the MAI did provoke discussion of how the agreement could intrude on Australia's sovereignty and regulatory space. Some of these concerns related to particular proposals for the content of the MAI, which might bind state governments as well as the federal government, or require the removal of screening processes for foreign investment.[123] In addition to these specific concerns noted by the government, some commentators raised wider arguments about the

---

118 Foreign Investment Review Board, *Annual Report 1994–1995* (Australian Government Publishing Service, 1996) 8.

119 See JSCOT, *Report 4*, above n 117, [1.56], [1.65].

120 See Chapter 5.

121 See DFAT, Government of Australia, *Agreement between Australia and Uruguay on the Promotion and Protection of Investments: National Interest Analysis* (tabled 12 March 2002); DFAT, Government of Australia, *Agreement between Australia and Egypt on the Promotion and Protection of Investments: National Interest Analysis* (tabled 12 March 2002).

122 See JSCOT, *Report 4*, above n 117, [1.55], [1.63].

123 Foreign Investment Review Board, *Annual Report 1995–1996* (Australian Government Publishing Service, 1997) 8.

potential for investment protections in the MAI to narrow the policy space available to regulators in the future.[124] One point of particular concern was the nature of the country-specific exceptions provided in the agreement, which shielded only pre-existing measures or policies, precluding more restrictive future policies.[125] In addition, some regarded the definition of expropriation as too broad, covering a wide range of measures not directly related to foreign investment and placing foreign investors in a position superior to that of Australian companies.[126]

The greater concerns expressed about the MAI, compared to Australia's BITs, may be explained by a few factors. First, due to the size of the MAI and the nature of the parties involved (including the US and the EU), Australia would have been more likely to be affected by the agreement as a recipient of investment (rather than as a source of outward investment). Second, when Australia started to conclude its BITs in the late 1980s, very few known ISDS cases existed. By the time the MAI was being negotiated in the late 1990s, more cases had arisen, along with a general unease about the effects of globalisation and international economic law, as we now discuss.

V SECOND GENERATION: THE SHIFT TOWARDS PTAs

The conclusion of a PTA with Singapore in 2003 (SAFTA) marked an important turning point for Australia's international economic diplomacy. The government still made clear statements in favour of multilateralism as a tool for reducing trade barriers, but it had shifted towards viewing bilateral or regional PTAs as stepping stones towards this goal, rather than as antagonistic competitors with it.[127] In addition to the SAFTA, Australia concluded another four PTAs by the end of 2009, with the US, Thailand, Chile, and ASEAN (alongside New Zealand), as set out in Table 1.2.

---

124 JSCOT, *Report 18*, above n 102, [6.10]–[6.16].

125 Ibid [4.23]–[4.25], [6.34]–[6.62].

126 Ibid [6.63]–[6.76].

127 DFAT, *Advancing the National Interest: Australia's Foreign and Trade Policy White Paper* (Commonwealth of Australia, 2003) 49, 58–63; Statement of Minister for Foreign Affairs, Alexander Downer MP, 'Trade Influences: Where Next?', Hayman Island (8 September 2002).

Table 1.2 Australia's 'Second Generation' BITs and PTAs in Order of Signature

Year of signature	Agreement
2003	SAFTA
2004	AUSFTA
2004	TAFTA
2005	Australia–Turkey BIT
2005	Australia–Mexico BIT
2008	ACIFTA
2009	AANZFTA

Australia's move towards actively pursuing PTAs arose, in part, from the slow progress of multilateral negotiations in the WTO.[128] Progress at the multilateral level had been slowed by several factors: significant opposition to trade liberalisation (including major protests at WTO negotiating rounds, such as the Ministerial Conference held in Seattle in 1999);[129] intractable differences on issues such as agriculture, making it difficult for the WTO Members to move forward using the 'single undertaking' model according to which 'nothing is agreed until everything is agreed';[130] and the expanded and diversified WTO membership. Not only were multilateral talks beginning to stall, but Australia was also afraid of being left behind or disadvantaged by other countries' bilateral trade arrangements.[131] In addition to these external factors, domestic politics also played a role. When Prime Minister John Howard and the Coalition came to power in 1996, part of their campaign platform had been to pursue bilateral negotiations as a means of accessing export markets.[132] Thus, the 1997 White Paper 'In the National Interest' demonstrated a greater appetite for bilateral and regional trade negotiations, which could be 'the course that will bring Australia the most substantial gains in market access in the shortest time frame'.[133]

This context for Australia's embracing of bilateralism is important because it influenced the content of its negotiated agreements. PTAs were

---

128 See Capling, *Australia and Trade*, above n 54, ch 8.

129 Ibid.

130 Statement of Minister for Foreign Affairs, above n 127.

131 See, eg, JSCOT, *Report 102: Treaties Tabled on 12 and 16 March 2009* (June 2009) [2.13]–[2.14].

132 Capling, *Australia and Trade*, above n 54, 171.

133 DFAT, *In the National Interest* (1997) 42.

viewed as a tool for achieving liberalisation that had not yet been secured through the WTO framework: 'WTO-plus' obligations. Many of the commitments made in these PTAs took further steps in areas already covered by WTO rules, such as eliminating remaining barriers to trade in goods (tariffs and quantitative restrictions), liberalising additional services sectors, and (as discussed further in Chapter 2) increasing minimum standards of intellectual property protection. For Australia, one particular area of concern that motivated bilateral negotiations was the reduction of tariffs and quantitative restrictions that limited access for its agricultural goods in other markets, such as the quantitative restrictions imposed by the US on beef and sugar imports.[134] In addition to 'WTO-plus' obligations, whole new disciplines were included in some of the PTAs concluded in this era, covering topics such as e-commerce,[135] competition policy,[136] environment[137] (discussed further in Chapter 6), and labour.[138] Through the inclusion of chapters for the protection of foreign investors,[139] Australia began to incorporate obligations usually found in BITs into its PTAs: a significant contrast to the first generation of agreements, in which trade and investment were kept separate. The increasingly broad subject matter of PTAs creates further potential for these agreements to erode regulatory sovereignty, as we discuss in later chapters.

During this period, there was generally bipartisan support for entry into PTAs, although the AUSFTA was an exception.[140] Yet even where the treaties received broad support, they were not without controversy,

---

[134] Very little was actually achieved on these two points in the final agreement. See Capling, *All the Way*, above n 7, 66–69; Andrew D Mitchell, 'The Australia-United States Free Trade Agreement' in Ross P Buckley, Vai Io Lo and Laurence Boulle (eds), *Challenges to Multilateral Trade: The Impact of Bilateral, Preferential and Regional Agreements* (Kluwer Law International, 2008).

[135] See, eg, ACIFTA ch 16.

[136] See, eg, TAFTA ch 12.

[137] See, eg, AUSFTA ch 19.

[138] See, eg, AUSFTA ch 18.

[139] See, eg, SAFTA ch 8.

[140] The political rifts regarding this agreement are revealed by the two Parliamentary committee reports on the agreement. See JSCOT, *Report 61: The Australia—United States Free Trade Agreement* (June 2004); Parliament of Australia, Senate Select Committee Australia United States Free Trade Agreement, *Final Report* (August 2004). See also Bryan Mercurio, 'Should Australia Continue Negotiating Bilateral Free Trade Agreements? A Practical Analysis' (2004) 27 *University of New South Wales Law Journal* 667, 668.

reflecting the heightened public awareness of the potential impact of globalisation and international economic law on other policy areas, such as the protection of public health and the natural environment.

Concerns about the impact of the agreement on Australia's sovereignty were raised during the JSCOT process for the SAFTA, with some submissions to the inquiry noting that the agreement may 'limit the future actions of Australian governments'.[141] Of particular concern was the 'negative list' approach to coverage of the services obligations of the agreement, which meant that activities were covered unless they were specifically carved out.[142] JSCOT responded to these concerns regarding regulatory autonomy, noting that '[t]he Committee does not agree that FTAs impose limitations on sovereignty—they are, in fact, instances of the exercise of sovereignty'.[143] Moreover, the JSCOT report noted that if such problems were to arise, the agreement could be amended or terminated in the future, as well as the biennial review process allowing governments to add sectors to their list of reservations if necessary.[144] Finally, the JSCOT process considered the possibility, raised by some critics of the agreement, that the investment provisions could expose Australia to claims similar to those the US and Canada had experienced under the NAFTA.[145] In response to these concerns, DFAT provided a detailed analysis of how the ISDS provisions of the SAFTA differed from those of the NAFTA.[146]

Civil society wariness of PTAs and concern about regulatory autonomy varied greatly in relation to the five different trade agreements Australia concluded in this second generation. Although some issues were raised in relation to the first of these agreements (SAFTA), very little was said in relation to the last agreement, the 2009 AANZFTA.[147] In fact, the JSCOT report for that agreement noted the absence of provisions requiring the parties to promote human rights, high labour standards or environmental protection, expressing no concern that other provisions of the agreement might adversely impact the policy space available to Australia or other governments.[148] In contrast to the somewhat detailed discussion of ISDS

---

141 JSCOT, *Report 52: Treaties Tabled in March 2003* (June 2003) [2.175].

142 See Chapter 3.

143 JSCOT, *Report 52*, above n 141, [2.176].

144 Ibid [2.176]–[2.177].

145 Ibid [2.107].

146 Ibid. See also DFAT, 'SAFTA—Response to Query from the Joint Standing Committee on Treaties, 19 June 2003'.

147 See JSCOT, *Report 102*, above n 131, ch 2.

148 Ibid [2.57]–[2.61].

provisions undertaken in relation to the SAFTA, the JSCOT report on the ACIFTA, concluded five years later, referred to only one submission raising concerns about ISDS and its potential impact on health and environmental policy.[149] This discrepancy suggests that civil society concern about regulatory autonomy is sensitive to the specific context of each agreement, including the identity of the parties and the scope of the obligations.

The most controversial and influential PTA Australia entered into during this period was the AUSFTA.[150] As noted earlier, some commentators and community groups viewed several aspects of this agreement as threats to Australia's regulatory autonomy. These included provisions that would require specific alterations to Australia's existing laws, such as intellectual property protections or the process for listing pharmaceuticals on the PBS,[151] as well as more general concerns that investment protection norms may undermine national sovereignty.[152] In what was, at the time, a unique move for a developed country, Australia responded to these concerns by pushing for ISDS not to be included in the PTA.[153] Australia succeeded in this regard, making this agreement a rare example of a US PTA with investment obligations but no ISDS.

The second generation of Australia's modern trade and investment agreements was dominated by PTAs, but two final BITs were also concluded in this period.[154] Australia's BITs with Mexico and Turkey were both concluded in 2005. However, although they came after PTAs such as SAFTA and AUSFTA, they were based on the earlier Australian model BIT and their text is similar to that of first generation BITs.[155] Although, in terms of chronology, they appear in the second generation of Australia's agreements, these two BITs are perhaps better viewed as late examples of the first generation. Negotiations for the Turkey BIT

---

[149] JSCOT, *Report 95: Treaties Tabled on 4 June, 17 June, 25 June and 26 August 2008* (October 2008) [3.52].

[150] On the controversies surrounding the agreement, see generally Linda Weiss, Elizabeth Thurbon and John A Mathews, *How to Kill a Country: Australia's Devastating Trade Deal with the United States* (Allen & Unwin, 2004); Capling, *All the Way*, above n 7; Burrell and Weatherall, above n 5; Mitchell, above n 134.

[151] Capling, *All the Way*, above n 7, 59–65.

[152] JSCOT, *Report 61*, above n 140, [12.18], [12.22]–[12.25].

[153] Instead, the parties to AUSFTA merely agreed to the possibility of future consultations on ISDS. See AUSFTA art 11.16.

[154] See Table 1.2 above.

[155] JSCOT, *Report 72: Treaties Tabled on 29 November 2005 (2)* (February 2006) [5.12].

began in 1999,[156] while the Mexico BIT built on a general trade and investment agreement concluded in 1997.[157] Yet, the general concerns that had arisen regarding regulatory autonomy were reflected in the review of the Mexico BIT. Perhaps informed by Mexico's own experience with ISDS cases under the NAFTA,[158] the Queensland government expressed concerns that the BIT might require Australian governments to pay compensation for actions consistent with domestic law, such as the revocation of a licence or approval.[159] In response to these concerns:

> DFAT advised that it was unlikely that regulatory action by States, such as the imposition of taxation or the lawful revocation of licences or permits, would constitute expropriation at international law.[160]

Although this interaction was not a full or thorough discussion of the potential risks to regulatory autonomy posed by BITs or IIAs, the fact that these questions were even raised in relation to the Mexico BIT, when they had not been raised in relation to Australia's 19 previous BITs, demonstrates the increase in concern about regulatory autonomy that characterised the second generation of Australia's trade and investment agreements.

VI THIRD GENERATION: BACKLASH AND '21ST CENTURY PTAs'

Concerns about the impact of PTAs on Australia's regulatory autonomy have escalated in recent years, in the wake of disputes brought against it and other developed countries relating to health and environmental

---

156 Ibid [5.2].

157 *Trade and Investment Agreement between the Government of Australia and the Government of the United Mexican States*, signed 13 November 1994, [1997] ATS 15 (entered into force 3 April 1997).

158 Mexico was a respondent in notable cases relating to licences and approvals. See, eg, *Metalclad v Mexico*, Award; *Tecmed v Mexico*, Award.

159 JSCOT, *Report 83: Treaties Tabled on 20 June (2), 17 October, 28 November (2) 2006 and CO_2 Sequestration in Sub-Seabed Formations* (February 2007) [2.13].

160 Ibid [2.14].

policies.[161] In 2010, the Australian Productivity Commission issued a report on bilateral and regional trade agreements, which also considered the investment aspects of these agreements.[162] The Productivity Commission is an independent authority established by Commonwealth statute, which provides research and advice to governments on a range of policy issues, either at the request of a Minister or on its own initiative.[163] The Commission's 2010 Report was prepared because:

> The Commission was asked by the Government to examine the effects of such agreements on a range of matters, including trade and investment barriers, prospects for multilateral reform, regional integration and Australia's economy generally.[164]

Among many other findings, the Commission's Report gave the following advice related to regulatory autonomy:

> The Australian Government should not include matters in bilateral and regional trade agreements that would serve to increase barriers to trade, *raise costs or affect established social policies without a comprehensive review of the implications and available options for change.*[165]

Further, the Commission made specific recommendations about the process of ISDS, suggesting that the government should 'seek to avoid the inclusion of investor–state dispute settlement provisions in [PTAs] that grant foreign investors in Australia substantive or procedural rights greater than those enjoyed by Australian investors'.[166] Not long after the release of this report, the first ever ISDS case against Australia was launched by Philip Morris, challenging the consistency of cigarette plain-packaging requirements with the 1993 Australia–Hong Kong BIT, as discussed further in Chapter 2. That agreement was one of Australia's first generation BITs, concluded before many ISDS cases had been brought and concerns about their potential impact on 'regulatory

---

161 See, eg, the tobacco-related disputes discussed in Chapter 2; Appellate Body Report, *US—Clove Cigarettes*; Appellate Body Reports, *EC—Seal Products*; Appellate Body Report, *US—Tuna II (Mexico)*; *Vattenfall v Germany*, Notice of Arbitration.

162 Productivity Commission, Australian Government, *Bilateral and Regional Trade Agreements: Productivity Commission Research Report* (November 2010) ('Productivity Commission Report').

163 *Productivity Commission Act 1998* (Cth) s 6(1).

164 Productivity Commission Report, above n 162, iii.

165 Ibid recommendation 4.

166 Ibid recommendation 4(b).

autonomy' had begun to develop.[167] In December 2015, Philip Morris' claim was dismissed on jurisdictional grounds,[168] but the litigation has still had a significant impact on the third generation of Australia's PTAs. The Productivity Commission Report, along with the Philip Morris arbitration, contributed to ISDS becoming a focal point for concerns regarding regulatory autonomy and PTAs in Australia.

Initially, the government endorsed the Productivity Commission's recommendation that ISDS provisions not be included in future PTAs, through the Gillard Trade Policy Statement of April 2011.[169] This policy changed when the Liberal–National Coalition was elected in September 2013. Since that time, the inclusion of ISDS provisions in PTAs has been considered on a case-by-case basis.[170] Outside the major political parties there has been even stronger opposition to ISDS, with Australian Greens' Senator Peter Whish-Wilson introducing a private Senator's Bill in 2014 that would prevent the government concluding any future treaties that included an ISDS mechanism.[171] Although the Bill was never voted on, its discussion by Senate Foreign Affairs, Defence and Trade Legislation Committee provides further insight into the views of Australia's political parties on ISDS. The Coalition members maintained that ISDS may be a worthwhile inclusion in some agreements.[172] The Labor Party Senators on the Committee felt that ISDS was 'unnecessary', but that it was also 'not desirable to radically constrain'

[167] For further detail on the frequency of disputes initiated under ISDS mechanisms, see UNCTAD, *World Investment Report 2015: Reforming International Investment Governance* (United Nations, 2015) 114.

[168] See *Philip Morris v Australia*, Jurisdictional Decision.

[169] DFAT, *Gillard Government Trade Policy Statement: Trading Our Way to More Jobs and Prosperity* (April 2011) 14.

[170] Parliament of Australia, Senate Foreign Affairs, Defence and Trade Legislation Committee, *Trade and Foreign Investment (Protecting the Public Interest) Bill 2014* (August 2014) [2.7].

[171] See Trade and Foreign Investment (Protecting the Public Interest) Bill 2014 (Cth); Explanatory Memorandum Trade and Foreign Investment (Protecting the Public Interest) Bill 2014 (Cth).

[172] Parliament of Australia, Senate Foreign Affairs, Defence and Trade Legislation Committee, *Trade and Foreign Investment (Protecting the Public Interest) Bill 2014* (August 2014) 17.

the government's treaty making power through the proposed legislation.[173] The majority of the Committee suggested that concerns regarding ISDS would be better addressed through careful treaty drafting and the inclusion of appropriate safeguards.[174]

Another focal point of concern and backlash regarding PTAs in this third generation of Australia's agreements has been the process of treaty negotiation. In June 2015, the Senate Foreign Affairs, Defence and Trade References Committee released a report titled 'Blind Agreement', discussing the need for greater transparency and consultation in the making of treaties.[175] The report was not limited to discussion of trade and investment agreements, applying more broadly to Australia's treaty making process. However, negotiation of the ChAFTA and TPP were cited by the Committee as important context for its inquiry.[176] The majority of the Committee recommended, *inter alia*, that parliamentarians and their advisors and non-governmental stakeholders be given greater opportunity to consult on the negotiation of treaties, and to review and comment on the text of treaties before their signature. As well as confidentiality of negotiations being unenforceable in a digital age,[177] the Committee noted evidence that 'international trade agreements can sometimes have unintended consequences, especially with regard to intellectual property provisions negotiated in the context of bilateral or regional trade deals'.[178] These and other factors suggested to the majority of the Committee that treaty-making processes in Australia required reform, because 'the context of treaty making—particularly in relation to trade treaties—had changed dramatically in recent decades'.[179] The Coalition government disagreed with all of the Committee's findings, creating doubt as to whether or not Australia's treaty process will be reformed to allow for greater involvement of parliamentarians or the community.[180]

173 Ibid 19–21.

174 Ibid 17.

175 Parliament of Australia, Senate Foreign Affairs, Defence and Trade References Committee, *Blind Agreement: Reforming Australia's Treaty-Making Process* (June 2015).

176 Ibid ix, [2.27]–[2.34].

177 Ibid [2.35]–[2.36].

178 Ibid [2.33].

179 Ibid [3.46].

180 See ibid, Dissenting Report by Coalition Senators; Australian Government, *Australian Government Response to the Senate Foreign Affairs, Defence and Trade References Committee Report: Blind Agreement: Reforming Australia's Treaty-Making Process* (February 2016).

Since 2010, Australia has concluded four new PTAs, including with three of Australia's largest trading partners in North Asia (Korea, Japan and China), as well as an Investment Protocol to the ANZCERTA, as set out in Table 1.3. In 2016, Singapore and Australia agreed significant amendments to the SAFTA, aligning that agreement more closely with Australia's recent PTA practice.

Table 1.3 Australia's 'Third Generation' BITs and PTAs in Order of Signature

Year of signature	Agreement
2011	ANZCERTA Investment Protocol
2012	MAFTA
2014	KAFTA
2014	JAEPA
2015	ChAFTA
2016	TPP

Despite the Productivity Commission report and the Philip Morris arbitration, two of these PTAs—KAFTA and ChAFTA—include ISDS mechanisms.[181] The Coalition government has emphasised the economic benefits of these treaties, while also noting that they include adequate safeguards to protect Australia's ability to regulate in the public interest.[182] In this third generation of PTAs, the drafting of investment obligations has evolved considerably when compared to the first generation of Australia's BITs,[183] while the ChAFTA ISDS provisions include a novel mechanism for the resolution of disputes regarding 'public welfare measures', as elaborated in Chapter 5. As a result of ongoing concerns about regulatory autonomy, many of these agreements include general exceptions clauses that apply to investment obligations,[184] as well as clarifications of the scope of concepts such as indirect expropriation and fair and equitable treatment,[185] as detailed in Chapter 4.

181 ChAFTA art 9.12; KAFTA art 11.16. However, as discussed in greater detail in Chapter 5, the ChAFTA mechanism is limited in scope.

182 See, eg, Regulation Impact Statement, KAFTA (4 February 2013) [72]–[74]; Regulation Impact Statement, ChAFTA (23 March 2015) [152].

183 These drafting changes are discussed in Chapter 4.

184 See, eg, MAFTA art 12.18.

185 See, eg, KAFTA annex 11–B and art 11.5.2(a).

In addition to the four PTAs that have entered into force, a number of other third generation PTAs are being negotiated or have recently been finalised. Most notable among these is the TPP, which was signed in February 2016 by 12 nations accounting for over 35 per cent of world GDP.[186] As well as being significant simply for its size, the TPP is noteworthy as an example of a '21st century' trade agreement, which seeks to include innovative provisions that achieve further liberalisation than that achieved in earlier PTAs. For example, the TPP includes chapters relating to regulatory coherence, small and medium-sized businesses, and State-owned enterprises,[187] as well as novel environmental provisions covering fisheries subsidies and other disciplines not often included in PTAs.[188] These new provisions demonstrate a tension inherent in the TPP and other contemporary PTAs, between recognising the parties' 'inherent right to regulate' and 'safeguard public welfare',[189] and their desire to pursue deeper economic integration and expand the reach of PTAs.[190] The TPP also exemplifies the impact of tobacco-related disputes on subsequent negotiations, as the agreement includes a special carve-out from ISDS for tobacco control measures.[191] A similar clause was also included in the 2016 agreement to amend SAFTA, signalling that Australia may seek to include this provision in future agreements.[192]

The TPP was signed by the 12 negotiating parties, but it cannot enter into force in its current form absent some unexpected developments in the US. After President Trump took office in the US in January 2017, one of his first executive acts was to withdraw the US from the TPP.[193] Under the terms of the TPP, the treaty can enter into force only if at least six of its original signatories complete their applicable legal requirements to ratify it, provided that those parties represent at least 85 per cent of the combined gross domestic product of the 12 original signatories (based on

---

186 DFAT, *TPP*, <http://dfat.gov.au/trade/agreements/tpp/pages/trans-pacific-partnership-agreement-tpp.aspx> (last visited 7 April 2017).

187 TPP ch 17, 24, 25.

188 TPP ch 20 art 20.16.

189 TPP preamble.

190 For a discussion of these tensions in relation to regulatory coherence provisions, see Elizabeth Sheargold and Andrew D Mitchell, 'The TPP and Good Regulatory Practices: An Opportunity for Regulatory Coherence to Promote Regulatory Autonomy?' (2016) 15 *World Trade Review* 587.

191 The mechanism is a denial of benefits clause, which TPP parties may elect to use. See TPP art 29.5 and discussion in Chapter 5 of this volume.

192 SAFTA 2016 ch 8 art 22. See also Chapter 5 of this volume.

193 Letter from Maria L Pagan, Acting USTR, to the Trans-Pacific Partnership Depositary (30 January 2017).

2013 figures).[194] This requirement means that the TPP cannot enter into force without the US (and Japan), because it would be impossible for the other parties to reach the 85 per cent threshold. However, this does not necessarily mean that the agreement is dead. The remaining 11 TPP signatories may negotiate a new means of entry into force for the agreement as among themselves, or the agreement may be used as a template for future agreements between these and other parties.

The negotiation of the TPP sparked a new wave of concern among civil society about the impact of the agreement on regulatory autonomy, particularly in relation to IP protections and ISDS.[195] Unlike previous JSCOT reports, which had downplayed the risk of ISDS cases being brought against Australia, the report on the TPP suggested that the Australian government 'be open about the prospect that ISDS cases may be brought against it'.[196] In responding to concerns regarding the potential impact of the ISDS provisions in the TPP on regulatory autonomy, the Committee noted that the benefits of ISDS for Australian investors had been largely overlooked in the debate,[197] and that the TPP ISDS mechanism included 'new qualifications and improvements' that 'will protect Australia public interest regulation from claims'.[198] Although it acknowledged that investors may bring unmeritorious cases, the Committee considered that 'should a case be brought against Australia in relation to public interest regulation under the TPP ISDS provisions it would most likely fail'.[199] A majority of the Committee approved these findings.[200]

The pursuit of PTAs retains support, even though their potential risks (especially through ISDS) for regulatory autonomy are now well known and understood by the Australian government. Aside from the small period when the Gillard government stated that it would not include ISDS mechanisms in future treaties, Australia's response to increased concerns regarding regulatory autonomy has been to make small but significant changes in the drafting of key disciplines, as will be demonstrated in more detail through the following chapters.

---

194 See TPP arts 30.5.1–30.5.3.

195 JSCOT, *Report 165*, above n 18, ch 6, 7.

196 Ibid [6.68]. See also [6.81].

197 Ibid [6.28], [6.73].

198 Ibid [6.79]. See also [6.34], [6.44].

199 Ibid [6.42].

200 The Australian Greens Party member of the committee released a dissenting report. See JSCOT ibid 196.

VII CONCLUSIONS AND OUTLINE

Concerns regarding regulatory autonomy, as that concept is conceived today, were not a major influence or consideration in the conclusion of the first generation of Australia's BITs or the ANZCERTA. In these agreements, Australia was typically the larger and more developed economy. However, by the late 1990s, concerns about the impact of economic agreements on policy space in other areas, such as public health and environmental protection, had begun to emerge. This change coincided with Australia's shift in policy towards approving bilateral PTAs, in its second generation of agreements. Following the Productivity Commission Report in 2010 and the initiation of arbitration by Philip Morris against Australia, concerns about regulatory autonomy grew and have become a prominent feature of parliamentary and public consideration of Australia's PTAs. However, Australia has nevertheless continued to embrace these agreements. As we will demonstrate in the chapters that follow, these concerns have manifested in modifications to treaty drafting such as the addition of new safeguards to agreements, although the efficacy of these provisions is not always clear.

In the following chapters, we consider how the range of different BITs and PTAs that Australia has concluded since 1983 may influence the country's regulatory autonomy in three key areas: the protection of intellectual property, the regulation of services, and the protection of foreign investors. As foreshadowed in this introductory chapter, these three areas have often given rise to the greatest concerns about potential constraints on regulatory autonomy.

We begin in Chapter 2 with an analysis of intellectual property standards contained in Australia's PTAs, which have received considerable public attention, particularly in our PTAs negotiated with the US: the AUSFTA and TPP. Chapter 3 examines rules relating to trade in services, with a particular focus on how the structure of commitments through either a 'positive' or 'negative' list of commitments shapes the extent of both trade liberalisation and policy space. Given the particular prominence of concerns regarding the substance of protections for foreign investors and enforcement of those standards through ISDS, Chapters 4 and 5, respectively, are dedicated to these topics. To provide a more detailed illustration of how these disciplines may impact on domestic policy making, Chapter 6 considers the impact of Australia's PTAs and BITs on the ability to regulate for the protection of the environment. The chapter includes a detailed consideration of how investment standards may apply to a range of environmental measures, using cases that have been decided under the NAFTA, as well as considering Australian PTA exceptions and obligations that relate specifically to the environment.

This book does not suggest that regulatory autonomy is an absolute good, or that any limitations imposed by Australia's PTAs and BITs are negative from a policy perspective. As Associate Commissioner Andrew Stoler noted in his comments on the 2010 Productivity Commission Report, 'there is reason to believe that a little bit of "regulatory chill" might be a good thing, even in Australia'.[201] Similarly, Australia's Chief TPP Negotiator Elizabeth Ward stated before a JSCOT hearing in 2016 in relation to regulatory chill arising from ISDS: 'if it gives regulators en masse, including the public sector, pause for thought about the sort of legislation we are putting in place, that is no bad thing'.[202] The very purpose of international economic law is to constrain States from enacting regulations that create barriers to trade or infringe on investor rights, in order to pursue the wider economic and welfare objectives underlying international trade law and international investment law.

Thus, the question we are examining in this book cannot be stated as simply as: do Australia's PTAs and BITs protect regulatory autonomy? Instead, the study we undertake in this book seeks to examine the extent to which Australia's PTAs and BITs constrain the ability of government to take legitimate regulatory actions in areas such as the protection of public health or the environment, and to examine alternative options for clarifying the scope of agreements or safeguarding regulatory space in areas where we believe it may be necessary. By examining all of Australia's PTAs and BITs, and, where relevant, making comparisons to other agreements, we hope to shed light on the overlapping web of agreements that currently shape not only Australia's regulatory autonomy but also Australia's gains from liberalisation of trade and the promotion and protection of inward and outward foreign investment. Changing patterns of Australia's treaty drafting over time reveal the complexity and nuance of the relationship between international economic law and regulatory autonomy, which is relevant to Australia and countries around the world as they face the ongoing challenges of globalisation.

---

[201] Productivity Commission Report, above n 162, iii.

[202] Evidence to JSCOT, Canberra (7 November 2016) 1 (Elizabeth Ward, Chief Negotiator, TPP, DFAT).

2. Intellectual Property: Increasing Protections under US Influence

I INTRODUCTION

A September 2016 report by Australia's independent Productivity Commission on Australia's intellectual property arrangements found that IP provisions in Australia's PTAs 'substantially constrain domestic policy flexibility'.[1] In particular, the Productivity Commission explained that Australia's obligations under the AUSFTA 'required substantive changes to IP laws' and that many of the AUSFTA's IP provisions have been duplicated in subsequent PTAs such as ACIFTA, KAFTA and the TPP, resulting in 'overlapping and complex rules'.[2] Moreover, these changes tended to go in one direction, namely increasing IP protections:

> Some PTAs embody stronger standards of protection than multilateral agreements, tipping the balance in favour of rights holders and elevating the costs of IP protection. This imposes greater costs on Australia as a net importer of IP, and impedes further creation and innovation.[3]

The Productivity Commission's concern about the necessary 'balance' in IP protection reflects the recognition in the TRIPS Agreement that:

> The protection and enforcement of intellectual property rights should contribute to the promotion of technological innovation and to the transfer and dissemination of technology, to the mutual advantage of producers and users of technological knowledge and in a manner conducive to social and economic welfare, and to a balance of rights and obligations.[4]

---

[1] Productivity Commission, Australian Government, *Intellectual Property Arrangements: Productivity Commission Inquiry Report* (No 78, 23 September 2016) ('*Productivity Commission 2016*') 527.

[2] Ibid 539.

[3] Ibid 527.

[4] TRIPS Agreement art 7.

The same 'Objectives' provision appears in the TPP.[5] Similarly, TRIPS and the TPP contain 'Principles' confirming that parties may adopt measures otherwise consistent with the relevant treaty that are necessary: 'to protect public health and nutrition and to promote the public interest in sectors of vital importance to their socio-economic and technological development'; or 'to prevent the abuse of [IP] rights by right holders or the resort to practices which unreasonably restrain trade or adversely affect the international transfer of technology'.[6] The TPP also adds in its IP chapter a provision on 'Understandings in Respect of this Chapter' that recognises the needs to 'promote innovation and creativity', 'facilitate the diffusion of information, knowledge, technology, culture and the arts' and 'foster competition and open and efficient markets' as well as the 'principles of transparency and due process' and the 'interests of relevant stakeholders, including right holders, service providers, users and the public'.[7] These kinds of principles and objectives may influence the interpretation of other treaty provisions pursuant to customary rules of treaty interpretation, including as codified in the VCLT.[8]

Some of Australia's other PTAs explain the objectives of IP provisions (and their role in trade agreements) in different ways. TAFTA articulates the objective of its IP chapter as being 'to increase the benefits from trade and investment through the protection and enforcement of intellectual property rights',[9] emphasising the link that is said to justify the inclusion of IP provisions in trade agreements. AANZFTA also emphasises this link as well as the balance required in protecting IP and the needs of countries at different levels of development:

> Each Party confirms its commitment to reducing impediments to trade and investment by promoting deeper economic integration through effective and adequate creation, utilisation, protection and enforcement of intellectual property rights, taking into account the different levels of economic development and capacity and differences in national legal systems and the need to maintain an appropriate balance between the rights of intellectual property

---

5 TPP art 18.2.

6 TRIPS Agreement art 8; TPP art 18.3.

7 TPP art 18.4.

8 VCLT art 31(1) refers to both 'context' and 'object and purpose'. In the WTO context see also, eg, DSU art 3.2; Appellate Body Report, *US—Gasoline* 16–17; Appellate Body Report, *US—Carbon Steel*, [61]; Andrew D Mitchell, *Legal Principles in WTO Disputes* (Cambridge University Press, 2008) ch 3.

9 TAFTA art 1301.1.

owners and the legitimate interests of users in subject matter protected by intellectual property rights.[10]

Notwithstanding the recognition in the TRIPS Agreement and Australia's PTAs of these various interests and the need for balance, the question arises whether these treaties have indeed pushed Australia's IP laws too far in one direction, to the detriment of IP users and the nation as a whole. IP experts such as Kimberlee Weatherall put forward a strong view that Australia's IP provisions in PTAs, including the TPP, have become unnecessarily prescriptive and detailed, reducing flexibility for Australian policy-makers in IP-related areas and restricting the possibility of future reforms in the domestic IP system.[11]

In this chapter, we examine three key types of intellectual property, all of which raise important issues for Australia's regulatory autonomy regarding matters such as cultural life and public health: copyright (in part II), trade marks (in part III), and patents (in part IV). Within those areas, we consider only certain significant issues, including the implications of international trade and investment claims against tobacco control measures, the term of protection, and parallel imports. Many other vital issues regarding IP in Australia and internationally are not addressed, such as the treatment of indigenous traditional knowledge and cultural expressions,[12] and the potential liability of 'intermediaries' such as internet service providers for copyright infringement.[13]

---

[10] AANZFTA ch 13 art 1.

[11] See, eg, *Productivity Commission 2016*, 542; Kimberlee Weatherall, *Submission 168 to JSCOT Inquiry into the TPP* (2016); Kimberlee Weatherall, 'Intellectual Property in the TPP: Not "The New *TRIPS*"' (2016) 17(2) *Melbourne Journal of International Law* 257.

[12] See TPP art 29.8; Peru–US side letter; Malaysia–US side letter. See also Kimberlee Weatherall, 'The Emergence and Development of Intellectual Property Law in Australia and New Zealand' in Rochelle C Dreyfuss and Justine Pila (eds), *The Oxford Handbook of Intellectual Property Law* (forthcoming, Oxford University Press) available at <http://ssrn.com/abstract=2821342> (last visited 8 April 2017), 22–23; Tania Voon, 'The World Trade Organization, the *TRIPS Agreement* and Traditional Knowledge' in Matthew Rimmer (ed), *Indigenous Intellectual Property: A Handbook of Contemporary Research* (Edward Elgar, 2015) 64; Peter Drahos and Susy Frankel (eds), *Indigenous Peoples' Innovation: Intellectual Property Pathways to Development* (Australian National University E Press, 2012).

[13] See generally, eg, Sean M Flynn et al, 'The US Proposal for an Intellectual Property Chapter in the Trans-Pacific Partnership Agreement' (2012) 28(1) *American University International Law Review* 105.

We conclude that Australia's PTA obligations (in particular under the AUSFTA) impose substantial constraints on Australia's regulation of intellectual property in the public interest. In some instances (such as the extended term of protection for copyright works) these constraints have been reinforced in subsequent PTAs, further limiting the scope for future reforms. At the same time, several more stringent aspects of Australia's intellectual property system (such as prohibitions on parallel importation of books) are not currently dictated by Australia's obligations under the TRIPS Agreement or PTAs. Our review demonstrates the powerful role of the AUSFTA in shaping Australia's intellectual property laws and international trade arrangements, highlighting the dangers of unthinkingly duplicating PTA provisions in subsequent agreements. The TPP would have strengthened and arguably worsened Australia's position in relation to IP regulation, while potentially improving certain aspects of the AUSFTA provisions.

The tobacco disputes mentioned below highlight the practical significance of the intersection between intellectual property law and international economic law and thus the importance of continuing to scrutinise Australia's intellectual property obligations in existing and future treaties. In the absence of the TPP in the form signed in 2016, and with the AUSFTA potentially open to termination or renegotiation under the Trump administration, Australia has the opportunity to re-examine its IP provisions in the light of the Productivity Commission recommendations as well as earlier proposals by the ALRC and other bodies, in relation to areas covered by PTAs as well as those going beyond PTA requirements. This kind of reassessment has the potential to contribute to the progressive development of the intellectual property system in Australia as well as the broader pursuit of improvements in the Australian treaty process, particularly in the context of international economic law.[14]

[14] See Hilary Charlesworth et al, *No Country is an Island: Australia and International Law* (UNSW Press, 2006) ch 4 ('Trade'), especially as regards the secrecy of Australia's negotiation of the AUSFTA.

II COPYRIGHT

A Overview: TRIPS-Plus Obligations from the AUSFTA Onwards

As with patents, the AUSFTA required substantive changes to Australian law, generally increasing copyright protections[15] and going beyond TRIPS obligations. The TPP imposed similarly detailed and strong copyright provisions, whereas Australia's other PTAs are less prescriptive, as shown in Table 2.1. Weatherall has explained that the implementation of the AUSFTA coincided with major reforms to Australian copyright laws that were not required by that treaty, with the various amendments reflecting neither a 'coherent theory' nor a 'holistic appraisal of the best law for Australian cultural and economic interests'.[16] Insufficient consideration of public policy objectives in relation to intellectual property matters appeared to afflict not only the domestic copyright reform process[17] but also the related negotiation of the AUSFTA, perhaps in part due to the leading role of DFAT negotiators: 'the attitude towards copyright of trade negotiators for whom IP is one of many horses to trade could not possibly be the same as that of those who have spent much of their professional lives dealing with copyright and walking the halls of the WIPO'.[18] Others have similarly lamented Australia's apparent lack of a 'positive agenda regarding the IP chapters of the TPP'.[19]

---

15 See generally Robert Burrell and Kimberlee Weatherall, 'Exporting Controversy? Reactions to the Copyright Provisions of the US–Australia Free Trade Agreement: Lessons for US Trade Policy' [2008] *University of Illinois Journal of Law, Technology & Policy* 259.

16 Kimberlee Weatherall, 'Of Copyright Bureaucracies and Incoherence: Stepping Back from Australia's Recent Copyright Reforms' (2007) 31 *Melbourne University Law Review* 967, 984.

17 Ibid 987.

18 Ibid 977.

19 Tony Harris, Dianne Nicol and Nicholas Gruen, *Pharmaceutical Patents Review Report* (Commonwealth of Australia, 2013) xx.

Table 2.1 Selected Copyright Provisions in the WTO and Australia's PTAs

Treaty	Entry into force	Minimum copyright term from death of author or publication or creation	Restriction on parallel imports	Anti-circumvention	Exceptions: 3-step test
ANZCERTA	1983	✘	✘	✘	✘
TRIPS	1995	50 years	✘	✘	✔
SAFTA original	2003	✘	✘	✘	✘
TAFTA	2005	✘	✘	✘	✘
AUSFTA	2005	70 years	✘	✔	✔
ACIFTA	2009	70 years	✘	✔	✔
AANZFTA	2009	✘	✘	✔	✘
SAFTA amended	2011	70 years	✘	✔	✘
MAFTA	2013	✘	✘	✔	✔
KAFTA	2014	70 years	✘	✔	✔
JAEPA	2015	✘	✘	✔	✔
ChAFTA	2015	✘	✘	✘	✘
TPP	–	70 years	✘[20]	✔	✔
SAFTA 2016[21]	–	70 years	✘	✔	✘

B Copyright Term

The TRIPS Agreement essentially requires WTO Members to provide a minimum term of protection for copyright works of 50 years. First, TRIPS art 9.1 requires WTO Members to comply with certain provisions of the Berne Convention (1971), including art 7(1), which specifies the general term of copyright protection as the life of the author plus 50

[20] But AUSFTA prevails in relation to parallel imports as between Australia and the US: TPP art 18.11, n 8.

[21] Most of the IP provisions remain unamended in SAFTA 2016 so the SAFTA 2011 version continues to apply.

years,[22] and art 7(3), which provides for a term of 50 years from the work being lawfully made available to the public in the case of 'anonymous or pseudonymous works'. In addition, the TRIPS Agreement provides:

> Whenever the term of protection of a work, other than a photographic work or a work of applied art, is calculated on a basis other than the life of a natural person, such term shall be no less than 50 years from the end of the calendar year of authorized publication, or, failing such authorized publication within 50 years from the making of the work, 50 years from the end of the calendar year of making.[23]

The TRIPS Agreement established a minimum term of protection for performers and producers of phonograms of 50 years from 'the end of the calendar year in which the fixation was made or the performance took place'.[24]

For Australia, the AUSFTA extended this minimum copyright term (essentially from 50 years to 70 years) and also extended it to photographic works and to circumstances in which the term is calculated by reference to the life of a natural person:

> Each Party shall provide that, where the term of protection of a work (including a photographic work), performance, or phonogram is to be calculated:
>
> (a) on the basis of the life of a natural person, the term shall be not less than the life of the author and 70 years after the author's death; and
> (b) on a basis other than the life of a natural person, the term shall be:
>   (i) not less than 70 years from the end of the calendar year of the first authorised publication of the work, performance, or phonogram; or
>   (ii) failing such authorised publication within 50 years from the creation of the work, performance, or phonogram, not less than 70 years from the end of the calendar year of the creation of the work, performance, or phonogram.[25]

The approach of the TPP to the copyright term is slightly modified. For example, paragraph (b)(ii) begins 'failing such authorised publication

---

[22] Certain different provisions apply eg to cinematographic works, photographic works and works of applied art: see, eg, Berne Convention (1971) art 7(2), 7(4).

[23] TRIPS Agreement art 12.

[24] TRIPS Agreement art 14.5.

[25] AUSFTA art 17.4.4.

within 25 years'[26] rather than 50 years, potentially limiting the term in respect of works not published within 25 years but published within 50 years (to which paragraph (b)(ii) rather than (b)(i) will apply). This is a relatively minimal change, notwithstanding the explicit recognition in the TPP IP chapter of 'the importance of a rich and accessible public domain'.[27] The imposition of a minimum copyright term under the TPP, well beyond that required under the TRIPS Agreement, would have been of greater significance to those TPP countries that had not already adopted the US 70-year model. The TPP text implicitly recognises, through bilateral side letters with Japan, the difficulty created by extending the term of copyright, in relation to administrative costs and royalty calculations. Japan exchanged letters with the US, New Zealand and Australia to confirm that 'industry-led dialogue' will be required 'between individual collective management societies and affected rights holders with a view to addressing and resolving these matters in a manner consistent with their respective governing documents and applicable law'.[28]

The change in Australia's agreed minimum copyright term flowed from the AUSFTA to four of the eight PTAs that Australia subsequently negotiated, as at the time of writing (including the TPP).[29] Only the PTAs with ASEAN/New Zealand, Malaysia, Japan, and China exclude a minimum copyright term. Australia's bilateral PTA partnerships with States with PTAs with the US include the minimum copyright term: Chile,[30] Korea,[31] and Singapore[32] all have PTAs with the US that include this minimum as well. (Along the same lines, the dominance of the United States in TPP negotiations has been well documented, for

---

26 TPP art 18.63(b)(ii).

27 TPP art 18.15.1.

28 Exchange of letters between Andrew Robb, Minister for Trade and Investment, and Shuichi Takatori, State Minister of Cabinet Office of Japan (4 February 2016) [ii]; Exchange of letters between Shuichi Takatori, State Minister of Cabinet Office of Japan and Todd McClay, Minister of Trade (New Zealand) (4 February 2016) [ii]; Exchange of letters between Shuichi Takatori, State Minister of Cabinet Office of Japan and Michael Froman, United States Trade Representative (4 February 2016) [ii].

29 ACIFTA art 17.27; SAFTA ch 13 art 4.1 (not amended in 2016); KAFTA art 13.5.5; TPP art 18.63 (see discussion following regarding modifications to the AUSFTA approach).

30 US–Chile FTA art 17.5.4.

31 US–Korea FTA art 18.4.4 (with modified para (b)(ii) as in the TPP as discussed below).

32 US–Singapore FTA art 16.4.4.

example leading to empirical calculations of 80 per cent similarity between the TPP text and US PTAs.)[33]

The status of the bilateral trading relationship between the US and Australia's PTA partners may explain the distinction between Australia's PTAs containing this minimum copyright term and those omitting it. Those partners that had already agreed to the minimum term (including Australia in the AUSFTA) were comfortable including it in subsequent PTAs not including the US. As discussed further below in relation to patents, intellectual property standards are typically applied across the board, meaning that the longer copyright term applied in Australia to the US would be applied to other nations and their nationals anyway. Nevertheless, cementing the longer term in not only PTAs with the US but also PTAs with other countries, in the absence of a US role in negotiating those PTAs (that is, in the absence of US pressure to do so, in return for market access under the PTA, for example), seems to assume that the US PTAs and relationships will continue and that no future reform will seek to revisit the term. That approach might be understandable if the term were evidence-based and internationally agreed. However, as noted in the following paragraphs, the length of the term is questionable and arguably harmful both nationally and internationally. Given the developments in the US with the election of Donald Trump in 2016, the expectation of continuing unchanging relations with the US now also appears misguided.

In its 2016 report, the Productivity Commission explained:

> The scope and term of copyright protection in Australia has expanded over time, often with no transparent evidence-based analysis, and is now skewed too far in favour of copyright holders. While a single optimal copyright term is arguably elusive, it is likely to be considerably less than 70 years after death.[34]

---

[33] See Todd Allee and Andrew Lugg, 'Who Wrote the Rules for the Trans-Pacific Partnership?' (July–September 2016) *Research and Politics* 1. See also Wolfgang Alschner and Dmitriy Skougarevskiy, 'The New Gold Standard? Empirically Situating the Trans-Pacific Partnership in the Investment Treaty Universe' (2016) 17 *Journal of World Investment and Trade* 339, 341, 349; Tomer Broude, Yoram Z Haftel and Alexander Thompson, 'The Trans-Pacific Partnership and Regulatory Space: A Comparison of Treaty Texts', International Law Forum Research Paper No 02–17, Hebrew University of Jerusalem Faculty of Law (2 April 2017); 'Language in NAFTA Draft Notice Similar to TPP Text on Investment, IP, SOE' (7 April 2017) 35 *Inside US Trade* (online).

[34] *Productivity Commission 2016*, 131.

The Productivity Commission concluded that the extension of the copyright term as required under the AUSFTA had imposed a net cost on Australia,[35] as a 'significant net importer of copyright material'.[36] As a result of the 'overly broad reach' of copyright (through both the long copyright term and Australia's approaches to other copyright matters such as fair use, parallel imports, and anti-circumvention), concerns have also arisen about potential breaches of copyright through 'every day actions undertaken by most Australians'.[37]

Certain reforms may be possible even within the constraints of Australia's PTA obligations. For example, Burrell and Weatherall have identified practical problems with the minimum copyright term required under the TPP, which rather than harmonising the term does not specify how to calculate it, meaning that the term would expire on different days in different TPP countries.[38] To address the logistical difficulty of 'orphan' works (whose owner cannot be identified—a more significant concern the longer the copyright term), Weatherall points out that the TPP would allow a TPP country such as Australia to impose a registration requirement for later parts of the copyright term, such that copyright continues only upon registration by the owner.[39]

The Productivity Commission also endorsed a 2015 proposal by the Australian government to restrict the copyright term for unpublished works to 70 years beyond the life of the author where the author is known, and 70 years from the making of the work where the author is unknown.[40] The Copyright Amendment (Disability Access and Other Measures) Bill 2017, introduced into the Commonwealth of Australia's House of Representatives on 22 March 2017, would implement this proposal (among a number of other reforms), 'seek[ing] to harmonise the term of copyright protection for published and unpublished works, films and sound recordings' by establishing a term of protection for

---

35 Ibid 166.

36 Ibid 106.

37 Ibid 113.

38 Burrell and Weatherall, above n 15, 307. See also Weatherall, above n 11, 270.

39 Kimberlee Weatherall, *Section by Section Commentary on the TPP Final IP Chapter Published 5 November 2015—Part 2—Copyright* (version 0, 7 November 2015) 12, available at <http://works.bepress.com/kimweatherall/32/> (last visited 8 April 2017).

40 *Productivity Commission 2016*, 133.

unpublished materials instead of protecting them 'in perpetuity' under copyright.[41]

C Fair Use

The TRIPS Agreement contains in art 13 a provision in relation to copyright requiring WTO Members to 'confine limitations or exceptions to exclusive rights to certain special cases which do not conflict with a normal exploitation of the work and do not unreasonably prejudice the legitimate interests of the right holder'. While imposing an obligation that restricts the types of permissible limitations or exceptions, TRIPS art 13 can also be understood as an exception to copyright obligations in that it allows WTO Members to limit copyright holders' rights. The provision sets out what is known as the 'three-step test', corresponding to the allowable exceptions to patent rights in TRIPS art 30 as discussed below:

> Article 13 of the TRIPS Agreement requires that limitations and exceptions to exclusive rights (1) be confined to certain special cases, (2) do not conflict with a normal exploitation of the work, and (3) do not unreasonably prejudice the legitimate interests of the right holder.[42]

The same provision appears, as shown in Table 2.1, in most of Australia's modern PTAs, including the AUSFTA[43] and the TPP.[44] The TPP also explicitly refers to the role of exceptions in assisting in achieving *balance* in copyright regulation:

> Each Party shall endeavour to achieve an appropriate balance in its copyright and related rights system, among other things by means of limitations or exceptions that are consistent with Article 18.65 (Limitations and Exceptions), including those for the digital environment, giving due consideration to legitimate purposes such as, but not limited to: criticism; comment; news reporting; teaching, scholarship, research, and other similar purposes; and facilitating access to published works for persons who are blind, visually impaired or otherwise print disabled.[45]

---

[41] Parliament of the Commonwealth of Australia, House of Representatives, *Copyright Amendment (Disability Access and Other Measures) Bill 2017: Explanatory Memorandum* (2017) 10. See also *Copyright Amendment (Disability Access and Other Measures) Bill 2017* (Cth) sch 2 s 4, substituting a new s 33 for ss 33–34.

[42] Panel Report, *US—Section 110(5) Copyright Act* [6.97].

[43] AUSFTA art 17.4.10(a).

[44] TPP art 18.65.

[45] TPP art 18.66 (footnotes omitted).

Although this TPP provision is merely a requirement to 'endeavour' to achieve balance and would be difficult to enforce, '[t]he inclusion of positive language on exceptions in copyright is a welcome development'.[46]

As with Australia's restrictions on parallel imports discussed below, the approach taken in the Australian copyright system to exceptions is necessarily dictated by the boundaries of TRIPS art 13 or the corresponding provisions in Australia's PTAs. Rather, the doctrine of 'fair dealing' under Australian law specifies in detail the activities that are allowed and do not infringe copyright, such as:

(a) for the purpose of research or study,[47] criticism or review,[48] parody or satire,[49] or reporting news;[50]
(b) incidentally making a 'temporary reproduction' of a work 'as a necessary part of a technical process of using a copy of the work';[51] or
(c) copying a computer program for the purpose of testing the security of the program.[52]

The specificity of these exceptions may limit their ability to adapt to changing circumstances and technologies: 'The drafters looked at existing technology and current practice, and narrowly wrote the exceptions to fit'.[53]

A different approach (adopting a broad exception of 'fair use') is found in other countries including the US.[54] That approach has been recommended for Australia following a range of enquiries over the years, including by JSCOT in relation to implementation of the AUSFTA in

46 Weatherall, *Section by Section*, above n 39, 15.
47 *Copyright Act 1968* (Cth) s 40.
48 *Copyright Act 1968* (Cth) s 41.
49 *Copyright Act 1968* (Cth) s 41A.
50 *Copyright Act 1968* (Cth) s 42.
51 *Copyright Act 1968* (Cth) s 43B.
52 *Copyright Act 1968* (Cth) s 47F.
53 Weatherall, 'Of Copyright Bureaucracies', above n 16, 996.
54 17 USC § 107 (2017).

2004,[55] the ALRC in 2013,[56] and the Productivity Commission in 2016.[57] According to the ALRC, '[f]air use builds on Australia's current fair dealing exceptions, retaining the focus on fairness, but removing unnecessary limitations to particular types of use'.[58] According to the Productivity Commission, the introduction of an 'open-ended fair use exception' could allow use of orphan works (a problem exacerbated by long copyright terms, as noted above), generating new economic activity worth AUD10 to 20 million per annum, while saving taxpayers AUD18 million per annum in the avoidance of statutory licence fees paid by education and government users for free online material.[59] The Productivity Commission maintains that such a shift would be consistent with the TRIPS Agreement.[60]

A fair use exception would preclude copyright infringement for 'fair' use of copyright material, as determined by considering specified factors including 'the purpose and character of the use and any harm that might be done to a rights holder's interests by the use',[61] and with an illustrative list of purposes such as criticism, comment, reporting, teaching or research. Thus, for example, the relevant US provision on 'Limitations on exclusive rights: Fair use' reads:

> Notwithstanding the provisions of sections 106 and 106A, the fair use of a copyrighted work, including such use by reproduction in copies or phonorecords or by any other means specified by that section, *for purposes such as criticism, comment, news reporting, teaching (including multiple copies for classroom use), scholarship, or research*, is not an infringement of copyright. In determining whether the use made of a work in any particular case is a fair use the factors to be considered shall include—
>
> (1) the *purpose* and character of the use, including whether such use is of a commercial nature or is for nonprofit educational purposes;
> (2) the *nature* of the copyrighted work;
> (3) the *amount and substantiality* of the portion used in relation to the copyrighted work as a whole; and
> (4) the *effect* of the use upon the potential market for or value of the copyrighted work.

---

55 JSCOT, *Report 61: The Australia–United States Free Trade Agreement* (June 2004) 240.

56 ALRC, *Report 122: Copyright and the Digital Economy—Final Report* (November 2013) [4.1].

57 *Productivity Commission 2016*, 33.

58 ALRC, above n 56, [4.38].

59 *Productivity Commission 2016*, 28.

60 *Productivity Commission 2016*, 184.

61 ALRC, above n 56, [4.2].

> The fact that a work is unpublished shall not itself bar a finding of fair use if such finding is made upon consideration of all the above factors.[62]

One difficulty with a fair use exception that closely models the US provisions—notwithstanding its appeal to JSCOT, the ALRC and Productivity Commission—is that it could require more decision-making to be left to the judiciary rather than providing more concrete statutory direction and certainty. The difficulties arising from vague wording and discretion in dispute settlement are exemplified in Chapters 4 and 5 of this book in relation to investment and ISDS. Moreover, an overly broad exception provision risks inconsistency with the three-step test in TRIPS art 13, at least in its application in some instances. This area remains under debate.[63]

D Parallel Imports

Unlike the situation as regards patents discussed below, the AUSFTA does not prohibit parallel importation of copyright material. Rather, a footnote indicates that parties have the right to determine the conditions under which copyright is exhausted after the first authorised sale.[64] Thus, consistent with the AUSFTA, Australia could allow the importation of copyright works that have been sold—with the authorisation of the copyright owner—outside Australia. An exchange of diplomatic notes preceding entry into force of the AUSFTA suggests some restriction on Australia's right in this regard by agreeing to disallow the exception for temporary and necessary reproductions where the reproduction is made from a parallel import.[65] The legal status of these notes is unclear, but they might well constitute relevant context for the interpretation of the AUSFTA pursuant to VCLT art 31(2)(a) ('any agreement relating to the treaty which was made between all the parties in connection with the conclusion of the treaty') or VCLT art 31(2)(b) ('any instrument which was made by one or more parties in connection with the conclusion of the treaty and accepted by the other parties as an instrument related to the

---

62 17 USC § 107 (2017) (emphasis added).

63 See, eg, Sam Ricketson and Jane C Ginsburg, *International Copyright and Neighbouring Rights: The Berne Convention and Beyond* (Cambridge University Press, 2nd ed, 2006) ch 13; Ruth L Okediji (ed), *Copyright Law in an Age of Limitations and Exceptions* (Cambridge University Press, 2017).

64 AUSFTA n 17–46.

65 Exchange of letters between Mark Vaile, Minister for Trade (Australia) and Robert Zoellick, United States Trade Representative (17 November 2004). See Burrell and Weatherall, above n 15, n 119.

treaty'). The non-application of this exception in relation to parallel imports might have continued to apply under the TPP, which specifically maintains obligations under earlier international agreements regarding exhaustion[66] (as discussed further below in relation to parallel imports of patented products).

As it stands, Australia's PTAs do not require Australia to prohibit parallel importation of copyright material, but Australia does impose certain restrictions on parallel imports. We would also regard the TRIPS Agreement as not addressing this question because of its allowance for WTO Members to adopt their own approaches to exhaustion of IP rights,[67] as discussed further below in relation to patents.[68] Several independent studies have criticised Australia's prohibition on parallel importation of books by booksellers (while allowing individuals to purchase books online from outside the country),[69] which is said to increase prices for consumers and harm booksellers in Australia:[70] 'Parallel import restrictions are similar to other import restrictions (such as tariffs) in that they benefit local producers by shielding them from international competition. They are an implicit tax on Australian consumers and businesses',[71] which is 'used largely to subsidise foreign copyright holders'.[72]

E Anti-Circumvention

The AUSFTA created detailed obligations regarding anti-circumvention of copyright that have been included in all of Australia's subsequent PTAs apart from the ChAFTA. The AUSFTA obligations include creating criminal procedures and penalties for certain activities, when undertaken

---

66 TPP art 18.1, n 8.

67 TRIPS Agreement art 6. However, it might be possible to argue that the principle of 'independence of protection' in the Berne Convention (1971) requires controls on parallel imports.

68 Berne Convention (1971) art 5(2).

69 *Copyright Act 1968* (Cth) s 37 (subject to fair dealing exception in s 44A).

70 See, eg, *Productivity Commission 2016*, 13; Productivity Commission, *Restrictions on the Parallel Importation of Books* (June 2009) xxv; Ian Harper et al, *Competition Policy Review: Final Report* (Commonwealth of Australia, March 2015) 178.

71 Harper et al, above n 70, 47.

72 Ibid 167. See also, eg, Matthew Rimmer, 'It's Time to Future-Proof Australia's Copyright Laws for the 21st Century' (5 May 2016) *The Conversation* (online).

for commercial advantage or financial gain, such as manufacturing devices intended to circumvent an 'effective technological measure'[73] (often referred to as a 'technological protection measure' or TPM), meaning 'any technology, device, or component that … *controls access* to a protected work … *or* protects any copyright'.[74] A party may apply certain exceptions such as in relation to non-profit libraries[75] or 'non-infringing reverse engineering activities … for the sole purpose of achieving interoperability of an independently created computer program with other programs'.[76] The TPP contains comparable provisions,[77] although the allowed exceptions seem less detailed and prescriptive.[78]

Weatherall explains that the broad wording 'controls access' in both the AUSFTA and the TPP suggests that a TPM could include a device that does more than preventing copyright infringement, also preventing acts that might be both legitimate and exempt, for example under the three-step test in TRIPS art 13 (or fair use or fair dealing at the domestic level).[79] She highlights the importance of 'sensible interpretation' in making anti-circumvention provisions 'workable'.[80] To the extent that the wording in Australia's PTAs is ambiguous or flexible, Australia may be able to interpret that wording so as to allow conduct that is legitimate and that should not be precluded by copyright law, within the scope of the VCLT.

For example, the practice of 'geoblocking' often prevents Australian consumers from accessing digital services such as video streaming (or allows such access at a much higher price than in other markets)[81] or prevents a consumer having purchased a legitimate copyright product (for example, a DVD) in one market from playing that product on a legitimate multi-region player in another region.[82] A committee of the Australian House of Representatives found in 2013 that 'Australians have tolerated higher prices for a range of goods' (particularly information

---

73 AUSFTA art 17.4.7(a)(ii).

74 AUSFTA art 17.4.7(b) (emphasis added). See also SAFTA 2011 ch 13 art 5.1(a) (not amended in 2016); KAFTA art 13.5.9(a).

75 AUSFTA art 17.4.7(a).

76 AUSFTA art 17.4.7(e)(i).

77 TPP art 18.68.

78 TPP art 18.68.4.

79 Weatherall, *Section by Section*, above n 39, 20.

80 Weatherall, *Section by Section*, above n 39, 18.

81 *Productivity Commission 2016*, 142.

82 House of Representatives, Standing Committee on Infrastructure and Communications, *At What Cost? IT Pricing and the Australia Tax* (Commonwealth of Australia, July 2013) [4.53].

technology products) 'for much of their history',[83] referring to such strategies and price discrimination as the 'Australia tax'.[84] The committee recommended amendments to Australian copyright law 'to clarify and secure consumers' rights to circumvent [TPMs] that control geographic market segmentation'.[85]

The legality of various circumvention methods remains unclear under both Australian copyright law[86] and Australia's PTAs. Under Australian copyright law, a limited exception removes from the definition of TPM (with respect to cinematograph films and computer programs) a device that 'controls geographic market segmentation by preventing the playback in Australia of a non-infringing copy of the work ... acquired outside Australia'.[87] Footnote 82 of the TPP intellectual property chapter states:

> Nothing in this Agreement requires a Party to restrict the importation or domestic sale of a device that does not render effective a technological measure the only purpose of which is to control market segmentation for legitimate physical copies of a cinematographic film, and is not otherwise a violation of the law.

However, each of these exceptions is limited to particular activities (for example, importing or selling a circumvention device in the case of the TPP) and particular kinds of copyright works (film and computer program in the case of Australian copyright law, and film in the case of the TPP). Moreover, the AUSFTA does not refer in its anti-circumvention provisions to any exception in relation to geographic market segmentation, leaving the question to interpretation of words such as 'controls access' and parallels with the specified allowable exceptions.

The approach of some of Australia's other PTAs provides more room for circumvention of geoblocking. For example, ACIFTA refers to TPMs used 'in connection with the exercise of ... copyright and related rights, and that restrict acts ... which are not ... permitted by law'.[88] This wording would seem to prevent TPMs that go beyond copyright infringement and restrict activities that are otherwise legal. AANZFTA imposes

---

83 Ibid [1.14].

84 Ibid vii.

85 Ibid 108.

86 Ibid 105–106.

87 *Copyright Act 1968* (Cth) s 10(1) (definition of 'technological protection measure').

88 ACIFTA art 17.28. See also MAFTA art 13.2(d) (definition of 'effective technological measure'); JAEPA art 16.12.1(b).

similar wording and also makes the obligation to provide effective legal remedies against circumvention of TPMs an obligation to 'endeavour' to do so.[89] MAFTA provides a broad 'three-step test' approach for exceptions to the anti-circumvention provisions.[90] However, as with the impact of the AUSFTA on patents as discussed in part IVB below, the additional flexibilities in other PTAs are of limited significance while the AUSFTA remains in place because the AUSFTA imposes minimum standards on Australian copyright law.

III TRADE MARKS

A Trade Mark-Related Tobacco Disputes

A number of disputes with respect to tobacco control have arisen in recent years under Australian constitutional law, international trade law, and international investment law, which have implications for the treatment of trade marks in the intellectual property chapter of Australia's PTAs. In this section we reflect on the trade mark aspects of these disputes (some of which are ongoing at the time of writing) as a basis for considering Australian PTAs' conception of the nature of trade mark rights and exceptions to those rights. These disputes also illustrate the complexity of relationships between international trade law, international investment law, and national and international intellectual property laws.[91]

The potential for challenges to intellectual property regulation under ISDS[92] (which is explored further in Chapter 5 of this book) has been

---

[89] AANZFTA ch 13 art 5.2(b).

[90] MAFTA art 13.14.3.

[91] See also Sergio Puig, 'Tobacco Litigation in International Courts' (2016) 57(2) *Harvard International Law Journal* 383.

[92] See generally Tania Voon, Andrew D Mitchell and James Munro, 'Intellectual Property Rights in International Investment Agreements: Striving for Coherence in National and International Law' in Chin Lim and Bryan Mercurio (eds), *International Economic Law After the Global Crisis: A Tale of Fragmented Disciplines* (Cambridge University Press, 2015) (with Andrew Mitchell and James Munro) 380; Henning Grosse Ruse-Khan, 'Challenging Compliance with International Intellectual Property Norms in Investor–State Dispute Settlement' (2016) 19 *Journal of International Economic Law* 241; Carlos Correa and Jorge E Viñuales, 'Intellectual Property Rights as Protected Investments: How Open are the Gates?' (2016) 19 *Journal of International Economic Law* 91; James Gathii and Cynthia Ho, 'Regime Shifting of IP Law Making and Enforcement

recently highlighted by the two unsuccessful investment treaty claims brought by Philip Morris, as explained in this section, as well as the unsuccessful claim brought by Eli Lilly against Canada in relation to Canadian courts' interpretation and application of Canadian patent law.[93] ISDS is generally available only in respect of alleged breaches of investment obligations (contained in a BIT or the investment chapter of a PTA, or in some cases in an investment agreement between a foreign investor and the relevant national authority, or an authorisation granted by a party's foreign investment authority),[94] rather than to enforce the intellectual property chapter or other chapters in a PTA.[95] Nevertheless, intellectual property provisions in the relevant PTA, the WTO or domestic law may be relevant in interpreting or applying investment obligations.[96]

The disputes involving Australia centre on Australia's introduction of standardised (so-called 'plain') packaging of tobacco products, which was fully implemented from December 2012.[97] As Australia was the first country in the world to introduce such a measure (which excludes the use of promotional colours, graphics, logos and lettering), the tobacco industry fought it on numerous fronts.[98] Australia's population may be relatively small (24.4 million)[99] and its current smoking rate relatively

---

from the WTO to the International Investment Regime' (2017) 18 *Minnesota Journal of Law, Science and Technology* (forthcoming).

93 *Eli Lilly v Canada*, Final Award. See also Kathleen Liddell and Michael Waibel, 'Fair and Equitable Treatment and Judicial Patent Decisions' (2016) 19 *Journal of International Economic Law* 145.

94 See, eg, KAFTA art 11.16.1(a) and definitions of 'investment agreement' and 'investment authority' in art 11.28.

95 See, eg, in relation to the non-application of ISDS to the IP chapter in ChAFTA: Evidence to JSCOT, Canberra (17 August 2015) 24 (Jan Ward, Deputy Secretary, DFAT).

96 See generally Jarrod Hepburn, *Domestic Law in International Investment Arbitration* (Oxford University Press, 2017).

97 *Tobacco Plain Packaging Act 2011* (Cth). See generally Simon Chapman and Becky Freeman, *Removing the Emperor's Clothes: Australia and Tobacco Plain Packaging* (Sydney University Press, 2014).

98 In addition to the legal disputes mentioned below, see also, eg, Andrew D Mitchell and Tania Voon, 'Someone to Watch Over Me: The Use of FOI Requests by the Tobacco Industry' (2014) 22 *Australian Journal of Administrative Law* 18.

99 Australian Bureau of Statistics, *Population Clock* <http://www.abs.gov.au/ausstats/abs@.nsf/Web+Pages/Population+Clock?opendocument> (last visited 8 April 2017): 24,419,185.

low (12.8 per cent),[100] but if standardised packaging succeeds the greater risk to the industry is its adoption in countries around the world. The aggressive response of the industry belies its claims that such measures are ineffective. In Australia, strong evidence suggests the positive impact on public health that plain packaging has already had[101] (although it is a long-term strategy with effects to be seen after generations), and other countries are at various stages of introducing similar measures,[102] while also warding off legal challenges by the tobacco industry.[103] Implementing guidelines adopted by the Conference of the Parties to the WHO FCTC also encourage the 180 contracting parties to that treaty to consider adopting plain packaging.[104]

One question that has arisen in these disputes, which is particularly relevant to trade mark provisions under Australia's PTAs, is whether trade mark owners have a 'positive' right to use their registered trade marks or merely a 'negative' right to exclude others from using them. Davison and Emerton explain this distinction in a more nuanced fashion:

> The right to exclude others from using a trademark creates the conditions under which a trademark owner obtains both the exclusive privilege of using

---

[100] Australian Government, Australian Institute of Health and Welfare, *National Drug Strategy Household Survey detailed report* (2013) 19 (referring to the percentage of people in Australia aged 14 or older who were daily smokers).

[101] Australian Government, Department of Health, *Post-Implementation Review: Tobacco Plain Packaging* (2016) 4, 35–37. See also, eg, Melanie Wakefield et al, 'Australian Adult Smokers' Responses to Plain Packaging with Larger Graphic Health Warnings 1 Year After Implementation: Results from a National Cross-Sectional Tracking Survey' (2015) 24 *Tobacco Control* ii17.

[102] See, eg, *Public Health (Standardised Packaging of Tobacco) Act 2015* (Ireland); *The Standardised Packaging of Tobacco Products Regulations 2015* (UK); *Décret no 2016–334 du 21 mars 2016 relatif au paquet neutre des cigarettes et de certains produits du tabac* (France, 21 March 2016: decree concerning the neutral packaging of cigarettes and certain tobacco products).

[103] See, eg, *British American Tobacco UK Limited, British American Tobacco (Brands) Inc, British American Tobacco (Investments) Limited, JT International SA, Gallaher Limited, Imperial Tobacco Limited, Tann UK Limited, Tannpapier GmbH, Benkert UK Limited and Deutsche Benkert GmbH & Co KG v Secretary of State for Health* [2016] EWCA Civ 1182 (30 November 2016).

[104] *Guidelines for Implementation of Article 11 of the WHO Framework Convention on Tobacco Control (Packaging and Labelling of Tobacco Products)*, [46]; *Guidelines for implementation of Article 13 of the WHO Framework Convention on Tobacco Control (Tobacco Advertising, Promotion and Sponsorship)*, [17].

> the trademark as a trademark and the power to authorize others, such as licensees, to use the trademark exclusively.[105]

The characterisation of trade mark rights affects the legal claims against Australia in different ways.

In the High Court of Australia, a number of tobacco companies[106] alleged that Australia's plain packaging laws are unconstitutional,[107] on the grounds that they constitute an acquisition of property other than on just terms (that is, without compensation), contrary to s 51(xxxi) of the Australian Constitution. A majority of the Court rejected this claim,[108] essentially on the basis that an acquisition for the purposes of this provision requires the conferral of a 'proprietary' benefit,[109] which was absent in this case. The characterisation of trade mark rights was not essential to this conclusion. However, a majority of the Court suggested that trade mark rights under Australian trade mark law are negative rights,[110] notwithstanding the language of the relevant provision, which states that the registered owner of a trade mark has 'the exclusive rights: (a) to use the trade mark; and (b) to authorise other persons to use the

---

[105] Mark Davison and Patrick Emerton, 'Rights, Privileges, Legitimate Interests, and Justifiability: Article 20 of TRIPS and Plain Packaging of Tobacco' (2014) 29(3) *American University International Law Review* 505, 522.

[106] *JT International SA v Australia; British American Tobacco Australasia Ltd v Australia* [2012] HCA 43 ('*JT/BAT v Australia*'), [66]: Philip Morris Ltd, Van Nelle Tabak Nederland BV and Imperial Tobacco Australia Ltd intervening in support of the plaintiffs; the Northern Territory and the Australian Capital Territory intervening in support of the Commonwealth.

[107] See generally Sam Ricketson, 'Plain Packaging Legislation for Tobacco Products and Trade Marks in the High Court of Australia' (2013) 3(3) *Queen Mary Journal of Intellectual Property* 224; Tania Voon, 'Acquisition of Intellectual Property Rights: Australia's Plain Tobacco Packaging Dispute' [2013] 2 *European Intellectual Property Review* 113; Jonathan Liberman, 'Plainly Constitutional: The Upholding of Plain Tobacco Packaging by the High Court of Australia' (2013) 39 *American Journal of Law & Medicine* 361; Matthew Rimmer, 'The High Court of Australia and the Marlboro Man: The Battle over the Plain Packaging of Tobacco Products' in Tania Voon, Andrew D Mitchell and Jonathan Liberman (eds), *Regulating Tobacco, Alcohol and Unhealthy Foods: The Legal Issues* (Routledge, 2014) 337.

[108] *JT/BAT v Australia*, [43]–[44] (French CJ); [101], [155] (Gummow J); [188]–[189] (Hayne and Bell JJ); [296] (Crennan J); [372] (Kiefel J).

[109] *JT/BAT v Australia*, [169] (Hayne and Bell JJ); [42] (French CJ); [118], [131], [147] (Gummow J); [305] (Crennan J); [365] (Kiefel J).

[110] *JT/BAT v Australia*, [36], [43] (French CJ); [248] (Crennan J); [348] (Kiefel J); cf [107] (Gummow J).

trade mark' in relation to the goods or services in respect of which the trade mark is registered.[111]

The corresponding provision of the TRIPS Agreement is more obviously directed at trade mark rights as negative rights. TRIPS art 16.1 commences:

> The owner of a registered trademark shall have the *exclusive right to prevent* all third parties not having the owner's consent from using in the course of trade identical or similar signs for goods or services which are identical or similar to those in respect of which the trademark is registered where such use would result in a likelihood of confusion.[112]

The characterisation of trade mark rights in this provision is likely to be significant for the interpretation and application of other TRIPS provisions in addressing complaints brought in the WTO dispute settlement system against Australia's plain packaging laws by Cuba,[113] the Dominican Republic,[114] Honduras[115] and Indonesia[116] (Ukraine's claim having lapsed).[117] If, as TRIPS art 16.1 suggests and Australia maintains, TRIPS does not mandate a 'right to use' trade marks, many of the claims under

---

[111] *Trade Marks Act 1995* (Cth) s 20(1).

[112] Emphasis added.

[113] *Australia—Certain Measures Concerning Trademarks, Geographical Indications and Other Plain Packaging Requirements Applicable to Tobacco Products and Packaging: Request for the Establishment of a Panel by Cuba*, WTO Doc WT/DS458/14 (14 April 2014).

[114] *Australia—Certain Measures Concerning Trademarks, Geographical Indications and Other Plain Packaging Requirements Applicable to Tobacco Products and Packaging: Request for the Establishment of a Panel by the Dominican Republic*, WTO Doc WT/DS441/15 (13 November 2012).

[115] *Australia—Certain Measures Concerning Trademarks, Geographical Indications and Other Plain Packaging Requirements Applicable to Tobacco Products and Packaging: Request for the Establishment of a Panel by Honduras*, WTO Doc WT/DS435/16 (17 October 2012).

[116] *Australia—Certain Measures Concerning Trademarks, Geographical Indications and Other Plain Packaging Requirements Applicable to Tobacco Products and Packaging: Request for the Establishment of a Panel by Indonesia*, WTO Doc WT/DS467/15 (6 March 2014).

[117] *Australia—Certain Measures Concerning Trademarks and Other Plain Packaging Requirements Applicable to Tobacco Products and Packaging: Request for the Establishment of a Panel by Ukraine*, WTO Doc WT/DS434/11 (17 August 2012); *Australia—Certain Measures Concerning Trademarks and Other Plain Packaging Requirements Applicable to Tobacco Products and Packaging: Communication from the Chairperson of the Panel*, WTO Doc WT/DS434/16 (3 June 2015).

the TRIPS Agreement arguably fall away.[118] The greater uncertainty may be in relation to claims under TRIPS art 20, which states:

> The use of a trademark in the course of trade shall not be unjustifiably encumbered by special requirements, such as … use in a special form or use in a manner detrimental to its capability to distinguish the goods or services of one undertaking from those of other undertakings …

In our view, Australia has a strong defence to these claims as well. At the time of writing, the Panel Reports are pending in these disputes (with the final report expected to be issued to the parties not before May 2017)[119] and likely to be appealed in due course. Global interest in these disputes is reflected in the record numbers of third party WTO Members participating in them (more than 30 in each, including the EU representing its 28 member countries).[120] At least some of these complaints are being supported by tobacco companies, according to statements on the public record.[121]

---

118 *Australia—Certain Measures Concerning Trademarks, Geographical Indications and Other Plain Packaging Requirements Applicable to Tobacco Products and Packaging: Integrated Executive Summary of Australia's Submissions* (23 March 2016) [125]. See also *Australia—Certain Measures Concerning Trademarks, Geographical Indications and Other Plain Packaging Requirements Applicable to Tobacco Products and Packaging: Third Party Submission of Canada* (10 April 2015) [40], [46]. For further analysis of the claims in these disputes in relation to the TRIPS Agreement and the TBT Agreement in particular, see, eg, Andrew D Mitchell and Tania Voon, 'Face Off: Assessing WTO Challenges to Australia's Scheme for Plain Tobacco Packaging' (2011) 22(3) *Public Law Review* 218.

119 See, eg, *Australia—Certain Measures Concerning Trademarks, Geographical Indications and Other Plain Packaging Requirements Applicable to Tobacco Products and Packaging: Communication from the Chairperson of the Panel*, WTO Doc WT/DS435/21 (6 December 2016).

120 Cuba (33); Dominican Republic (34); Honduras (37); Indonesia (33). See WTO, *Index of Disputes Issues: Tobacco* <https://www.wto.org/english/tratop_e/dispu_e/dispu_subjects_index_e.htm> (last visited 8 April 2017).

121 See, eg, Christopher Thompson, 'Big Tobacco Backs Australian Law Opposers' (29 April 2012) *Financial Times* (online); Stephanie Nebehay, 'Australia Says Big Tobacco Aiding WTO Challengers' (23 May 2012) *Reuters* (online); Michael Goldhaber, 'Smoke and Lawyers' (1 January 2015) *The American Lawyer* (online).

Philip Morris Asia Ltd also brought a direct claim against Australia with respect to plain packaging under the Australia–Hong Kong BIT,[122] pursuant to the ISDS mechanism discussed further in Chapter 5. That claim failed on jurisdictional grounds because the tribunal determined that Philip Morris had engaged in an 'abuse of rights'[123] by making its investment in Australia (almost a year after the government's announcement of its intention to introduce plain tobacco packaging),[124] with the sole or predominant purpose of bringing the claim.[125] At the time of writing, the tribunal's decision with respect to the allocation of the costs of the proceedings has not yet been made public.[126]

Had the investment treaty claim against Australia proceeded to the merits, we believe that Australia would have had a strong defence,[127] as in the WTO disputes. The outcome may have depended in part on the tribunal's characterisation of trade mark rights under Australian law,[128] which would have been influenced by the High Court's reasoning in the constitutional case. Further insight into that issue, from the perspective of international investment law, can be gleaned from the reasoning of the tribunal in the unsuccessful investment treaty claims brought by Philip Morris against Uruguay under the Switzerland-Uruguay BIT with respect to other requirements regarding tobacco product packaging and labelling.[129] Similarly to Davison and Emerton as noted above, the tribunal stated:

---

122 *Philip Morris v Australia*, Notice of Claim.

123 *Philip Morris v Australia*, Jurisdictional Decision, [588].

124 Prime Minister of Australia, 'Anti-Smoking Action' (Media Release, 29 April 2010).

125 *Philip Morris v Australia*, Jurisdictional Decision, [584].

126 On 7 July 2017, while this book was in press, the tribunal's final award regarding costs of 8 March 2017 was released to the public. The tribunal required the claimant to pay Australia a portion of Australia's costs incurred and a portion of Australia's share of the arbitration costs. However, the proportions and amounts were redacted from the decision.

127 See Tania Voon and Andrew D Mitchell, 'Implications of International Investment Law for Plain Tobacco Packaging: Lessons from the Hong Kong–Australia BIT' in Tania Voon, Andrew D Mitchell and Jonathan Liberman with Glyn Ayres (eds), *Public Health and Plain Packaging of Cigarettes: Legal Issues* (Edward Elgar, 2012) 137.

128 See, eg, *Philip Morris v Uruguay*, Award, [270]–[271].

129 See generally Benn McGrady, 'Implications of ongoing trade and investment disputes concerning tobacco: Philip Morris v Uruguay' in Voon et al, above n 127, 173; Tania Voon and Andrew D Mitchell, 'Philip Morris vs tobacco control: two wins for public health, but uncertainty remains' (12 September 2016) 182 *Columbia FDI Perspectives* (online); Tania Voon, 'Philip Morris v

> [b]oth Parties have focused on a dichotomy between a right to use and a right to protect. However, it may be more fruitful to view the case as a question of an absolute versus exclusive right to use … [U]nder Uruguayan law or international conventions to which Uruguay is a party the trademark holder does not enjoy an absolute right of use, free of regulation, but only an exclusive right to exclude third parties from the market so that only the trademark holder has the possibility to use the trademark in commerce, subject to the State's regulatory power.[130]

Although one arbitrator dissented in part, the dissent did not relate to this aspect of the decision. Thus, these statements can be understood as the unanimous approach of the tribunal to trade mark rights. This approach provided one basis for the tribunal's unanimous rejection of the claims by Philip Morris of expropriation, and similar reasoning would have supported Australia's defence as well.

B Rights of Trade Mark Owners in Australia's PTAs

As demonstrated by the tobacco control disputes just discussed, the conception of trade mark rights in Australia's PTAs may have important implications for Australia's obligations under both international trade law and international investment law. The wording of Australia's PTAs may therefore prove crucial in ensuring Australia is able to regulate in good faith with respect to matters of public health such as tobacco control in effective ways that may not necessarily have been envisaged at the time of each treaty's conclusion. The characterisation of trade mark rights in Australia's PTAs could directly affect a State-to-State claim under a PTA of a breach of intellectual property provisions in the PTA, or indirectly affect an ISDS claim under a PTA alleging a breach of investment protections in the PTA.

The AUSFTA states in relation to trade mark rights:

> Each Party shall provide that the owner of a registered mark shall have the *exclusive right to prevent* all third parties not having the owner's consent from using in the course of trade identical or similar signs, including geographical indications, for goods or services that are *related to* those goods or services in respect of which the owner's mark is registered, where such use would result in a likelihood of confusion.[131]

Uruguay: Implications for Public Health' (2017) 18(2) *Journal of World Investment and Trade* 320.

[130] *Philip Morris v Uruguay*, Award, [267], [271].

[131] AUSFTA art 17.2.4 (emphasis added).

The ACIFTA,[132] KAFTA[133] and TPP[134] contain similar wording. Thus, although these treaties (all flowing from the AUSFTA) maintain the 'negative' type reference of TRIPS art 16.1, they also appear to strengthen the TRIPS protection by extending the rights beyond the goods or services in respect of which the trade mark is registered to goods and services that are 'related to' those in respect of which the trade mark is registered. This provision also appears to enhance protections for geographical indications, although a footnote to the TPP specifies that the provision is not to be 'interpreted to affect' the parties' rights and obligations under two of the three TRIPS provisions targeting geographical indications (that is, TRIPS arts 22 and 23).[135] The ANZCERTA does not address trade marks at all, while Australia's other PTAs do address trade marks but do not directly specify whether trade mark owners have positive or negative rights.

Grosse Ruse-Khan describes 'the concept of "negative rights"' as 'the most important TRIPS flexibility', contending that '[l]imiting IP rights as mere "negative rights" allows governments to impose further regulatory controls on their utilisation and exploitation'.[136] That flexibility is retained to some extent in Australia's PTAs in relation to trade mark rights, either through explicit wording corresponding to that in TRIPS art 16.1 or through an absence of specification. Although this omission may create uncertainty about the drafters' intentions, the broader context of the TRIPS Agreement and domestic and international laws regarding trade mark rights may support the interpretation of these PTAs as not imposing on parties obligations to accord positive rights to use trade marks, particularly given the more limited nature of trade mark provisions in these PTAs.

Flexibility is also enhanced by the reference to allowed exceptions in several of Australia's PTAs. These exceptions derive from TRIPS art 17, which provides:

> Members may provide limited exceptions to the rights conferred by a trademark, such as fair use of descriptive terms, provided that such exceptions

---

[132] ACIFTA art 17.10.

[133] KAFTA art 13.2.3.

[134] TPP art 18.20.

[135] TPP art 18.20 n 12.

[136] Henning Grosse Ruse-Khan, 'Protecting intellectual property rights under BITs, FTAs and TRIPS: Conflicting regimes or mutual coherence?' in Chester Brown and Kate Miles, *Evolution in Investment Treaty Law and Arbitration* (Cambridge University Press, 2011) 485, 489.

take account of the legitimate interests of the owner of the trademark and of third parties.

Similar wording appears in the four Australian PTAs that adopt TRIPS art 16.1-type language (AUSFTA,[137] ACIFTA,[138] KAFTA,[139] and the TPP)[140] as well as MAFTA.[141] The need for express exceptions may be diminished in those PTAs that contain less detailed obligations regarding trade marks.

The tobacco cases reveal how concepts such as the rights of trade mark owners and the scope of exceptions to such rights may come to play an important role in justifying regulatory approaches of Australia and other countries, particularly in circumstances where ISDS may be used to enforce obligations in PTAs and BITs. The current drafting of Australia's PTAs does not raise concerns in relation to Australia's plain tobacco packaging measure or tobacco control more generally. Nevertheless, the difference between the more particularised US-based provisions on trade marks (building on the relevant TRIPS provisions) and Australia's other less prescriptive PTAs demonstrates how increasing intellectual property protections beyond the minimum standards imposed by the TRIPS Agreement may have unintended and unforeseeable consequences. These treaties are difficult to modify and may remain in place for decades, during which time new regulatory challenges (for example in relation to alcohol labelling or unhealthy foods)[142] may emerge that will be assessed according to the precise language adopted in the relevant provisions.

IV PATENTS

A TRIPS-Plus Obligations in the AUSFTA and the TPP

As noted in earlier chapters, requirements regarding patent regulation have been of particular concern to the Australian community in connection with PTAs such as the AUSFTA, especially due to the potential

[137] AUSFTA art 17.2.5.
[138] ACIFTA art 17.11.
[139] KAFTA art 13.2.4.
[140] TPP art 18.21.
[141] MAFTA art 13.9.4.
[142] See, eg, Paula O'Brien et al, 'Marginalising Health Information: Implications of the Trans-Pacific Partnership for Alcohol Labelling' (2017) *Melbourne University Law Review* (forthcoming); Mark Davison, 'International Intellectual Property Law' in Voon, Mitchell and Liberman, above n 107, 131.

impact on pharmaceuticals, and in particular the PBS.[143] As shown in Table 2.2, the TRIPS Agreement[144] required an increase in the patent term under Australian law from 16 years from filing to 20 years[145] from filing. Although subsequent PTAs have not required an increase in that term *per se*, the AUSFTA required the introduction of additional protections for patent owners that may have the effect of increasing the term in practice beyond 20 years. These kinds of 'TRIPS-plus' obligations[146] have been targeted (including as they appear in the AUSFTA in particular) in the UN Secretary-General's high level panel report on access to medicines.[147]

For example, the AUSFTA requires the US and Australia to provide the means to increase the term of a patent at the request of the patent owner to compensate for 'unreasonable delays', which would include a delay of more than four years from filing an application or two years from a request for examination of an application (whichever is later).[148] In calculating delays, 'periods attributable to actions of the patent applicant or any opposing third person need not be included'.[149] With respect to pharmaceutical products, patent term adjustment must also be available

---

143 See, eg, Harris, Nicol and Gruen, above n 19, 268, 292, 298; Thomas Faunce and Ruth Townsend, 'Public Health and Medicine Policies' in Jane Kelsey (ed), *No Ordinary Deal: Unmasking the Trans-Pacific Partnership Free Trade Agreement* (Allen & Unwin, 2010) 149, 154–155; Andrew D Mitchell and Tania Voon, 'Australia–United States Free Trade Agreement' in Simon Lester and Bryan Mercurio (eds), *Bilateral and Regional Trade Agreements: Case Studies* (Cambridge University Press, 2009) 6, 17–19, 18–33; Bryan Mercurio, 'The Impact of the Australia–United States Free Trade Agreement on the Provision of Health Services in Australia' (2005) 26 *Whittier Law Review* 1051. Cf Andrew L Stoler, 'The Australia–United States FTA as a "Third Wave" Trade Agreement: Beyond the WTO Envelope' in Andrew D Mitchell, *Challenges and Prospects for the WTO* (Cameron May, 2005) 253, 264–265.

144 TRIPS Agreement art 33.

145 *Patents (World Trade Organization Amendments) Act 1994* (Cth) s 4, amending *Patents Act 1990* (Cth) s 67.

146 See generally Bryan Mercurio, 'TRIPS-Plus Provisions in FTAs: Recent Trends' in Lorand Bartels and Federico Ortino (eds), *Regional Trade Agreements and the WTO Legal System* (Oxford University Press, 2006) 215.

147 UN, *Report of the United Nations Secretary-General's High-Level Panel on Access to Medicines: Promoting innovation and access to health technologies* (September 2016) 25–26. See also Matthew Rimmer, 'The *Trans-Pacific Partnership*: Intellectual Property, Public Health, and Access to Essential Medicines' (2017) 29 *Intellectual Property Journal* 275.

148 AUSFTA art 17.9.8(a).

149 AUSFTA art 17.9.8(a).

for 'unreasonable curtailment of the effective patent term as a result of the marketing approval process', although the AUSFTA does not specify a time period for such curtailment.[150]

In addition, the AUSFTA imposes a data exclusivity period for pharmaceuticals:

> If a Party requires, as a condition of approving the marketing of a new pharmaceutical product, the submission of undisclosed test or other data concerning safety or efficacy of the product, the Party shall not permit third persons, without the consent of the person who provided the information, to market the same or a similar product on the basis of that information, or the marketing approval granted to the person who submitted such information, for *at least five years* from the date of marketing approval by the Party.[151]

A similar provision imposes an exclusivity period of ten years for new agricultural chemical products.[152] The specification of these minimum periods of exclusivity goes beyond the general TRIPS requirements: TRIPS art 39(3) requires WTO Members to protect 'against unfair commercial use' undisclosed (that is, confidential) test data submitted for marketing of pharmaceutical or agricultural chemical products using new chemical entities. Australian PTAs often reaffirm parties' commitment to TRIPS provisions.[153]

As shown in Table 2.2, the TPP maintains the stringent requirements introduced into Australian patent law as a result of the AUSFTA: an extension to the term of patent protection to compensate for unreasonable delays in issuing a patent[154] or (in the case of pharmaceuticals) granting marketing approval;[155] and a period of data exclusivity for five years from the date of marketing approval for a new pharmaceutical product[156] and ten years for a new agricultural chemical product.[157] However, the TPP increases the amount of delay that is 'unreasonable' for the issuing of a patent to more than five (instead of four) years from the date of filing or three (instead of two) years from a request for examination of the application (whichever is later).[158] The TPP also adds to the periods

---

150 AUSFTA art 17.9.8(b).
151 AUSFTA art 17.10.1(a) (emphasis added).
152 AUSFTA art 17.10.1(b).
153 See, eg, TAFTA art 1301; SAFTA 2011 art 2.
154 TPP art 18.46.4.
155 TPP art 18.48.2.
156 TPP art 18.50.1(a).
157 TPP art 18.47.1.
158 TPP art 18.46.4.

Table 2.2 Selected Patent Obligations in the WTO and Australia's PTAs

Treaty	Entry into force	Minimum patent term	Patent term extension for unreasonable delays in issuing patent or (for pharmaceuticals) marketing approval	Data exclusivity period for pharmaceuticals: protection of undisclosed data submitted for marketing approval	Data exclusivity period for pharmaceuticals that are/contain biologics
ANZCERTA	1983	✘	✘	✘	✘
TRIPS[159]	1995	20 years from filing	✘	✘	✘
SAFTA original	2003	✘	✘	✘	✘
TAFTA	2005	✘	✘	✘	✘
AUSFTA	2005	✘	✔	5 years from marketing approval	✘
ACIFTA	2009	✘	✘	✘	✘
AANZFTA	2009	✘	✘	✘	✘
SAFTA amended	2011	✘	✘	✘	✘
MAFTA	2013	✘	✘	✘	✘
KAFTA	2014	✘	✘	✘	✘
JAEPA	2015	✘	✘	✘	✘
ChAFTA	2015	✘	✘	✘	✘
TPP	–	✘	✔	5 years from marketing approval	8 years from marketing approval; or 5 years plus other measures and market circumstances for comparable outcome
SAFTA 2016	–	✘	✘	✘	✘

159 See above reference to TRIPS art 39.3 and its incorporation in other PTAs.

of time that need not be included in calculating the amount of delay: a TPP party may exclude from the calculation of the amount of delay not only periods attributable to the patent applicant (as in the AUSFTA) but also periods that do not occur during the processing or examination of the application by the granting authority, and periods that are not directly attributable to that authority.[160] These changes have some potential to limit the duration of the patent term in comparison to the AUSFTA, as a side letter between the two countries confirms that these particular TPP provisions would replace the corresponding AUSFTA provisions.[161]

The TPP also introduces additional data exclusivity requirements regarding each pharmaceutical product that is or contains a 'biologic', meaning at least a product that is or contains 'a protein produced using biotechnology processes, for use in human beings for the prevention, treatment, or cure of a disease or condition'.[162] A strange and complicated provision allows TPP parties to protect such a product in one of two ways in relation to the product's first marketing approval. Each Party shall provide 'effective market protection' *either*: by extending the period of data exclusivity to 'at least eight years from the date of first marketing approval of that product in that Party'[163] (instead of the usual five applicable to pharmaceutical products);[164] or by extending the period of data exclusivity to:

> (i) … at least five years from the date of first marketing approval of that product in that Party,
> (ii) through other measures, and
> (iii) recognising that market circumstances also contribute to effective market protection
>
> to deliver a comparable outcome in the market.[165]

The second, rather uncertain, option for protecting biologics under the TPP allowed Australia to maintain that its current system of providing a five-year period of data exclusivity for pharmaceutical products (as

---

[160] TPP art 18.46.4.

[161] Exchange of letters between Andrew Robb, Minister for Trade and Investment (Australia) and Michael Froman, United States Trade Representative (4 February 2016) [3].

[162] TPP art 18.51.2.

[163] TPP art 18.51.1(a).

[164] TPP art 18.50.1(a).

[165] TPP art 18.51.1(b).

required under the AUSFTA) meets the TPP requirements.[166] Australia touted this drafting of the TPP text as a significant achievement in protecting Australian regulatory approaches,[167] as part of its broader claim that the TPP would not require any changes to IP laws or regulations in Australia[168] (a claim that some have contested with respect to particular issues, while also querying its relevance as a benchmark:[169] 'The simplistic view of many … IP negotiators that there is no harm in agreeing to provisions which simply mirror current practice is based on the entirely false premise that the current system is worth preserving forever').[170] The Productivity Commission found in its report that although '[b]iologic drugs differ from standard pharmaceuticals' (in that they are generally more difficult and more expensive to both produce and copy), extending the period of data protection for these products would 'likely overcompensate most products and increase consumer costs'.[171] However, the outcome on biologics caused significant consternation among some US interests, given the initial US proposal for a 12-year period of data exclusivity, consistent with its own laws.[172]

The AUSFTA contains certain exceptions regarding patent obligations, including a provision equivalent to TRIPS art 30,[173] but these other provisions do not substantially affect the TRIPS-plus obligations outlined above. The AUSFTA also contains a number of other TRIPS-plus provisions in relation to patents,[174] such as a restriction of the grounds

---

166 See, eg, *National Interest Analysis (Australia)* [2016] ATNIA 4 (4 February 2016) [42].

167 See, eg, DFAT, *TPP Outcomes: Biologics* (Fact Sheet updated 6 October 2015). See also 'Chile Sees Win on Sensitive TPP IP Provisions Such as Biologics, Linkage' (27 November 2015) 33 *Inside US Trade* (online).

168 See, eg, *National Interest Analysis (Australia)* [2016] ATNIA 4 (4 February 2016) [39].

169 See, eg, Weatherall, *Submission 168*, above n 11, 3; Senate Foreign Affairs, Defence and Trade References Committee, *Proposed Trans-Pacific Partnership (TPP) Agreement* (February 2017) [3.53]–[3.54].

170 Hazel VJ Moir, 'The Patent Price of Market Access in the AUSFTA' (2015) 69(5) *Australian Journal of International Affairs* 559, 564, 571–572.

171 *Productivity Commission 2016*, 285.

172 See, eg, 'TPP Allows Five Years on Biologic Data Exclusivity' (9 October 2015) *International Trade Daily* (online); *Productivity Commission 2016*, 19.

173 AUSFTA art 17.9.3.

174 See Moir, above n 170, 565–568.

for revoking a patent.[175] The TPP also contains numerous TRIPS-plus provisions, many similar to those of the AUSFTA.[176] Nevertheless, the TPP appears to include some improvements on the AUSFTA in connection with patents. As noted above, the TPP slightly increases the period of time that constitutes an 'unreasonable' delay for the purposes of patent term extension.[177] The TPP,[178] like the TRIPS Agreement,[179] allows parties to determine their own approach to the 'exhaustion' of intellectual property rights (or at least excludes WTO dispute settlement as regards such questions), meaning for example that parties are free to allow 'parallel' imports of patented products sold in other countries. However, the AUSFTA requires Australia to allow patent owners to prevent importation of a patented product without consent, 'at least where the patentee has placed restrictions on importation by contract or other means'.[180] As between Australia and the US, this AUSFTA provision on parallel importation would have prevailed even if the TPP had entered into force in the form signed in 2016.[181] In contrast, pursuant to the side letter between Australia and the US regarding intellectual property, the broader TPP provision requiring parties to implement a 'regulatory review exception'[182] (an exception to patent rights to enable a third party during the term of the patent to obtain regulatory approval for the marketing of a generic product after the end of the patent term) would have replaced the more prescriptive AUSFTA provision.[183]

In addition to a TRIPS art 30-type provision,[184] the TPP contains provisions concerning compulsory licensing and public health that also provide more scope for regulatory autonomy than those of the AUSFTA.

---

[175] AUSFTA art 17.9.5. See also Exchange of letters between Mark Vaile, Minister for Trade (Australia) and Robert Zoellick, United States Trade Representative (18 May 2004) [4].

[176] See, eg, TPP art 18.39.

[177] See above nn 160–62 and corresponding text.

[178] TPP art 18.11. See also, eg, ChAFTA art 11.8.

[179] TRIPS Agreement art 6.

[180] AUSFTA art 17.9.4.

[181] TPP art 18.11 n 8.

[182] TPP art 18.49. In the WTO, a WTO Panel (not appealed) has interpreted a Canadian regulatory review exception as falling within the allowable exceptions under TRIPS art 30: Panel Report, *Canada—Pharmaceutical Patents*, [7.84].

[183] AUSFTA art 17.9.6. See also Exchange of letters between Mark Vaile, Minister for Trade (Australia) and Robert Zoellick, United States Trade Representative (18 May 2004) [1].

[184] TPP art 18.40.

The AUSFTA restricts the circumstances in which the parties may issue compulsory licences[185] (specifically, to remedy an anti-competitive practice under the relevant domestic law, or in cases of public non-commercial use, national emergency, or other circumstances of extreme urgency).[186] In contrast, TRIPS art 31 imposes conditions on compulsory licences without specifying the circumstances in which a WTO Member may issue them. TRIPS art 31(b) refers to national emergency, other circumstances of extreme urgency and cases of public non-commercial use, not as criteria for issuing compulsory licences but as criteria for waiving the requirement to seek authorisation from the right holder on reasonable commercial terms. An amendment to the TRIPS Agreement entered into force on 23 January 2017 following its acceptance by two-thirds of the WTO membership[187] (with Australia having accepted on 12 September 2007),[188] inserting a new art 31*bis* to allow further scope for the use of compulsory licences to assist developing countries lacking sufficient pharmaceutical manufacturing capacity. In Chapter 4, we explain how most of Australia's PTAs partially exclude compulsory licensing and other intellectual property restrictions from the expropriation obligation in the investment chapter.

The TPP takes a less restrictive approach than the AUSFTA, aligning more closely with the pre-existing TRIPS flexibilities. To begin with, as a general matter, under TPP art 18.6, the parties 'affirm their commitment'[189]

---

185 Grosse Ruse-Khan, 'Protecting Intellectual Property Rights', above n 136, 492.

186 AUSFTA art 17.9.7.

187 WTO General Council, *Amendment of the TRIPS Agreement: Decision of 6 December 2005*, WTO Doc WT/L/641 (8 December 2005); WTO, 'WTO Members welcome entry into force of amendment to ease access to medicines', News Item (30 January 2017). See also Thomas Pogge, Matthew Rimmer and Kim Rubenstein (eds), *Incentives for Global Public Health: Patent Law and Access to Medicines* (Cambridge University Press, 2010); Andrew D Mitchell and Tania Voon, 'Patents and Public Health in the WTO, FTAs and Beyond: Tension and Conflict in International Law' (2009) 43(3) *Journal of World Trade* 571; Frederick Abbott, 'The WTO Medicines Decision: World Pharmaceutical Trade and the Protection of Public Health' (2005) 99(2) *American Journal of International Law* 317.

188 See WTO, *Amendment of the TRIPS Agreement* <https://www.wto.org/english/tratop_e/trips_e/amendment_e.htm> (last visited 8 April 2017).

189 TPP art 18.6.1.

to the *Doha Declaration on TRIPS and Public Health*[190] and also specify certain 'understandings',[191] including that:

> The obligations of this Chapter do not and should not prevent a Party from taking measures to protect public health. Accordingly, while reiterating their commitment to this Chapter, the Parties affirm that this Chapter can and should be interpreted and implemented in a manner supportive of each Party's right to protect public health and, in particular, to promote access to medicines for all.[192]

The TPP also specifies that each TPP party 'shall notify, if it has not already done so, the WTO of its acceptance of the *Protocol amending the TRIPS Agreement*, done at Geneva on December 6, 2005'.[193] More specifically, TPP art 18.41 provides:

> *Other Use Without Authorisation of the Right Holder*
>
> The Parties understand that nothing in this Chapter limits a Party's rights and obligations under Article 31 of the TRIPS Agreement, any waiver or any amendment to that Article that the Parties accept.

Finally, as regards data exclusivity and biologics, the TPP makes clear that TPP parties 'may take measures to protect public health'[194] in accordance with the *Doha Declaration on TRIPS and Public Health*,[195] and any waiver or amendment of the TRIPS Agreement to implement that declaration 'that enters into force with respect to the Parties'.[196]

These TPP provisions arguably go further in promoting TRIPS flexibilities than does ChAFTA, which nevertheless reaffirms the parties' 'commitment to contribute to the international efforts' towards this TRIPS amendment[197] and 'confirm[s] that the provisions of this Chapter are without prejudice to the Doha Declaration'.[198] The TPP provisions also provide more flexibility to governments in relation to compulsory

---

190 WTO Ministerial Conference, *Declaration on the TRIPS Agreement and Public Health Adopted on 14 November 2001*, WTO Doc WT/MIN(01)/Dec/2 (20 November 2001).
191 TPP art 18.6.1.
192 TPP art 18.6.1(a).
193 TPP art 18.6.2.
194 TPP art 18.50.3.
195 TPP art 18.50.3(a).
196 TPP art 18.50.3(b)–(c).
197 ChAFTA art 11.7.2.
198 ChAFTA art 11.7.1.

licensing and data exclusivity than does the AUSFTA, because of their stronger recognition of existing TRIPS flexibilities. Unlike the TPP, the AUSFTA is currently in force for Australia and undermines flexibilities directed at public health that are in force under the TRIPS Agreement in the WTO.

B Impact of the AUSFTA on Australia's Other International Trade Obligations

These additional patent protections required under the AUSFTA and the TPP do not form part of Australia's other PTAs, concluded before or since the AUSFTA. Indeed, DFAT has identified the AUSFTA as 'the only PTA that has required changes to Australia's IP laws'.[199] Thus, in the absence of the TPP, Australia is left with the obligations already assumed under the AUSFTA and may have more freedom in enacting reforms to patent law. This freedom is supported by explicit exceptions to patent obligations in Australia's PTAs (in addition to the omission of extensive TRIPS-plus obligations regarding patents in most of its PTAs).[200] For example, the patent obligations in MAFTA include various exceptions including under art 13.11.4: 'Nothing in this Article will limit the scope of exceptions to patentability available in each Party's laws and regulations at the time that this Agreement enters into force.' In a sense, this provision may be understood as grandfathering for each party any existing non-conforming measures imposed by that party (although perhaps it was needed due to a significant TRIPS-plus provision in MAFTA that would otherwise create a presumption of patent validity).[201] MAFTA, alongside other Australian PTAs, also duplicates the allowance in TRIPS art 30 for parties to 'provide limited exceptions to the exclusive rights conferred by a patent, provided that such exceptions do not unreasonably conflict with a normal exploitation of the patent and do not unreasonably prejudice the legitimate interests of the patent owner, taking account of the legitimate interests of third parties'.[202]

However, these exceptions and the omission of extensive patent obligations from most Australian PTAs do little to assist Australia in relation to the high standards already accepted under the AUSFTA. The TRIPS Agreement and the AUSFTA impose minimum standards of

---

199 *Productivity Commission 2016*, 611. Cf Moir, above n 170, 570.

200 But on the inclusion of some TRIPS-plus provisions see Moir, above n 170, 566.

201 MAFTA art 13.8.2. See Moir, above n 170, 568.

202 MAFTA art 13.11.3; ACIFTA art 17.20; KAFTA art 13.8.3.

intellectual property protection,[203] which have become the floor for intellectual property protection in Australia in general, with respect to the nationals of not only all WTO Members but also all countries. Australia's obligation to provide a patent term of at least 20 years from filing under Article 33 of the TRIPS Agreement is enforceable by any WTO Member pursuant to the WTO dispute settlement system.[204] In addition, Article 4 of the TRIPS Agreement imposes an MFN obligation on each WTO Member, such that Australia must accord any 'advantage' granted to United States nationals under the AUSFTA 'immediately and unconditionally to the nationals of all other Members'. This MFN obligation means that in effect Australia must apply the TRIPS-plus protections for patents under the AUSFTA discussed above (patent term extension for unreasonable delays and data exclusivity periods) to nationals of all WTO Members.[205] Moreover, as a practical matter, intellectual property standards tend to be applied generally rather than distinguishing between nationals of different countries (which is why cross-retaliation under the TRIPS Agreement to enforce DSB rulings has not been successfully implemented in practice,[206] notwithstanding DSB authorisation to do so).[207] Accordingly, in practice, the increased patent protections under the AUSFTA apply across the board in Australia, even though the WTO-consistency of such TRIPS-plus provisions is questionable.[208]

---

[203] TRIPS Agreement art 1.1; AUSFTA art 17.1.1.

[204] TRIPS Agreement art 64.1.

[205] See, eg, Antony Taubman, Hannu Wager and Jayashree Watal (eds), *A Handbook on the WTO TRIPS Agreement* (Cambridge University Press, 2012) 18; Grosse Ruse-Khan, above n 136, 491, n 19; Thomas Cottier, 'The Agreement on Trade-Related Aspects of Intellectual Property Rights' in Patrick Macrory, Michael Plummer and Arthur Appleton (eds), *The World Trade Organization* (Springer, 2005) vol I, 1041, 1068–1069.

[206] See, eg, Andrew D Mitchell and Constantine Salonidis, 'David's Sling: Cross-Agreement Retaliation in International Trade Disputes' (2011) 45(2) *Journal of World Trade* 457, 480–485.

[207] See the summary of cases in Taubman, Wager and Watal, above n 205, 165.

[208] See Mitchell and Voon, above n 187, 596–599 regarding the difficulties of characterising more stringent intellectual property protections as advantages under TRIPS art 4, the potential for at least some TRIPS-plus provisions to be contrary to WTO law and public international law more generally, and the uncertainty surrounding the possible application of GATT art XXIV to the TRIPS Agreement. See also Henning Grosse Ruse-Khan, 'Time for a Paradigm Shift? Exploring Maximum Standards in International Intellectual Property Protection' (2009) 1(1) *Journal of Trade, Law and Development* 56; Grosse Ruse-Khan, 'Protecting Intellectual Property Rights', above n 136, 510–515.

C Costs of Excessive Patent Protection

Although in some respects the TPP might have marginally improved the approach to patents in the AUSFTA from Australia's perspective, concerns about the impact of TPP on medicine prices and innovation extend beyond Australia. In particular, while Australia has already agreed to many of the key TRIPS-plus provisions in the TPP because of their existence in the AUSFTA, some other TPP countries (such as Viet Nam and Malaysia)[209] have not done so and would be agreeing to strengthen patent protections significantly under the TPP. This change would also directly affect Australia (aside from any moral or humanitarian concerns), for example because of the impact of such increases on international prices and innovation. According to Doctors Without Borders:

> [T]he TPP will … fail to address the urgent need for reform in the biomedical innovation system. The sole reliance on high medicine prices, backed by monopolies expanded and further entrenched by the TPP, is a flawed paradigm for funding innovation. This leads to unaffordable prices while failing to stimulate innovation for diseases disproportionately affecting developing countries, where patients have limited purchasing power.[210]

The costs of an unbalanced patent system that disproportionately benefits patent owners have been documented elsewhere.[211] Harris, Nicol and Gruen concluded in 2013:

> Australia's patent system has allowed and will continue for some time to allow patents to be granted which would not be granted elsewhere; it has awarded a longer effective patent life than is provided in the United States or than seems necessary to underpin drug development in Australia; it has allowed patents to expire later in Australia than in its major trading partners. All of this has limited the generic manufacturing base, employment and exports and it has increased Australia's pharmaceutical costs.[212]

Moir contended in 2015 that 'the social cost of patent policy is both absolutely high and substantially higher than the cost of alternative more efficient policies. The gains to producers are between an eighth and a

---

209 Doctors Without Borders/Médecins Sans Frontières, *Submission No 28 to the Senate Foreign Affairs, Defence and Trade References Committee Inquiry into the TPP* (October 2016) 5.

210 Ibid 7.

211 See, eg, Moir, above n 170, 569.

212 Harris, Nicol and Gruen, above n 19, xiv.

sixth of the cost to consumers'.[213] In its 2016 report on Australia's intellectual property arrangements, the Productivity Commission estimated 'the cost to the Australian Government (and ultimately taxpayers)' of extensions of pharmaceutical patent terms at AUD260 million per annum:[214] 'This cost only accounts for government expenditure on the PBS, which makes up 80 per cent of the cost of all PBS medicines. Consumer costs make up the remaining 20 per cent.'[215]

Nevertheless, the Productivity Commission concluded that reform of the Australian patent system is not only needed but also possible within the limits of Australia's international trade obligations:

> Australia provides stronger patent rights than most other advanced countries. As a large net importer of patented technology, overcompensation is particularly costly for Australia …
>
> While achieving a more effective and efficient patent system is constrained by international agreements, reform can be achieved.[216]

Reforms recommended by the Productivity Commission in 2016 include, for example, changes to the extension of patent terms for pharmaceuticals,[217] the introduction of an 'objects clause' specifying the purpose of the *Patents Act 1990* (Cth) as 'enhancing the wellbeing of Australians by promoting technological innovation and the transfer and dissemination of technology',[218] in order to 'better balance the patent rights of software innovators and users'.[219]

V CONCLUSION

In its 2010 report on Australia's PTAs, the Productivity Commission concluded:

> Australia should not generally seek to include IP provisions in further [PTAs], and that any IP provisions that are proposed for a particular agreements

---

213 Moir, above n 170, 569.
214 *Productivity Commission 2016*, 298.
215 Ibid.
216 Ibid 199.
217 Ibid 310.
218 Ibid 219.
219 Ibid 281.

> should only be included after an economic assessment of the impacts, including on consumers, in Australia and partner countries.[220]

In its 2016 report on Australia's IP arrangements, the Productivity Commission recommended a review of the TRIPS Agreement.[221] The evidence examined in this chapter supports these notes of caution as regards future Australian PTAs as well as the need to review existing IP arrangements. With the current text of the TPP no longer being viable, and with the potential for the TPP and RCEP to proceed in the absence of the US, Australia has the chance to demonstrate leadership and circumspection in relation to IP protection at the national and international levels. If the AUSFTA is renegotiated, Australia needs to be ready to counter US demands for further increasing IP protection in a manner that is likely to upset the balance of the IP regime and undermine the purpose of IP rules in encouraging innovation while ensuring dissemination and access to protected material. A renegotiation would not necessarily be disadvantageous to Australia, if the opportunity can be seized to pull back on some of the more extreme aspects of the AUSFTA, perhaps drawing on some of the improvements found in the TPP (such as longer periods to amount to an 'unreasonable' delay in issuing a patent, a broader regulatory review exception, and a return to the TRIPS position on exhaustion of patent rights).

In addition, sensible reforms have been repeatedly suggested to improve Australia's IP system in a manner consistent with Australia's current international trade obligations, such as by repealing the prohibition on parallel importation of books, and considering the potential for broader 'fair use' type exceptions for copyright in place of the multiple detailed 'fair dealing' exceptions. Enhancing clarity on the anti-circumvention provisions under Australian law could also help encourage clarity at the international level, to ensure legitimate practices are not unwittingly caught.

The collapse of the TPP and the major shift in US trade policy should encourage a period of reflection as regards a number of broad approaches towards IP in Australia's PTAs. First, Australia should hesitate before unnecessarily imposing heightened IP standards demanded by the US in Australia's PTAs with other countries (such as the extended copyright term), because of the impact on both Australia (in further tying its hands)

---

220 Productivity Commission, Australian Government, *Bilateral and Regional Trade Agreements: Productivity Commission Research Report* (November 2010) 264. See also Harris, Nicol and Gruen, above n 19, 55–58.

221 *Productivity Commission 2016*, 550.

and those other countries (in unbalancing their IP systems). Second, before agreeing to extended IP protections in future PTAs (especially with the US), Australia must take account of the impact on the balance achieved in Australia's IP system, particularly as the higher standards will generally apply across the board and not only with respect to US IP materials or US nationals. Third, Australia needs to consider the impact of any IP obligations in its PTAs on the past and the future, keeping in mind the purpose of IP laws and the intended balance between the rights of users and rights holders. As regards the past, retroactive application of increased IP protections[222] cannot retrospectively increase incentives to innovate.[223] As regards the future, even a PTA obligation that simply mirrors existing Australian practice may prove unwise as Australia seeks to keep its IP system aligned with changing technology, tastes and practices. Finally, the claims that Australia has already faced in relation to plain tobacco packaging in domestic and international forums (alongside other claims regarding intellectual property in investment treaty arbitration in particular) demonstrate the potential for liability arising from overly stringent intellectual property protections.

[222] See, eg, TPP art 18.10.1; AUSFTA art 17.1.9; cf TRIPS Agreement art 70.

[223] See *Productivity Commission 2016*, 131–132; Kimberlee Weatherall, *Section by Section Commentary on the TPP Final IP Chapter Published 6 November 2015—Part 1—General Provisions, Trade Mark, GIs, Designs* (version 0, 7 November 2015) 15–16, available at <http://works.bepress.com/kimweatherall/31/> (last visited 8 April 2017).

3. Trade in Services: Lumbering Towards More Open Markets

I INTRODUCTION

> There are likely to be substantial gains from liberalizing trade in services, immediately and in the longer term provided the regulatory framework is adequate.[1]

> Producers gain from access to a larger market and higher prices, and consumers gain because they get access to both a wider variety of goods and services and to lower-priced imported goods and services.[2]

Trade liberalisation and sovereign regulatory autonomy are both important concepts to bear in mind—and to balance—in devising or evaluating a PTA, and especially one that encompasses services. The relationship between liberalisation of trade in services and regulatory autonomy is complex and not necessarily linear. Thus, increased trade liberalisation does not necessarily correspond with decreased regulation or decreased autonomy: 'it is by now generally accepted that liberalization requires re-regulation or sometimes original regulation'.[3] Nor, as explained in Chapter 1, is regulatory autonomy an absolute good. Too much autonomy allowed under a services PTA (or other international trade agreement) may leave less scope for the agreement to have a positive impact on development and national and global welfare, in accordance with its underlying goals.

---

1 Brian Copeland and Aaditya Mattoo, 'The Basic Economics of Services Trade' in Aaditya Mattoo, Robert M Stern and Gianni Zanini (eds), *A Handbook of International Trade in Services* (Oxford University Press, 2008) 84, 128.

2 Ibid 88–89.

3 Markus Krajewski, 'Domestic Regulation and Services Trade: Lessons from Regional and Bilateral Free Trade Agreements' in Pierre Sauvé and Martin Roy (eds), *Research Handbook on Trade in Services* (Edward Elgar, 2016) 216, 216. See also Aaditya Mattoo and Pierre Sauvé, 'The Preferential Liberalization of Services Trade: Economic Insights' in Pierre Sauvé and Anirudh Shingal (eds), *The Preferential Liberalization of Trade in Services: Comparative Regionalism* (Edward Elgar, 2014) 37, 45.

In the multilateral context, the WTO's services agreement (GATS) aims, through a 'fine balance', 'to re-regulate domestic policy in order to establish competition and market access in service sectors without curtailing the freedom of Members to regulate so as to meet national policy objectives'.[4] This balance is captured in the preamble to the GATS:

> *Wishing* to establish a multilateral framework of principles and rules for trade in services with a view to the expansion of such trade under conditions of transparency and progressive liberalization and as a means of promoting the economic growth of all trading partners and the development of developing countries;
>
> *Desiring* the early achievement of progressively higher levels of liberalization of trade in services through successive rounds of multilateral negotiations aimed at promoting the interests of all participants on a mutually advantageous basis and at securing an overall balance of rights and obligations, while giving due respect to national policy objectives;[5]

Natens has used a case study of the EU to investigate the relationship between trade in services and regulatory autonomy. We adopt a comparable approach in this chapter, focusing on services aspects of Australia's PTAs. Natens emphasises the importance of services trade to the global economy, as services facilitate economic growth,[6] for example with '[t]ransport, logistics, finance, communication, other business, and professional services' all being 'prerequisites for global value chains'.[7] He also points out the heightened difficulty of balancing liberalisation and autonomy in the context of trade in services due to the wide scope of services and their extensive regulation,[8] which is often more difficult to identify, measure and assess than barriers to trade in goods such as tariffs.[9]

---

[4] Jan Wouters and Dominic Coppens, 'GATS and Domestic Regulation: Balancing the Right to Regulate and Trade Liberalization' in Kern Alexander and Mads Andenas, *The World Trade Organization and Trade in Services* (Martinus Nijhoff, 2008) 207, 210.

[5] Italics in original; underlining added.

[6] Bregt Natens, *Regulatory Autonomy and International Trade in Services* (Edward Elgar, 2016) 7. See also IMF, World Bank and WTO, *Making Trade an Engine of Growth for All: The Case for Trade and for Policies to Facilitate Adjustment* (2017) [70].

[7] Natens, above n 6, 8.

[8] Ibid 8–9. See also Copeland and Mattoo, above n 1, 127.

[9] Copeland and Mattoo, above n 1, 103–104.

Before turning to the substantive aspects of Australia's PTAs on services, we note in part II of this chapter that a number of areas are typically excluded from the scope of the core services chapter in Australia's PTAs. In part III, we explain changes in Australia's approach to positive and negative lists in its PTAs over time, while also examining the inclusion of key services obligations in Australia's PTAs: national treatment, MFN treatment, local presence, and domestic regulation. In part IV, we summarise Australia's own services commitments in particular sectors (in positive list PTAs) and Australia's listed non-conforming measures (in negative list PTAs), taking particular note of the unusual approach of Australia's first services PTA: the ANZCERTA Services Protocol concluded in 1988. In part V, we address the 'general exceptions' included in Australia's PTAs, as modelled on the general exceptions in GATS art XIV.

Although it is difficult to generalise from this brief survey, some patterns emerge. In particular, three services agreements appear to have played an important role in the development of Australia's PTAs, with other PTAs following and building on them: first, the GATS, typically understood as a 'positive list' agreement in which only those sectors listed are bound by particular GATS obligations; second, the AUSFTA, which adopts instead a 'negative list' approach according to which services and service sectors are covered by core obligations unless otherwise specified by the relevant party; and now, third, the TPP, another negative list agreement that contains additional innovations and flexibilities. The use of TPP provisions in the amendments agreed to the SAFTA in 2016 suggests that the TPP may play an important role in future negotiations and treaties of Australia and other TPP countries (and, indeed, non-TPP countries), even though the entry into force of the TPP in its current form now appears impossible. In the future, the TiSA—currently under negotiation with co-leaders Australia, the EU and the United States—may take up a fourth influential role in the development of services PTAs.

Our examination of the provisions and annexes of Australia's PTAs suggests that Australian negotiators have identified certain 'sensitive' areas and seek to protect Australia's regulatory autonomy in those areas, with an eye to future sensitivities as well. Australia's general shift towards negative rather than positive lists in its PTAs may be understood as an effort by Australia to encourage greater liberalisation among its trading partners, while the inclusion of strong NCMs, exceptions and exclusions from the scope of the core services chapter simultaneously enables preservation of policy space by both parties. Australia's awareness of community concerns about sectors such as social services appears reflected in the various mechanisms incorporated in Australia's services chapters in PTAs to avoid or soften particular obligations.[10] However, these concerns may be rooted in mercantilist impulses of the kind that PTAs and international trade law more generally are designed to overcome. Greater services liberalisation, with its attendant economic benefits, may require a scaling back of exceptions, exclusions and NCMs, the proliferation of which also raises questions in relation to GATS-compatibility.

II SCOPE OF SERVICES CHAPTERS

Australia's post-GATS PTAs follow GATS in excluding from (at least) the scope of their core services obligations: government procurement[11] and services supplied in the exercise of governmental authority.[12] These PTAs also exclude from their services chapters subsidies or grants.[13] (In contrast, although the GATS contains no specific subsidies disciplines,[14] subsidies are not excluded from other GATS obligations such as non-discrimination.)[15] Australia's only PTA pre-dating the GATS is the

---

[10] With respect to the low level of GATS commitments in health and social services, see Rudolf Adlung, 'The GATS Negotiations: Implications for Health and Social Services' (2003) 38(3) *Intereconomics* 147.

[11] GATS art XIII:1; TAFTA art 803.2(c); AUSFTA art 10.1.4(b); ACIFTA art 9.2.3(b); AANZFTA ch 8 art 1.4(a); MAFTA art 8.1.4(b); KAFTA art 7.1.3(b); JAEPA art 9.1.2(b); ChAFTA art 8.1.2(b); TPP art 10.2.3(b); SAFTA 2016 ch 7 art 1.2(d).

[12] GATS art I:3(b); TAFTA art 803.2(b); AUSFTA art 10.1.4(e); ACIFTA art 9.2.3(d); AANZFTA ch 8 art 1.4(c); MAFTA art 8.1.4(a); KAFTA art 7.1.5; JAEPA art 9.1.2(e); ChAFTA art 8.1.2(c); TPP art 10.2.3(c); SAFTA 2016 ch 7 art 2.3(c).

[13] TAFTA art 803.2(a); AUSFTA art 10.1.4(d); ACIFTA art 9.2.3(c); AANZFTA ch 8 art 1.4(b); MAFTA art 8.1.4(c); KAFTA art 7.1.3(c); JAEPA art 9.1.2(c); ChAFTA art 8.1.2(d); TPP art 10.2.3(d); SAFTA 2016 ch 7 art 2.3(b).

[14] GATS art XV.

[15] See, eg, WTO, Trade in Services, *Guidelines for the Scheduling of Specific Commitments under the General Agreement on Trade in Services (GATS)*, WTO Doc S/L/92 (28 March 2001) [16]; Rudolf Adlung, 'Export Policies and the General Agreement on Trade in Services' (2015) 18(3) *Journal of International Economic Law* 487, 501; Markus Krajewski, 'Public Services and Trade Liberalization: Mapping the Legal Framework' (2003) 6(2) *Journal of International Economic Law* 341, 361. Australia also recognises the existence of national treatment disciplines for subsidies, for example by scheduling 'unbound' for research and development subsidies under mode 3: GATS, *Australia:*

ANZCERTA Services Protocol, which excludes government procurement and subsidies from the national treatment obligation[16] and also does not apply to taxation measures.[17] Australia's other PTAs take a more nuanced approach to taxation measures, while providing that they do not apply to taxation measures except to the limited extent specified.[18] Negative list PTAs generally apply national treatment and MFN treatment obligations under the core services chapter to taxation measures in some circumstances,[19] while the 2016 amendments to SAFTA provide for only national treatment to apply to taxation measures.[20] Some PTAs provide for rights and obligations to be imposed regarding taxation measures to the extent applicable under a WTO agreement[21] and also in some instances under other PTA provisions (for example, regarding investment).[22]

These limitations on the scope of the core services chapter in Australia's PTAs grant additional leeway to the parties in regulating services (although some other obligations may apply under separate chapters on government procurement, etc.). For example, government procurement may make up a large portion of services transactions in a given country. Governments may also be able to use taxation measures and subsidies as effective tools to achieve their regulatory goals in the services sector or potentially as tools of protectionism. The relatively limited variation among Australia's PTAs in relation to these exclusions may suggest that there is no intention to remove them on the path to progressively greater liberalisation in services trade, such that they represent significant scope for regulatory autonomy (or to put it differently, protectionism and discrimination) in relation to government procurement, taxation and subsidies, even if the depth and breadth of services obligations increase.

Schedule of Specific Commitments, WTO Doc GATS/SC/6 (15 April 1994) 2 (horizontal commitments).

16 ANZCERTA Services Protocol art 5.4.

17 ANZCERTA Services Protocol art 15.

18 TAFTA art 1607.1; AUSFTA art 22.3.1; ACIFTA art 22.3.1; AANZFTA ch 15 art 3.1; MAFTA art 18.3.1; KAFTA art 22.3.1; JAEPA art 1.8.1; ChAFTA art 16.4.2; TPP art 29.4.2; SAFTA 2016 ch 17 art 3.2.

19 AUSFTA 22.3.4(a)–(b); ACIFTA art 22.3.4(a)–(b); KAFTA art 22.3.2(b)–(c); JAEPA art 1.8.2(c)–(d); TPP art 29.4.6(a)–(b).

20 SAFTA 2016 ch 17 art 3.3.

21 TAFTA art 1607.1(a); AANZFTA ch 15 art 3.2(a); ChAFTA art 16.4.3.

22 AANZFTA ch 15 art 3.2(b)–(c); MAFTA art 18.3.2(b)–(c); SAFTA 2016 ch 17 art 3.3.

III CORE OBLIGATIONS

A Non-Discrimination, Market Access and Local Presence: Listing and Modes

In understanding Australia's PTA obligations with respect to particular service sectors, we must first explain the concept of negative and positive listing approaches. The MFN rule in GATS art II adopts a typical negative list approach, whereby all measures covered by GATS are subject to the rule except to the extent that a WTO Member has listed a relevant MFN exemption:

> 1. With respect to any measure covered by this Agreement, each Member shall accord immediately and unconditionally to services and service suppliers of any other Member *treatment no less favourable* than that it accords to like services and service suppliers of *any other country*.
> 2. A Member may maintain a measure inconsistent with paragraph 1 provided that such a *measure is listed in*, and meets the conditions of, the Annex on Article II Exemptions.[23]

In contrast, the market access and national treatment obligations under GATS adopt a positive list approach, whereby they apply only in the sectors listed in the relevant Member's GATS Schedule, and subject to any limitations listed in the Schedule:

> With respect to *market access* through the modes of supply identified in Article I, each Member shall accord services and service suppliers of any other Member treatment no less favourable than that provided for under the terms, limitations and conditions agreed and specified in its Schedule.[24]
>
> In the sectors inscribed in its Schedule, and subject to any conditions and qualifications set out therein, each Member shall accord to services and service suppliers of any other Member, in respect of all measures affecting the supply of services, *treatment no less favourable* than that it accords to its *own like services and service suppliers*.[25]

Among Australia's PTAs, as shown in Table 3.1, only the ANZCERTA Services Protocol entered into force before GATS, and it adopts what

---

[23] GATS art II (emphasis added).
[24] GATS art XVI:1 (emphasis added; footnote omitted).
[25] GATS art XVII:1 (emphasis added; footnote omitted).

may be understood as the opposite approach: a negative list[26] for market access[27] and national treatment[28] and a positive list for MFN.[29] (This agreement has been credited as the first PTA adopting a negative list approach for trade in services in the absence of an investment chapter, before both services and investment being taken up in the NAFTA.)[30] In contrast, like GATS, TAFTA, AANZFTA and MAFTA adopt a positive list approach for market access[31] and national treatment,[32] although they lack a traditional MFN obligation.[33] Most other Australian PTAs adopt a negative list approach for MFN (where an MFN obligation is included),[34] market access,[35] and national treatment.[36] The exception is ChAFTA, in which, unusually, Australia adopts a negative list approach[37] and China adopts a positive list approach.[38] As in the investment chapter of ChAFTA (discussed in Chapters 4 to 5 of this volume), the ChAFTA provision for review of the services chapter specifies that the 'next round of the negotiation on trade in services' is to be conducted 'in the form of

---

[26] The negative list approach is effected through a general annex removing certain services from the scope of the agreement: ANZCERTA Services Protocol art 2.4: 'Except as otherwise provided in particular Articles, this Protocol shall not apply to the provision within or into the territory of one Member State of the services inscribed by that Member State in the Annex until such time as such services inscribed by it have been removed from the Annex in accordance with Article 10 of this Protocol.'

[27] ANZCERTA Services Protocol art 4.

[28] ANZCERTA Services Protocol art 5.1.

[29] ANZCERTA Services Protocol art 6.

[30] Aaditya Mattoo and Pierre Sauvé, 'Services' in Jean-Pierre Chauffour and Jean-Christophe Maur (eds), *Preferential Trade Agreement Policies for Development: A Handbook* (World Bank, 2011) 235, 251.

[31] TAFTA art 809.1; AANZFTA ch 8 art 4; MAFTA art 8.5.1.

[32] TAFTA art 810.1; AANZFTA ch 8 art 3.1; MAFTA art 8.3.1.

[33] AANZFTA ch 8 art 7 provides for a consultative process in relation to MFN treatment.

[34] AUSFTA arts 10.3, 10.6; ACIFTA arts 9.4, 9.7; KAFTA arts 7.3, 7.6; JAEPA arts 9.5, 9.7; TPP arts 10.4, 10.7.1, 10.7.2; SAFTA 2016 ch 7 arts 5, 7.1, 7.2.

[35] AUSFTA arts 10.4, 10.6; ACIFTA arts 9.5, 9.7; KAFTA arts 7.4, 7.6; JAEPA arts 9.3, 9.7; TPP arts 10.5, 10.7.1, 10.7.2; SAFTA 2016 ch 7 arts 3, 7.1, 7.2.

[36] AUSFTA arts 10.2, 10.6; ACIFTA arts 9.3, 9.7; KAFTA arts 7.2.1, 7.6; JAEPA arts 9.4.1, 9.7; TPP arts 10.3.1, 10.7.1, 10.7.2; SAFTA 2016 ch 7 arts 4, 7.1, 7.2.

[37] ChAFTA arts 8.9, 8.12.1, 8.11, 8.10.1.

[38] ChAFTA arts 8.4, 8.7.1, 8.6.1, 8.5.1.

negative listing approach'.[39] In March 2017 the parties indicated their intention to commence the services and investment reviews in 2017.[40] The proposed approach for TiSA is also unusual in the context of Australian PTAs, but perhaps less so in the context of GATS: TiSA is proposed to adopt a negative list approach for MFN and a positive list approach for market access (both as in GATS) but moves to a negative list approach for national treatment.[41]

The GATS provisions generally apply to all four modes of service supply (mode 1: cross-border supply by a supplier into the consumer's territory;[42] mode 2: consumption by a consumer abroad;[43] mode 3: commercial presence, that is, local presence;[44] mode 4: presence of natural persons, where the supplier rather than the consumer moves).[45] GATS also includes annexes on specific sectors such as financial services and telecommunications. Some of Australia's PTAs follow this four-mode approach.[46] Several of Australia's (especially newer, negative list-focused) PTAs contain a core services chapter targeting 'cross-border' trade in services[47] (defined to include modes 1, 2 and 4 but not 3)[48] while they and other Australian PTAs contain separate provisions or chapters

---

39 ChAFTA art 8.24.3.

40 *Declaration of Intent by the Government of Australia and the Government of the People's Republic of China Regarding Review of Elements of the China–Australia Free Trade Agreement* (signed 24 March 2017).

41 'How to Read a Trade in Services Agreement Schedule', available at DFAT, *Free Trade Agreements: TiSA Scheduling Approach* <http://dfat.gov.au/trade/agreements/trade-in-services-agreement/Pages/tisa-scheduling-approach.aspx> (last visited 7 April 2017); *Trade in Services Agreement (TiSA) Core Text (April 2015)*, released by wikileaks (1 July 2015) 4.

42 GATS art I:2(a): supply of a service 'from the territory of one Member into the territory of any other Member'.

43 GATS art I:2(b): supply of a service 'in the territory of one Member to the service consumer of any other Member'.

44 GATS art I:2(c): supply of a service 'by a service supplier of one Member, through commercial presence in the territory of any other Member'.

45 GATS art I:2(d): supply of a service 'by a service supplier of one Member, through presence of natural persons of a Member in the territory of any other Member'.

46 TAFTA art 802(i); AANZFTA ch 8 art 2(s); MAFTA art 8.2(o); JAEPA art 9.2(n); ChAFTA art 8.2(x).

47 AUSFTA ch 10; ACIFTA ch 9; KAFTA ch 7; TPP ch 10; SAFTA 2016 ch 7.

48 AUSFTA art 10.14.1; ACIFTA art 9.1(d); KAFTA art 7.13; TPP art 10.1; SAFTA 2016 ch 7 art 1.

regarding telecommunications,[49] financial services,[50] electronic commerce,[51] and movement of natural persons.[52]

The separation of mode 3 in many of Australia's PTAs may indicate a greater level of comfort with modes 1, 2 and 4 of trading services (and particularly mode 1, which is most easily analogous to trade in goods (supply across borders)). Sensitivities (connected with migration issues) that are reflected in limited GATS commitments with respect to mode 4[53] can be separately addressed in a PTA chapter on movement of natural persons. Similarly, technicalities and sector-specific concerns in relation to telecommunications, electronic commerce and financial services can also be separately addressed with dedicated PTA chapters.

The Australian PTAs containing core services chapters that exclude mode 3 include an additional (negative list) obligation with regard to local presence, first exemplified in the AUSFTA:

> Neither Party may require a service supplier of the other Party to establish or maintain a representative office or any form of enterprise, or to be resident, in its territory as a condition for the cross-border supply of a service.[54]

This obligation builds on the GATS, which imposes various disciplines on residency requirements and registration requirements, particularly if discriminatory and in the face of full commitments under mode 1.[55]

Before the AUSFTA, the ANZCERTA took a slightly different approach, providing a more restricted obligation in relation to local

---

[49] AUSFTA ch 12; MAFTA ch 9; ACIFTA ch 11; AANZFTA ch 8 annex on telecommunications; KAFTA ch 9; JAEPA ch 10; TPP ch 13; SAFTA ch 10. Cf ChAFTA art 8.19.

[50] AUSFTA ch 13; MAFTA ch 8 annex on financial services; ACIFTA ch 12; AANZFTA ch 8 annex on financial services; KAFTA ch 8; JAEPA ch 11; ChAFTA annex 8–B; TPP ch 11; SAFTA ch 9.

[51] TAFTA ch 11; AUSFTA ch 16; ACIFTA ch 16; AANZFTA ch 10; MAFTA ch 15; KAFTA ch 15; JAEPA ch 13; ChAFTA ch 12; SAFTA ch 14; TPP ch 14.

[52] TAFTA ch 10; AANZFTA ch 9; MAFTA ch 10; KAFTA ch 10; JAEPA ch 12; ChAFTA ch 10; SAFTA ch 11. See also ACIFTA ch 13; TPP ch 12.

[53] WTO, Council for Trade in Services, *Presence of Natural Persons (Mode 4): Background Note by the Secretariat*, WTO Doc S/C/W/301 (15 September 2009) [74]; WTO, Working Party on Domestic Regulation, *Regulatory Issues in Sectors and Modes of Supply: Note by the Secretariat*, WTO Doc S/WPDR/W/48 (13 June 2012) [182]–[183].

[54] AUSFTA art 10.5. See also ACIFTA art 9.6; KAFTA art 7.5; TPP art 10.6; SAFTA 2016 ch 7 art 6.

[55] See, eg, WTO *Scheduling Guidelines*, above n 15, [14], 16–17.

presence requirements that draws on language from the chapeau of GATT art XX and GATS art XIV:

Discriminatory or restrictive measures

> Notwithstanding that such measures may be consistent with Articles 4, 5, 6 and 7 of this Protocol, neither Member State shall introduce any measure, including a measure requiring the establishment or commercial presence by a person of the other Member State in its territory as a condition for the provision of a service, *that constitutes* a means of arbitrary or unjustifiable discrimination against persons of the other Member State or a disguised restriction on trade between them in services.[56]

JAEPA also applies a local presence prohibition to all modes of supply apart from mode 3 (commercial presence),[57] which by definition requires local presence.

Australia's PTAs also deal in different ways with the overlapping nature of services and investment, in the sense that the supply of services through mode 3 (commercial presence) normally involves foreign investment. This link is important[58] because of the large proportion of trade in services that occurs via mode 3: according to a 2009 WTO Secretariat estimate, mode 3 accounts for 'approximately 55–60 per cent of all services trade falling under the GATS', while FDI in services accounts for 'about two-thirds of FDI inflows worldwide'.[59] For Australia, data for 2014–2015 shows most majority foreign-owned affiliates operating in the services sector.[60] The link between investment and mode 3 services trade is more pronounced in Australia's PTAs than in the WTO agreements because of the inclusion of significant investment obligations in most of these PTAs, and particularly where ISDS is included. In contrast, the WTO's TRIMS Agreement is confined to merchandise trade and contains

---

56 ANZCERTA Services Protocol art 8 (emphasis added).

57 JAEPA art 9.6 note.

58 See generally Rudolf Adlung, 'International Rules Governing Foreign Direct Investment in Services: Investment Treaties versus the GATS' (2016) 17 *Journal of World Investment & Trade* 47; Martín Molinuevo, *Protecting Investment in Services: Investor–State Arbitration versus WTO Dispute Settlement* (Wolters Kluwer, 2012).

59 WTO, Working Party on Domestic Regulation, above n 53, [269]. See also UNCTAD, *World Investment Report 2015: Reforming International Investment Governance* (2015) 13.

60 DFAT, *International Investment Australia 2015* (November 2016) 22–23.

only minimal investment protections such as a national treatment requirement with respect to trade-related investment measures.[61]

Under MAFTA, certain investment provisions in chapter 12 (including the minimum standard of treatment and expropriation) 'apply, *mutatis mutandis*, to' mode 3 services, 'but only to the extent that any such measure relates to a covered investment and an obligation under this Chapter, regardless of whether such a service sector is scheduled in a Party's Schedule of Specific Services Commitments'.[62] AANZFTA adopts a similar approach, while also allowing ISDS in respect of mode 3 services supply.[63] In contrast, the SAFTA amendments agreed in 2016 explicitly state, '[f]or greater certainty', that nothing in the services chapter is subject to ISDS.[64] The TPP explicitly excludes from chapter 10 (on Cross-Border Trade in Services) 'the supply of a service in the territory of a Party by a covered investment' (that is, the supply of a service through mode 3 (commercial presence),[65] to the extent that this amounts to a covered investment).[66]

In our view, a negative list approach is inherently more liberalising than a positive list approach because everything is covered unless otherwise specified.[67] In theory, a negative or positive list approach could be used to achieve the same outcomes, and the negotiating dynamics and bargains reached may affect the resulting liberalisation more than the listing approach.[68] The distinction between negative and positive lists is also admittedly somewhat artificial, since a listing of sectors covered typically also includes limitations, conditions or reservations to that

---

61 TRIMS Agreement art 2.1.

62 MAFTA art 12.3.2.

63 AANZFTA ch 8 art 22.2(f).

64 SAFTA 2016 ch 7 n 1.

65 TPP art 10.1 (definition of 'cross-border trade in services or cross-border supply of services').

66 Cf CETA art 9.1 (definition of 'cross-border trade in services or cross-border supply of services') to cover only modes 1 and 2. See also the discussion in Natens, above n 6, 325.

67 See, eg, Productivity Commission, Australian Government, *Bilateral and Regional Trade Agreements: Productivity Commission Research Report* (November 2010) 73.

68 Rudolf Adlung and Hamid Mamdouh, 'How to Design Trade Agreements in Services: Top Down or Bottom–Up?' (2014) 48(2) *Journal of World Trade* 191, 216. See also Tomer Broude and Shai Moses, 'The Behavioural Dynamics of Positive and Negative Listing in Services Trade Liberalization: A Look at the Trade in Services Agreement (TiSA) Negotiations' in Sauvé and Roy, above n 3, 385, 411.

Table 3.1 Non-Discrimination, Market Access and Local Presence in Australia's PTAs

Treaty	Entry into force	MFN	Market access	National treatment	Local presence
ANZCERTA Services Protocol	1989	positive list	negative list	negative list	negative list
GATS	1995	negative list	positive list	positive list	✘
SAFTA original	2003	✘	negative list	negative list	✘
TAFTA	2005	✘	positive list	positive list	✘
AUSFTA	2005	negative list	negative list	negative list	negative list
ACIFTA	2009	negative list	negative list	negative list	negative list
AANZFTA	2009	✘	positive list	positive list	✘
SAFTA amended	2011	✘	negative list	negative list	✘
MAFTA	2013	✘	positive list	positive list	✘
KAFTA	2014	negative list	negative list	negative list	negative list
JAEPA	2015	negative list	negative list	negative list	negative list
ChAFTA	2015	Australia: negative list China: positive list	Australia: negative list China: positive list	Australia: negative list China: positive list	✘
TPP	–	negative list	negative list	negative list	negative list
SAFTA 2016	–	negative list	negative list	negative list	negative list
TiSA	–	negative list	positive list	negative list	negative list

coverage.[69] However, behavioural analysis tentatively suggests that factors such as framing effects and status quo bias may make negative lists more conducive to liberalisation.[70] More importantly, a negative list is more likely to cover 'new' services, as technology develops (unless a reservation covering future NCMs is allowed), whereas a positive list may not;[71] in that sense a negative list approach is automatically progressive.

Under the GATS, for example, some WTO Members have undertaken commitments for services sectors that lack specific sub-sector categories

[69] Broude and Moses, above n 68, 392 (referring to Adlung and Mamdouh, above n 68).

[70] Broude and Moses, above n 68, 390, 395–397.

[71] Mattoo and Sauvé, above n 30, 253.

under the commonly used GATS classification (such as 2.E 'Communication Services: Other' and 4.E 'Distribution Services: Other'),[72] meaning that future communication or distribution services not mentioned in other categories would be covered. The proper interpretation and application of a given PTA (or GATS Schedule) may also sometimes enable coverage of unspecified services in a positive list setting. In *China—Publications and Audiovisual Products*, the Appellate Body held that China's commitment in respect of the distribution of sound recordings extended to electronic distribution:[73] a different approach to the evolution of GATS commitments could have led to a gradual reduction in the scope of commitments, particularly in dynamic sectors such as telecommunications and other technology-related services.[74]

We consider that Australia's overall move away from a positive list approach and towards a negative list approach can be understood in principle as increasing the liberalising effect of Australia's PTAs in relation to services. However, the premise of a negative list may encourage negotiators to list more exempted measures than they otherwise might, in order to avoid accidentally making greater commitments than intended in particular sectors. Thus, in particular cases, a negative list approach may end up being less liberalising than a positive list approach;[75] that is the risk of endless NCMs.

Australia appears to have a clear preference for negative listing (modified in TiSA in response to other parties' preferences),[76] and its experience with this approach makes it easier for it to apply such an approach.[77] For other countries without treaty practice embracing the negative list, the review necessary to allow the listing of NCMs can be

---

[72] WTO, *Services Sectoral Classification List: Note by the Secretariat*, WTO Doc MTN.GNS/W/120 (10 July 1991) 4.

[73] Appellate Body Report, *China—Publications and Audiovisual Products*, [396]–[397], [408].

[74] See Tania Voon, Introductory Note to WTO Appellate Body Report, *China—Measures Affecting Trading Rights and Distribution Services for Certain Publications and Audiovisual Entertainment Products* (2010) 49(2) *International Legal Materials* 516, 517.

[75] Mattoo and Sauvé, above n 30, 252; Broude and Moses, above n 68, 398.

[76] See Daniel Pruzin, 'Punke Cites Positive Movement In Geneva Talks on Services, ITA' (27 September 2012) *International Trade Daily* (online) (referring to the EU preference for a positive list); Broude and Moses, above n 68, 409 (referring to the compromise proposed by the co-leaders Australia, the EU and the US).

[77] Broude and Moses, above n 68, 405.

significant and burdensome, particularly for developing countries.[78] However, by encouraging PTA partners to engage in such an exercise, Australia may pursue several benefits in connection with transparency. To begin with, listing Australia's NCMs (such as those mentioned below) provides a basis for pointing to areas of concern for the Australian community that are explicitly carved out of the agreement or of particular obligations (increasing the chances of community acceptance of the agreement). Moreover, a list of NCMs of PTA partners, particularly an extensive list, can provide a basis for Australia to seek further liberalisation in subsequent reviews of the PTA or new PTAs encompassing the same parties (much as the process of 'tariffication'—that is, conversion of import quotas to tariffs—in the Uruguay Round was said to provide a clearer basis for progressive reduction of tariffs in future rounds).[79] The same applies to Australia: the list of NCMs may be usefully whittled down over time to facilitate international trade in services for the overall benefit of Australian consumers and service suppliers, where certain NCMs are not considered necessary for the protection of regulatory autonomy.

B Domestic Regulation

Australia's PTAs address the different components of the domestic regulation provisions in GATS art VI in different ways, including in some cases through broader transparency provisions in a separate chapter on transparency (which is also covered separately in GATS art III). The extent to which Australia's PTAs maintain four key aspects of GATS art VI is summarised in Table 3.2. To some degree the extent of alignment with GATS corresponds with whether the PTA takes a positive list approach to the national treatment and market access obligations, as in the GATS (see Table 3.1). Those PTAs tend to follow GATS in limiting certain obligations to sectors or services in relation to which the relevant party has made 'specific commitments' (that is, national treatment, market access, or additional commitments). That approach makes less sense for negative list PTAs, since they do not generally have explicit commitments to particular sectors or services. Since the domestic regulation obligations are not generally limited to particular sectors or services in negative list PTAs, those PTAs have sometimes adopted

---

[78] Mattoo and Sauvé, above n 30, 253; Broude and Moses, above n 68, 406.

[79] See, eg, John Jackson, *The World Trading System: Law and Policy of International Economic Relations* (2nd ed, MIT Press, 1997) 140.

alternative means of ensuring regulatory flexibility in the face of these procedural requirements, such as subjecting them to listed NCMs.

Beginning with the positive list PTAs, the ANZCERTA Services Protocol does not contain the GATS art VI provisions, having been concluded in 1988 (well before the GATS entered into force in 1995). However, the ANZCERTA Services Protocol does contain general obligations concerning licensing and certification,[80] transparency,[81] and notification.[82]

TAFTA incorporates GATS art VI:1, 2, 3, 5 and 6 by way of reference.[83] The other positive list PTAs tend to mirror the wording of GATS art VI. Article VI:1 provides that, '[i]n sectors where specific commitments are undertaken, each Member shall ensure that all measures of general application affecting trade in services are administered in a reasonable, objective and impartial manner'.[84] This general requirement can be understood as being parallel to GATT art X:3(a), which requires each WTO Member to 'administer in a uniform, impartial and reasonable manner all its laws, regulations, decisions and rulings of the kind described in paragraph 1 of this Article', being '[l]aws, regulations, judicial decisions and administrative rulings of general application' pertaining to matters such as customs valuation, tariffs, taxes, restrictions on imports or exports, or affecting sale, distribution, or transportation.[85]

AANZFTA and MAFTA (also positive list PTAs) adopt the GATS art VI:1 wording,[86] meaning that the requirement of reasonable, objective and impartial administration applies only to measures of general application, and only to sectors in which the relevant Member has made specific commitments (that is, national treatment or market access commitments). Somewhat strangely, ChAFTA also adopts this language,[87] even though Australia (unlike China) has a negative list approach to national treatment and market access under ChAFTA. Presumably, for Australia under ChAFTA, the requirement of reasonable,

---

80 ANZCERTA Services Protocol art 9.

81 ANZCERTA Services Protocol art 13.

82 ANZCERTA Services Protocol art 16.

83 TAFTA art 807.

84 See generally Andrew Mitchell and Tania Voon, 'Reasonableness, impartiality and objectivity' in Aik Hoe Lim and Bart De Meester (eds), *WTO, Domestic Regulation and Services Trade: Putting Principles into Practice* (Cambridge University Press, 2014) 65.

85 GATT 1994 art X:1.

86 AANZFTA ch 8 art 10.1; MAFTA art 8.9.1.

87 ChAFTA art 8.13.1.

objective and impartial administration applies to measures of general application in any service sector that has not been completely eliminated in Australia's NCMs lists in annex IIIA or IIIB.

Among the negative list PTAs, ACIFTA, JAEPA, TPP and the SAFTA amendments agreed in 2016 adopt the GATS art VI:1 language, but without the restriction to sectors in which specific commitments are made,[88] which is logical as that reference makes more sense for positive list PTAs. However, all of the SAFTA's domestic regulation obligations are subject to the NCMs listed in annexes 4–I and 4–II,[89] with the TPP taking an analogous approach.[90] The ANZCERTA Services Protocol contains no obligation corresponding to GATS art VI:1 (which, as noted above, did not exist when the Protocol was concluded). KAFTA contains a broader obligation to this effect in the transparency chapter.[91] The AUSFTA contains specific obligations of reasonable, objective and impartial administration of measures in the telecommunications[92] and financial services[93] settings. The AUSFTA transparency chapter imposes on each party a more limited general obligation to provide notice and an opportunity to present arguments to administrative agencies '*[w]ith a view to* administering its laws, regulations, procedures, and administrative rules of general application … in a consistent, impartial and reasonable manner'.[94]

The second key aspect of GATS art VI is the requirement in art VI:2 (not limited to sectors in which commitments have been made) to 'maintain or institute as soon as practicable judicial, arbitral or administrative tribunals or procedures' to allow for prompt review and remedies for 'administrative decisions affecting trade in services'.[95] All of Australia's PTAs apart from the ANZCERTA Services Protocol contain the same or a similar requirement, in either their services chapter[96] or their transparency chapter.[97] However, SAFTA's obligation is not to establish such tribunals or procedures but to apply any such tribunals or procedures on a non-discriminatory

88 ACIFTA art 9.8.1; JAEPA art 9.8.1; TPP art 10.8.1; SAFTA ch 7 art 11.1.

89 SAFTA 2016 ch 7 art 7.3.

90 TPP art 10.8.8.

91 KAFTA art 19.3.1.

92 AUSFTA art 12.22(c).

93 AUSFTA art 13.11.2.

94 AUSFTA art 20.4 (emphasis added).

95 GATS art VI:2(a).

96 TAFTA art 807; AANZFTA ch 8 art 12.2; JAEPA art 9.8.2; ChAFTA art 8.13.2(a).

97 AUSFTA art 20.5.1; ACIFTA art 19.6.1; MAFTA art 17.6.1; KAFTA art 19.4.1; TPP art 26.4.1.

Table 3.2 Domestic Regulation Requirements in Australia's PTAs

<table>
<tr><th></th><th>Reasonable, objective, impartial administration</th><th>Judicial, arbitral or administrative tribunals or procedures</th><th>Procedures regarding application for authorization to supply service</th><th>Criteria regarding qualification requirements and procedures, technical standards and licensing requirements</th></tr>
<tr><td colspan="5">Positive lists for market access and national treatment:</td></tr>
<tr><td>ANZCERTA Services Protocol</td><td>✘</td><td>✘</td><td>✘</td><td>✘</td></tr>
<tr><td>GATS</td><td rowspan="5">where specific commitments made</td><td rowspan="3">✓</td><td rowspan="5">where specific commitments made</td><td rowspan="5">where specific commitments made</td></tr>
<tr><td>TAFTA</td></tr>
<tr><td>AANZFTA</td></tr>
<tr><td>MAFTA</td><td>in transparency chapter</td></tr>
<tr><td>ChAFTA[98]</td><td>✓</td></tr>
<tr><td colspan="5">Negative lists for market access and national treatment:</td></tr>
<tr><td>AUSFTA</td><td>in transparency, telecommunications and financial services chapters</td><td rowspan="3">in transparency chapter</td><td>subject to NCMs in annex II</td><td>endeavour only</td></tr>
<tr><td>ACIFTA</td><td>✓</td><td>✓</td><td>✓</td></tr>
<tr><td>KAFTA</td><td>in transparency chapter</td><td>subject to NCMs in annex II</td><td>endeavour only</td></tr>
<tr><td>JAEPA</td><td>✓</td><td>✓</td><td>✓</td><td>✓</td></tr>
<tr><td>TPP</td><td rowspan="2">subject to NCMs in both annexes</td><td>in transparency chapter</td><td rowspan="2">subject to NCMs in both annexes</td><td rowspan="2">endeavour only; subject to NCMs in both annexes</td></tr>
<tr><td>SAFTA 2016</td><td>subject to NCMs in annexes 4–I/II</td></tr>
</table>

98 As noted in part IIIA above, in relation to services, ChAFTA adopts a positive list approach for China and a negative list approach for Australia. However, its domestic regulation provisions are the same for both parties and adopt the general model of Australia's positive list PTAs.

basis: 'Each Party shall ensure that its judicial, arbitral or administrative tribunals or procedures which provide for the prompt review of, and where justified, appropriate remedies for, administrative decisions affecting trade in services are open on a non-discriminatory basis to a service supplier of the other Party …'.[99] Again, this obligation is subject to the NCMs in annexes 4–I and 4–II.[100]

GATS art VI:3 provides:

> Where authorization is required for the supply of a *service on which a specific commitment has been made*, the competent authorities of a Member shall, within a *reasonable period of time* after the submission of an application considered complete under domestic laws and regulations, *inform the applicant of the decision* concerning the application. At the request of the applicant, the competent authorities of the Member shall provide, without undue delay, information concerning the *status* of the application.[101]

Australia's positive list PTAs (TAFTA, AANZFTA and MAFTA, as well as ChAFTA) follow GATS in imposing such procedural requirements where 'authorization is required for the supply of a service on which a specific commitment has been made'.[102] As for the negative list PTAs, the AUSFTA and KAFTA follow the GATS language subject to annex II NCMs.[103] ACIFTA and JAEPA contain similar obligations without the restriction to services in relation to which a specific commitment has been made.[104] These provisions also add procedural elements such as requirements to provide written reasons for a decision not to grant an application[105] and to identify additional information required to complete an incomplete application.[106] The TPP and SAFTA 2016 contain further procedural elements but subject to NCMs in both annexes.[107]

Under GATS art VI:5 (pending the entry into force of disciplines that were expected to be developed by the Council for Trade in Services under art VI:4), a WTO Member must not 'apply licensing and qualification requirements and technical standards that nullify or impair'

---

99 SAFTA 2016 ch 7 art 11.2.

100 SAFTA 2016 ch 7 art 7.3.

101 Emphasis added.

102 TAFTA art 807; AANZFTA ch 8 art 10.5; MAFTA art 8.9.5; ChAFTA art 8.13.3.

103 AUSFTA art 10.7.1; KAFTA art 7.7.1.

104 ACIFTA art 9.8.3(b); JAEPA art 9.8.6(b).

105 ACIFTA art 9.8.3(b)(iv); JAEPA art 9.8.6(b)(v).

106 JAEPA art 9.8.6(b)(iii) (see also (iv)).

107 TPP arts 10.8.4, 10.8.8; SAFTA 2016 ch 7 arts 7.3, 11.4.

specific commitments made by that Member in a manner that 'could not reasonably have been expected of that Member at the time the specific commitments … were made' and does not comply with one or more of these criteria from art VI:4:

> (a) based on objective and transparent criteria, such as competence and the ability to supply the service;
> (b) not more burdensome than necessary to ensure the quality of the service;
> (c) in the case of licensing procedures, not in themselves a restriction on the supply of the service.

GATS art VI:5(b) adds that, in determining whether a Member complies with this obligation, 'account shall be taken of international standards of relevant international organizations applied by that Member'. Footnote 3 adds that such organisations are 'international bodies whose membership is open to the relevant bodies of at least all Members of the WTO'.

Australia's positive list PTAs (TAFTA, AANZFTA and MAFTA, as well as ChAFTA) all adopt provisions aligned with GATS arts VI:5 and VI:6.[108] However, apart from ACIFTA,[109] Australia's negative list PTAs limit the obligation, so that parties must only 'endeavour' to ensure rather than being *obliged* to ensure compliance with the specified criteria.[110] This change in the language may reflect the fact that this obligation is not, in negative list PTAs, restricted to any particular service or service sector.

The TPP and SAFTA 2016 not only refer to a 'right to regulate' (whatever that means) but also remove the criterion of 'not more burdensome than necessary', which may be seen as analogous to art 2.2 of the WTO's TBT Agreement:

> With a view to ensuring that measures relating to qualification requirements and procedures, technical standards and licensing requirements do not constitute unnecessary barriers to trade in services, while recognising the *right to regulate* and to introduce new regulations on the supply of services in order to meet its policy objectives, each Party shall *endeavour to ensure* that any such measures that it adopts or maintains are:
>
> (a) based on objective and transparent criteria, such as competence and the ability to supply the service; and

---

108 TAFTA art 807; AANZFTA ch 8 arts 10.3, 10.4; MAFTA arts 8.9.3, 8.9.4, 8.9.6; ChAFTA arts 8.13.5, 8.13.6.

109 ACIFTA art 9.8.2.

110 AUSFTA art 10.7.2; KAFTA art 7.7.2; JAEPA art 9.8.4.

(b) in the case of licensing procedures, not in themselves a restriction on the supply of the service.[111]

Finally, TPP and SAFTA 2016 make this obligation subject to the NCMs listed in either annex.[112] TPP and SAFTA are Australia's only negative list PTAs that include the GATS reference to the relevance of international standards in determining compliance with this obligation.[113]

These changes, particularly in the TPP and the SAFTA 2016, may reflect a growing understanding of the potential breadth and uncertainty of a no 'more burdensome than necessary to ensure the quality of the service' requirement,[114] as well as the criteria regarding objectivity and restrictions on the supply of a service. The multilayered approach of SAFTA 2016 to this problem—invoking the NCMs lists in both annexes with respect to all domestic regulation obligations and removing the obligation regarding the burden of such measures—may represent a concerted effort to preserve regulatory autonomy, particularly in relation to sensitive service sectors such as health and education. However:

> In order for regulations to achieve their perceived objectives, certain conditions need to be met. In particular, the adverse social impact of an unregulated market should be higher than the risks associated with 'regulatory failure' on the part of the governments and administrations involved. The latter cannot simply be assumed to be impartial advocates of the public interest ... and to have more accurate information and foresight than private individuals or groups. The regulatory process ... is subject to vested interests lobbying for influence ... Inventors and innovators, consumers and taxpayers typically play second fiddle.[115]

WTO jurisprudence suggests these overlapping protections of policy space may unnecessarily undermine the purpose of the domestic regulation obligations (and trade liberalisation in general), for example to prevent unduly burdensome regulation that stifles competition and innovation, privileging incumbents. To date, the WTO Appellate Body has never found a violation of the requirement in TBT art 2.2 that technical

---

111 TPP art 10.8.2. See also SAFTA 2016 ch 7 art 11.6.

112 TPP art 10.8.8; SAFTA 2016 ch 7 art 7.3.

113 TPP art 10.8.3; SAFTA 2016 ch 7 art 11.7.

114 In respect of accountancy, WTO Members modified this obligation to a requirement that relevant measures be 'not more trade-restrictive than necessary to fulfil a legitimate objective', aligning more closely with the language of TBT art 2.2 as discussed below: WTO, Trade in Services, *Disciplines on Domestic Regulation in the Accountancy Sector*, WTO Doc S/L/64 (17 December 1998) [2].

115 Adlung, 'Social Services', above n 10, 148.

regulations not be 'more trade-restrictive than necessary to fulfil a legitimate objective, taking account of the risks non-fulfilment would create', instead adopting a deferential approach to this provision, in contrast to its analysis under TBT art 2.1 with respect to discriminatory measures.[116] Although these results would not determine or necessarily even influence the outcome under Australia's services PTAs, they indicate the potential for appropriate analysis and understanding of government regulatory approaches in interpreting and applying obligations of proportionality such as GATS art VI:4(b).

IV AUSTRALIA'S COMMITMENTS AND NON-CONFORMING MEASURES

A ANZCERTA Services Protocol: Annex

Australia's first 'positive list' entailed commitments to the MFN obligation for sectors inscribed in the annex to the ANZCERTA Services Protocol.[117] Yet this annex serves two purposes: both to apply the MFN obligation to listed sectors[118] (pursuant to a positive list approach) and to apply—through additional descriptions under the listed sectors—limitations and conditions to not only the MFN obligation but also (pursuant to a negative list approach) the national treatment and market access commitments.[119] This approach has led to unusual developments through progressive negotiation. Over time, Australia has removed certain sectors from the annex, consequently removing not only the corresponding limitations and conditions on commitments but also the MFN obligation with respect to those sectors. These revisions appear to have taken place on two occasions, as shown in Table 3.3.

The most recent revision of the annex was effected by a letter that is publicly available, in which the Australian Minister for Trade and Investment advises the New Zealand Minister of Trade that the Australian

---

116 See generally Tania Voon, Andrew Mitchell and Catherine Gascoigne, 'Consumer information, consumer preferences and product labels under the TBT Agreement' in Tracey Epps and Michael J Trebilcock (eds), *Research Handbook on the WTO and Technical Barriers to Trade* (Edward Elgar, 2013) 454.

117 ANZCERTA Services Protocol art 6, annex.

118 ANZCERTA Services Protocol art 6.

119 ANZCERTA Services Protocol art 2.4; annex: '(Where an activity is described further, the exemption in terms of Article 2.4 of this Protocol applies to the description only.)'.

government 'is removing from the Annex to the Protocol the inscription "*Broadcasting and Television: Limits on foreign ownership as set out in the Broadcasting Services Act 1992*" with effect from the date of this letter'.[120] The letter attaches a copy of the amended annex, which removes not only the specified inscription regarding limits on foreign ownership, but the sector 'Broadcasting and Television' itself (while retaining the separate sector of 'Broadcasting and television (short-wave and satellite broadcasting)').

Table 3.3 Australia's MFN Obligations under the ANZCERTA Services Protocol

	18 August 1988	9 March 1999	20 April 2015
MFN coverage (* indicates limitations and conditions on MFN/national treatment/market access)	• Telecommunications* • Banking* • Airport services* • Domestic air services* • International aviation: passenger and freight services* • Coastal shipping* • Construction, engineering and general consultancy* • Broadcasting and television* • Broadcasting and television (short-wave and satellite broadcasting) • Basic health insurance services • Third-party insurance • Workers Compensation insurance • Postal services*	• Air services* • Coastal shipping* • Broadcasting and television* • Broadcasting and television (short-wave and satellite broadcasting) • Third party insurance* • Postal services*	• Air services* • Coastal shipping* • Broadcasting and television (short-wave and satellite broadcasting) • Third party insurance* • Postal services*

As shown in Table 3.3, as Australia has gradually reduced the list of sectors inscribed in the annex, the limitations and conditions on its commitments have decreased, but at the same time the sectors covered by the MFN obligation have also decreased. This may be an unintended quirk arising from the use of the annex as both a positive and negative

[120] Letter from Andrew Robb, Minister for Trade and Investment, Australia, to Tim Groser, Minister of Trade, New Zealand (20 April 2015).

list, in contrast to several of Australia's other PTAs, which adopt a negative list approach to MFN, national treatment and market access, and also in contrast to the GATS, which contains separate schedules of MFN exemptions (pursuant to a negative list approach) and national treatment/ market access commitments (pursuant to a positive list approach). The unusual example of the ANZCERTA Services Protocol may caution against combining annexes or other lists of negative and positive list commitments (notwithstanding the blurring of the two approaches as acknowledged above), given the potential for unwittingly (or deliberately) reducing commitments over time instead of engaging in progressive liberalisation of trade in services.

Rather than referring to foreign investment policy in the annex as a limitation on national treatment or market access, the text of the ANZCERTA Services Protocol itself specifies that the 'provisions of this Protocol shall apply subject to the foreign investment policies of the Member States'.[121] Similar provisions are included in other ways in other Australian PTAs, as discussed further below.

B Positive Lists: Commitments, Limitations and Conditions

Apart from the ANZCERTA Services Protocol, Australia's three PTAs adopting positive lists follow the GATS approach, namely a schedule of commitments to accord national treatment and market access. TAFTA, AANZFTA and MAFTA also adopt a structure similar to GATS schedules, so that the schedules look quite similar, except that the TAFTA schedule is not divided into columns for market access, national treatment and additional commitments. (As noted above, unlike GATS, these three PTAs contain no MFN obligation and therefore no list of MFN exemptions.)

Some commitments that Australia has made in these three PTAs that are not found in its GATS schedule are with respect to:

(a) basic telecommunications services (for example, 'voice telephone services' and 'digital cellular services'), subject to mode 3 restrictions regarding Telstra's ownership, offices and directorship, and certain structural requirements regarding entities holding new carrier licences; and
(b) environmental services: increasing coverage of sub-sectors and removal of limitations and conditions.

---

121 ANZCERTA Services Protocol art 2.2.

Some common limitations and conditions on Australia's services obligations under these three PTAs are with respect to:

(a) Australia's foreign investment policy (with respect to all sectors included in the schedule);
(b) secondary, higher and other education services: unbound with respect to market access for mode 3 (commercial presence), meaning no market access commitments for these sectors in this mode; and
(c) health services: 'other' human health services unbound under GATS/AANZFTA with respect to market access and national treatment in mode 1 (cross-border supply); MAFTA applies the same approach to these services and also to private hospital services (which are not covered at all in GATS/AANZFTA/TAFTA); 'other' human health services not 'unbound' under TAFTA but permanent residency requirement with respect to some of these services specified for some States.

Australia's most recently concluded PTAs—the TPP and the amendments to SAFTA agreed in 2016—adopt a different approach, facilitating comparisons with GATS commitments. Even though these agreements adopt a negative list approach for the MFN, market access and national treatment obligations (which are therefore subject to specified NCMs as discussed below), the relevant negative list annexes also include an Appendix A setting out Australia's 'market access improvements' in comparison with Australia's GATS commitments (that is, in a positive list manner).[122] Appendix A nevertheless forms part of the negative list approach by virtue of a reservation or NCM that specifies for market access with respect to all service sectors:

> Australia reserves the right to adopt or maintain any measure at the *regional level of government* that is not inconsistent with Australia's obligations under Article XVI of GATS.
>
> For the purposes of this entry, Australia's Schedule of Specific Commitments is modified as set out in Appendix A.[123]

The GATS commitments are also subject to change, as the reservation is specified to include commitments made under GATS art XVI 'after the

---

[122] SAFTA 2016 annex 4–II(A) (Australia) appendix A; TPP annex II (Australia) appendix A.

[123] SAFTA 2016 annex 4–II(A) (Australia) 4 (emphasis added); TPP annex II (Australia) 4 (emphasis added).

date of entry into force of this Agreement'.[124] As with Australia's more positive list PTAs, the market access improvements include additional coverage of telecommunications and environmental services.

C Negative Lists: Non-Conforming Measures

Australia's seven PTAs employing negative lists for the MFN, market access and national treatment obligations are, as shown above in Table 3.1: AUSFTA, ACIFTA, KAFTA, JAEPA, ChAFTA (although China adopts a positive list approach to all three obligations), the 2016 agreed SAFTA amendments, and the TPP. These lists are in theory more easily comparable, given that they should all include measures imposed by Australia that do not conform to these three core services obligations. However, the complexity of the descriptions and their separation into different schedules makes comparisons more difficult.

The AUSFTA can be seen as establishing the new model of negative lists for Australia's PTAs, which subsequent PTAs have tended to follow. The AUSFTA provides in relation to measures that do not conform with the obligations regarding national treatment (art 10.2), MFN treatment (art 10.3), market access (art 10.4) and local presence (art 10.5) in respect of cross-border trade in services (mode 1):

> 1. Articles 10.2, 10.3, 10.4, and 10.5 do not apply to:
>
> (a) any *existing non-conforming measure* that is maintained by a Party at:
> (i) the central level of government, as set out by that Party in its Schedule to Annex I;
> (ii) a regional level of government, as set out by that Party in its Schedule to Annex I; or
> (iii) a local level of government;
>
> (b) the *continuation or prompt renewal* of any non-conforming measure referred to in subparagraph (a); or
>
> (c) an *amendment* to any non-conforming measure referred to in subparagraph (a) to the extent that the amendment does not decrease the conformity of the measure, as it existed immediately before the amendment, with Articles 10.2, 10.3, 10.4, or 10.5.
>
> 2. Articles 10.2, 10.3, 10.4, and 10.5 do not apply to any measure that a Party adopts or maintains with respect to sectors, sub-sectors, or activities as set out in its Schedule to Annex II.[125]

---

124 SAFTA 2016 annex 4–II(A) (Australia) 4; TPP annex II (Australia) 4.

125 AUSFTA art 10.6 (emphasis added).

The lists of NCMs in Australia's PTAs are typically common to the services and investment chapters. That is, for example, annexes I and II referred to above contain NCMs in connection with both services and investment obligations under the AUSFTA. The significance of the different annexes is also common to the two areas. Thus, as we see in Chapter 4 of this volume in relation to investment, the above wording means with respect to annex I that: (i) existing NCMs of local government are exempt even if not specifically listed as NCMs; (ii) amendments to NCMs are covered only to the extent that they do not decrease the conformity of the measures (known as a 'standstill' mechanism); and (iii) amendments that enhance the conformity of NCMs are covered, and subsequent amendments cannot return to a lower degree of conformity (a 'ratchet' mechanism). In addition, a party may list in annex II 'sectors', 'sub-sectors' or 'activities' in which NCMs are exempt, without the need to list them and regardless of whether they exist at the time the treaty is concluded. The standstill and ratchet mechanisms do not apply to measures falling within the scope of the areas listed in annex II. Annex II thus provides a much greater degree of flexibility to parties and less trade-liberalising effects.

These seven 'negative list' PTAs include certain key areas of interest from the perspective of regulatory autonomy, as set out in Table 3.4.

As shown in Table 3.4, some of the listing approaches are not always consistent, for example as to whether particular NCMs are listed in annex I or annex II (or their equivalents). However, apart from this distinction they are often similar in scope and content. For example, the typical annex II-type NCM listing for social services applies to non-conformity with national treatment, MFN treatment and local presence provisions as well as certain investment obligations (regarding performance requirements and senior management) and reads:

> Australia reserves the right to adopt or maintain any measure with respect to the provision of law enforcement and correctional services, and the following services to the extent that they are social services established or maintained for a public purpose: income security or insurance, social security or insurance, social welfare, public education, public training, health, and child care.[126]

---

[126] AUSFTA annex II (Australia) 4.

Table 3.4 Key Areas of Non-Conformity in Australia's Positive List PTAs

	Social services incl health, education	Tobacco, alcohol, firearms (wholesale/ retail)	Culture (incl broad-casting, newspapers)	Indigenous persons	Foreign investment policy	Existing international agreements
AUSFTA	annex I/II	annex II	annex I/II	annex II	annex I/II	annex II
ACIFTA	annex I/II	annex I	annex II	annex II	annex I/II	annex II
KAFTA	annex I/II	annex I/II	annex II	annex II	annex I/II	annex II
JAEPA[127]	annex 6/7	annex 6/7	annex 7	annex 7	annex 6/7	annex 7
ChAFTA[128]	annex IIIA/B	annex IIIA/B	annex IIIB	annex IIIB	annex IIIA/B	annex IIIB
TPP	annex I/II	annex II	annex II	annex II	annex I/II	annex II
SAFTA 2016[129]	annex 4–I/ 4–II	annex 4–I/4–II	annex 4–I/ 4–II	annex 4–II	annex 4–I/ 4–II	annex 4–II

A footnote to this provision in the most recent two PTAs specifies, '[f]or greater certainty', that 'measures adopted or maintained with respect to the provision of services covered by this entry include measures for the protection of personal information relating to health and children'.[130] An additional footnote to this provision in some newer PTAs specifies '[f]or the avoidance of doubt' that such services include 'any measure with respect to: the collection of blood and its components; the distribution of blood and blood-related products, including plasma derived products; plasma fractionation services; and the procurement of blood and blood-related products and services'.[131] Rather than a footnote, KAFTA

[127] JAEPA annexes 6 and 7 broadly correspond with AUSFTA annexes I and II respectively.

[128] ChAFTA sections A and B of annex III broadly correspond with AUSFTA annexes I and II respectively. ChAFTA also includes a side letter on education services.

[129] SAFTA 2016 annexes 4–I and 4–II broadly correspond with AUSFTA annexes I and II respectively.

[130] SAFTA 2016 annex 4–II(A) (Australia) n 6; TPP annex II (Australia) n 6.

[131] ChAFTA annex IIIB (Australia) n 25. See also JAEPA annex 7 (Australia) n 6; SAFTA 2016 annex 4–II(A) (Australia) n 7; TPP annex II (Australia) n 7. A side letter applies under AUSFTA with respect to blood-related products and services, which is focused on the government procurement chapter rather than the cross-border trade in services chapter.

contains instead a separate entry for such blood-related matters, specifying existing legislation with respect to 'Australia's policy on blood self-sufficiency'.[132]

The typical annex II-type NCM listing for tobacco, alcoholic beverages and firearms applies to non-conformity with the market access obligation for distribution services and states: 'Australia reserves the right to adopt or maintain any measure with respect to wholesale and retail trade services of tobacco products, alcoholic beverages, or firearms'.[133] Extensive provisions regarding broadcasting tend to relate to matters such as 'transmission quotas for local content' and '[s]ubsidies or grants for investment in Australian cultural activity where eligibility for the subsidy or grant is subject to local content or production requirements'.[134] NCMs with respect to the MFN obligation apply to 'preferential co-production arrangements for film and television productions'.[135] Foreign investment limits are sometimes specifically included with respect to national treatment in the newspapers sector.[136] NCMs with respect to culture are sometimes linked to those with respect to indigenous matters, such as in the SAFTA amendments agreed in 2016:

> Australia reserves the right to adopt or maintain any measure with respect to the creative arts, Indigenous traditional cultural expressions and other cultural heritage.[137]

The general indigenous-focused listing applies to all sectors and to market access, national treatment, local presence, and investment obligations concerning performance requirements and senior management, including with respect to services:

> Australia reserves the right to adopt or maintain any measure according preferences to any Indigenous person or organisation or providing for the favourable treatment of any Indigenous person or organisation in relation to acquisition, establishment or operation of any commercial or industrial undertaking in the service sector.[138]

---

132 KAFTA annex II (Australia).
133 AUSFTA annex II (Australia).
134 AUSFTA annex II (Australia).
135 AUSFTA annex II (Australia).
136 AUSFTA annex I (Australia).
137 SAFTA 2016 annex 4–II(A) (Australia) (footnotes omitted). See also TPP annex II (Australia).
138 SAFTA 2016 annex 4–II(A) (Australia). See also TPP annex II (Australia) 3.

The various NCM listings for foreign investment policies are broad and note several different legislative components of 'Australia's foreign investment framework', which imposes notification and approval requirements on foreign investments above certain thresholds (for example, AUD252 million) in sectors such as telecommunications and in other sectors above higher thresholds (for example, AUD1.094 million).[139]

As discussed below, some of Australia's PTAs contain exceptions regarding other international agreements. Moreover, Australia's annex 4–II of the 2016 agreed SAFTA amendments contains a general reservation for all sectors with respect to the MFN obligation in the services and investment chapters under which 'Australia reserves the right to adopt or maintain any measure that accords more favourable treatment to the service suppliers or investors of non-Parties under any bilateral or multilateral international agreement in force on, or signed prior to', SAFTA's entry into force.[140] That description could extend to pre-existing PTAs, the WTO agreements, and BITs. (AUSFTA contains a similar NCM listing in Australia's annex II.)[141] A footnote to this provision confirms that it extends to 'subsequent review or amendment' of such an agreement, including 'any existing or future protocol' to the ANZCERTA Services Protocol.[142] ACIFTA,[143] KAFTA,[144] JAEPA[145] and ChAFTA[146] adopt a similar approach, as does the TPP, which also adds a reference to measures according more favourable treatment 'to any service supplier or investor of a Pacific Island Forum member state under any international agreement' whether signed or in force before or after the TPP.[147]

139 SAFTA 2016 annex 4–I(A) (Australia).
140 SAFTA 2016 annex 4–II(A) (Australia).
141 AUSFTA annex II (Australia).
142 SAFTA 2016 annex 4–II(A) (Australia) n 18.
143 ACIFTA annex II (Australia).
144 KAFTA annex II (Australia).
145 JAEPA annex 7 (Australia).
146 ChAFTA annex IIIB (Australia).
147 TPP annex II (Australia) 19.

In addition to those types of NCMs summarised in Table 3.4, some common listings apply to:

(a) existing measures at the regional level of government (that is, Australian State and territory governments), subject in some cases to WTO-consistency;[148]
(b) the ownership and management of Telstra (with respect to telecommunications), Qantas (with respect to transport) and CSL (with respect to health services);[149] and
(c) gambling and betting services.[150]

V GENERAL EXCEPTIONS

In this section we examine common exceptions in Australia's PTAs, pursuant to which States parties may derogate from their services obligations subject to certain conditions. As we have focused on the 'cross-border trade in services' and 'trade in services' chapters of Australia's FTAs rather than the chapters specific to financial services, telecommunications services, or movement of natural persons, we do not analyse exceptions in the PTAs that are specific to financial services,[151] telecommunications services,[152] or movement of natural persons.[153] All

[148] See, eg, AUSFTA annex I (Australia) 1, annex II (Australia) 2; KAFTA annex I (Australia) introductory note, annex II (Australia); JAEPA annex 6 (Australia) pt 1 s 1 [6], annex 7 (Australia) pt 1 s 1 [3]; ChAFTA annex IIIA (Australia) pt 1 s 1 introductory notes [3], annex IIIB (Australia) 1; TPP annex I (Australia) 2, annex II (Australia) 4. See also above nn 122–123 and corresponding text; SAFTA 2016 annex 4–I(A) (Australia) introductory notes [1], annex 4–II(A) (Australia) 4.

[149] See, eg, KAFTA annex I (Australia); JAEPA annex 6 (Australia); ChAFTA annex IIIA (Australia); TPP annex I (Australia); SAFTA 2016 annex 4–I (Australia).

[150] See, eg, JAEPA annex 7 (Australia); TPP annex II (Australia) 15; SAFTA 2016 annex 4–II (Australia) 15.

[151] See, eg, TAFTA art 1606 (prudential measures); ACIFTA art 12.8 (information); MAFTA ch 8 annex on financial services art 7; ChAFTA ch 8 annex 8B financial services art 3.

[152] See, eg, SAFTA 2016 ch 10 art 18.

[153] See, eg, TAFTA art 803.4.

of Australia's PTAs, as well as the GATS, contain security exceptions,[154] exceptions regarding the disclosure of confidential information,[155] and 'general exceptions'.[156] Australia's PTAs tend to follow the relevant GATS provisions with respect to these matters. We focus here on the general exceptions and related extensions to the GATS provisions in the PTAs, before turning to some additional exceptions regarding international agreements.

GATS art XIV (general exceptions) provides:[157]

> Subject to the requirement that such measures are not applied in a manner which would constitute a means of arbitrary or unjustifiable discrimination between countries where like conditions prevail, or a disguised restriction on trade in services, nothing in this Agreement shall be construed to prevent the adoption or enforcement by any Member of measures:
>
> (a) necessary to protect *public morals* or to maintain public order;[5]
> (b) necessary to protect human, animal or plant life or *health*;
> (c) necessary to *secure compliance* with laws or regulations which are not inconsistent with the provisions of this Agreement including those relating to:
> (i) the prevention of deceptive and fraudulent practices or to deal with the effects of a default on services contracts;
> (ii) the protection of the privacy of individuals in relation to the processing and dissemination of personal data and the protection of confidentiality of individual records and accounts;
> (iii) safety;
> (d) inconsistent with Article XVII [national treatment], provided that the difference in treatment is aimed at ensuring the equitable or effective imposition or collection of direct *taxes* in respect of services or service suppliers of other Members; [footnote omitted]

---

154 GATS art XIV*bis*; ANZCERTA Services Protocol art 18(a); TAFTA art 1602; AUSFTA art 22.2; ACIFTA art 22.2; AANZFTA ch 15 art 2; MAFTA art 18.2; KAFTA art 22.2; JAEPA art 1.10; ChAFTA art 16.3; TPP art 29.2; SAFTA 2016 ch 17 art 2.

155 GATS art III*bis*; ANZCERTA Services Protocol art 13.3; TAFTA art 1603; AUSFTA art 22.4.1; ACIFTA art 22.5.2; AANZFTA ch 8 art 13; MAFTA art 21.4; KAFTA art 22.4; JAEPA art 1.7.2; ChAFTA art 16.1.1; TPP art 29.7; SAFTA 2016 ch 7 art 10.

156 GATS art XIV; ANZCERTA Services Protocol art 18; TAFTA art 1601.2; AUSFTA art 22.1.2; ACIFTA art 22.1.2; AANZFTA ch 15 art 1.2; MAFTA art 18.1.2; KAFTA art 22.1.2; JAEPA art 1.9.2; ChAFTA art 16.2.2; TPP art 29.1.3; SAFTA 2016 ch 7 art 16.

157 Emphasis added.

(e) inconsistent with Article II [MFN treatment] provided that the difference in treatment is the result of an agreement on the avoidance of double taxation or provisions on the avoidance of *double taxation* in any other international agreement or arrangement by which the Member is bound.

---

[5] The public order exception may be invoked only where a genuine and sufficiently serious threat is posed to one of the fundamental interests of society.

Most Australian PTAs simply incorporate GATS art XIV, *mutatis mutandis*, into the agreement. However, some variation exists. AANZFTA, in addition to incorporating GATS art XIV,[158] adds an exception (subject to chapeau-type language) for 'measures necessary to protect national treasures or specific sites of historical or archaeological value, or measures necessary to support creative arts of national value'.[159] A footnote defines 'creative arts' broadly to include 'the performing arts', 'visual arts and craft, literature, film and video, language arts, creative on-line content, indigenous traditional practice and contemporary cultural expression, and digital interactive media and hybrid art work', among other details.[160] The reference to 'national treasures' is reminiscent of GATT art XX(f), which refers to measures 'imposed for the protection of national treasures of artistic, historic or archaeological value'.

While following the general structure of GATS art XIV, the ANZCERTA Services Protocol general exceptions add measures necessary 'to prevent disorder or crime'[161] or 'to prevent unfair, deceptive, or misleading practices'[162] (without such measures having to be necessary to secure compliance with laws relating to these matters). The general exceptions also incorporate a security exception[163] and an exception regarding international agreements as noted below.

The ANZCERTA Services Protocol also adds a gloss to the national treatment obligation, which in retrospect appears something like the gloss that the WTO Appellate Body has added to the non-discrimination obligation in TBT art 2.1 (that is, a detrimental impact on imports that

---

158 AANZFTA ch 15 art 1.2.
159 AANZFTA ch 15 art 1.4.
160 AANZFTA ch 15 art 1.4 n 2.
161 ANZCERTA Services Protocol art 18(b).
162 ANZCERTA Services Protocol art 18(d).
163 ANZCERTA Services Protocol art 18(a).

stems exclusively from a legitimate regulatory distinction is not discrimination contrary to art 2.1).[164] The WTO Appellate Body has cited the absence of a general exceptions provision in the TBT Agreement corresponding to GATT art XX/GATS art XIV as one reason for introducing this gloss on TBT art 2.1[165] and as a reason for not introducing it into the national treatment obligation in GATT art III:4 or the MFN obligation in GATT art I:1.[166] The Appellate Body has adopted a similar approach, albeit in *obiter dicta*, in excluding regulatory distinctions and the TBT 'gloss' from both likeness and less favourable treatment under GATS arts II:1 (MFN) and XVII (national treatment).[167]

Moving away from the Appellate Body approach to less favourable treatment under GATT 1994 and GATS, the ANZCERTA Services Protocol allows differential treatment provided that it 'is no greater than that necessary for prudential, fiduciary, health and safety or consumer protection reasons'.[168] That restriction operates in addition to, rather than in the place of, the general exceptions clause. An even broader exception applies under TAFTA, again in addition to the incorporation of GATS art XIV:[169]

> Nothing in this Chapter shall prevent a Party from maintaining and introducing measures to regulate service sectors within its territory, provided that such measures are applied on a non-discriminatory basis without the intention to nullify or impair the benefits accruing to the other Party under the terms of this Chapter.[170]

More recently, in addition to the general exceptions provisions in SAFTA and the TPP, a footnote specifies that 'whether treatment is accorded in "like circumstances"' in relation to national treatment or MFN treatment 'depends on the totality of the circumstances, whether the relevant treatment distinguishes between services or service suppliers on the basis of legitimate public welfare objectives'.[171] Rather than 'doubling up' on

---

164 See, eg, Appellate Body Report, *US—Clove Cigarettes*, [215].

165 See, eg, Appellate Body Report, *US—Clove Cigarettes*, [109].

166 Appellate Body Reports, *EC—Seal Products*, [5.125].

167 Appellate Body Report, *Argentina—Financial Services*, [6.106], [6.111], [6.112], [6.115], [6.121].

168 ANZCERTA Services Protocol art 5.2(a).

169 TAFTA art 1601.2.

170 TAFTA art 803.3.

171 TPP ch 10 n 2; SAFTA 2016 ch 7 n 3. A corresponding footnote appears in the investment chapters as well: TPP ch 9 n 14; SAFTA 2016 ch 8 n 8. The latter footnotes are discussed further in Chapter 6 of this volume.

the general exceptions (as the Appellate Body's reasoning might suggest), this kind of qualification acknowledges that legitimate policy objectives exist beyond those enumerated in GATS art XIV or the corresponding PTA provisions, and therefore that the general exceptions provisions may be insufficient to protect all legitimate regulation.

As regards taxation measures and taxation agreements (which are addressed in GATS art XIV(d)–(e)), Australia's PTAs have different approaches to exceptions, in addition to the limitations on scope as discussed in part II of this chapter. The ANZCERTA Services Protocol is distinct from the others as it does not apply to any taxation measures, as noted above. The other Australian PTAs do apply to taxation measures to some extent and therefore have a number of exceptions. Australia's positive list PTAs (apart from the ANZCERTA Services Protocol and SAFTA) provide exceptions for existing non-conforming tax measures, the continuation or prompt renewal of such measures, and amendments to such measures that do not decrease the level of conformity.[172] ACIFTA adds to these an exception for the replacement of an existing non-conforming measure with a substantially similar measure.[173] These PTAs and also SAFTA provide an exception of some kind for measures allowed under GATS art XIV(d) (without regard to its limitation to direct taxes): that is, measures aimed at ensuring the equitable or effective imposition or collection of taxes.[174]

Most Australian PTAs contain an exception (often MFN-specific) for double taxation agreements[175] and/or a statement that double taxation agreements prevail to the extent of any inconsistency.[176] More narrowly, TAFTA provides that the double taxation agreement between Australia and Thailand prevails to the extent of any inconsistency.[177] More

---

[172] AUSFTA art 22.3.4(d)–(f); ACIFTA art 22.3.4(e)–(g); KAFTA art 22.3.3(b)–(d); JAEPA art 1.8.3(a)–(c); ChAFTA art 16.4.4(b); TPP art 29.4.6(e)–(g).

[173] ACIFTA art 22.3.4(h).

[174] AUSFTA art 22.3.4(g); ACIFTA art 22.3.4(i); KAFTA art 22.3.3(e); JAEPA art 1.8.3(d); ChAFTA art 16.4.4(c); TPP art 29.4.6(h); SAFTA ch 17 art 3.3.

[175] AUSFTA art 22.3.4(c); ACIFTA art 22.3.4(d); AANZFTA ch 15 art 3.6; MAFTA art 18.3.7; KAFTA art 22.3.3(a); ChAFTA art 16.4.4(a); TPP art 29.4.6(d).

[176] AUSFTA art 22.3.2(a); ACIFTA art 22.3.2; AANZFTA ch 15 art 3.5; MAFTA art 18.3.4; KAFTA art 22.3.6; JAEPA art 1.8.4; ChAFTA art 16.4.5; TPP art 29.4.3; SAFTA 2016 ch 17 art 3.4.

[177] TAFTA art 1607.3.

unusually, JAEPA specifies that the dispute settlement procedures provided under ch 19 do not apply to the national treatment provisions in the trade in services chapter with respect to a measure falling 'within the scope of an international agreement between the Parties relating to the avoidance of double taxation'.[178] Finally, in the TPP but not the SAFTA, an exception applies to taxation measures by Singapore that are not 'more trade restrictive than necessary to address Singapore's public policy objectives arising out of its specific constraints of space'.[179]

GATS arts V and V*bis* provide exceptions from GATS obligations for economic integration agreements and labour markets integration agreements respectively. These exceptions determine the GATS-consistency of PTAs, as discussed in part VI of this chapter below. Only some of Australia's PTAs include exceptions that might be understood as corresponding in part to these GATS exceptions. For example, under ChAFTA, an MFN exception applies to differential treatment 'in accordance with any free trade agreement or multilateral international agreement in force or signed prior to the date' of ChAFTA's entry into force.[180] That description appears directed to PTAs (including those with an investment chapter) and the WTO agreements, but would not appear to cover a BIT. (In contrast, Australia's negative list PTAs include existing international agreements including BITs in their annex II-type NCM lists, as discussed above.) The ANZCERTA Services Protocol includes as part of its general exceptions measures necessary 'in pursuance of obligations under international agreements',[181] which could arguably provide an MFN exception for existing and even future agreements covering trade and/or investment as well as other kinds of agreements.

Some Australian PTAs provide an exception with respect to 'actions authorised by the Dispute Settlement Body of the WTO'[182] or (in the case of the TPP) 'authorised by the Dispute Settlement Body of the WTO or … taken as a result of a decision by a dispute settlement panel under a free trade agreement to which the Party taking action and the Party against which the action is taken are party'.[183] Several Australian PTAs also contain more general provisions (not positive exceptions) regarding their relationship to other international agreements in general[184] or

---

178 JAEPA art 9.4.2.
179 TPP art 29.4.9.
180 ChAFTA arts 8.7.2, 8.12.2. See also AANZFTA ch 8 arts 7.2, 7.4.
181 ANZCERTA Services Protocol art 18(e).
182 KAFTA art 22.1.4; ACIFTA art 22.1.3.
183 TPP art 29.1.4.
184 See, eg, AUSFTA art 1.1.2; AANZFTA ch 18 art 2; MAFTA art 21.2.

particular kinds of agreements, such as the WTO agreements[185] or multilateral environmental agreements.[186]

VI WTO-CONSISTENCY OF AUSTRALIA'S PTAs

We have elsewhere raised questions about the GATS-compatibility of the approach to international mobile roaming favoured as between Australia and New Zealand[187] and now reflected in the TPP text.[188] Those questions relate to an apparent MFN violation not clearly exempted under GATS or other PTAs. Similar questions could arise in relation to the various deviations from GATS in Australia's PTAs as outlined in this chapter. In order to comply with Australia's GATS obligations, any treatment Australia provides under a PTA that is *more* favourable than treatment accorded under GATS must fall within the parameters of the exception for economic integration in GATS art V or for labour markets integration agreements in GATS art V*bis* (or conceivably a general exception in GATS art XIV). Otherwise, the more favourable treatment is likely to violate the MFN obligation in GATS art II, which is a negative list obligation. Australia has listed an MFN exemption only with respect to audiovisual services[189] and not more generally (or with respect to its bilateral investment treaties).[190]

Notwithstanding the apparent reluctance of WTO Members to raise complaints under the WTO dispute settlement system regarding PTAs, a third country could conceivably invoke the MFN rule to demand the

---

185 See, eg, AUSFTA art 1.1.2; AANZFTA ch 18 art 2; MAFTA art 21.2.

186 See, eg, AUSFTA art 19.8.

187 Tania Voon, 'Discrimination in International Mobile Roaming Regulation: Implications of WTO Law' (2013) 16(1) *Journal of International Economic Law* 91, 116–117.

188 Danny Kotlowitz and Tania Voon, 'Telecommunications Services in the Trans-Pacific Partnership: Will the Mobile Roaming Provisions Benefit Tourists and Traders?' (2016) 17(2) *Melbourne Journal of International Law* 404, 435–437; Danny Kotlowitz and Tania Voon, 'Services in the TPP: A Case Study of Telecommunications' in Tania Voon (ed), *Trade Liberalisation and International Co-operation: A Legal Analysis of the Trans-Pacific Partnership Agreement* (Edward Elgar, 2013) 131, 152–154.

189 WTO, GATS, *Australia: Final List of Article II (MFN) Exemptions*, WTO Docs GATS/EL/6 (15 April 1994) and suppl.1 (26 February 1998).

190 See, eg, WTO, GATS, *United States of America: Final List of Article II (MFN) Exemptions*, WTO Doc GATS/EL/90 (15 April 1994) 1. See also Rudolf Adlung, 'Trade in Healthcare and Health Insurance Services: WTO/GATS as a Supporting Actor (?)' (2010) 45(4) *Intereconomics* 227, 237.

more favourable treatment under a PTA to the extent that it falls outside the GATS exceptions. Such a claim would be enhanced by the WTO Appellate Body's stringent interpretation of the corresponding exception for PTAs in GATT art XXIV.[191] Based on the Appellate Body Report in *Turkey—Textiles* (with respect to GATT art XXIV:1), more favourable treatment might be exempted under GATS art V:1 only if introduced at the formation of the relevant PTA and if necessary for that formation.[192] In addition, GATS art V:4 (similarly to GATT art XXIV:5) specifies that an agreement exempt under GATS art V:1:

> Shall be designed to facilitate trade between the parties to the agreement and shall not in respect of any Member outside the agreement raise the overall level of barriers to trade in services within the respective sectors or subsectors compared to the level applicable prior to such an agreement.

Furthermore, any *less* favourable treatment under Australia's PTAs than under GATS[193] (or even under other PTAs)[194] may also raise concerns regarding GATS-compatibility. For example, an NCM that is listed under a PTA but not under GATS might not comply with GATS. As discussed above, while some Australian PTAs (for example, the 2016 amendments agreed to SAFTA and the TPP) define certain NCMs with reference to GATS obligations,[195] others such as the AUSFTA include NCMs lists that are not explicitly restricted by GATS-compatibility.[196] The coverage of the MFN obligation in the ANZCERTA Services Protocol has reduced in some respects over time, as discussed in part IVA of this chapter. Some Australian FTAs do not even contain an MFN obligation, as illustrated in Table 3.1 above. Several Australian FTAs contain sweeping reservations

---

[191] See generally Andrew D Mitchell and Nicolas JS Lockhart, 'Legal Requirements for PTAs under the WTO' in Simon Lester, Bryan Mercurio and Lorand Bartels, *Bilateral and Regional Trade Agreements: Commentary and Analysis* (Cambridge University Press, 2nd ed, 2015) 81.

[192] Appellate Body Report, *Turkey—Textiles*, [46], [58]. See also Rudolf Adlung, 'The Trade in Services Agreement (TISA) and Its Compatibility with GATS: An Assessment Based on Current Evidence' (2015) 14(4) *World Trade Review* 617, 623.

[193] See generally Rudolf Adlung and Sébastien Miroudot, 'Poison in the Wine? Tracing GATS-Minus Commitments in Regional Trade Agreements' (2012) 46(5) *Journal of World Trade* 1045.

[194] See Adlung, 'TISA', above n 192, 622–624.

[195] See above n 122 and corresponding text.

[196] See above n 125 and corresponding text.

with respect to other agreements including other PTAs, as noted earlier.[197] As explained in part V of this chapter, AANZFTA and the ANZCERTA Services Protocol add to the list of general exceptions recognised in GATS art XIV.

All these reductions in the levels of preferential treatment in Australia's PTAs risk undermining Australia's reliance on GATS art V:1, which exempts a PTA provided that it:

> (a) has substantial sectoral coverage; and
> (b) provides for the absence or elimination of substantially all discrimination, in the sense of Article XVII [national treatment], between or among the parties, in the sectors covered under subparagraph (a), through:
>   (i) elimination of existing discriminatory measures, and/or
>   (ii) prohibition of new or more discriminatory measures,
>
> either at the entry into force of that agreement or on the basis of a reasonable time-frame, except for measures permitted under Articles XI [payments and transfers], XII [restrictions to safeguard the balance of payments], XIV [general exceptions] and XIV*bis* [security exceptions].[198]

Just as a third country might use GATS-plus or GATS-minus provisions to challenge an Australian PTA's compliance with GATS art V:1, so too might one of Australia's PTA partners use the WTO dispute settlement system to enforce compliance with GATS commitments notwithstanding their relaxation in the relevant PTA. The Appellate Body in *Peru—Agricultural Products* took a restrictive approach to *inter se* agreements between WTO Members (modifying their WTO obligations as between themselves). The Appellate Body noted the conditions specified in *Turkey—Textiles*[199] and stating that the references in GATT art XXIV:4 'to facilitating trade and closer integration are not consistent with an interpretation of Article XXIV as a broad defence for measures in FTAs that *roll back on Members' rights and obligations under the WTO* covered agreements'.[200] That sentiment would seem even more applicable to the GATS, which refers in several places to progressive liberalisation of services,[201] including in the preamble, as noted at the start of this chapter.

---

197 See above nn 140–147 and corresponding text.

198 Footnote omitted.

199 Appellate Body Report, *Peru—Agricultural Products*, [5.115].

200 Appellate Body Report, *Peru—Agricultural Products*, [5.116] (emphasis added).

201 See, eg, GATS art XIX:1.

VII CONCLUSION

The analysis of Australia's services PTAs in this chapter makes clear the different mechanisms that Australia has used to preserve regulatory autonomy with respect to trade in services. These include: excluding areas from the scope of the core services chapter (in particular government procurement, taxation, subsidies, and the exercise of governmental authority); limiting the content of core obligations, such as through changing 'hard' obligations to 'best endeavours' type obligations with respect to domestic regulation, and explicitly recognising a right to regulate in this regard; listing limitations to commitments in positive list PTAs and NCMs in negative list PTAs (whether in annex I (subject to standstill and ratchet requirements) or annex II (providing more flexibility for future regulatory change) or their equivalents); and incorporating general exceptions in both positive and negative list PTAs, whether or not such exceptions overlap with limitations on commitments or specified NCMs. Social services in general, including health and education services, are well protected in both positive list PTAs (as conditions on obligations) and negative list PTAs (as NCMs). NCMs in Australia's modern PTAs extend specifically to regional regulation, indigenous peoples, culture, tobacco, alcohol, firearms, gambling, foreign investment policy, Qantas, CSL, and Telstra. Exceptions now tend to apply to other pre-existing international agreements, for example allowing what might otherwise amount to MFN violations to the extent reflected in a PTA (or, in some but not all cases, a BIT).

Australia's apparent preference for negative list services PTAs may assist in enhancing transparency and the potential for increasing liberalisation, particularly in relation to new services and new technologies. However, that potential may be undermined by overuse of the tools just mentioned (exclusion of large areas from the scope of services chapters, general exceptions overlaid with specific NCMs, and weakening of obligations with reference to best endeavours). An increasing focus on 'policy space' also risks potential conflicts with Australia's WTO obligations under the GATS. The value of a negative list may also be diluted if the two parties adopt different approaches, as in ChAFTA. Similarly, the use of a hybrid approach in TiSA (to accommodate the preferences of other negotiating parties) may not be ideal (although it has arguably worked in the GATS). Structural problems may be avoided by ensuring separate annexes are used instead of using the same annex to list both exemptions for a negative list obligation and inscriptions for a positive list obligation (as in the ANZCERTA Services Protocol). Just as the

GATS and the AUSFTA appeared to provide a focal point for Australia's services PTAs, the TPP may be set to do the same, and subsequently the TiSA. Given the compromises made by Australia in these negotiations, the TiSA hybrid listing approach should not be automatically applied to future Australian PTAs; nor the substantive services provisions of the TPP and TiSA without considered reflection on a case-by-case basis (particularly given the withdrawal of the US from the TPP).

This chapter has briefly addressed investment issues in the context of their treatment in Australia's services PTAs. The overlap between services and investment is a crucial aspect of Australia's trade and investment framework, which must be carefully resolved, for example by removing mode 3 services from the core services chapter, as under the TPP, or otherwise through exceptions and NCMs or similar mechanisms. However, the precise mechanism used will be important. Allowing the investment chapter to do all the work once done by GATS with respect to mode 3 services may provide clarity but will also make the content of the investment chapter all the more significant, including as regards ISDS. The investment chapter may be less well-equipped to preserve regulatory autonomy than the services chapter in Australia's PTAs. For example, as we discuss in Chapter 4, not all Australian PTAs and BITs include general exceptions akin to GATT art XX/GATS art XIV, whereas Australia's PTAs do all include general exceptions of this kind with respect to trade in services.[202] These exceptions may be particularly important in relation to matters that arise in the future and are not specified in footnotes or NCMs because they do not yet exist.

---

202 See also generally Adlung, 'Healthcare', above n 190.

4. Investment: Haphazard Responses to Expansive Obligations

I INTRODUCTION

The coverage of foreign investment forms one of the most controversial aspects of Australia's obligations under international economic law. In this chapter, we outline core aspects of Australia's IIAs, taking account of the traditional approaches in BITs as well as the more modern approaches in investment chapters of PTAs. Our aim is to identify patterns and developments over time in order to assess the extent to which these treaties have been drafted so as to protect Australia's regulatory sovereignty with respect to matters such as public health and other non-trade/investment policy objectives.

We begin in part II by reviewing Australia's IIA provisions in respect of three key substantive investment obligations: MFN treatment, the minimum standard of treatment (including the FET standard), and expropriation. Our analysis demonstrates significant variance in the terms of these obligations, even among Australia's PTAs. We also show that although some progressive changes have been made that enhance Australia's policy space with respect to these obligations, other reforms adopted in some of Australia's IIAs but not others or witnessed in other countries' treaty practice could further enhance policy space without undermining Australia's investment objectives.

In part III, we refer to two main types of 'exceptions' to investment obligations, namely specified 'non-conforming measures' that are not subject to particular obligations, and 'general exceptions' with respect to particular legitimate policy objectives. Here, too, we see inconsistency and a failure to adopt consistently the approach most favourable to regulatory autonomy. In this regard, the treaty practice of the United States appears influential, for example in omitting general exceptions or applying them only to certain obligations, not including expropriation and the FET standard.

When viewed as a whole, Australia's approach to the reform of IIAs to protect policy space is clear but perhaps half-hearted. The existence of inconsistency among Australia's 20 BITs in force and 11 PTAs with investment chapters (including the SAFTA amendments agreed in 2016 and the TPP) itself creates difficulties, as elaborated in Chapter 5. Yet such inconsistency is inevitable in the absence of a concerted effort to reform the suite of treaties in a systematic fashion (for example, through renegotiation, amendment or termination). In addition, the adoption of minor changes to substantive obligations appears to have been hampered by an inability to maintain the better approaches in all agreements, as well as the exclusion of 'general exceptions' for the most important investment obligations in most IIAs.

II KEY SUBSTANTIVE OBLIGATIONS

A MFN Treatment

1 The MFN obligation in Australia's BITs

The obligation to accord MFN treatment is a significant part of international investment law, widening the scope and significance of investment protections as the number of IIAs has grown. Although the number of IIAs concluded each year has slowed in the last 15 years,[1] and notwithstanding the termination of certain IIAs,[2] the cumulative number of IIAs in force continues to rise at present.[3] The MFN obligation is a key reason for the de facto 'multilateralisation' of international investment law described by Schill.[4] The MFN obligation is also one of two significant reasons for older style IIAs remaining crucial even after more modern IIAs have entered into force (the other significant reason being the ability of multinational corporations to

---

1 UNCTAD, 'Recent Trends in IIAs and ISDS', *IIA Issues Note No 1* (February 2015) 2.

2 See generally Tania Voon, Andrew D Mitchell and James Munro, 'Parting Ways: The Impact of Mutual Termination of Investment Treaties on Investor Rights' (2014) *ICSID Review* 451; Tania Voon and Andrew D Mitchell, 'Denunciation, Termination and Survival: The Interplay of Treaty Law and International Investment Law' (2016) 31(2) *ICSID Review* 413.

3 UNCTAD, above n 1, 2.

4 Stephan W Schill, *The Multilateralization of International Investment Law* (Cambridge University Press, 2009) ch IV.

restructure to take advantage of more favourable IIAs,[5] albeit subject to certain limitations).[6] These two factors mean that a country such as Australia cannot succeed in modernising its IIAs simply by adopting new provisions (for example, additional exceptions or clarifications of substantive investment obligations in order to enhance regulatory sovereignty) one by one in each new negotiated IIA. If older IIAs are not terminated or revised, investors can fairly easily restructure or select the appropriate existing subsidiary to take advantage of the IIA with the most favourable terms from the perspective of the claimant. Thus, in the case of *Philip Morris v Australia*,[7] the claim was brought (albeit unsuccessfully) under the Australia–Hong Kong BIT, which contains few if any clarifications and exceptions of the kind seen in more modern Australian IIAs.

Table 4.1 summarises certain key elements of the MFN provisions in Australia's current BITs (that is, excluding the Australia–Chile BIT, which was terminated on the entry into force of ACIFTA,[8] and the Australia–India BIT, which India unilaterally terminated as of 23 March 2017).[9] The Australia–Viet Nam BIT (signed and entered into force in 1991) contains a typical older-style MFN provision, which does not explicitly extend to the establishment of investments (that is, MFN does

---

[5] See generally Tania Voon, Andrew D Mitchell and James Munro, 'Legal Responses to Corporate Manoeuvring in International Investment Arbitration' (2014) 5(1) *Journal of International Dispute Settlement* 41. See also Schill, above n 4, ch V.

[6] See, eg, *Philip Morris v Australia*, Jurisdictional Decision, [539], [554], [588]. The investment treaty claims brought by Philip Morris against Australia and Uruguay are discussed further in Chapter 2.

[7] *Philip Morris v Australia*, Jurisdictional Decision.

[8] The Australia–Chile BIT continued to apply to investments made before the entry into force of ACIFTA on 6 March 2009 'with respect to any act, fact or situation which originated before' that date, but ISDS remained available for only three years from that date: ACIFTA annex 10–E: 'Termination of the Bilateral Investment Agreement', [2]–[3].

[9] The Australia–India BIT continues to apply to investments made on or before 22 March 2017 by way of a 15-year survival clause: Australia–India BIT art 17.3; Australian Government, Department of Foreign Affairs & Trade, *Australia and foreign investment; Australia's bilateral investment treaties* <http://dfat.gov.au/trade/topics/investment/Pages/australias-bilateral-investment-treaties.aspx> (last visited 7 April 2017).

Table 4.1 MFN in Australia's Current BITs

Treaty	Entry into force	Extension to establishment of investments	Exception for PTAs	Restriction to like circumstances	Dispute settlement excluded
China BIT	1988	✗	✓	✗	✗
Viet Nam BIT	1991	✗	✓	✗	✗
Papua New Guinea BIT[10]	1991	✗	✓	✗	✗
Poland BIT	1992	✗	✓	✗	✗
Hungary BIT	1992	✗	✓	✗	✗
Indonesia BIT	1993	✗	✓	✗	✗
Hong Kong BIT[11]	1993	✗	✓	✗	✗
Romania BIT	1994	✗	✓	✗	✗
Czech Republic BIT	1994	✗	✓	✗	✗
Lao PDR BIT	1995	✗	✓	✗	✗
Philippines BIT	1995	✗	✓	✗	✗
Argentina BIT[12]	1997	✗	✓	✗	✗
Peru BIT	1997	✗	✓	✗	✗
Pakistan BIT	1998	✗	✓	✗	✗
Lithuania BIT	2002	✗	✓	✗	✗
Egypt BIT	2002	✗	✓	✗	✗
Uruguay BIT	2002	✗	✓	✗	✗

[10] Under art 4.2 of the Australia–Papua New Guinea BIT, 'Special incentives granted by one Contracting Party only to its nationals or companies in order to stimulate the creation of local industries are considered compatible with this Article'.

[11] Under art 3.3 of the Australia–Papua New Guinea BIT, 'each Contracting Party shall permit investors of the other Contracting Party who have made investments in the first Contracting Party's area to employ within its area, key technical and managerial personnel of their choice, and permit physical persons who are investors of the other Contracting Party and personnel employed by companies of that other Contracting Party to enter and remain in its area for the purpose of engaging in activities related to investments. Such personnel employed from abroad shall be entitled to transfer abroad, subject to the provisions of Article 8 of this Agreement, unspent earnings and other remuneration in connection with investments'.

[12] Under art 5(c) of the Australia–Argentina BIT, also excluded from the MFN obligation are 'the bilateral agreements providing for concessional financing concluded by the Argentine Republic with the Republic of Italy on 10 December 1987 and with the Kingdom of Spain on 3 June 1988'.

Treaty	Entry into force	Extension to establishment of investments	Exception for PTAs	Restriction to like circumstances	Dispute settlement excluded
Sri Lanka BIT	2007	✘	✔	✘	✘
Mexico BIT[13]	2007	✘	✔	✔	✘
Turkey BIT[14]	2009	✔	✔	✔	✘

not apply to the pre-establishment phase) and includes exceptions for other PTAs and double taxation arrangements:

> A Contracting Party shall at all times treat investments in its own territory on a basis *no less favourable* than that accorded to investments of nationals of *any third country*, provided that a Contracting Party shall not be obliged to extend to investments any treatment, preference or privilege resulting from:
>
> (a) any customs union, economic union, *free trade area* or regional economic integration agreement to which the Contracting Party belongs; or
> (b) the provisions of a double *taxation* agreement with a third country.[15]

Nearly all of Australia's BITs contain this type of MFN clause, although the wording may differ, the provision may be incorporated into broader obligations,[16] and additional clarifications or specific exceptions may apply.[17]

Australia's BITs do not generally include any restriction regarding 'like circumstances' or coverage of dispute settlement, as seen later in Australia's FTAs. The exceptions are Australia's BITs with Mexico (which entered into force in 2007) and Turkey (2009), which do refer to 'like circumstances'[18] and 'similar situations' respectively,[19] after this terminology had been introduced into Australia's treaties through the AUSFTA in 2005.[20] The BIT with Turkey is also unusual among

[13] The exception from MFN treatment in art 4.5 of the Australia–Mexico BIT applies to 'taxation measures' generally (as defined in art 4.6) rather than taxation arrangements.

[14] The restriction in the MFN obligation in arts 4.1 and 4.2 of the Australia–Turkey BIT is phrased as 'similar situations' rather than 'like circumstances'.

[15] Australia–Viet Nam BIT art 4 (emphasis added).

[16] See, eg, Australia–China BIT art III (incorporating the FET obligation).

[17] See, eg, below nn 10, 12, 14.

[18] Australia–Mexico BIT art 4.3.

[19] Australia–Turkey BIT arts 4.1, 4.2.

[20] AUSFTA art 11.4.

Australia's BITs in implicitly extending the MFN obligation to the pre-establishment phase,[21] again as occurred in the AUSFTA.[22]

2 Developments from the AUSFTA to the TPP

The changes in the MFN clause in Australia's PTAs compared with its BITs are summarised in Table 4.2. The AUSFTA, unlike all of Australia's BITs, dispenses with the exception for PTAs in the MFN provision. That means that more 'favourable' arrangements concluded with other countries will need to be accorded to the investors of the other State party pursuant to the MFN obligation unless some other exemption applies. However, such an exemption does apply under the AUSFTA and other Australian PTAs through negotiated NCM lists as noted below and in Chapter 3. AUSFTA art 11.4 reads:

> 1. Each Party shall accord to investors of the other Party treatment no less favourable than that it accords, *in like circumstances*, to investors of any non-Party with respect to the *establishment*, acquisition, expansion, management, conduct, operation, and sale or other disposition of investments in its territory.
> 2. Each Party shall accord to covered investments treatment no less favourable than that it accords, *in like circumstances*, to investments in its territory of investors of any non-Party with respect to the *establishment*, acquisition, expansion, management, conduct, operation, and sale or other disposition of investments.[23]

These three newer elements from AUSFTA—restriction to like circumstances; extension to pre-establishment phase; no exception for PTAs in the MFN obligation itself—are followed in ACIFTA (2009),[24] MAFTA (2013)[25] (although the MAFTA MFN obligation is not yet operative),[26] ANZCERTA Investment Protocol (2013),[27] and KAFTA (2014).[28] However, TAFTA (which entered into force on 1 January 2005, the same day as the AUSFTA) does not extend to the pre-establishment phase;[29] nor does JAEPA (2015).[30]

---

21 Australia–Turkey BIT art 4.1.
22 AUSFTA art 11.4.
23 Emphasis added.
24 ACIFTA art 10.4.
25 MAFTA art 12.5.
26 MAFTA art 12.16.4.
27 ANZCERTA Investment Protocol art 6.1.
28 KAFTA art 11.4.
29 TAFTA art 910.
30 JAEPA art 14.4.

Although these PTAs do not exclude pre-existing international agreements (such as PTAs and BITs) in the MFN provision itself, as noted in Chapter 3 with respect to the common NCM annexes for services and investment in Australia's PTAs taking a negative list approach to MFN in the services context, pre-existing agreements are excluded through NCM annexes. Such an NCM also appears in the ANZCERTA Investment Protocol with respect to the MFN obligation,[31] and TAFTA contains a similar exception for existing and future agreements.[32] These limitations regarding other international agreements provide a powerful restriction on the otherwise expansive nature of the MFN obligation, although most preclude the application of the MFN rule to past but not future agreements. Similarly, although Australia's PTAs do not contain MFN-specific exceptions directly addressing double tax arrangements, they tend to contain general provisions limiting the application of the investment chapter (or the agreement as a whole) to taxation measures, explicitly mentioning tax treaties (sometimes termed as agreements or conventions).[33]

The most modern form of the MFN obligation in Australia's PTAs also includes a fourth element, introduced in the ANZCERTA Investment Protocol in 2013. That element is a clarification that the MFN obligation does not apply to dispute settlement procedures, meaning that a claimant cannot invoke the MFN obligation in order to gain access to preferential dispute settlement procedures under another IIA, such as access to ISDS under an IIA that does not otherwise contain an ISDS mechanism. Such clauses have been more recently introduced in IIAs by many countries[34] following concerns arising from the jurisdictional decision in *Maffezini v Spain*, which allowed the claimant investor Maffezini to dispense with the requirement under the Argentina–Spain BIT of exhausting domestic remedies on the basis that the Chile–Spain BIT imposed no such requirement.[35] The MFN obligation in art 6 of the ANZCERTA Investment Protocol reads:

---

31 ANZCERTA Investment Protocol art 9.2, annex II (Australia).

32 TAFTA art 1907.

33 SAFTA 2003 ch 8 art 2.3; SAFTA 2011 ch 8 art 2.3; SAFTA 2016 ch 17 art 3.2; AUSFTA art 22.3; TAFTA art 1607; ACIFTA art 22.3; AANZFTA ch 15 art 3; MAFTA arts 12.2(b), 18.3; ANZCERTA Investment Protocol art 21; KAFTA art 22.3; JAEPA art 1.8; ChAFTA art 16.4; TPP art 29.4.

34 See, eg, CETA art 8.7.4; China–New Zealand FTA, art 139.2.

35 *Maffezini v Spain*, Jurisdictional Decision, [39], [54], [56], [64]. See also, eg, Pavel Šturma, 'Goodbye, *Maffezini*? On the Recent Developments of Most-Favoured-Nation Clause Interpretation in International Investment Law' (2016)

1. Each Party shall accord to investors of the other Party and covered investments treatment no less favourable than that it accords, in like circumstances, to investors of any non-Party and their investments with respect to the establishment, acquisition, expansion, management, conduct, operation, and sale or other disposition of investments in its territory.
2. For greater certainty, this Article does not apply to dispute settlement procedures.

This clause can be seen as the modern incarnation of the MFN obligation in Australia's PTAs, followed in the TPP[36] and the amendments to SAFTA agreed in 2016[37] (along with clarifications on the meaning of 'like circumstances', addressed by footnotes in these three PTAs as discussed in Chapter 3). Strangely, KAFTA does not include this exclusion of dispute settlement proceedings from the MFN rule. Perhaps this omission arises from the fact that KAFTA already contains an ISDS mechanism, reducing concerns about using the MFN obligation to bring in ISDS from another treaty. However, ChAFTA, the TPP and SAFTA also include both ISDS and the *Maffezini*-directed exclusion. The omission of this exclusion from KAFTA appears risky in the face of significant case law and State practice on the issue: the States parties must have been aware of the potential problem, hindering arguments against a broad reading of the MFN provision. ISDS mechanisms differ greatly in their scope and conditions, as discussed further in Chapter 5. Accordingly, an investor could attempt to use the MFN obligation in KAFTA to bring in a range of more favourable procedures or dispute settlement provisions from other PTAs or BITs, even if the possibility of ISDS itself is already agreed in KAFTA. A reductionist approach to the inclusion or exclusion of specific safeguards undermines the efforts of Australian negotiators to improve treaty drafting and protect Australian policy space.

15 *Law and Practice of International Courts and Tribunals* 81; Martins Paparinskis, 'MFN Clauses and International Dispute Settlement: Moving beyond *Maffezini* and *Plama*?' (2011) 26(2) *ICSID Review* 14.

[36] TPP art 9.5.

[37] SAFTA 2016 ch 8 art 5.

Table 4.2 MFN in Australia's Current PTAs

Treaty	Entry into force	Extension to establishment of investments	Exception for PTAs in the MFN provision[38]	Restriction to like circumstances	Dispute settlement excluded
TAFTA	2005	✗	✗	✓	✗
AUSFTA	2005	✓	✗	✓	✗
ACIFTA	2009	✓	✗	✓	✗
AANZFTA[39]	2010	–	–	–	–
MAFTA[40]	2013	✓	✗	✓	✗
ANZCERTA Investment Protocol	2013	✓	✗	✓	✓
KAFTA	2014	✓	✗	✓	✗
JAEPA	2015	✗	✗	✓	✓
ChAFTA[41]	2015	✓	✓	✓	✓
TPP	–	✓	✗	✓	✓
SAFTA 2016 amendments[42]	–	✓	✗	✓	✓

The contours of changes to the MFN obligation in Australia's IIAs over the last three decades reflect both expansion of the obligation (to cover the pre-establishment phase and without excepting existing PTAs) and clarification or restriction of the obligation (to 'like circumstances' and excluding dispute settlement). The approach can be understood as

38 This column refers to exceptions in the MFN provision itself. As noted above and elaborated in Chapter 3 of this book, Australia's negative list PTAs exclude pre-existing international agreements such as PTAs and BITs from the MFN provision by listing them in an NCM annex.

39 AANZFTA contains no MFN obligation.

40 Pursuant to MAFTA art 12.16.4, the MAFTA national treatment, MFN treatment and NCM provisions will not apply until the parties have agreed NCM schedules.

41 Under art 9.4.3 of the ChAFTA, an exception from MFN treatment applies to measures that accord with 'any bilateral or multilateral international agreement in force prior to the date of entry into force of this Agreement' (which would extend to PTAs and double tax arrangements). In addition, under art 9.4.4, an MFN exception applies to measures that accord with any such agreement whether in force before or after the entry into force of ChAFTA 'involving (a) aviation; (b) fisheries; or (c) maritime matters, including salvage'.

42 The original SAFTA and the SAFTA as amended in 2011 contained no MFN obligation.

generally static in Australia's BITs until the entry into force of the AUSFTA in 2005, with the substance of MFN provisions in the areas we have focused on in the table varying more significantly in the last ten years. The differing modern approaches in KAFTA, JAEPA and ChAFTA in particular demonstrate the apparent significance of the interests and approaches of the negotiating partner in agreeing the final wording, even for this most basic form of investment protection. ChAFTA goes further in restricting the MFN obligation, adding a broad exception for existing international agreements and an additional exception for future international agreements in particular sectors.[43]

The approach adopted in the TPP and in the 2016 agreed amendments to SAFTA might be expected to dominate in future agreements, at least to the extent that negotiating partners accept such an approach. By allowing the MFN obligation to be used to invoke substantive preferential treatment from both BITs and PTAs, including in the pre-establishment phase, this approach provides strong protection to inbound and outbound investment, notwithstanding the reference to like circumstances and the exclusion of dispute settlement. This strong protection might be thought to allow for sovereign regulatory autonomy only to a minimal degree. However, the obligation is subject to any listed NCMs or general exceptions as discussed further below; in practice, Australia excludes other international agreements from the MFN obligation, typically through its NCM schedule.

B Minimum Standard of Treatment

1 Minimum standard of treatment in Australia's BITs

The minimum standard of treatment, including in particular the FET obligation, is a crucial part of international investment law—'the most relied upon and successful basis for IIA claims by investors'[44]—which creates significant concerns from the perspective of State regulatory autonomy because of its amorphous or subjective nature.[45] As with the MFN provisions in Australia's IIAs, the FET obligation is fairly uniform in Australia's BITs, with greater clarification developing in Australia's FTAs. Most FET provisions in Australia's BITs are very brief and

---

[43] See above n 41.

[44] UNCTAD, *Fair and Equitable Treatment: UNCTAD Series on Issues in International Investment Agreements II* (United Nations, 2012) 1.

[45] See Rudolf Dolzer, 'Fair and Equitable Treatment: Today's Contours' (2013) 12 *Santa Clara Journal of International Law* 7, 15.

without clarification or definition. For example, art III of the Australia–China BIT provides simply that each State party 'shall at all times: (a) ensure fair and equitable treatment in its own territory to investments and activities associated with such investments'. Other Australian BIT provisions are in similar terms,[46] often omitting the express reference to associated 'activities',[47] and occasionally also omitting the restriction to investments 'in its own territory'.[48] Article III(b) of the Australia–China BIT also requires each party, *inter alia*, to 'accord within its territory protection and security to investments and activities associated with investments'. Such a reference to protection and security is also common in Australia's other BITs, without further clarification, but generally 'subject to its laws'[49] and sometimes with the descriptor 'full' protection and security.[50]

2 Customary international law and NAFTA

SAFTA (which entered into force in 2003) was Australia's first FTA to include investment provisions, although it did not contain an FET clause. Changes to the BIT formulation of the FET obligation began with the entry into force of the AUSFTA in 2005. AUSFTA art 11.5 provides:

> 1. Each Party shall accord to covered investments treatment in accordance with the *customary international law minimum standard* of treatment of aliens, including fair and equitable treatment and full protection and security.
> 2. For greater certainty, the concepts of 'fair and equitable treatment' and 'full protection and security' do not require treatment in addition to or beyond that which is required by that standard, and do not create additional substantive rights. The obligation in paragraph 1 to provide:
>   (a) 'fair and equitable treatment' includes the obligation not to deny justice in criminal, civil, or administrative adjudicatory proceedings in accordance with the principle of due process embodied in the principal legal systems of the world; and

---

46 See, eg, Australia–Poland BIT art 3.2.

47 See, eg, Australia–Viet Nam BIT art 3.2; Australia–Papua New Guinea BIT art 3.3; Australia–Hungary BIT art 3.2; Australia–Indonesia BIT art II:2. See also Australia–India BIT art 4.1 (now terminated).

48 See, eg, Australia–Philippines BIT art 3.2; Australia–Argentina BIT art 4.1.

49 See, eg, Australia–Viet Nam BIT art 3.3; Australia–Poland BIT art 3.3; Australia–Hungary BIT art 3.3; Australia–Indonesia BIT art II:3.

50 See, eg, Australia–Papua New Guinea BIT art 3.3; Australia–Hong Kong BIT art 2.2.

(b) 'full protection and security' requires each Party to provide the level of police protection required under customary international law.

3. A determination that there has been a breach of another provision of this Agreement, or of a separate international agreement, does not establish that there has been a breach of this Article.[51]

Annex 11–A of the AUSFTA adds:

> The Parties confirm their shared understanding that 'customary international law' generally and as specifically referenced in Article 11.5 and Annex 11–B results from a general and consistent practice of States that they follow from a sense of legal obligation. With regard to Article 11.5, the customary international law minimum standard of treatment of aliens refers to all customary international law principles that protect the economic rights and interests of aliens.

In stark contrast, TAFTA art 909 (entering into force the same day) provides simply (like the Australia–China BIT):

2. Each Party shall ensure fair and equitable treatment in its own territory of investments.
3. Each Party shall accord within its territory protection and security to investments.

Australia's BITs with Sri Lanka (2007) and Turkey (2009), both of which followed the AUSFTA, similarly adopt the older style FET provision[52] without the AUSFTA clarifications. Nevertheless, the AUSFTA provision on the minimum standard of treatment seems to have had a profound impact, not only on all of Australia's subsequent FTAs[53] (excluding ChAFTA, which presently contains no FET/minimum standard of treatment provision)[54] but also on its BIT with Mexico,[55] which entered into force in 2007. This discrepancy with the BITs with Sri Lanka and Turkey can perhaps be attributed to Mexico's participation in NAFTA. In a JSCOT hearing on ChAFTA, DFAT explained the exclusion of FET (and expropriation) from that treaty as follows:

---

[51] Emphasis added.

[52] Australia–Sri Lanka BIT art 3.2; Australia–Turkey BIT art 3.2.

[53] ACIFTA art 10.5, annex 10–A; AANZFTA ch 11 art 6; MAFTA art 12.7; ANZCERTA Investment Protocol art 12; KAFTA art 11.5, annex 11–A; JAEPA art 14.5; TPP art 9.6, annex 9–A; SAFTA 2011 ch 8 art 4; SAFTA 2016 ch 8 art 6.

[54] ChAFTA art 9.9.3(b)(i) provides for future consideration of such a provision.

[55] Australia–Mexico BIT Protocol art 4.1.

> China is in the midst of what is a bilateral investment treaty negotiation with the US and is also negotiating with the EU. At this stage of its investment policy development, we decided to have a short-form chapter which really covers a non-discrimination and an MFN commitment, and to commit to in three years time coming back to negotiating a fuller investment chapter with China.[56]

As explained in Chapter 3 with respect to services, the ChAFTA review process is scheduled to commence in 2017.[57] In the meantime, as discussed further in Chapter 5, the Australia–China BIT continues to operate.

Article 1105 of NAFTA, which entered into force in 1994, contains a standard older style reference to FET.[58] However, in 2001, the NAFTA Free Trade Commission ('comprising cabinet-level representatives of the [NAFTA] Parties or their designees')[59] adopted interpretations of NAFTA ch 11 'in order to clarify and reaffirm the meaning of certain of its provisions'.[60] These interpretations were in part prompted by arbitral decisions in investor–State disputes arising under NAFTA ch 11.

Traditionally, as set out in the *Neer* claim, the FET standard under customary international law was violated only by State conduct amounting to 'an outrage, to bad faith, to wilful neglect of duty, or to an insufficiency of governmental action so far short of international standards that every reasonable and impartial man would readily recognize its insufficiency'.[61] However, in 2001, the tribunal in *Pope & Talbot v Canada* held that the FET obligation under NAFTA art 1105.1 contains 'fairness elements' in addition to the international minimum standard of treatment[62] and is not limited to egregious, outrageous, shocking or otherwise extraordinary conduct.[63] In addition, in *SD Myers v Canada*, the tribunal held that 'the fact that a host Party has breached a rule of international law that is specifically designed to protect investors will

---

[56] Evidence to JSCOT, Canberra (17 August 2015) 22 (Jan Adams, Deputy Secretary, DFAT).

[57] *Declaration of Intent By the Government of Australia and the Government of the People's Republic of China Regarding Review of Elements of the China–Australia Free Trade Agreement* (signed 24 March 2017).

[58] NAFTA art 1105.1.

[59] NAFTA art 2001.1.

[60] NAFTA Free Trade Commission, *Notes of Interpretation of Certain Chapter 11 Provisions* (31 July 2001) preamble.

[61] *Neer v Mexico*, Opinion, [4].

[62] *Pope & Talbot v Canada*, Merits Award Phase 2, [111].

[63] *Pope & Talbot v Canada*, Merits Award Phase 2, [118].

tend to weigh heavily in favour of finding a breach of Article 1105'.[64] In the circumstances of the case, a majority of the tribunal[65] also found that a breach of the national treatment standard in NAFTA art 1102 'essentially establishes a breach of Article 1105 as well'.[66]

In response particularly to these kinds of decisions,[67] the NAFTA Free Trade Commission's interpretation of the minimum standard of treatment incorporated key features now found in the AUSFTA, including an express limitation to the customary international law standard and a reference to the relationship to other agreements and provisions:

1. Article 1105(1) prescribes the *customary international law* minimum standard of treatment of aliens as the minimum standard of treatment to be afforded to investments of investors of another Party.
2. The concepts of 'fair and equitable treatment' and 'full protection and security' do not require treatment in addition to or beyond that which is required by the customary international law minimum standard of treatment of aliens.
3. A determination that there has been a breach of another provision of the NAFTA, or of a separate international agreement, does not establish that there has been a breach of Article 1105(1).[68]

The *Pope & Talbot* tribunal considered this interpretation in making its determination on damages but determined that, even pursuant to that interpretation, the customary international law standard evolves over time and has moved beyond the *Neer* standard to encompass other forms of breach.[69] Other tribunals such as that in *Mondev* have supported this view of an evolving FET standard, which extends beyond *Neer* to requirements such as according transparency and due process (including non-denial of justice and lack of arbitrariness).[70] More controversially,[71] many tribunals have explicitly or implicitly suggested that the FET obligation requires adherence to the 'legitimate expectations' of investors,[72] to the extent that, since 2003, 'arbitral tribunals and commentators have generally

---

[64] *SD Myers v Canada*, Partial Award, [264].

[65] *SD Myers v Canada*, Partial Award, [267], [268].

[66] *SD Myers v Canada*, Partial Award, [266].

[67] See also, eg, *Metalclad v Mexico*, Award, [104].

[68] NAFTA Free Trade Commission, above n 60, [2] (emphasis added).

[69] *Pope & Talbot v Canada*, Damages Award, [47], [51], [58]–[65].

[70] *Mondev v United States*, Award, [115]–[116], [123]–[125].

[71] See generally, eg, Christopher Campbell, 'House of Cards: The Relevance of Legitimate Expectations under Fair and Equitable Treatment Provisions in Investment Treaty Law' (2013) 30(4) *Journal of International Arbitration* 361.

[72] See, eg, *Tecmed v Mexico*, Award, [122].

treated the legitimate expectations of investors as the central substantive pillar of the FET standard'.[73] In contrast, the Australia–China BIT imposes a specific obligation on the host State to 'adhere to any written undertakings given by a competent authority to a national of the other Contracting Party with regard to an investment in accordance with its law and the provisions of this Agreement'.[74] Two other Australian BITs contain similar obligations regarding written undertakings.[75]

Bilcon was the first and so far only NAFTA award following the Commission's interpretation finding a violation of the FET obligation. In that dispute, the majority applied the usual *Waste Management*[76] description of the FET standard:

> While no single arbitral formulation can definitively and exhaustively capture the meaning of Article 1105, the Tribunal finds this quote from *Waste Management* to be a particularly apt one. Acts or omissions constituting a breach must be of a serious nature. The *Waste Management* formulation applies intensifying adjectives to certain items—but by no means all of them—in its list of categories of potentially nonconforming conduct. The formulation includes 'grossly' unfair, 'manifest' failure of natural justice and 'complete' lack of transparency.[77]

Applying that standard, the tribunal found that a Canadian rejection of a development project on environmental grounds entailed a breach of the FET obligation in NAFTA art 1105.1.[78] In a vigorous dissent, Professor Donald McRae contended that the majority had improperly converted a potential violation of Canadian law into a NAFTA breach.[79] He described the majority's decision as 'not only an intrusion into the way an environmental review process is to be conducted, but also an intrusion into the environmental public policy of the state'.[80]

The significance of aligning the FET obligation to the customary international law standard is uncertain, to the extent that the latter

---

[73] Lucy Reed, Pedro Caeiro and Simon Consedine, 'Fair and Equitable Treatment: Legitimate Expectations and Transparency' in Meg N Kinnear et al (eds), *Building International Investment Law: The First 50 Years of ICSID* (Kluwer Law International, 2015) 283, 286. See also, eg, *Electrabel v Hungary*, Award, [7.75].

[74] Australia–China BIT art XI.

[75] Australia–Papua New Guinea BIT art 11; Australia–Poland BIT art 10.

[76] *Waste Management v Mexico*, Award, [98].

[77] *Clayton and Bilcon v Canada*, Award, [443].

[78] *Clayton and Bilcon v Canada*, Award, [592], [600], [604].

[79] *Clayton and Bilcon v Canada*, Dissent [43].

[80] *Clayton and Bilcon v Canada*, Dissent [49].

standard may have evolved in any case,[81] and the nature and scope of that evolution may be subject to debate. However, some tribunals have emphasised that the burden falls on the claimant to establish the evolution of the standard it is alleging.[82] In general, the threshold for a breach of the FET standard is still understood as being high.[83] Furthermore, even if an investor's legitimate expectations are relevant to the assessment of FET, the prevailing view is that investors cannot expect regulation to remain frozen:[84] 'the host State is entitled to maintain a reasonable degree of regulatory flexibility to respond to changing circumstances in the public interest',[85] even more so in traditionally regulated industries or in relation to unhealthy products such as tobacco.[86]

As noted above, Australia's more recent FTAs have followed the AUSFTA and the NAFTA Free Trade Commission in including an express restriction to the customary international law standard, as have many other IIAs concluded by countries around the world.[87] This restriction appears to convey the States parties' intentions to restrict the scope of the FET obligation and reduce the risk of tribunals expansively interpreting that obligation so as to unduly limit regulatory autonomy (although the relevant JSCOT reports do not appear to address this intention explicitly in relation to FET).

3 Other provisions and international agreements

The objective of enhancing regulatory freedom can be understood as underlying the FET restriction that prevents tribunals from equating a breach of one provision of an IIA with a breach of the FET standard in the same IIA, or indeed equating a breach of another international law with a breach of the FET standard. These kinds of issues also arise under the so-called 'umbrella clause' of some BITs, which is sometimes used to elevate contractual breaches (that is, breaches of contracts between a host State and an investor) to treaty breaches (that is, breaches of IIAs,

---

81 See, eg, *Murphy v Ecuador*, Partial Award, [206].

82 See, eg, *Glamis Gold v United States*, Award, [21]–[22]; *Cargill v Mexico*, Award, [273].

83 See, eg, *Waste Management v Mexico*, Award, [98].

84 *Saluka v Czech Republic*, Partial Award, [305].

85 *Electrabel v Hungary*, Award, [7.77].

86 *Philip Morris v Uruguay*, Award, [269].

87 See, eg, Canada–Korea FTA art 8.5.2; Colombia Model BIT (2007) art III. Cf France Model BIT (2006) art 3.

allowing invocation of the ISDS mechanism),[88] or at least to ensure compliance with specific government undertakings to investors.[89] This kind of FET limitation may prevent an investor from claiming, for example, that a WTO breach amounts to an IIA breach, which Philip Morris originally claimed in its case against Australia[90] under the umbrella clause of the Australia–Hong Kong BIT,[91] before later abandoning the umbrella clause claim.[92]

Philip Morris also brought a claim under the umbrella clause of the Switzerland–Uruguay BIT[93] in its dispute against Uruguay's tobacco packaging laws. Rather than referring to extraneous international law or another BIT provision, that claim ultimately centred on Uruguay's alleged breach of domestic law. The tribunal rejected the claim,[94] maintaining the view, 'repeatedly held by investment tribunals, that clauses such as Article 11—referring to "commitments entered into [by the host State] with respect to the investment of the investor" of the other State—do not cover general obligations imposed by the law of the host State'.[95] The risk of conversion of a domestic law breach to a treaty breach under the umbrella clause may not be problematic in view of this kind of jurisprudential approach. However, in the light of *Bilcon*, an additional modern qualification that could usefully be added to the FET obligation in Australia's IIAs would be a clarification that a breach of domestic law does not of itself give rise to an FET breach.

---

88 See, eg, *Philip Morris v Uruguay*, Award, [472]; *SGS v Philippines*, Jurisdictional Decision, [127], [128], [135]. Cf *SGS v Pakistan*, Jurisdictional Decision, [166]. See also Andrés Rigo Sureda, 'The Umbrella Clause' in Meg N Kinnear et al, above n 73, 375.

89 See, eg, Australia–Poland BIT art 10: 'A Contracting Party shall, subject to its law, do all in its power to ensure that a written undertaking given by a competent authority to a national of the other Contracting Party with regard to investment is respected'.

90 *Philip Morris v Australia*, Notice of Claim, [46]: 'contravention of Australia's international trade treaty obligations results in a failure by Australia to observe obligations it entered into with regard to investments of investors in its territory'.

91 Australia–Hong Kong BIT art 2.2: 'Each Contracting Party shall observe any obligation it may have entered into with regard to investments of investors of the other Contracting Party'.

92 *Philip Morris v Australia*, Procedural Order 8, [34].

93 Switzerland–Uruguay BIT art 11: 'Each Contracting Party shall constantly guarantee the observance of the commitments it has entered into with respect to the investments of the investors of the other Contracting Party'.

94 *Philip Morris v Uruguay*, Award, [482].

95 *Philip Morris v Uruguay*, Award, [478].

4 Subsidies and investor expectations

The TPP and the 2016 agreed SAFTA amendments do add two additional qualifications to the minimum standard of treatment/FET obligation, again in the direction of ensuring sufficient space for host State regulation. Specifically, they limit the force of an investor's expectations in establishing an FET breach, and they specifically address the relevance of the FET obligation to subsidies (which the Australian government says includes Australia's PBS):[96]

> 4. For greater certainty, the mere fact that a Party takes or fails to take an action that may be inconsistent with an investor's expectations does not constitute a breach of this Article, even if there is loss or damage to the covered investment as a result.
> 5. For greater certainty, the mere fact that a subsidy or grant has not been issued, renewed or maintained, or has been modified or reduced, by a Party, does not constitute a breach of this Article, even if there is loss or damage to the covered investment as a result.[97]

Unfortunately, the reference to an investor's expectations, while ostensibly designed to enhance regulatory autonomy,[98] may conversely give weight to arguments that an investor's legitimate expectations are indeed *relevant* to the assessment of whether an FET breach has occurred. At the same time, the reference to subsidies in SAFTA seems unnecessary given that the investment chapter as a whole is expressed not to apply to 'subsidies or grants provided by a Party or to any conditions attached to the receipt or continued receipt of such subsidies or grants, whether or not [they] are offered exclusively to domestic investors and investments'.[99] Perhaps the qualification is included out of an abundance of caution and in view of the possibility that the general exclusion of subsidies might be later removed.[100]

---

[96] DFAT, *TPP Outcomes: Investment* (Fact Sheet updated 12 October 2015) 3.

[97] SAFTA 2016 ch 8 art 6; TPP art 9.6.

[98] See, eg, DFAT, *TPP Outcomes: Investment* (Fact Sheet updated 12 October 2015) 3, referring to the reference to investors' expectations in a list of 'robust safeguards' included in the TPP investment chapter 'to preserve the right of the Government to continue regulating in the public interest'.

[99] SAFTA 2016 ch 8 art 2.2(a).

[100] See SAFTA 2016 ch 8 art 17.

5 Alternative approaches: exhaustive list of breaches

In addition, Australia's newest approaches to the FET standard as reflected in the TPP and the 2016 SAFTA agreed amendments have not taken up the opportunity offered by alternative approaches to curbing the expansive interpretation of the FET obligation by, for example, setting out an exhaustive rather than inclusive list of possible FET breaches. TPP and the 2016 SAFTA amendments both specify that FET '*includes* the obligation not to deny justice in criminal, civil or administrative adjudicatory proceedings in accordance with the principle of due process embodied in the principal legal systems of the world'.[101] In contrast, for example, the agreed CETA text includes (in addition to two provisions addressing the relevance of an investor's expectations,[102] a reference to breaches of international and domestic laws alone not establishing an FET violation,[103] and restrictions on subsidy-related decisions amounting to a breach of an investment obligation)[104] a reaffirmation of the right to regulate to achieve legitimate policy objectives,[105] and the following *exclusive* list of FET breaches:

> A Party breaches the obligation of fair and equitable treatment referenced in paragraph 1 if a measure or series of measures constitutes:
>
> (a) denial of justice in criminal, civil or administrative proceedings;
> (b) fundamental breach of due process, including a fundamental breach of transparency, in judicial and administrative proceedings;
> (c) manifest arbitrariness;
> (d) targeted discrimination on manifestly wrongful grounds, such as gender, race or religious belief;
> (e) abusive treatment of investors, such as coercion, duress and harassment; or
> (f) a breach of any further elements of the fair and equitable treatment obligation adopted by the Parties in accordance with paragraph 3 of this Article.[106]

Similar provisions are also contained in the EU's proposal for the investment chapter in the TTIP.[107] Greater certainty could be introduced

---

[101] SAFTA 2016 ch 8 art 6.2(a) (emphasis added); TPP art 9.6.2(a) (emphasis added).
[102] CETA arts 8.9.2, 8.10.4.
[103] CETA arts 8.10.6, 8.10.7.
[104] CETA arts 8.9.3, 8.9.4.
[105] CETA art 8.9.1.
[106] CETA art 8.10.2.
[107] EU TTIP ch II proposal (12 November 2015) arts 2, 3.2, 3.4, 3.6.

by specifying that an FET breach arises 'only' if a measure falls within one of these scenarios. The revised India Model BIT (2015) goes perhaps even further, eschewing reference to the problematic 'FET' standard altogether, and providing instead a short exclusive list of conduct that would be unauthorised where it violates 'customary international law'.[108]

C Expropriation

1 Lawful and unlawful, direct and indirect expropriation

Expropriation is a core investment obligation. Expropriation lies at the heart of the international investment regime, in the sense that the regime was originally established to address such classical problems as host States nationalising foreign assets, particularly in industries requiring high set-up costs such as energy or infrastructure.[109] Concerns about international investment law in the context of expropriation in more recent years have primarily involved the more amorphous concept of 'indirect' expropriation, involving not direct taking of assets but rather devaluation of assets through regulation or other action.[110] Much of the recent treaty practice in this field, as explained in the following section, has been directed at clarifying the scope of indirect expropriation in order to avoid over-expansive interpretations that infringe unduly on regulatory autonomy.

Australia's BITs take a broadly similar approach to expropriation. For example, the Australia–Egypt BIT provides:

> Neither Party shall nationalise, expropriate or subject to measures having effect *equivalent to nationalisation* or expropriation (hereinafter referred to as 'expropriation') the investments of investors of the other Party unless the following conditions are complied with:
>
> (a) the expropriation is in the public interest which is related to the internal needs of that Party and under due process of law;
> (b) the expropriation is non-discriminatory; and
> (c) the expropriation is accompanied by the payment of prompt, adequate and effective *compensation*.[111]

The words 'equivalent to nationalisation' refer to indirect expropriation. The reference to compensation means that even if an expropriation is

---

[108] India Model BIT (2015) art 3.1.

[109] See, eg, Andrew Newcombe and Lluís Paradell, *Law and Practice of Investment Treaties: Standards of Treatment* (Kluwer Law International, 2009) 18, 24.

[110] See, eg, ibid 325–328.

[111] Australia–Egypt BIT art 7.1 (emphasis added).

non-discriminatory and in the public interest, it is unlawful in the absence of the appropriate level and manner of compensation. In that context, the meaning of 'expropriation' becomes crucial. If a measure constitutes expropriation then compensation will need to be paid, but if a measure falls outside the definition of expropriation then compensation will not be payable. However, the BITs do not define expropriation, although they tend to provide additional details such as how to calculate the relevant compensation.[112]

Table 4.3 summarises certain key features of the expropriation provision in Australia's PTAs, which generally narrow the scope of the obligation and so enhance regulatory autonomy. Below, we investigate some of these common features in more detail.

The Australian government might perceive these restrictions as more important for PTAs that allow for ISDS. The omission from the ANZCERTA Investment Protocol, for example, of the requirement of interference with a property right or interest might be seen as less significant from Australia's perspective in the absence of an ISDS mechanism in that treaty (such that only the New Zealand government, and not a New Zealand investor, could bring a claim of unlawful expropriation). However, the potential for invasive State–State disputes should not be underestimated, as reflected in Australia's experiences as respondent in the WTO. In that context, Australia has faced claims from close allies including New Zealand,[113] Canada,[114] and the United States.[115] In the ongoing claims against Australia's tobacco plain packaging laws, mentioned in Chapter 2, Indonesia is one of the four remaining complainants and is simultaneously a major trading partner of Australia. Moreover, inconsistency across Australia's PTAs (such as through imposing an apparently lower threshold for a finding of expropriation under the ANZCERTA Investment Protocol) may create regulatory difficulties in view of the potential breadth of the MFN obligation discussed above. That is, an investor bringing a claim under any given Australian BIT or PTA could attempt to invoke any more stringent investment obligation—lacking modern clarifications—in other Australian BITs or PTAs.[116]

---

[112] See, eg, Australia–Egypt BIT arts 7.2, 7.3.

[113] See, eg, Appellate Body Report, *Australia—Apples*.

[114] See, eg, Appellate Body Report, *Australia—Salmon*.

[115] See, eg, Panel Report, *Australia—Automotive Leather II*.

[116] On possible restrictions of the scope of the MFN obligation with respect to invoking substantive investment protections, where terms such as 'in similar situations' appear in the MFN provision, see *İçkale v Turkmenistan*, Award, [329], [332].

Table 4.3 Expropriation in Australia's PTAs

PTA	Entry into force	Requires interference with property right/ interest	Excludes compulsory licences consistent with TRIPS	Excludes IP restrictions consistent with IP chapter	Contains inclusive list of relevant factors	Excludes non-discriminatory regulatory actions for legitimate objectives
SAFTA	2003	✘	and consistent with IP chapter	and consistent with TRIPS	✘	✘
TAFTA	2005	✘	✘	✘	✘	✘
AUSFTA	2005	✔	and consistent with IP chapter	✔	✔	except in rare circumstances
ACIFTA	2009	✔	✔	✔	✔	except in rare circumstances
AANZFTA	2010	✔	✔	✘	✔	✔
MAFTA	2013	✔	✔	✘	✔	✔
ANZCERTA Investment Protocol	2013	✘	✔	✘	✘	except in rare circumstances
KAFTA	2014	✔	and consistent with IP chapter	✔	✔	except in rare circumstances
JAEPA	2015	✔	and consistent with IP chapter	✔	✔	except in rare circumstances
ChAFTA[117]	2015	–	–	–	–	–
TPP	–	✔	and consistent with IP chapter	and consistent with TRIPS	✔	except in rare circumstances
SAFTA amendments 2016	–	✔	✔	consistent with TRIPS, not IP chapter	✔	except in rare circumstances

117 ChAFTA contains no expropriation obligation: see art 9.9.3(b)(ii).

2 Land and intellectual property

Australia's early PTAs provide little additional assistance in identifying expropriation. TAFTA adopts essentially the same approach as the BITs, also confirming that taxation measures could effect an expropriation.[118] SAFTA in its original form introduced two additional provisions, which were retained in the 2011 amendments to that treaty. First, the treaty specified that compensation for an expropriatory measure relating to land would be determined according to the relevant domestic legislation and subsequent amendments to that legislation where they 'follow the general trends in the market value of the land'.[119] The same kind of provision appears in the 2016 agreed amendments to SAFTA.[120] (Certain country-specific exceptions also apply in relation to expropriation under the TPP, including for Singapore.)[121] Second, excluded from the original SAFTA provision on expropriation were 'the issuance of compulsory licenses granted in relation to intellectual property rights' and 'the revocation, limitation or creation of intellectual property rights' to the extent consistent with the TRIPS Agreement and SAFTA's intellectual property chapter.[122] Slightly different exclusions regarding intellectual property have been included in subsequent Australian PTAs (and the 2016 SAFTA amendments), as explained further below.

More extensive changes to the expropriation obligation in Australia's PTAs began with the AUSFTA and have generally been followed since then (although not in the TAFTA negotiated at the same time, or the subsequent BITs with Mexico, Sri Lanka and Turkey). First, the expropriation provision itself specifies that it does not apply to the issuance of compulsory licences granted in accordance with the TRIPS Agreement and the intellectual property chapter of AUSFTA or to the revocation, limitation, or creation of intellectual property rights consistent with that chapter.[123] A footnote also makes clear that the reference to the TRIPS Agreement includes any waiver of TRIPS obligations granted by WTO Members,[124] taking account of the pre-existing waiver of TRIPS arts

---

118 TAFTA art 1607.1(b), n 10.

119 SAFTA 2003 ch 8 art 9.3; SAFTA 2011 ch 8 art 11.3.

120 SAFTA 2016 ch 8 art 13.5.

121 TPP annex 9–C (re Singapore and Viet Nam); see also art 9.8.1(a), n 18 (re meaning of public purpose in connection with land for Brunei Darussalam and Malaysia).

122 SAFTA 2003 ch 8 art 9.4; SAFTA 2011 ch 8 art 11.4.

123 AUSFTA art 11.7.5.

124 AUSFTA art 11.7.5, n 11–10.

31(f) and 31(h) to address problems faced by Members lacking manufacturing capacity in the pharmaceutical sector in extreme public health situations.[125] As noted in Chapter 2, WTO Members have crafted a corresponding amendment to the TRIPS Agreement,[126] which entered into force on 23 January 2017.[127]

Essentially the same provision regarding intellectual property appears in KAFTA,[128] JAEPA[129] and the TPP,[130] except that KAFTA strangely (and perhaps unintentionally) omits the clarification regarding the TRIPS waiver. The 2016 amendments to SAFTA alter the provision so as to require compliance with TRIPS but not the intellectual property chapter[131] (while retaining the note about the TRIPS waiver).[132] ACIFTA is slightly more flexible, excluding from the expropriation provision compulsory licences consistent with the TRIPS Agreement (without mentioning the intellectual property chapter of ACIFTA) and other intellectual property rights restrictions consistent with the intellectual property chapter of ACIFTA (without mentioning TRIPS).[133] The ACIFTA approach seems the most logical, although the reference to the TRIPS waiver is again omitted.[134] More restrictive are AANZFTA,[135] MAFTA[136] and the

---

[125] WTO General Council, *Implementation of Paragraph 6 of the Doha Declaration on the TRIPS Agreement and Public Health: Decision of 30 August 2003*, WTO Doc WT/L/430 (1 September 2003).

[126] WTO General Council, *Amendment of the TRIPS Agreement: Decision of 6 December 2005*, WTO Doc WT/L/641 (8 December 2005).

[127] WTO, 'WTO IP rules amended to ease poor countries' access to affordable medicines', News Item (23 January 2017).

[128] KAFTA art 11.7.5 (TRIPS Agreement defined in art 1.4).

[129] JAEPA art 14.11.6 and accompanying 'Note'.

[130] TPP art 9.8.5 (TRIPS Agreement defined in art 1.2 with reference to TRIPS waiver in n 2).

[131] SAFTA 2016 ch 8 art 13.6.

[132] SAFTA 2016 ch 8 art 1(u) n 6.

[133] ACIFTA art 10.11.5. This provision achieves this difference compared with say AUSFTA art 11.7.5 by omitting the word 'issuance' (which refers to the issuance of compulsory licences) from the final clause to read: 'This Article does not apply to the issuance of compulsory licences granted in relation to intellectual property rights in accordance with the TRIPS Agreement, or to the revocation, limitation, or creation of intellectual property rights, to the extent that such revocation, limitation, or creation is consistent with Chapter 17 (Intellectual Property).'

[134] ACIFTA art 2.1(cc) defines TRIPS Agreement.

[135] AANZFTA ch 11 art 9.5.

[136] MAFTA art 12.8.5.

ANZCERTA Investment Protocol,[137] which allow for compulsory licensing under the TRIPS Agreement but not other intellectual property restrictions consistent with the TRIPS Agreement or the intellectual property chapter.

Although all these references to the TRIPS Agreement may impose limits on the extent of the expropriation obligation, Henning Grosse Ruse-Khan has pointed out that they also create difficulties in potentially requiring or allowing an investment treaty tribunal to interpret and apply TRIPS obligations in the context of an ISDS claim.[138]

3 Customary international law

AUSFTA also introduced an annex on expropriation,[139] which has been duplicated in subsequent Australian PTAs[140] that include an expropriation obligation,[141] apart from the ANZCERTA Investment Protocol. The annex contains a number of elements, which we will examine in turn. The exclusion of such an annex from the ANZCERTA Investment Protocol is curious and means that most of the clarifications contained in the AUSFTA annex on expropriation are missing from the ANZCERTA Investment Protocol. Although the implications of the omission for regulatory autonomy are not necessarily adverse, the omission of an annex on expropriation does mean that the States parties to the ANZCERTA Investment Protocol give less guidance to tribunals in a State-State dispute concerning expropriation, for example regarding how to address an investor's expectations and the relevant factors to consider in determining whether an expropriation exists. Presumably the annex was thought unnecessary given that ANZCERTA does not contain an ISDS mechanism.

In its first paragraph, the AUSFTA annex on expropriation confirms the States parties' 'shared understanding' that the expropriation obligation 'is intended to reflect customary international law concerning the obligation

---

137 ANZCERTA Investment Protocol art 14.4.

138 See, eg, Henning Grosse Ruse-Khan, 'Protecting Intellectual Property Rights under BITs, FTAs and TRIPS: Conflicting Regimes or Mutual Coherence?' in Chester Brown and Kate Miles (eds), *Evolution in Investment Treaty Law and Arbitration* (Cambridge University Press, 2011) 485, 505–508.

139 AUSFTA annex 11–B.

140 ACIFTA annex 10–B; AANZFTA Annex on Expropriation and Compensation; MAFTA Annex on Expropriation; JAEPA annex 12; KAFTA annex 11–B; TPP annex 9–B; SAFTA 2016 annex 8–A.

141 ChAFTA includes no expropriation obligation.

of States with respect to expropriation'.[142] In contrast, the TPP and the 2016 amendments to SAFTA specify in a footnote, '[f]or greater certainty', that for the purposes of the expropriation provision 'the term "public purpose" refers to a concept in customary international law' and that '[d]omestic law may express this or a similar concept by using different terms, such as "public necessity", "public interest", or "public use"'.[143] However, the term public purpose relates to the conditions for lawful expropriation (which include compensation, as noted above), rather than the definition of expropriation. The clarification of the meaning of public purpose in this context therefore does little to enhance regulatory autonomy in connection with allegedly expropriatory measures. Other Australian PTAs do not refer to customary international law in their provision or annex on expropriation.

4 Property rights

The second paragraph of the AUSFTA annex on expropriation specifies that '[a]n action or a series of actions by a Party cannot constitute an expropriation unless it interferes with a tangible or intangible property right or property interest in an investment'.[144] All subsequent PTAs of Australia apart from the ANZCERTA Investment Protocol (and ChAFTA, which includes no expropriation obligation) include such a specification.[145] This inclusion appears directed towards certain investment treaty awards allowing contractual rights to be the subject of expropriation.[146] More recently, debate has continued among investment treaty tribunals as to whether expropriation is limited to property rights[147] or can extend to contractual rights.[148] Moreover, some tribunals have even suggested that 'residual contractual rights under the investment as crystallised' in an arbitral award constitute property capable of expropriation.[149] The explicit restriction to property rights in most Australian PTAs thus might

---

142 AUSFTA annex 11–B, [1].

143 TPP art 9.8.1(a) n 17; SAFTA 2016 ch 8 art 13.1(a) n 13.

144 AUSFTA annex 11–B, [2].

145 ACIFTA annex 10–B, [1]; AANZFTA Annex on Expropriation and Compensation, [1]; MAFTA Annex on Expropriation, [1]; JAEPA annex 12, [1]; KAFTA annex 11–B, [1]; TPP annex 9–B, [1]; SAFTA 2016 annex 8–A, [1].

146 See generally Zachary Douglas, 'Property Rights as the Object of an Expropriation' in Kinnear et al, above n 73, 331.

147 See, eg, *Emmis v Hungary*, Award, [159], [165].

148 See, eg, *Tidewater v Venezuela*, Award, [118].

149 See especially *Saipem v Bangladesh*, Award, [128]; followed in *White Industries v India*, Award, [7.6.10]; cf *GEA v Ukraine*, Award, [161]–[162]. See generally Richard Garnett, 'National Court Intervention in Arbitration as an

not prevent these debates, if tribunals maintain that contractual rights or arbitral awards amount to or derive from intangible property rights or interests.

5 Relevant factors including investor expectations

The fourth paragraph of the AUSFTA annex on expropriation introduces an inclusive list of factors that are relevant to determining whether an indirect expropriation has taken place:

> The determination of whether an action or series of actions by a Party, in a specific fact situation, constitutes an indirect expropriation, requires a case-by-case, fact-based inquiry that considers, among other factors:
>
> (i) the *economic impact* of the government action, although the fact that an action or series of actions by a Party has an adverse effect on the economic value of an investment, standing alone, does not establish that an indirect expropriation has occurred;
> (ii) the extent to which the government action interferes with distinct, reasonable investment-backed *expectations*; and
> (iii) the *character* of the government action.[150]

Again, all of Australia's subsequent PTAs that include such an annex include a similar list, with some minor variation in language.[151] The AUSFTA list makes clear that an investor's 'reasonable' expectations are relevant to the expropriation obligation. MAFTA refers instead to 'whether the government action breaches the government's *prior binding written commitment*, where applicable, to the investor whether by contract, licence or other legal document',[152] while also adding that the 'character of the government action' includes 'its objective and whether the action is *disproportionate* to the public purpose'.[153] AANZFTA also adopts these two qualifications,[154] which appear to increase deference to the host State. KAFTA adds two related footnotes to the inclusive list of

Investment Treaty Claim' (2011) 60 *International and Comparative Law Quarterly* 485.

150 AUSFTA annex 11–B, [4(a)] (emphasis added).

151 ACIFTA annex 10–B, [3(a)]; AANZFTA Annex on Expropriation and Compensation, [3]; MAFTA Annex on Expropriation, [3]; JAEPA annex 12, [3]; KAFTA annex 11–B, [4]; TPP annex 9–B, [3(a)]; SAFTA 2016 annex 8–A, [3(a)].

152 MAFTA Annex on Expropriation, [3(b)] (emphasis added).

153 MAFTA Annex on Expropriation, [3(c)] (emphasis added).

154 AANZFTA Annex on Expropriation and Compensation, [3(b)], [3(c)].

relevant factors, in relation to the investor's expectations and the character of the government action ('including its objectives and context')[155] respectively:

> For greater certainty, whether an investor's investment-backed expectations are reasonable may include consideration of the nature and extent of governmental *regulation* in the relevant sector.[156]
>
> For *Korea*, a relevant consideration could include whether the investor bears a *disproportionate* burden such as a special sacrifice that exceeds what the investor or investment should be expected to endure for the public interest.[157]

The TPP adds a footnote recalling aspects of the approach in MAFTA, AANZFTA and KAFTA:

> For greater certainty, whether an investor's investment-backed expectations are reasonable depends, to the extent relevant, on factors such as whether the government provided the investor with *binding written assurances* and the nature and extent of governmental *regulation* or the potential for government regulation in the relevant sector.[158]

The TPP approach provides less certainty than the MAFTA and the AANZFTA, which confirm the relevance to expropriation of only binding written commitments rather than reasonable expectations more generally. The SAFTA provides even less certainty again, since the 2016 agreed amendments contain no clarification or footnote regarding the meaning or relevance of 'reasonable investment-backed expectations'.[159] The reference in the TPP to governmental regulation relates to the point made above in relation to the FET obligation, that investors cannot expect regulation to remain frozen. An additional reference to proportionality as in MAFTA, AANZFTA and the KAFTA (albeit for Korea only) might assist in showing that a governmental action need not be perfect or optimal but should be proportionate to its objectives.[160] However, the method for establishing proportionality could vary, leaving room for

---

155 KAFTA annex 11–B, [4(c)].

156 KAFTA annex 11–B, [4(b)], n 18 (emphasis added).

157 KAFTA annex 11–B, [4(c)], n 19 (emphasis added).

158 TPP annex 9–B, [3(a)], n 36 (emphasis added).

159 SAFTA 2016 annex 8–A, [3(a)(ii)].

160 See, eg, Benedict Kingsbury and Stephan W Schill, 'Public Law Concepts to Balance Investors' Rights with State Regulatory Actions in the Public Interest—The Concept of Proportionality' in Stephan W Schill (ed), *International Investment Law and Comparative Public Law* (Oxford University Press, 2010) 75.

widely differing approaches, as is seen in other areas of law including WTO law.[161]

6 Regulatory actions for public welfare objectives

The final paragraph of the AUSFTA annex on expropriation contains an important restriction recognising the non-expropriatory nature of certain types of regulatory actions:

> *Except in rare circumstances*, nondiscriminatory regulatory actions by a Party that are designed and applied to achieve *legitimate public welfare objectives*, such as the protection of public health, safety, and the environment, do not constitute indirect expropriations.[162]

This qualification, followed in all of Australia's subsequent PTAs containing an expropriation obligation, recognises the breadth of regulatory objectives that the host State may have, classifying them as 'legitimate public welfare objectives'[163] together with an inclusive list of such objectives. This approach contrasts with some later narrower approaches discussed below, such as the 'carve-out' from ISDS for tobacco products in the TPP and the 2016 amendments agreed to the SAFTA. The broader wording is more effective in protecting the wide range of a host State's potential objectives rather than targeting one particular product or objective. The word 'legitimate'[164] may impose some constraint and is arguably superfluous, since a public welfare objective that is illegitimate might properly be regarded as something other than a public welfare objective.

More importantly, the opening words '[e]xcept in rare circumstances'[165] constrain the qualification for non-discriminatory regulatory actions, leaving it for arbitrators (in the case of an ISDS dispute, for example) to determine whether the circumstances before them are 'rare'. Perhaps even to get to the stage of an arbitral dispute might suggest that

---

161 See, eg, Caroline Henckels, *Proportionality and Deference in Investor–State Arbitration: Balancing Investment Protection and Regulatory Autonomy* (Cambridge University Press, 2015); Gebhard Bücheler, *Proportionality in Investor–State Arbitration* (Oxford University Press, 2015); Peter Van den Bossche, 'Looking for Proportionality in WTO Law' (2008) 35(3) *Legal Issues of Economic Integration* 283; Andrew D Mitchell, 'Proportionality and Remedies in WTO Disputes' (2006) 17(5) *European Journal of International Law* 985.

162 AUSFTA annex 11–B, [4(b)] (emphasis added).

163 AUSFTA annex 11–B, [4(b)].

164 AUSFTA annex 11–B, [4(b)].

165 AUSFTA annex 11–B, [4(b)].

the circumstances are rare to begin with: most disputes would presumably be resolved at an earlier stage. These words may also represent a step backwards in terms of the protection of Australian policy space, given that the doctrine of 'police powers' that has developed through investment treaty jurisprudence as a limit on expropriation[166] contains no such qualification, and the requirement of a 'legitimate public welfare objective' just mentioned already imposes limits on allowable measures. Yet these same words appear in nearly all of Australia's PTAs containing an expropriation obligation: this element of the AUSFTA annex on expropriation is the only one contained in the ANZCERTA Investment Protocol, in a footnote, which also includes the 'rare circumstances' exception;[167] this exception also appears in ACIFTA,[168] JAEPA,[169] KAFTA,[170] the TPP,[171] and the SAFTA 2016 agreed amendments.[172] The two exceptions to the AUSFTA approach here are AANZFTA[173] and MAFTA,[174] which exclude the words 'except in rare circumstances'.[175]

Although most of Australia's post-AUSFTA PTAs include the 'except in rare circumstances' language, some additional clarifications appear in some treaties. JAEPA provides an additional gloss, making clear that 'rare circumstances' entail rather extreme situations, 'such as when an action or a series of actions by a Party is *so severe in light of its purpose* that it cannot be reasonably viewed as having been applied in *good faith*'.[176] The JAEPA approach is perhaps the second most protective of policy space when compared to not including the 'rare circumstances' language at all. However, Australia's three more recent FTAs including an expropriation obligation adopt narrower, product-specific qualifications instead of more broadly excluding 'rare circumstances' or setting a high threshold for finding such circumstances. In particular, KAFTA contains in footnotes an exception for Korea regarding real estate price stabilisation,[177] an (obvious) confirmation that the list of objectives is

---

166 See, eg, *Philip Morris v Uruguay*, Award, [287].
167 ANZCERTA Investment Protocol art 14.1, n 7.
168 ACIFTA annex 10–B, [3(b)].
169 JAEPA annex 12, [4].
170 KAFTA annex 11–B, [5].
171 TPP annex 9–B, [3(b)].
172 SAFTA 2016 annex 8–A, [3(b)].
173 AANZFTA Annex on Expropriation and Compensation, [4].
174 MAFTA Annex on Expropriation, [4].
175 See also India Model BIT (2015) art 5.5.
176 JAEPA annex 12, [4] (emphasis added).
177 KAFTA annex 11–B, [5], n 22.

'not exhaustive',[178] and an inclusive list of areas covered by the reference to public health:

> For greater certainty and without limiting the scope of paragraph 5, such regulatory actions to protect public health *include* regulation, supply and reimbursement with respect to *pharmaceuticals*, diagnostics, vaccines, medical devices, health-related aids and appliances and *blood* and blood products.[179]

This latter footnote is replicated in the TPP and the SAFTA 2016 agreed amendments, with the addition of references to 'pharmaceuticals (including *biological* products)', 'gene therapies and technologies', and 'blood-*related* products'.[180] One wonders whether the continuous attempt to foresee the specific areas in which an ISDS claim (for example) might arise can succeed, particularly if Australia's IIAs are updated one by one as they are negotiated without rectifying older provisions.

7 Subsidies

The TPP and the 2016 agreed amendments to SAFTA introduce one additional qualification to the expropriation obligation (within the core expropriation provision rather than the annex on expropriation) in connection with subsidies, mirroring that discussed above in relation to the FET standard:

> For greater certainty, a Party's decision not to issue, renew or maintain a subsidy or grant, or decision to modify or reduce a subsidy or grant,
>
> (a) in the absence of any specific commitment under law or contract to issue, renew or maintain that subsidy or grant; or
> (b) in accordance with any terms or conditions attached to the issuance, renewal, modification, reduction and maintenance of that subsidy or grant,
>
> standing alone, does not constitute an expropriation.[181]

This restriction can be understood as relating to investor expectations, in that it would seem to limit the relevance of such expectations where not

---

[178] KAFTA annex 11–B, [5], n 20.
[179] KAFTA annex 11–B, [5], n 21 (emphasis added).
[180] TPP annex 9–B, [3(b)], n 37 (emphasis added); SAFTA 2016 annex 8–A, [3(b)], n 22 (emphasis added).
[181] TPP art 9.7.6; SAFTA 2016 ch 8 art 13.7.

contained in a 'specific commitment under law or contract'.[182] Yet these words provide more certainty and greater limits on expropriation claims than do the words included in the specific reference to investor expectations elsewhere in these agreements, as discussed above.[183] Again, a narrow focus on subsidies seems to have overtaken the drafting rather than a broader focus on all possible uses and implications of the expropriation obligation.

III KEY EXCEPTIONS

A Non-Conforming Measures

Australia's PTAs including investment chapters, commencing with SAFTA in 2003, include lists of specific 'non-conforming measures' exempt from particular investment obligations. These lists often apply to both investment obligations and services obligations as discussed in Chapter 3 of this volume. Under the original SAFTA, the non-conforming measures applied to the national treatment obligation.[184] Since the 2011 amendments to SAFTA, the lists of non-conforming measures have also applied to the prohibition of performance requirements.[185] The 2016 agreed SAFTA amendments extend the lists to the MFN obligation and the obligations regarding senior management and boards of directors. Focusing on the MFN obligation, the relevant provision reads:

> [Article 5] (Most-Favoured-Nation Treatment) … shall not apply to:
>
> (a) any *existing non-conforming* measure that is maintained by a Party at:
> (i) the *central level* of government or a *regional level* of government, as set out by that Party in its Schedule to Annex 4–I; or
> (ii) a *local level* of government; or
>
> (b) the *continuation or prompt renewal* of any non-conforming measure referred to in subparagraph (a); or
>
> (c) an amendment to any non-conforming measure referred to in subparagraph (a) to the extent that *the amendment does not decrease the conformity* of the measure, as it existed immediately before the amendment, with [Article 5] …[186]

---

[182] TPP art 9.7.6(a); SAFTA 2016 ch 8 art 13.7(a).
[183] See above nn 157–158 and corresponding text.
[184] SAFTA 2003 ch 8 art 5.
[185] SAFTA 2011 ch 8 art 7.
[186] SAFTA 2016 ch 8 art 11.1 (emphasis added).

This provision contains a number of elements common to Australia's other FTAs. First, existing non-conforming measures of local government are covered without needing to be explicitly listed. Second, a 'standstill' mechanism applies, meaning that the States parties cannot increase the existing degree of non-conformity with the MFN provision. An existing non-conforming measure will continue to be covered (that is, exempt from the MFN obligation) as long as it is maintained, promptly renewed, or amended without increasing the level of non-conformity. Third, a 'ratchet' mechanism can be understood as applying. If an existing non-conforming measure is repealed or not promptly renewed pursuant to paragraph (b), that non-conforming measure will no longer be covered. At the same time, if an existing non-conforming measure is amended to decrease the level of non-conformity, that new (more compliant) measure will be covered, and further amendments cannot revert to a higher level of non-conformity, pursuant to paragraph (c).

TAFTA includes no list of non-conforming measures. However, Australia's other PTAs tend to adopt a similar approach to the SAFTA 2016 agreed amendments, while adding an additional list of exempted 'sectors, sub-sectors and activities'.[187] AANZFTA's list applies only to national treatment and (only 'in the case of Lao PDR') to the prohibition of performance requirements,[188] while MAFTA's and ChAFTA's apply only to national treatment and MFN treatment.[189] JAEPA and TPP include procedural requirements regarding consultations and notification with respect to non-conforming measures and amendments to such measures.[190] JAEPA and ChAFTA impose an obligation on the parties to 'endeavour' to reduce or eliminate the non-conforming measures.[191] Separate from the lists of non-conforming measures, Australia's PTAs tend to exclude the application of the investment chapter or particular investment obligations such as non-discrimination obligations (national treatment and/or MFN treatment) to the provision of subsidies,[192]

187 AUSFTA arts 11.13.1, 11.13.2; ACIFTA arts 10.9.1, 10.9.2; ANZCERTA Investment Protocol arts 9.1, 9.2; KAFTA arts 11.12.1, 11.12.2; JAEPA arts 14.10.1, 14.10.2; TPP arts 9.11.1, 9.11.2.

188 AANZFTA ch 11 arts 12.1, 12.2.

189 MAFTA arts 12.14.1, 12.14.2; ChAFTA art 9.5.

190 JAEPA art 14.10.4; TPP arts 9.11.3, 9.11.7.

191 JAEPA art 14.10.5; ChAFTA art 9.5.4.

192 TAFTA art 902.1; AUSFTA art 11.13.5(a); ACIFTA art 10.9.5(b); ANZCERTA Investment Protocol art 9.4(b); KAFTA art 11.12.5(b); JAEPA art 14.10.7(b); SAFTA 2016 ch 8 art 2.2(a) (see also art 17); TPP art 9.11.6(b). See

government procurement,[193] and certain measures allowed under the TRIPS Agreement or the intellectual property chapter of the relevant PTA.[194]

ChAFTA adopts an unusual approach whereby Australia includes a list of non-conforming measures but China does not. That is, Australia adopts a 'negative list' approach whereby the investment obligations under ChAFTA (currently just national treatment and MFN treatment, since no obligations regarding expropriation or the minimum standard of treatment are presently included, as noted above) apply in general except to those non-conforming measures specified. In contrast, for China those obligations do not apply to 'any existing non-conforming measures maintained within its territory' or the continuation of such measures, without specifying what those measures are.[195] Also rather strangely, whereas Australia's non-conforming measures remain covered if they are amended or modified 'to the extent that the amendment or modification does not decrease the conformity of the measure',[196] China's non-conforming measures remain covered if they are amended 'to the extent that the amendment does not *increase the non-conformity* of the measure',[197] which would seem to be the same thing stated in different words. The review of ChAFTA is specified to include 'scheduling of investment commitments by China on a negative list basis'.[198]

The NCMs listed by Australia and its PTA partners were discussed in Chapter 3. Some NCMs particularly focused on investment include with respect to indigenous people and health services. With respect to indigenous persons, SAFTA (pursuant to the amendments agreed in 2016) states:

---

also parts IIB4 and IIC7 above regarding the limitations to the minimum standard of treatment and expropriation in connection with subsidies.

[193] TAFTA art 902.2; AUSFTA art 11.13.5(b); ACIFTA art 10.9.5(a); MAFTA art 12.14.4; ANZCERTA Investment Protocol art 9.4(a); KAFTA art 11.12.5(a); JAEPA art 14.10.7(a); SAFTA 2016 ch 8 art 11.1.5; TPP art 9.11.6(a).

[194] AUSFTA art 11.13.4; ACIFTA art 10.9.4; ANZCERTA Investment Protocol art 7.4(a); KAFTA art 11.12.4; JAEPA art 14.10.6; SAFTA 2016 ch 8 art 11.1.4; TPP art 9.11.5(b). See also part IIC2 above regarding the limitations to expropriation in connection with intellectual property.

[195] ChAFTA arts 9.5.2(a), 9.5.2(b).

[196] ChAFTA art 9.5.1(c).

[197] ChAFTA art 9.5.2(c) (emphasis added).

[198] ChAFTA art 9.9(3)(c).

> Australia reserves the right to adopt or maintain any measure with respect to investment that accords preferences to any Indigenous person or organisation or providing for the favourable treatment of any Indigenous person or organisation.[199]

With respect to health services, the TPP makes clear in a footnote:

> For greater certainty, the subsidies programmes under Australia's Pharmaceutical Benefits Scheme and Medicare Benefits Scheme, or successor programmes, are not subject to Article 9.4 (National Treatment), Article 9.5 (Most-Favoured-Nation Treatment), and Article 9.11 (Senior Management and Boards of Directors), in accordance with Article 9.12(6)(b) (Non-Conforming Measures).[200]

KAFTA also contains a separate NCM listing for Australia with respect to investment obligations in connection with the sector 'Disadvantaged Groups':

> Australia reserves the right to adopt or maintain any measure that accords rights or preferences to socially or economically disadvantaged groups, such as the disabled, persons who have rendered distinguished services to the state and minority groups.[201]

These newer specifications would arguably be covered by some of the NCM listings discussed in Chapter 3 of this volume with respect to services, for example in relation to health and other social services, and preferences for indigenous persons.

B General Exceptions

Australia's PTAs make relatively liberal use of general exceptions provisions for investment, in comparison with most IIAs, which follow a more traditional approach of excluding such exceptions. However, these types of provisions are increasingly appearing in more modern IIAs, at least for some countries such as Canada.[202]

Although the Australia–India BIT (now terminated) contained an exception for 'measures necessary for the protection of its own essential security interests or for the prevention of diseases or pests',[203] the

---

199 SAFTA 2016 annex 4–II(A) (Australia).
200 TPP annex II (Australia) n 8.
201 KAFTA annex–II (Schedule of Australia).
202 See, eg, CETA art 28.3.2; India Model BIT art 32.1.
203 See, eg, Australia–India BIT art 15 (now terminated).

concept of a 'general exception' akin to GATT art XX did not arise until SAFTA entered into force in 2003. The original SAFTA provided, in very similar terms to GATT art XX:

> Subject to the requirement that such measures are not applied in a manner which would constitute a means of arbitrary or unjustifiable discrimination between the Parties where like conditions prevail, or a disguised restriction on investments in the territory of a Party by investors of the other Party, *nothing in this Chapter shall be construed to prevent* the adoption or enforcement by a Party of measures:
>
> (a) necessary to protect public morals or to maintain public order;
> (b) necessary to protect human, animal or plant life or health;
> (c) necessary to secure compliance with laws or regulations which are not inconsistent with the provisions of this Chapter including those relating to:
> (i) the prevention of deceptive and fraudulent practices or to deal with the effects of a default on a contract;
> (ii) the protection of the privacy of individuals in relation to the processing and dissemination of personal data and the protection of confidentiality of individual records and accounts;
> (iii) safety;
> (d) imposed for the protection of national treasures of artistic, historic or archaeological value;
> (e) relating to the conservation of exhaustible natural resources if such measures are made effective in conjunction with restrictions on domestic production or consumption.[204]

That provision was maintained in the 2011 amendments to SAFTA[205] and the 2016 amendments to SAFTA[206] (albeit in the latter case with the addition of 'or' in two places in a manner that can be understood as not altering the meaning). MAFTA adopts a similar approach, adding to the list certain tax measures.[207] AANZFTA specifies for the investment chapter that GATS art XIV is incorporated *mutatis mutandis*[208] and also sets out GATT art XX-like terms with respect to national treasures and creative arts.[209]

As set out in Table 4.4, Australia's other PTAs are more restrictive in providing general exceptions for the investment chapter. TAFTA specifies

---

204 SAFTA 2003 ch 8 art 19 (emphasis added).
205 SAFTA 2011 ch 8 art 21.
206 SAFTA 2016 ch 8 art 19.
207 MAFTA art 12.18.1.
208 AANZFTA ch 15 art 1.2.
209 AANZFTA ch 15 art 1.4.

with respect to the investment chapter that GATT art XX(e)–(g) 'is incorporated into and made part of Chapter 9, *mutatis mutandis*'[210] (thereby excluding the paragraphs regarding public morals, health, and securing compliance). JAEPA[211] and the ANZCERTA Investment Protocol[212] include a general exception covering only some investment obligations: obligations such as national treatment and MFN treatment are covered but not the—often more important—obligations such as expropriation and the minimum standard of treatment/FET. The ANZCERTA Investment Protocol also omits the reference to measures necessary to secure compliance with other laws or regulations.

Table 4.4 General Exceptions Applicable to the Investment Chapter in Australia's PTAs

PTA	Entry into force	Covers expropriation/ FET	Public morals	Health	Securing compliance	National treasures	Natural resources
SAFTA original	2003	✔	✔	✔	✔	✔	✔
TAFTA	2005	✔	✘	✘	✘	✔	✔
AUSFTA	2005	✘	✘	✘	✘	✘	✘
ACIFTA	2009	✘	✘	✘	✘	✘	✘
AANZFTA	2010	✔	✔	✔	✔	✔	✔
SAFTA amended	2011	✔	✔	✔	✔	✔	✔
MAFTA	2013	✔	✔	✔	✔	✔	✔
ANZCERTA Investment Protocol	2013	✘	✔	✔	✘	✔	✔
KAFTA	2014	✔	✘	✔	✔	✔	✔
JAEPA	2015	✘	✔	✔	✔	✔	✔
ChAFTA[213]	2015	–	✘	✔	✔	✔	✔
TPP	–	✘	✘	✘	✘	✘	✘
SAFTA 2016 amendments	–	✔	✔	✔	✔	✔	✔

210 TAFTA art 1601.3.

211 JAEPA art 14.15.

212 ANZCERTA Investment Protocol art 19.

213 ChAFTA contains no expropriation obligation: see art 9.9.3(b)(ii).

KAFTA[214] and ChAFTA[215] (which has no fair and equitable treatment or expropriation obligation to exempt) omit the reference to measures necessary to protect public morals or maintain public order. ChAFTA nevertheless adds:

> The Parties understand that the measures referred to in subparagraph 1(a) include environmental measures to protect human, animal or plant life or health, and that the measures referred to in subparagraph 1(d) include environmental measures relating to the conservation of living or non-living exhaustible natural resources.[216]

This note calls to mind WTO case law, which has had to establish that the term 'exhaustible natural resources' in GATT art XX(g) extends to living resources such as endangered turtles,[217] and which has also addressed environmental measures connected to health such as restrictions on retreaded tyres, which may house mosquitoes.[218]

Presumably reflecting the position of the United States, the AUSFTA and ACIFTA have a general exception for some chapters but not the investment chapter.[219] The TPP has a GATT art XX-type exception in the investment chapter, but only with respect to certain obligations regarding performance requirements.[220] The TPP investment chapter contains the following provision regarding regulatory objectives:

> Nothing in this Chapter shall be construed to prevent a Party from adopting, maintaining or enforcing any measure *otherwise consistent with this Chapter* that it considers appropriate to ensure that investment activity in its territory is undertaken in a manner sensitive to environmental, health or other regulatory objectives.[221]

This provision is similar to one contained in the ANZCERTA Investment Protocol, limited to environmental matters:

---

214 KAFTA art 22.1.3.

215 ChAFTA art 9.8.1.

216 ChAFTA art 9.8.2. See also KAFTA art 22.1.1 (not applicable to the investment chapter); JAEPA art 14.15(b); ANZCERTA Investment Protocol art 19, n 8.

217 Appellate Body Report, *US—Shrimp*, [132], [134].

218 Appellate Body Report, *Brazil—Retreaded Tyres*, [163].

219 AUSFTA art 22.1; ACIFTA art 22.1.

220 TPP art 9.10.3(d).

221 TPP art 9.16 (emphasis added).

> Nothing in this Protocol shall be construed to prevent either Party from adopting, maintaining, or enforcing any measure *otherwise consistent with this Protocol* that it considers appropriate to ensure that investment activity in its territory is undertaken in a manner sensitive to environmental concerns.[222]

This provision is mirrored in the AUSFTA.[223] The words 'otherwise consistent with' this Chapter/Protocol detract from the force of these provisions. A measure that is otherwise consistent is unlikely to need justification pursuant to these provisions, which are not true exceptions. Nevertheless, the provisions may have interpretative weight as context and representations of the object and purpose of the treaty.[224] In the context of the WTO, for example, in interpreting TBT art 2.2, the Appellate Body has referred to the sixth preambular recital of the TBT Agreement,[225] which recognises that 'no country should be prevented from taking measures necessary to ensure … the protection of human, animal or plant life or health, or of the environment … at the levels it considers appropriate' subject to certain requirements including that the measures '*are otherwise in accordance with the provisions of this Agreement*'.[226]

The absence of a general exception for the TPP investment chapter could signal the way forward for many countries, to the extent that the US position continues to influence trade and investment negotiations. However, the fact that Australia has maintained such an exception in the SAFTA investment chapter (in the 2016 agreed amendments) suggests that its preference is to include such exceptions. The omission of a general exception may be in part offset by more specific references to public policy measures in the lists of non-conforming measures as discussed earlier or the specific carve-outs from ISDS as discussed in Chapter 5 of this volume. However, as we elaborate below, these more specific exceptions run the risk of becoming out of date and being incapable of foreseeing future sensitivities and developments in areas including policy and technology.

Some commentators have questioned the 'importation' of GATT art XX-type exceptions from the international trade law context to the international investment law context, suggesting that they may be

---

[222] ANZCERTA Investment Protocol art 24 (emphasis added).

[223] AUSFTA art 11.11.

[224] VCLT art 31(1).

[225] Appellate Body Report, *US—COOL (Article 21.5—Canada and Mexico)*, [5.201], [5.214], [5.253].

[226] Emphasis added.

superfluous or have unknown or unintended implications in the latter context.[227] For example, the use of such exceptions could conceivably impact the interpretation and application of substantive investment obligations, since those obligations evolved in the absence of general exceptions and therefore tend to contain inherent acknowledgment of regulatory objectives. For instance, the doctrine of 'police powers' developed in the absence of general exceptions or specific references to non-discriminatory regulatory actions for public welfare purposes as discussed above.[228]

States including Australia must therefore be cautious in entrusting too much to these kinds of exceptions, particularly in the absence of significant guidance in arbitral awards as to their interpretation and application,[229] and also in view of the stringent approach of the WTO Appellate Body to the invocation of GATT art XX and GATS art XIV even in the trade context.[230] At the same time, if Australia's position is that including such exceptions is preferable to excluding them, narrowing down the exceptions (for example to apply only to certain investment obligations or to a smaller number than those under GATT art XX, which itself is recognised as failing to include the entire universe of legitimate regulatory objectives)[231] may result in the worst of both worlds. That is, the full potential protection of the exception may not be realised, while its inclusion might nevertheless negatively affect the interpretation of other investment provisions from the perspective of regulatory sovereignty. For example, if an exception inserted in the investment chapter does not apply to expropriation, could that exclusion suggest that the expropriation obligation somehow does not encompass the police powers doctrine? Or if the exception does apply to expropriation, could a strict interpretation of the exception (for example through the application of a 'necessity' test as in the WTO with respect to several of the exceptions)

---

[227] See, eg, Julien Chaisse, 'Exploring the Confines of International Investment and Domestic Health Protections—Is a General Exceptions Clause a Forced Perspective?' (2013) 39 *American Journal of Law and Medicine* 332, 359.

[228] See above part IIC6.

[229] See Andrew Newcombe, 'The use of general exceptions in IIAs: increasing legitimacy or uncertainty?' in Armand de Mestral and Céline Lévesque (eds), *Improving International Investment Agreements* (Routledge, 2014) 267, 277.

[230] See, eg, Appellate Body Report, *Brazil—Retreaded Tyres*, [228]; Appellate Body Report, *US—Gambling*, [369].

[231] See, eg, Frieder Roessler, 'Diverging Domestic Policies and Multilateral Trade Integration' in Jagdish Bhagwati and Robert Hudec (eds), *Fair Trade and Harmonization: Prerequisites for Free Trade?* (vol II, MIT Press, 1996) 21, 30.

undermine the pre-existing broad police powers doctrine? The appropriate results pursuant to the VCLT might preclude such interpretations, but arbitral tribunals might not be sufficiently attentive in applying those rules of treaty interpretation.[232]

IV CONCLUSION

This chapter has displayed a relatively significant amount of consistency in Australia's *BITs* with respect to the key obligations of MFN treatment, the minimum standard of treatment, and expropriation, with less consistency between Australia's *PTAs* in relation to both these obligations and non-conforming measures and general exceptions. The powerful MFN obligation (in Australia's PTAs typically extending to the pre-establishment phase, albeit often subject to exclusion of pre-existing agreements through an NCM annex as noted in Chapter 3) and the multinational nature of many investors means they may be able to exploit this inconsistency in bringing ISDS claims under the most investment-friendly treaty, as discussed further in Chapter 5.

A comprehensive recalibration of all of Australia's IIAs is required to reduce uncertainty (including in relation to the question of consent to ISDS in Australia's BITs, as we explain in Chapter 5) and enhance consistency. However, proposals to renegotiate treaties are not politically saleable either domestically or with treaty partners: much less so in any case than ambitions to conclude new PTAs to open additional international markets.

Even apart from the risk of inconsistency over the decades, Australia has not chosen to (or has been unable to) safeguard its policy space to the maximum extent even in all its modern PTAs. For example, the following straightforward changes could protect Australia as a host State without severely limiting protections for Australian investors abroad or inbound investment:

(a) excluding the application of the MFN rule to dispute settlement procedures (as in most more recent Australian PTAs, but not KAFTA);

---

[232] See, eg, Andrew D Mitchell and James Munro, 'Someone Else's Deal: Interpreting International Investment Agreements in the Light of Third-Party Agreements' (2017) *European Journal of International Law* (forthcoming).

(b) confirming that a breach of domestic law is not sufficient of itself to establish a breach of the FET standard/minimum standard of treatment;
(c) providing an exhaustive list of possible breaches of the FET standard/minimum standard of treatment, instead of a non-exhaustive list;
(d) removing the words 'except in rare circumstances' in clarifying the application of the expropriation obligation to non-discriminatory regulatory measures, as has been achieved in AANZFTA and MAFTA;
(e) declining to agree to overarching non-reciprocal approaches to obligations or exceptions, such as the asymmetrical approach to non-conforming measures in ChAFTA; and
(f) adopting a broad general exception for the investment chapter, or at least to cover the obligations concerning the minimum standard of treatment and expropriation, as has been achieved in AANZFTA, MAFTA and SAFTA.

In Chapter 5, we continue our exploration of investment protection in Australia's PTAs and BITs by examining the role of ISDS and its impact on the substantive obligations and exceptions addressed in this chapter. Rather than alleviating the problems identified in this chapter, we find that Australia's approaches to ISDS also do not represent best practice in protecting regulatory autonomy and balancing the interests of investors with those of the Australian public.

5. Investor–State Dispute Settlement: Uncertainty, Inconsistency and Scope for Reform

I INTRODUCTION

The launch of the first investment treaty claim against Australia by Philip Morris in 2011 (as discussed in Chapter 2)[1] ignited community concerns about the impact of ISDS on Australia's sovereign regulatory autonomy. The suggestion that faceless and unaccountable decision-makers were able to rule on a crucial component of Australia's health policy seems abhorrent to the Australian community, which some commentators have used as a focal point for opposing agreements such as the TPP,[2] notwithstanding the inclusion of ISDS in Australia's BITs for nearly three decades. Even the Chief Justice of the High Court of Australia (Australia's highest court), reflected on the Philip Morris case—before the tribunal's decision declining jurisdiction—in cautioning against the implications of ISDS for Australia. His Honour noted the relationship of the investment treaty claim with the earlier High Court rejection of tobacco company claims that the Australian measure was unconstitutional as a matter of Australian law:[3]

> It is possible that the tribunal, in the context of an argument about expropriation, might be asked to form a view about the correctness of the High Court's conclusion that there was no acquisition within the meaning of s 51(xxxi) of the Constitution. There are therefore two issues of general

---

[1] See more recently *APR Energy v Australia*, Notice of Dispute.

[2] See, eg, Kyla Tienhaara, 'The dismissal of a case against plain cigarette packaging is good news for taxpayers' (20 December 2015) *Sydney Morning Herald* (online); Deborah Gleeson and Sharon Friel, 'Emerging Threats to Public Health from Regional Trade Agreements' (2013) 381 *The Lancet* 1507.

[3] *JT International SA v Commonwealth of Australia* [2012] HCA 43. See also Tania Voon, 'Acquisition of Intellectual Property Rights: Australia's Plain Tobacco Packaging Dispute' [2013] 2 *European Intellectual Property Review* 113.

> significance illuminated by this particular case—the use of ISDS to challenge legislative and administrative acts by governments and its use to call into question the decisions of national courts.[4]

In this chapter, we examine the impact of treaty-based ISDS, and in particular its role in expanding or tempering obligations in Australia's IIAs. We highlight Australia's ambivalent or fickle approach to ISDS, as evidenced in the wide variation in Australia's PTAs as to the inclusion or exclusion of ISDS (part III), and exacerbated by uncertainty in relation to consent to ISDS in Australia's BITs (part II). In part IV we review the reforms to ISDS in Australia's PTAs, including the use of joint decisions by the States parties with respect to interpreting treaty provisions or other specific questions. Although some of these PTAs contain significant modern reforms, on the whole they have not embraced the most policy-friendly approaches seen in some other jurisdictions. Instead, the most recent examples of innovation in Australia's treaty practice have been in providing a 'carve-out' from ISDS solely for tobacco control measures.

This piecemeal approach to safeguarding host State regulatory space, particularly when combined with the absence of a general exception for the investment chapter as in the TPP (as noted in Chapter 4), provides a rather shaky basis for future policy-making. The inconsistencies between the substantive obligations and exceptions of Australia's IIAs, as identified in Chapter 4, risk undermining attempts to reform Australia's approach to such treaties, because investors may simply choose the most investment-friendly (older-style) treaty to bring their ISDS claims (as was apparent in the Philip Morris claim brought under the Australia–Hong Kong BIT). The limited nature of reforms to standards of protection are only partially mitigated by reforms to the ISDS mechanism, with Australia failing to embrace the more radical approaches being promoted by jurisdictions such as Canada and the EU, as well as India through its Model BIT discussed in Chapter 4.[5]

---

[4] Speech by Chief Justice RS French AC, 'Investor–State Dispute Settlement—A Cut Above the Courts', *Supreme and Federal Courts Judges' Conference* (Darwin, 9 July 2014) 6.

[5] See India Model BIT (2015) ch IV.

II CONSENT TO ISDS IN AUSTRALIA'S BITs

ISDS mechanisms are included in all of Australia's 20 BITs currently in force,[6] as set out in Table 5.1. However, although Australia is a party to the ICSID Convention,[7] ISDS cannot be undertaken pursuant to the ICSID Convention with respect to disputes arising under BITs with States that are not also party to the ICSID Convention[8] (although the ICSID Additional Facility Rules provide a mechanism for arbitration where either the host State or the home State is a party to the ICSID Convention).[9] In addition, some uncertainty surrounds the extent to which some of these treaties themselves represent consent to ISDS on the part of the States parties, without requiring further action in the event of a dispute, as we explain in this section.

Article XI:2 of the Australia–Indonesia BIT allows an investor of either party to bring a dispute against the other Party in relation to an investment:

> (a) in accordance with the laws and regulations of the Party which has admitted the investment to the competent judicial or administrative bodies of that Party; or
> (b) to [ICSID] for the application of the conciliation or arbitration procedures provided by the [ICSID Convention].

In the event that both States parties are not party to the ICSID Convention at the time of the dispute, Article XI:3 provides for dispute settlement pursuant to other procedures as agreed by the disputing parties or the UNCITRAL Arbitration Rules. However, Australia and Indonesia are both party to the ICSID Convention and were also party to the ICSID Convention when they signed the BIT in 1992.[10]

---

[6] The Australia–Chile BIT was terminated upon the entry into force of ACIFTA: ACIFTA annex 10–E. The Australia–India BIT was terminated unilaterally by India as of 23 March 2017 although it persists to some extent pursuant by way of a survival clause as discussed in Chapter 4.

[7] Australia signed the ICSID Convention on 24 March 1975 and deposited its instrument of ratification on 2 May 1991. The ICSID Convention entered into force for Australia on 1 June 1991: ICSID, *Signatory and Contracting States* <https://icsid.worldbank.org/en/Pages/about/Database-of-Member-States.aspx> (last visited 7 April 2017).

[8] ICSID Convention art 25.1.

[9] ICSID Additional Facility Rules art 2(a).

[10] See above n 7. Indonesia signed the ICSID Convention on 16 February 1968 and deposited its instrument of ratification on 28 September 1968. The ICSID Convention entered into force for Indonesia on 28 October 1968: ICSID, *Signatory and Contracting States* <https://icsid.worldbank.org/en/Pages/about/Database-of-Member-States.aspx> (last visited 7 April 2017).

Table 5.1 ISDS in Australia's Current BITs

BIT partner	Current ICSID party?	ICSID arbitration	UNCITRAL arbitration	Other
Argentina	✔	✔	✔	As agreed by disputing parties
China[11]	✔	✔	✘	Under annex A
Czech Republic	✔	✔	✘	If *not* both ICSID parties: under annex B or as agreed
Egypt	✔	✔	✘	If *not* both ICSID parties: under annex B or as agreed or Cairo Regional Centre for International Commercial Arbitration
Hong Kong	✔	✘	If not otherwise agreed	As agreed by disputing parties
Hungary	✔	✔	✘	If *not* both ICSID parties: under annex B
Indonesia	✔	✔	If not otherwise agreed	If *not* both ICSID parties: as agreed
Lao PDR	✘	✔	✘	If *not* both ICSID parties: under annex B or as agreed
Lithuania	✔	✔	✘	If *not* both ICSID parties: under annex B or as agreed
Mexico	✘	✔	✔	ICSID Additional Facility Rules
Pakistan	✔	✔	✘	If *not* both ICSID parties: under annex B or as agreed
Papua New Guinea	✔	✔	✘	If *not* both ICSID parties: under annex B
Peru	✔	✔	✘	If *not* both ICSID parties: under annex B or as agreed
Philippines	✔	✔	✘	If *not* both ICSID parties: under Art 13 or as agreed
Poland	✘	✔	✘	If *not* both ICSID parties: under annex B
Romania	✔	✔	✘	If *not* both ICSID parties: under annex B or as agreed
Sri Lanka	✔	✔	✘	If *not* both ICSID parties: under annex B or as agreed
Turkey	✔	✔	✔	As agreed by disputing parties

[11] Under the Australia–China BIT, ISDS is limited to the amount of compensation for expropriation. See further discussion in part III below.

BIT partner	Current ICSID party?	ICSID arbitration	UNCITRAL arbitration	Other
Uruguay	✔	✔	✘	Under annex B or as agreed
Viet Nam	✘	✔	✘	If *not* both ICSID parties or disputing parties do not consent to ICSID: under annex B or as agreed

Article XI:4 states that where a dispute is referred to ICSID pursuant to Article XI:2(b):

> where that action is taken by an investor of one Party, *the other Party shall consent in writing* to the submission of the dispute to [ICSID] within forty-five days of receiving such a request from the investor ...[12]

In *Planet Mining v Indonesia*, the claimant Planet Mining, an Australian wholly-owned subsidiary of UK company Churchill Mining,[13] brought claims against Indonesia pursuant to the ICSID Convention and the Australia–Indonesia BIT in relation to a coal mining project.[14] Indonesia responded, *inter alia*, that it had not consented to arbitration under the ICSID Convention in relation to this dispute.[15] The tribunal agreed with Indonesia that:

> Article XI of the Australia-Indonesia BIT contains no standing offer to arbitrate Planet's claims before ICSID. Planet is therefore only entitled to resort to ICSID arbitration if Indonesia's consent was given through a further act.[16]

In the circumstances, the tribunal nevertheless found that Indonesia had consented to ICSID arbitration in relation to the alleged investments because of certain separate approvals, which constituted the necessary consent in writing under the BIT.[17] (However, subsequent to this jurisdictional decision, in its award on the merits the tribunal dismissed all the

[12] Emphasis added.
[13] *Planet Mining v Indonesia*, Jurisdictional Decision, [1].
[14] *Planet Mining v Indonesia*, Jurisdictional Decision, [48].
[15] *Planet Mining v Indonesia*, Jurisdictional Decision, [77(i)].
[16] *Planet Mining v Indonesia*, Jurisdictional Decision, [198].
[17] *Planet Mining v Indonesia*, Jurisdictional Decision, [217]–[218].

claims on the grounds of inadmissibility for unrelated reasons.[18] The claimants applied for annulment of that award on 31 March 2017.)[19]

In reaching its conclusion on the proper interpretation of Article XI of the Australia–Indonesia BIT, the tribunal referred to the usual elements (ordinary meaning, context, object and purpose, supplementary means) under Articles 31 and 32 of the VCLT.[20] The tribunal considered that the words 'shall consent in writing … within forty-five days' under Article XI:4(a) of the BIT indicate a sequence whereby consent is not granted in advance and can be granted only subsequent to the referral of the dispute to arbitration.[21] The tribunal also referred to Australian treaty practice:

> Australia deliberately entertains the distinction between advance consent and promise to consent. The foregoing review also demonstrates that Australia concluded BITs with unequivocal expressions of advance consent and thus knows how to express such an intent when it wishes to do so. Hence, the Tribunal is of the opinion that a review of Australia's treaty practice supports the conclusion it reached earlier, *i.e.* that the Australia–Indonesia BIT contains a promise to consent.[22]

As a matter of public international law and the VCLT, the reliance on extraneous treaties to interpret the Australia–Indonesia BIT is in itself problematic.[23] Further, simply comparing the final text of different treaties without knowledge of the reasons for the different language used or the negotiating context does little to explain the variance between a country's different IIAs. The tribunal appears to presume a level of consistency and strategy in Australia's negotiating approach that may not be borne out in the messy and pressure-filled practice of inter-State negotiations today, let alone more than two decades ago:

> Between 1990 and 2002, Australia concluded 12 BITs containing a dispute settlement clause similar to the one of the Treaty with Indonesia, suggesting that this wording corresponds to one of the model clauses employed by the Australian BIT negotiators.[24]

---

[18] *Planet Mining v Indonesia*, Award, [532].

[19] *Planet Mining v Indonesia*, Application for Annulment.

[20] *Planet Mining v Indonesia*, Jurisdictional Decision, [172]–[173].

[21] *Planet Mining v Indonesia*, Jurisdictional Decision, [162].

[22] *Planet Mining v Indonesia*, Jurisdictional Decision, [195].

[23] See Andrew D Mitchell and James Munro, 'Someone Else's Deal: Interpreting International Investment Agreements in the Light of Third-Party Agreements' (2017) *European Journal of International Law* (forthcoming).

[24] *Planet Mining v Indonesia*, Jurisdictional Decision, [189].

Nottage has explained the potentially grave implications of this decision (which he regards as incorrect)[25] for other BITs containing language in relation to consent that is similar to that in Australia's BIT with Indonesia:

> [I]f the tribunal is correct, Australia's outbound investors into Poland, Hungary, Romania, the Czech Republic, Lithuania, Peru, Pakistan, Egypt and perhaps Papua New Guinea (PNG)—and vice versa—will have only highly circumscribed rights to ISA in claims under those further nine BITs.[26]
>
> Similar complications may emerge for other countries in the region, such as Japan, with BITs containing similar wording to some of Australia's treaties.[27]

The tribunal's reading of the Australia–Indonesia BIT (and by extension other similarly worded BITs) removes the potential for ISDS not only pursuant to the ICSID Convention in the absence of an additional consent by the host State, but also pursuant to other arbitral rules where the BIT provides that those other rules are available only where the States parties to the BIT are *not* party to the ICSID Convention (as shown in Table 5.1).

Nottage has noted that some of these difficulties may be addressed by subsequent developments, such as the inclusion of ISDS in AANZFTA[28] (as noted further below), negotiations towards RCEP,[29] and the potential for termination of Australia's BIT with Peru[30] pursuant to a side letter

---

[25] Luke Nottage, 'Do Many of Australia's Bilateral Treaties Really Not Provide Full Advance Consent to Investor–State Arbitration? Analysis of Planet Mining v Indonesia and Regional Implications' (2015) 12(1) *Transnational Dispute Management* (online) 3, 5–6. See also Luke Nottage, 'The Limits of Legalization in Asia-Pacific Investment Treaty Arbitration' in Julien Chaisse and Tsai-yu Lin (eds), *International Economic Law and Governance: Essays in Honour of Mitsuo Matsushita* (Oxford University Press, 2016) 153.

[26] Nottage, 'Analysis of Planet Mining', above n 25, 3.

[27] Ibid 4.

[28] Ibid 13, 16, noting that AANZFTA ch 11 art 21 n 14 requires the disputing parties to agree for a claim to proceed against the Philippines under the ICSID Convention.

[29] Ibid 16.

[30] Ibid 14.

upon entry into force of the TPP[31] (an approach that also applies to Australia's BITs with Mexico[32] and Viet Nam).[33]

Another Australian investor is reported to have succeeded in an investment treaty claim:[34] *Tethyan Copper v Pakistan*, brought pursuant to the Australia–Pakistan BIT, which provides similarly to the Australia–Indonesia BIT that where an investor brings a claim pursuant to the ICSID Convention, the host State '*shall consent in writing* to the submission of the dispute to the Centre within thirty days of receiving such a request'.[35] In that dispute, as the *Planet Mining* tribunal noted,[36] the tribunal determined that 'it has *prima facie* jurisdiction over the merits of the dispute pursuant to'[37] ICSID Convention art 25(1) and the Australia–Pakistan BIT art 13. The *Tethyan Copper* tribunal did not even consider the 'shall consent' wording, perhaps because Pakistan apparently did not contend that it had not given consent to the arbitration[38] and did in fact provide the requisite written consent pursuant to the BIT.[39]

The third known ISDS treaty claim by an Australian investor was *White Industries v India*, brought pursuant to the UNCITRAL Arbitration Rules under the Australia–India BIT (now terminated), which indicates that—failing amicable settlement[40] or resolution through domestic procedures[41] or international conciliation[42]—a dispute may be referred 'to an

---

[31] Exchange of letters between Andrew Robb, Minister for Trade and Investment (Australia) and Ana María Sánchez de Ríos, Minister of Foreign Affairs (Peru) (6 November 2015).

[32] Exchange of letters between Andrew Robb, Minister for Trade and Investment (Australia) and Ildefonso Guajardo Villarreal, Minister of Economy (Mexico) (6 November 2015).

[33] Exchange of letters between Andrew Robb, Minister for Trade and Investment (Australia) and Vu Huy Hoang, Minister of Trade and Industry (Viet Nam) (6 November 2015).

[34] Barrick Gold Company, 'ICSID Issues Decision in Favor of Antofagasta plc and Barrick in Reko Diq Arbitration Proceedings' (Press Release, 21 March 2017), available at <http://www.italaw.com/cases/1631> (last visited 7 April 2017).

[35] Australia–Pakistan BIT art 13.3(a) (emphasis added).

[36] *Planet Mining v Indonesia*, Jurisdictional Decision, [132].

[37] *Tethyan Copper v Pakistan*, Provisional Measures Decision, [123] (italics in original).

[38] *Planet Mining v Indonesia*, Jurisdictional Decision, [132].

[39] *Tethyan Copper v Pakistan*, Provisional Measures Decision, [126].

[40] Australia–India BIT art 12.1.

[41] Australia–India BIT art 12.2(a).

[42] Australia–India BIT art 12.2(b).

ad hoc arbitral tribunal by either Party to the dispute'[43] in accordance with the UNCITRAL Arbitration Rules.[44] India unsuccessfully raised a number of objections to the tribunal's jurisdiction.[45] However, as this particular treaty wording did not expressly refer to prior consent from the host State, the question of consent as in *Planet Mining* did not arise. The tribunal found a breach of the obligation to provide 'effective means of asserting claims and enforcing rights'[46] and ordered India to pay White Industries approximately AUD4 million plus costs and interest.[47]

III THE INCLUSION OR EXCLUSION OF ISDS IN PTAs: AUSTRALIA'S VARIABLE APPROACH

As noted in Chapter 1, Australia has had a variable approach to the inclusion or exclusion of ISDS in its PTAs. Although all of Australia's BITs include ISDS (subject to the uncertainty regarding the language of consent to ISDS as discussed above), only some of Australia's PTAs include an ISDS mechanism, as summarised in Table 5.2.

How to make sense of this inconsistent approach to ISDS? ANZCERTA originally omitted not only ISDS but also investment obligations in general. When AANZFTA was concluded in 2009, side letters exchanged between the relevant Ministers of Australia and New Zealand again excluded the entire investment chapter, including ISDS.[48] Investment obligations without ISDS were then added under ANZCERTA by virtue of the 2011 protocol on investment, which entered into force in 2013.[49] In the TPP, ISDS was again excluded as between Australia and

---

43 Australia–India BIT art 12.3(c).

44 Australia–India BIT art 12.3(a) provides alternatively for ICSID arbitration (if 'both Parties to the dispute consent in writing') if the two States parties are party to the ICSID Convention, but India is not yet a party to the ICSID Convention.

45 *White Industries v India*, Award, part 5.1.

46 *White Industries v India*, Award, [16.1.1(a)].

47 *White Industries v India*, Award, [16.1.1(b)–(e)].

48 Letters exchanged between Tim Groser, Minister of Trade, New Zealand, and Simon Crean, Minister for Trade, Australia (27 February 2009).

49 *Protocol on Investment to the Australia–New Zealand Closer Economic Relations Trade Agreement,* signed 16 February 2011 [2013] ATS 1 (entered into force 1 March 2013).

Table 5.2 ISDS in Australia's PTAs

PTA partner	Signed	Entry into force	ISDS	ICSID arbitration	UNCITRAL arbitration	ICSID Additional Facility Rules or as agreed
Singapore (SAFTA)	2003	2003	✓	✓	✓	✗
United States (AUSFTA)	2004	2005	✗	✗	✗	✗
Thailand[50] (TAFTA)	2004	2005	✓	✗	✓	✓
Chile (ACIFTA)	2008	2009	✓	✓	✓	✓
Brunei Darussalam, Cambodia, Indonesia, Lao PDR,[51] Malaysia, Myanmar,[52] New Zealand, Philippines,[53] Singapore, Thailand, Viet Nam[54] (AANZFTA)	2009	2010	✓ (excl Aust–NZ)	✓	✓	✓
Malaysia (MAFTA)	2012	2013	✗	✗	✗	✗
New Zealand[55] (ANZCERTA Investment Protocol)	2013	2013	✗	✗	✗	✗
Korea (KAFTA)	2014	2014	✓	✓	✓	✓
Japan (JAEPA)	2014	2015	✗	✗	✗	✗
China (ChAFTA)	2015	2015	✓	✓	✓	✓

[50] TAFTA art 917.3 provides for ISDS using alternative forms agreed in subsequent agreements by either party. That would include ICSID Arbitration, pursuant to its inclusion in AANZFTA, if Australia and Thailand were both party to the ICSID Convention (see Nottage, 'Analysis of Planet Mining', above n 25, 15). Although Australia is party to the ICSID Convention, Thailand signed the ICSID Convention on 6 December 1985 but has not yet ratified it. Nevertheless, arbitration under the ICSID Additional Facility Rules could be available under TAFTA through invocation of the corresponding AANZFTA provision in accordance with TAFTA art 917.3.

[51] Lao PDR is not yet party to the ICSID Convention.

[52] Myanmar is not yet party to the ICSID Convention.

[53] See above n 28.

[54] Viet Nam is not yet party to the ICSID Convention.

[55] ANZCERTA did not contain investment provisions when it first entered into force. When the ANZCERTA Investment Protocol entered into force in 2013, ISDS was still excluded.

PTA partner	Signed	Entry into force	ISDS	ICSID arbitration	UNCITRAL arbitration	ICSID Additional Facility Rules or as agreed
Canada, Brunei Darussalam, Chile, Japan, Malaysia, Mexico,[56] New Zealand, Peru, Singapore, United States, Viet Nam (TPP)	2016	–	✓ (excl Aust–NZ)	✓	✓	✓
Singapore (SAFTA agreed amendments)	2016	–	✓	✓	✓	✓

New Zealand by means of side letters.[57] Although these various letters do not contain an official explanation of the rationale for excluding ISDS between the parties, this exclusion is consistent with both the ANZCERTA protocol on investment and a separate agreement between Australia and New Zealand[58] that recognises in its preamble the parties' 'longstanding friendship and close historic, political and economic relationship' and 'each Party's confidence in the judicial and regulatory institutions of the other Party'. Australia's Chief Negotiator for the TPP explained to JSCOT in a hearing on the TPP:

> There was never a question of a side letter, at any point, with the United States. The side letter with New Zealand was the exception, for several reasons. One is an historical reason. On several occasions we have negotiated FTAs with New Zealand and have agreed, on every occasion, not to enter into ISDS outcomes with them. At the same time, we agreed that we would not subject each other to antidumping measures—it is a package of things that we agree with the Kiwis …[59]

56 Mexico is not yet party to the ICSID Convention.

57 Letters exchanged between Todd McClay, Minister of Trade, New Zealand, and Andrew Robb, Minister for Trade and Investment, Australia (4 February 2016).

58 *Agreement between the Government of Australia and the Government of New Zealand on Trans-Tasman Court Proceedings and Regulatory Enforcement*, signed 24 July 2008, [2013] ATS 32 (entered into force 11 October 2013).

59 Evidence to JSCOT, Canberra (7 November 2016) 9 (Elizabeth Ward, Chief Negotiator, TPP, DFAT).

The SAFTA was the first of Australia's PTAs to include an ISDS mechanism,[60] but that facility was limited by the basic nature of the substantive investment obligations in the original agreement. In particular, the investment chapter of SAFTA included no general MFN obligation,[61] no obligation to accord fair and equitable treatment, and no prohibition on performance requirements. However, an FET obligation[62] and a prohibition on performance requirements[63] were added in amendments in 2011.[64] (Other amendments included updates to the intellectual property chapter to reflect changes to the domestic regimes of Australia and Singapore as a result of the conclusion of their respective PTAs with the United States.)[65] Despite the significance of adding an FET obligation (particularly in view of growing concern about the scope and nature of such an obligation in international investment law today), JSCOT concluded that it was 'satisfied that the amendments contained in this treaty are largely machinery [*sic*] in nature and will not result in significant change to the degree of market access each country accords its counterpart'.[66] This rather cursory review of the amendments is problematic given the inclusion of ISDS, particularly given DFAT's original contention before JSCOT in 2003 that SAFTA did not require a higher standard of treatment than investors would enjoy under Australia's domestic legal regime,[67] and its highlighting of the fact that substantive investment obligations determine the scope of exposure to ISDS claims.[68]

Subsequent to SAFTA, Australia succeeded in excluding ISDS from its PTA with the United States, officially declaring as the justification for the exclusion 'the Parties' open economic environments and shared legal traditions, and the confidence of investors in the fairness and integrity of

---

[60] SAFTA ch 8 art 16 (numbering as amended in 2011).

[61] Cf SAFTA ch 8 arts 12, 14.2(e), 17.1 (numbering as amended in 2011).

[62] SAFTA ch 8 art 4.1 (as introduced in 2011).

[63] SAFTA ch 8 art 5 (as introduced in 2011).

[64] See JSCOT, *Report 117: Treaties Tabled on 9 and 10 February, and 1 March 2011* (June 2011) ch 5: 'Amendments to the Singapore–Australia Free Trade Agreement'; *National Interest Analysis: Amendments to Singapore–Australia Free Trade Agreement, done at Singapore on 27 July 2009* [2011] ATNIF 1.

[65] See JSCOT, *Report 117*, above n 64, [5.21].

[66] Ibid [5.22].

[67] JSCOT, *Report 52: treaties Tabled in March 2003* (June 2003) ch 2: 'Singapore–Australia Free Trade Agreement', [2.69].

[68] Ibid [2.107].

their respective legal systems'.[69] AUSFTA does nevertheless provide that if either party 'considers that there has been a change in circumstances affecting the settlement of disputes on matters within the scope of' the investment chapter, the party may request consultations with the other party with a view to allowing an investor to submit a claim to arbitration and establishing appropriate procedures for such an arbitration'.[70]

In Australia's next three PTAs, with Chile, Thailand, and ASEAN/New Zealand, ISDS is included.[71] The ISDS mechanisms were perhaps of greater significance in these agreements than in SAFTA, at least initially, because they contained more comprehensive investment chapters, including an FET obligation[72] and (in the PTAs with Chile and Thailand) an MFN obligation.[73] In relation to TAFTA, JSCOT took note of the addition of ISDS despite its exclusion from the AUSFTA and concerns raised in some submissions to it but was 'assured by the response provided by the Attorney-General's Department',[74] which emphasised:

> [I]t is common to include these sorts of provisions when a developed state is concluding an agreement with a developing state ... To date, there has not been a single action brought against Australia under any of [its] 19 investment agreements or under [SAFTA] ... I think the kinds of comments made in some of the submissions are perhaps a little overstated in relation to investor–state provisions generally.[75]

While perhaps accurate in the assessment of 'overstatement', this rationale is less persuasive today, now that Australia has faced an ISDS claim under its BIT with Hong Kong, and States are increasingly realising the reciprocal nature of investment protections. Thus, for example, while the JSCOT report on TAFTA identified the benefits of ISDS in protecting Australian investors in Thailand,[76] it gave little consideration to the impact of a possible claim by a Thai investor in Australia. (One Australian investor in the mining sector has recently given formal notice

---

69 DFAT, *Australia–United States Free Trade Agreement: Guide to the Agreement* (March 2004) 121. See also JSCOT, *Report 61: The Australia–United States Free Trade Agreement* (June 2004) [4.23]–[4.24].

70 AUSFTA art 11.16.

71 TAFTA art 917; ACIFTA ch 10 s B; AANZFTA ch 11 s B.

72 TAFTA art 909.2; ACIFTA art 10.5; AANZFTA ch 11 art 6.

73 TAFTA art 910; ACIFTA art 10.4.

74 JSCOT, *Report 63: Treaties Tabled on 7 December 2004* (December 2004) [3.142].

75 Ibid [3.140].

76 See, eg, ibid [3,10], [3.11], [3.136].

of a potential claim against Thailand under TAFTA.)[77] JSCOT's original report on SAFTA also seemed to accept DFAT's reasoning that the inclusion of ISDS in that treaty posed few concerns because, *inter alia*, investors could only win such a dispute if Australia violated its treaty obligations, which Singapore could always enforce in State–State dispute settlement anyway.[78] As has become clearer in more recent years, this kind of rationale misses distinctions between these different forms of dispute settlement, such as a home State's broader perspective in deciding whether to launch an investment treaty claim, and an investor's potentially greater incentives and financial resources for doing so. In addition, Australia would now be much more acutely aware of the range and extent of costs imposed on a government respondent in an ISDS case, even where the claim fails.

With respect to ACIFTA, JSCOT's report again noted the alleged benefit of including ISDS to allow 'Australian investors to protect their investments'.[79] The report also referred to submissions raising concerns about the impact of ISDS on 'the ability of governments to regulate in the public interest' and in particular 'regulation aimed at protecting health and the environment'.[80] JSCOT supported Australia's ratification of the treaty[81] without responding to these concerns. Similarly, in its report on AANZFTA, JSCOT took note of submissions indicating the potential for the investment chapter to 'create greater transparency and certainty for Australian investors in the region'[82] and supported ratification of the treaty[83] with no mention of ISDS at all.

In April 2011, a statement by Julia Gillard's Labor government indicated that Australia had previously sought ISDS 'in trade agreements with developing countries at the behest of Australian businesses' but that it would no longer do so, as 'the Government does not support provisions that would confer greater legal rights on foreign businesses than those

---

[77] 'A Second Gold Mine Investor Puts Thailand on Notice of Arbitration Claim—This Time Under Australian Free Trade Agreement' (3 April 2017) *Investment Arbitration Reporter* (online).

[78] JSCOT, *Report 117*, above n 64, [2.104], [2.107].

[79] JSCOT, *Report 95: Treaties Tabled on 4 June, 17 June, 25 June and 26 August 2008* (October 2008) [3.10].

[80] Ibid [3.52].

[81] Ibid [3.64].

[82] JSCOT, *Report 102: Treaties Tabled on 12 and 16 March 2009* (2009) [2.6].

[83] Ibid [2.63].

available to domestic businesses'.[84] This anti-ISDS stance followed the Productivity Commission's recommendations against ISDS,[85] as noted in Chapter 1 of this volume. The change also roughly coincided with the commencement later in 2011 of the investment treaty arbitration by Philip Morris Asia Ltd against Australia's plain tobacco packaging laws.[86] Several months later, Australia signed a PTA with Malaysia, not surprisingly excluding ISDS. In its report on MAFTA, JSCOT noted that 'Malaysians invest significantly more in Australian shares than Australians invest in Malaysian shares',[87] while maintaining that the treaty 'includes better legal protections for Australian investments in Malaysia'.[88]

Not long after the MAFTA entered into force on 1 January 2013, a change of government occurred in Australia following the federal election on 7 September 2013, with the coalition of the Liberal/National parties taking power. This change had a significant impact on the country's approach to ISDS, with the new government declaring a return to an ad hoc approach, where ISDS is considered on a case-by-case basis in each negotiation.[89] ISDS was then included in KAFTA[90] but excluded from JAEPA. In its report on JAEPA, JSCOT noted the absence of an ISDS mechanism and the presence of a clause allowing for future

---

84 DFAT, *Gillard Government Trade Policy Statement: Trading our way to more jobs and prosperity* (April 2011) 14.

85 Productivity Commission, Australian Government, *Bilateral and Regional Trade Agreements: Productivity Commission Research Report* (November 2010). See also Jürgen Kurtz and Luke Nottage, 'Investment Treaty Arbitration "Down Under": Policy and Politics in Australia' (2015) 30(2) *ICSID Review* 465; Jürgen Kurtz, 'Australia's Rejection of Investor–State Arbitration: Causation, Omission and Implication' (2012) 27(1) *ICSID Review* 65; Leon Trakman, 'Investor State Arbitration or Local Courts: Will Australia Set a New Trend?' (2012) 46(1) *Journal of World Trade* 83.

86 *Philip Morris v Australia*, Notice of Claim; *Philip Morris v Australia*, Notice of Arbitration.

87 JSCOT, *Report 130: Treaty Tabled on 14 August 2012—Malaysia–Free Trade Agreement done at Kuala Lumpur on 22 May 2012* (October 2012) [2.13].

88 Ibid [2.19].

89 See, eg, Julie Bishop, 'Free Trade Focus' (28 March 2013) *On Line Opinion*; 'Australia May be More Open to ISDS in TPP with Government Change' (15 March 2013) 31 *Inside US Trade* (online).

90 KAFTA ch 11, s B.

consideration of such a mechanism.[91] JSCOT noted the benefits of the treaty's investment chapter for both Australian and Japanese investors.[92]

The JSCOT report on KAFTA similarly noted the treaty's benefits for both Australian investments in Korea and Korean investments in Australia,[93] stating (with reference to the Productivity Commission's 2010 report) that although ISDS mechanisms were '[o]riginally set up to protect foreign investors in developing countries', they 'are now included in the majority of FTAs'.[94] Moreover, according to DFAT, 'Korea had refused to sign' the treaty without ISDS.[95] JSCOT suggested that the inclusion of ISDS was tempered by 'a significant range of carve-outs and safeguards to protect regulation in areas of key public policy concerns including public welfare, health, culture and the environment', including exclusion of '[f]oreign investment screening decisions' from ISDS.[96] We discuss in part IV of this chapter below the gradual reforms to ISDS witnessed in Australian FTAs including KAFTA. JSCOT ultimately supported ratification of KAFTA,[97] while 'suggest[ing] that the Government exercise a cautious approach regarding the inclusion of ISDS provisions in upcoming FTAs'.[98]

Although ISDS is included in ChAFTA,[99] subject to advanced safeguards as discussed further below, the mechanism is (similarly to the original SAFTA) limited by the few substantive investment obligations

---

[91] JSCOT, *Report 144: Treaty Tabled on 14 July 2014—Agreement between Australia and Japan for an Economic Partnership* (October 2014) [2.45]. See JAEPA art 14.19.

[92] JSCOT, *Report 144*, above n 91, [2.44].

[93] JSCOT, *Report 142: Treaty Tabled on 13 May 2013—Free Trade Agreement between the Government of Australia and the Government of the Republic of Korea* (September 2014) [2.28].

[94] Ibid [4.4].

[95] Ibid [4.5].

[96] Ibid [4.7]. But see Dissenting Report of Kelvin Thomson and Melissa Parke (p 54, recommending renegotiation to exclude ISDS) and Dissenting Report of the Australian Greens (p 63, opposing the inclusion of ISDS 'in modern trade agreements which allow foreign corporations the right to sue sovereign governments if they feel changes to policy or Parliamentary laws negatively impact on their profits').

[97] Ibid [5.31].

[98] Ibid [5.5].

[99] ChAFTA ch 9 s B.

included in the treaty (essentially a narrow and lopsided MFN obligation[100] and a lopsided national treatment obligation),[101] as well as the explicit restriction of ISDS to national treatment claims.[102] Yet, at the time of writing, ISDS continues to be available pursuant to the Australia–China BIT.[103] The continued application of the BIT alongside the newer ChAFTA creates unusual circumstances and difficult questions of interpretation and application of treaty provisions under public international law. Our previous analysis[104] concluded that both treaties would continue to operate until amended, given the explicit statements in ChAFTA about the co-existence of the treaties[105] as well as relevant general rules under the VCLT.[106] Thus, a modern form of ISDS applies under ChAFTA to national treatment claims, while the Australia–China BIT provides consent to a much less nuanced form of ISDS with respect to the usual suite of investment obligations including (explicitly) as regards compensation for expropriation[107] and (arguably, for claims against Australia but not China)[108] fair and equitable treatment.[109]

Perhaps Australia's recognition of the well-established judicial systems in New Zealand and the United States could explain why ISDS was unnecessary or undesirable as between Australia and those two countries. More crudely, and taking account of the reference to developing countries in the Gillard Trade Policy Statement, Australia might have been seen as pursuing ISDS with developing but not developed country PTA partners. But that does not explain the ad hoc approach to ISDS in

---

[100] ChAFTA art 9.1 and n 4 to art 9.5 (providing for the application of non-conforming measures listed by China against the MFN obligation in other agreements).

[101] ChAFTA art 9.3 (providing pre-establishment rights to Chinese but not Australian investors).

[102] ChAFTA arts 9.12.2(a)(i) and 9.12.2(b)(i).

[103] Australia–China BIT art XII.

[104] Elizabeth Sheargold and Tania Voon, 'Australia, China, and the Co-Existence of Successive International Investment Agreements' in Colin Picker, Heng Wang and Weihuan Zhou (eds), *The China Australia Free Trade Agreement: A 21st Century Model* (Hart, forthcoming).

[105] See, eg, ChAFTA arts 1.2, 9.9.2.

[106] See, eg, VCLT arts 30(3), 31(3)(c).

[107] Australia–China BIT arts VIII, XII:2(b).

[108] See ICSID, *Contracting States and Measures Taken by them for the Purpose of the Convention, Notifications Concerning Classes of Disputes Considered Suitable or Unsuitable for Submission to the Centre (Art. 25(4) of the Convention) List ICSID/8–D* (27 September 2016).

[109] Australia–China BIT arts III:a, XII:4. See our further reasoning in Sheargold and Voon, above n 104.

subsequent agreements: in particular, the exclusion of ISDS from Australia's PTA with Malaysia (a developing country).[110] Singapore and Korea are also generally regarded as developing countries in the WTO context,[111] which allows Members to determine for themselves whether they are to be categorised as developing or developed. However, on other measures, Singapore and Korea are regarded as developed or 'high income' countries.[112] Therefore, one might have expected Australia *not* to include ISDS in its PTAs with Singapore and Korea. Perhaps the development divide is of little use in explaining these discrepancies, particularly given the decision by the World Bank to abandon the distinction between developed countries (which it previously defined as high-income countries) and developing countries (which it previously defined as low- and middle-income countries) in its *2016 World Development Indicators*.[113]

A more helpful explanation for Australia's variable approach to ISDS has two prongs. First, ISDS has become a party political issue, with the opposition Labor party continuing to eschew ISDS, declaring in advance of the 2016 federal election that if it won that election Australia would not accept ISDS in future agreements.[114] Labor members of JSCOT provided additional comments in JSCOT's report on the TPP indicating that they had unsuccessfully sought the inclusion of the following recommendation in the report:

> The Committee recommends the Australian government pursues any available opportunity to avoid being subject to any ISDS arrangements, or to the introduction of ISDS provisions between Australia and nations, like the USA, that are in any case low-risk in terms of direct expropriation that cannot be

---

[110] See, eg, *Formation of Asian Group of Developing Members: Communication from Pakistan*, WT/GC/COM/6 (27 March 2012) n 1.

[111] Ibid.

[112] See, eg, World Bank, *2015 World Development Indicators* (2015) preliminary pages. See also Luke Nottage, 'Investor–State Arbitration Policy and Practice in Australia', Investor–State Arbitration Series Paper No 6, Centre for International Governance Innovation (June 2016) 4–5.

[113] World Bank, *2016 World Development Indicators* (2016) iii.

[114] Australian Labor Party, *National Platform: A smart, modern, fair Australia* (July 2015) [71]: 'Labor in government will review ISDS provisions in existing trade and investment agreements and seek to work with Australia's trading partners to remove these provisions'.

> challenged within a domestic judicial system, and yet high-risk in terms of ISDS action that undermines public policy sovereignty.[115]

Second, with the coalition of the Liberal/National parties in power, Australia's traditional ad hoc approach to ISDS continues, with the result that ISDS has become a bargaining chip. Australia will accept ISDS where it obtains something of value in return in the negotiations. This conclusion would explain why Australia, having fought against considerable US interests to exclude ISDS from the AUSFTA,[116] and having only recently excluded ISDS from its PTA with Japan, ultimately agreed to ISDS in the TPP,[117] including with respect to both the US and Japan (excluding only New Zealand, as noted above). The nature of ISDS as a bargaining chip in the TPP negotiations is reflected in leaked drafts of the investment chapter, which changed from excluding Australia from the ISDS mechanism,[118] to specifying that the exclusion would be removed 'subject to certain conditions'.[119]

IV ISDS REFORMS IN AUSTRALIA'S PTAs

Table 5.3 sets out several reforms to the ISDS mechanism in the seven Australian PTAs that contain such a mechanism (including the TPP).[120] These reforms operate in addition to the exceptions and clarifications to substantive investment obligations discussed above, which may reduce the risk of a successful ISDS claim.

---

115 JSCOT, *Report 165: Trans-Pacific Partnership Agreement* (November 2016) 131. See also our discussion in Chapter 1 of Labor Senators' views on the Trade and Foreign Investment (Protecting the Public Interest) Bill 2014 (Cth).

116 See, eg, William H Cooper, *The US–Australia Free Trade Agreement: Provisions and Implications*, CRS Report for Congress (Library of Congress, 12 January 2005) 16.

117 TPP ch 9 s B.

118 Citizens Trade Campaign, 'Newly Leaked TPP Investment Chapter Contains Special Rights for Corporations' (13 June 2012) *Investment* n 20: '[Section B does not apply to Australia or an investor of Australia. Notwithstanding any provision of this Agreement, Australia does not consent to the submission of a claim to arbitration under this Section.]'

119 WikiLeaks, 'Trans-Pacific Partnership treaty: Advanced Investment Chapter working document for all 12 nations (January 20, 2015 draft)' (25 March 2015) *Investment* n 29.

120 See also Luke Nottage, 'The TPP Investment Chapter and Investor–State Arbitration in Asia and Oceania: Assessing Prospects for Ratification' (2016) 17(2) *Melbourne Journal of International Law* 313.

Table 5.3 ISDS Reform in Australia's PTAs Containing an ISDS Mechanism

PTA	Public hearings; transcripts; submissions	Binding decisions by States parties	ISDS carve-out for FIRB[121]	ISDS mechanism for public welfare measures	ISDS carve-out for tobacco control measures	Code of conduct
SAFTA 2011	✘	✘	✘	✘	✘	✘
TAFTA	✘	✘	✔	✘	✘	✘
ACIFTA	✔	✔	✔	✘	✘	✘
AANZFTA	✘	✔	✔	✘	✘	✘
KAFTA	✔	✔	✔	✘	✘	✘
ChAFTA	optional	✔	✔	✔	✘	✔
TPP	✔	✔	✔	✘	At host State's discretion	Through guidance of States parties
SAFTA 2016	✔	✔	✔	✘	✔	✔

A Forum Shopping

The earliest Australian PTAs including ISDS had only limited safeguards of the kind that might be seen today as narrowing the scope of ISDS or mitigating the risk of successful claims or claims in general. Nevertheless, SAFTA (before an agreement to amend it in 2016 as explained further below)[122] and TAFTA generally prevented States parties from using State–State dispute settlement (whether under an IIA or some other international agreement such as the WTO) with respect to matters that are already the subject of ISDS claims by their investors. For example, SAFTA provided:

[121] Australia's FTAs typically exclude FIRB decisions from at least certain investment obligations (eg in the NCM lists described in Chapter 4). This column of Table 5.3 relates only to exclusion of FIRB decisions from the ISDS mechanism itself. Similarly, the references to ISDS carve-outs for public welfare measures and tobacco control should be distinguished from exceptions discussed in Chapter 4, which may apply to such measures as well in the course of an ISDS claim.

[122] *Agreement to Amend the Singapore–Australia Free Trade Agreement*, signed 13 October 2016 (not yet in force).

> Neither Party shall give diplomatic protection, or bring an international claim, in respect of a dispute which one of its investors and the other Party shall have consented to submit or have submitted to conciliation or arbitration under this Article, unless such other Party has failed to abide by and comply with the award rendered in such dispute. Diplomatic protection, for the purposes of this paragraph, shall not include informal diplomatic exchanges for the sole purpose of facilitating a settlement of the dispute.[123]

TAFTA's corresponding limitation prevents a State party from 'pursu[ing] the dispute through diplomatic channels' unless the tribunal has determined that it lacks jurisdiction or the other State party has failed to comply with any determination of the tribunal.[124] SAFTA and TAFTA also prevented investors from bringing other arbitral claims or claims before domestic courts or tribunals of the host State with respect to the same matter: under SAFTA by requiring claimants to waive their right to initiate or continue other proceedings (except for interim relief);[125] and under TAFTA by providing the investor the 'choice' of bringing the dispute before the relevant domestic bodies 'or' an international ad hoc arbitral tribunal.[126] These kinds of provisions limiting State–State dispute settlement[127] and other claims by the investor[128] also appear in the subsequent treaties of ACIFTA and AANZFTA.

In contrast, the three most recent treaties (KAFTA, ChAFTA and the TPP) preclude certain claims by investors[129] but not State–State dispute settlement. The national interest analyses and regulatory impact statements regarding these three treaties do not appear to explain this change. Under this newer approach, the home State of a claimant investor could arguably bring an international claim against the host State (for example, Australia) in respect of a dispute already subject to ISDS (for example, under the same treaty or a different treaty, such as the WTO). Unlike other developments in more recent Australian FTAs, this change appears to *increase* the potential negative impact of IIAs on Australia's regulatory autonomy. Amendments to the SAFTA agreed by Australia and Singapore in 2016 will also remove the exclusion of State–State dispute

123 SAFTA ch 8 art 16.6 (numbering as amended in 2011).
124 TAFTA art 917.4.
125 SAFTA ch 8 art 16.4(b)(ii) (numbering as amended in 2011).
126 TAFTA art 917.2.
127 ACIFTA art 10.18.5; AANZFTA ch 11 art 22.3.
128 ACIFTA arts 10.18.2(b), 10.18.3; AANZFTA ch 11 art 22.1(c).
129 KAFTA art 11.18.2(b); ChAFTA art 9.14.2(d); TPP art 9.21.2(b).

settlement in respect of matters subject to ISDS.[130] These changes to the Australian approach to forum shopping in IIAs unfortunately increase the potential for conflict and inconsistency between arbitral decisions in parallel disputes,[131] while also reducing the potential for State–State dispute settlement to be used as a means of reasserting State control in the international investment law regime.[132]

B Exclusion of Decisions on Admission of Foreign Investment

TAFTA also contains a more unusual and substantive exclusion from ISDS of certain decisions by a foreign investment authority:

> This Article shall not be construed to allow an investor of a Party to pursue a claim against the other Party in relation to any decision that any foreign investment authority of that Party makes in relation to, or conditions that any foreign investment authority of that Party may have placed on, the establishment, acquisition or expansion of an investment by that investor, or in relation to the enforcement of any such conditions.[133]

In the case of Australia as host State, this exclusion would cover decisions by FIRB on the admission of investments from Thailand. KAFTA[134] and the TPP[135] contain similar exclusions of FIRB decisions from ISDS in particular, in addition to the exclusion of such decisions from substantive investment obligations, for example through lists of Australia's non-conforming measures as discussed in Chapter 4. The SAFTA amendments agreed in 2016 contain a corresponding exclusion.[136] ACIFTA, AANZFTA and ChAFTA also exclude FIRB decisions from ISDS by restricting ISDS to the post-establishment phase, through a

---

130 SAFTA 2016 ch 8 art 26 excludes other claims by the investor but not State–State dispute settlement.

131 See, eg, Hanno Wehland, 'The Regulation of Parallel Proceedings in Investor–State Disputes' (2016) 31(3) *ICSID Review* 576; August Reinisch, 'The Issues Raised by Parallel Proceedings and Possible Solutions' in Michael Waibel et al (eds), *The Backlash against Investment Arbitration* (Kluwer Law International, 2010) 113.

132 See Andreas Kulick, 'State–State Investment Arbitration as a Means of Reassertion of Control: From Antagonism to Dialogue' in Andreas Kulick (ed), *Reassertion of Control over the Investment Treaty Regime* (Cambridge University Press, 2016) 128.

133 TAFTA art 917.9.

134 KAFTA annex 11–G.

135 TPP annex 9–H, [1].

136 SAFTA 2016 ch 8 annex 8–B.

reference to ISDS applying to a covered investment made in accordance with the laws, regulations and *investment policies* of the host State[137] or a similar qualification in the definition of investment.[138]

C Transparency

All of Australia's PTAs following SAFTA and TAFTA—apart from AANZFTA[139]—contain more advanced transparency mechanisms with respect to ISDS. ACIFTA, KAFTA and the TPP require (in similar terms) public hearings and public release of hearing transcripts and party submissions, subject to confidentiality. KAFTA, for example, provides that '[t]he tribunal shall conduct hearings open to the public' and 'shall make appropriate arrangements to protect' information designated as 'protected information',[140] which is defined as 'confidential business information or information that is privileged or otherwise protected from disclosure under a Party's law'.[141] In addition, under KAFTA, subject to limitations regarding such types of information, the respondent in an ISDS dispute (that is, the host State) 'shall … make … available to the public' documents including the 'notice of intent', the 'notice of arbitration', 'pleadings, memorials and briefs submitted to the tribunal by a disputing party', 'minutes or transcripts of hearings of the tribunal, where available', and 'orders, awards, and decisions of the tribunal'.[142] The 2016 agreement to amend SAFTA contains corresponding transparency requirements.[143]

Inclusion of these requirements within IIAs is relatively unusual[144] and also significant, given concerns about the legitimacy of ISDS as a dispute

---

137 ACIFTA art 10.14; ChAFTA art 9.12.1.

138 AANZFTA ch 11 art 2(a).

139 AANZFTA merely *allows* the host State respondent to 'make publicly available all awards and decisions produced by the tribunal', subject to the usual confidentiality constraints: AANZFTA ch 11 art 26.1.

140 KAFTA art 11.21.2. See also ACIFTA art 10.22.2; TPP art 9.24.2.

141 KAFTA art 11.28. See also ACIFTA art 10.22.2; TPP 9.1.

142 KAFTA art 11.21.1. See also ACIFTA art 10.22.1; TPP art 9.24.1.

143 SAFTA 2016 ch 8 arts 1(r), 29.1, 29.2.

144 See generally Nathalie Bernasconi-Osterwalder and Lise Johnson, 'Transparency in the Dispute Settlement Process: Country best practices', Bulletin No 2, Best Practices Series, International Institute for Sustainable Development (February 2011).

resolution mechanism, in part because of its secrecy.[145] Not only are hearings usually closed and hearing transcripts and party submissions unavailable to the public, but tribunal decisions themselves are often not released. Moreover, the very existence of an ISDS dispute may be unknown. Hence, UNCTAD refers in its regular updates on developments in ISDS to 'known' claims.[146]

Responding to these difficulties, the UNCITRAL Transparency Rules entered into force on 1 April 2014 and apply by default to ISDS proceedings initiated under the UNCITRAL Arbitration Rules pursuant to treaties concluded from that date unless the States parties otherwise agree.[147] For treaties concluded before that date, the parties to a dispute under the UNCITRAL Arbitration Rules may agree to their application, and individual States may opt in to the rules by becoming party to the Mauritius Convention[148] (meaning that the rules will apply to ISDS under a given IIA where the States parties to that IIA have opted in, once the Mauritius Convention enters into force for those parties). The rules could also be adopted by consent in non-UNCITRAL ISDS proceedings,[149] as has already occurred,[150] or by a claimant investor's acceptance of a respondent's unilateral offer to apply those rules by becoming party to the Mauritius Convention, even if the claimant's home state is not a party.[151] The UNCITRAL Transparency Rules provide for disclosure of key documents to a repository, which in turn makes available to the public relevant documents and information (subject to confidentiality, etc),[152] including the initiation of a dispute,[153] the notice of arbitration, the statement of claim, parties' submissions, transcripts of hearings where

---

[145] But see generally Emilie M Hafner-Burton and David G Victor, 'Secrecy in International Investment Arbitration: An Empirical Analysis' (2016) 7 *Journal of International Dispute Settlement* 161.

[146] See, eg, UNCTAD, 'Investor–State Dispute Settlement: Review of Developments in 2015', *IIA Issues Note No 2* (June 2016) 1.

[147] UNCITRAL Transparency Rules art 1.1.

[148] UNCITRAL Transparency Rules art 1.2; Mauritius Convention art 2.1. On the Mauritius Convention, see generally Lise Johnson, 'The Mauritius Convention on Transparency: Comments on the treaty and its role in increasing transparency of investor–State arbitration', Policy Paper, Columbia Center on Sustainable Investment (September 2014).

[149] UNCITRAL Transparency Rules art 1.9.

[150] See, eg, *BSG v Guinea*, Procedural Order, [9]–[10].

[151] Mauritius Convention art 2.2.

[152] UNCITRAL Transparency Rules art 7.

[153] UNCITRAL Transparency Rules art 2.

available, and decisions of the tribunal.[154] The rules also generally require public hearings.[155]

The UNCITRAL Transparency Rules have been described as representing 'a carefully negotiated and widely approved template that can serve as a model for how to conduct investor-State arbitrations'.[156] The Mauritius Convention has similarly been lauded as an 'instrument with constitutional implications for the international investment regime', with the potential to 'bring about a paradigm shift' in ISDS, 'establish[ing] transparency as a general principle of international investment law'.[157] The Mauritius Convention has also been assessed for its potential as a mechanism for achieving broader investment law reform with respect to existing treaties, for example in relation to the European Commission's proposed appellate court for ISDS.[158] Together, the UNCITRAL Transparency Rules and the Mauritius Convention have the potential to achieve more ambitious goals, such as enhancing consistency in decision-making and legitimacy in ISDS more generally.[159]

Although Australia was active and supportive during the negotiation of the Rules,[160] at the time of writing it has neither signed nor ratified the

---

[154] UNCITRAL Transparency Rules art 3.1.

[155] UNCITRAL Transparency Rules art 6.1.

[156] Lise Johnson et al, 'New UNCITRAL Arbitration Rules on Transparency: Application, Content and Next Steps', Vale Columbia Center on Sustainable International Investment, International Institute for Sustainable Development, and Centre for International Environmental Law (August 2013) 2. But see generally Sophie Nappert, 'The other side of transparency' (16 February 2015) 141 *Columbia FDI Perspectives* (online).

[157] Stephan W Schill, 'Editorial: The Mauritius Convention on Transparency' (2015) 16(2) *Journal of World Investment & Trade* 201, 202.

[158] See Gabrielle Kaufmann-Kohler and Michele Potestà, 'Can the Mauritius Convention serve as a model for the reform of investor–State arbitration in connection with the introduction of a permanent investment tribunal or an appeal mechanism? Analysis and roadmap', Geneva Center for International Dispute Settlement (3 June 2016).

[159] See Esmé Shirlow, 'Dawn of a New Era? The UNCITRAL Rules and UN Convention on Transparency in Treaty-Based Investor–State Arbitration' (2016) 31(3) *ICSID Review* 622, 637, 647–654.

[160] See sources cited in Esmé Shirlow, 'Recent Developments in Australia's Approach to Confidentiality and Transparency in International Arbitration' (19 December 2015) *Kluwer Arbitration Blog* (online). Australia signed the Mauritius Convention on 18 July 2017, while this book was in press.

Mauritius Convention.[161] Nor has Australia included corresponding requirements in all its PTAs since the entry into force of the UNCITRAL Transparency Rules, or allowed the default mechanism to apply to those PTAs. In particular, ChAFTA merely *allows* this kind of transparency rather than requiring it. Although the respondent 'shall' (must) make available to the public (subject to confidentiality) the request for consultations, notice of arbitration, and decisions of the tribunal,[162] the respondent '*may* make … available to the public' party pleadings and minutes or transcripts of hearings.[163] Similarly, the respondent (host State) 'may make … available to the public' written submissions by the non-disputing party (that is, the home State of the claimant investor) 'provided that prior consent is obtained from the non-disputing Party'.[164] Thus, if Australia was the respondent host State, it could choose to make available to the public its own pleadings and those of the investor claimant, but it could not release any submissions by China as the relevant home State unless China agreed.

Nevertheless, a side letter to ChAFTA confirms the States parties' agreement to enter consultations within 12 months of the treaty's entry into force (that is, by 20 December 2016) 'on the future application' to ISDS under ChAFTA of the UNCITRAL Transparency Rules.[165] KAFTA in fact contains a similar side letter.[166] However, both side letters make clear that in the absence of future agreement the UNCITRAL Transparency Rules will *not* apply to ISDS proceedings commenced pursuant to ChAFTA/KAFTA under the UNCITRAL Arbitration Rules. (Nevertheless, the KAFTA requirements are aligned with the UNCITRAL Transparency Rules, and UNCITRAL has listed KAFTA as an example of a treaty containing 'provisions modelled on' the UNCITRAL Transparency

161 See UNCITRAL, *Status: United Nations Convention on Transparency in Treaty-based Investor–State Arbitration (New York, 2014)*, <http://www.uncitral.org/uncitral/en/uncitral_texts/arbitration/2014Transparency_Convention_status.html> (last visited 7 April 2017).

162 ChAFTA art 9.17.2(a).

163 ChAFTA art 9.17.2(b) (emphasis added).

164 ChAFTA art 9.17.2(c).

165 Exchange of letters between Andrew Robb, Minister for Trade and Investment, Australia, and Gao Hucheng, Minister of Commerce, The People's Republic of China (17 June 2015).

166 Exchange of letters between Andrew Robb, Minister for Trade and Investment, Australia, and Yoon Sang-jick, Minister of Trade, Industry and Energy, Republic of Korea (8 April 2014).

Rules.)[167] The TPP contains no such side letter, such that an ISDS proceeding commenced pursuant to the TPP (assuming it enters into force) under the UNCITRAL Arbitration Rules would be subject to the UNCITRAL Transparency Rules by virtue of their incorporation in the UNCITRAL Arbitration Rules. However, as noted above, the TPP already contains detailed transparency requirements,[168] which again are similar to the UNCITRAL Transparency Rules. To the extent of any inconsistency between the TPP itself and the UNCITRAL Transparency Rules, the TPP would prevail.[169] This analysis of the TPP applies equally to the SAFTA amendments agreed in 2016, apparently with no side letter.

D Joint Decisions, Public Welfare and Tobacco Control

Following SAFTA and TAFTA, all of Australia's PTAs included provisions allowing the States parties to make particular joint determinations that would bind the tribunal in an ISDS claim. First, under ACIFTA, a respondent may request from a 'Joint FTA Committee' an interpretation (which becomes binding on the tribunal)[170] as to whether a challenged measure falls within the scope of a listed non-conforming measure.[171] Next, under AANZFTA, '[t]he tribunal shall, on its own account or at the request of a disputing party, request a joint interpretation of any provision of this Agreement that is in issue in a dispute',[172] which then binds the tribunal.[173] (Although the word 'shall' appears to impose an obligation on the tribunal (to do so whether or not requested), the parties presumably intended that the tribunal request a joint interpretation if requested to do so by a disputing party or if the tribunal chose to do so, rather than the tribunal being bound to do so on every or any possible provision.)

These kinds of provisions may be understood as a means for States parties to IIAs to regain control over the ISDS process, restricting the tribunal's authority and the right of the claimant investor to determine or

---

167 UNCITRAL, *Status: UNCITRAL Rules on Transparency in Treaty-based Investor–State Arbitration (effective date: 1 April 2014)* <http://www.uncitral.org/uncitral/en/uncitral_texts/arbitration/2014Transparency_Rules_status.html> (last visited 7 April 2017).

168 TPP art 9.24.

169 UNCITRAL Transparency Rules art 1.7.

170 ACIFTA arts 10.23.2, 10.24.2.

171 ACIFTA art 10.24.1.

172 AANZFTA ch 11 art 27.2.

173 AANZFTA ch 11 art 27.3.

argue for particular interpretations.[174] The more recent Australian FTAs make additional use of such joint decisions. KAFTA allows a Joint Committee to make determinations binding on the tribunal regarding non-conforming measures[175] and interpretation of any provision of the treaty.[176] In addition, under KAFTA, at the request of a disputing Party (the respondent host State or the claimant investor), a 'Joint Committee' may override a determination by the tribunal 'that information claimed to be protected was not properly designated',[177] in connection with the transparency provisions discussed above. Richard Braddock, then Director of DFAT's Office of Trade Negotiations, emphasised in a JSCOT hearing on KAFTA that KAFTA contains:

> more explicit safeguards for legitimate public welfare regulation than in the vast majority of Australia's agreements. In fact, compared to other agreements worldwide, KAFTA is amongst the most protective of treaties in terms of its safeguards for legitimate government regulation.[178]

Under ChAFTA, as with the earlier treaties, the States parties may issue a joint decision regarding whether a challenged measure is included in the relevant lists of non-conforming measures,[179] and a Committee on Investment may issue an interpretation of any provision of the treaty.[180] Both are binding on the tribunal as well as *subsequent* tribunals.[181] Moreover, a respondent host State may issue a notice within 30 days of receiving a request for consultations stating that it considers the challenged measure to be[182] 'non-discriminatory and for the legitimate public welfare objectives of public health, safety, the environment, public morals or public order', which may not be the subject of an ISDS claim.[183] The States parties then engage in consultations during a 90 day

---

174 See generally Eleni Methymaki and Antonious Tzanakopoulos, 'Masters of Puppets? Reassertion of Control through Joint Investment Treaty Interpretations' in Kulick, above n 132, 155.

175 KAFTA art 11.23.

176 KAFTA arts 21.3.3(c), 11.22.3.

177 KAFTA art 11.21.4(e).

178 Evidence to JSCOT, Canberra (5 August 2014) 2–3 (Richard Braddock, Director, Office of Trade Negotiations, DFAT).

179 ChAFTA art 9.19.1.

180 ChAFTA art 9.18.2.

181 ChAFTA arts 9.18.2, 9.19.2, 9.19.3.

182 ChAFTA art 9.11.5.

183 ChAFTA art 9.11.4.

period.[184] If the States parties issue a joint decision that the challenged measure falls within that description, that decision is binding on the tribunal.[185] ChAFTA does not provide for joint decisions regarding 'protected information'; the parties may have regarded this possibility as unnecessary given that the transparency requirements are less demanding than under KAFTA and some of Australia's other FTAs. With reference to the public welfare provision, DFAT Deputy Secretary Jane Adams stated before a JSCOT hearing on ChAFTA: 'we have … included a very substantial number of regulatory safeguards in this [ISDS] mechanism—perhaps more so than in any of our existing agreements'.[186]

ChAFTA's broad 'public welfare' exclusion and notice procedure do not appear in the more recent treaty text in the TPP or the SAFTA amendments agreed in 2016. TPP provides for joint decisions on non-conforming measures and interpretation of treaty provisions,[187] while adding a novel and specific carve-out for tobacco control measures from ISDS. Article 29.5 of the TPP provides:

> **Tobacco Control Measures**[11]
>
> A Party may elect to deny the benefits of Section B of Chapter 9 (Investment) with respect to claims challenging a tobacco control measure[12] of the Party. Such a claim shall not be submitted to arbitration under Section B of Chapter 9 (Investment) if a Party has made such an election. If a Party has not elected to deny benefits with respect to such claims by the time of the submission of such a claim to arbitration under Section B of Chapter 9 (Investment), a Party may elect to deny benefits during the proceedings. For greater certainty, if a Party elects to deny benefits with respect to such claims, any such claim shall be dismissed.
>
> [11] For greater certainty, this Article does not prejudice: (i) the operation of Article 9.15 (Denial of Benefits); or (ii) a Party's rights under Chapter 28 (Dispute Settlement) in relation to a tobacco control measure.
>
> [12] A tobacco control measure means a measure of a Party related to the production or consumption of manufactured tobacco products (including products made or derived from tobacco), their distribution, labelling, packaging, advertising, marketing, promotion, sale, purchase, or use, as well as enforcement measures, such as inspection, recordkeeping, and reporting requirements. For greater certainty, a measure with respect to tobacco leaf that

---

[184] ChAFTA art 9.11.6.

[185] ChAFTA art 9.18.3.

[186] Evidence to JSCOT, Canberra (17 August 2015) 22 (Jan Adams, Deputy Secretary, DFAT).

[187] TPP arts 9.25.3, 9.26, 27.2.2(f).

is not in the possession of a manufacturer of tobacco products or that is not part of a manufactured tobacco product is not a tobacco control measure.

This provision is unusual in targeting one specific type of product, or its regulation. The provision is framed so as to allow a host State to preclude ISDS with respect to tobacco control measures, either before any dispute has commenced (including as a blanket announcement with respect to all such measures) or even with respect to a particular dispute after it has commenced. Australia and New Zealand have already indicated their intention to make a blanket announcement to this effect.[188] The structure of the provision suggests that the parties aimed to avoid having to defend a claim against a tobacco control measure (as Australia and Uruguay[189] had to do under ISDS) up to the point of making out a valid exception. Rather, the aim appears to be to ensure that the proceedings are promptly terminated to save time and expense. The provision has generated significant controversy. Some tobacco control advocates have argued that it is too narrow, for example because it requires a host State to take the positive step of electing to deny the benefits of ISDS, and it defines 'tobacco control measure' so as to exclude tobacco leaf itself.[190] We and others have highlighted the dangers of the provision's narrowness in other senses:[191] its inability to assist in relation to public health and public policy matters beyond tobacco control; its potential to detract from broader systemic reform of the investment treaty regime, which is problematic generally rather than only in relation to tobacco control; and its uncertain impact on ISDS in treaties lacking such a provision.[192]

---

188 *Notification by Australia pursuant to Article 29.5 of the Trans-Pacific Partnership Agreement* (15 February 2016); *National Interest Analysis (Australia)* [2016] ATNIA 4 (4 February 2016) [5]; *Trans-Pacific Partnership National Interest Analysis (New Zealand)* (25 January 2016) 252.

189 *Philip Morris v Uruguay*, Jurisdictional Decision; *Philip Morris v Uruguay*, Award. See further discussion in Chapter 2 of this volume.

190 See, eg, Katherine Hirono, Deborah Gleeson and Becky Freeman, 'To What Extent Does a Tobacco Carve-Out Protect Public Health in the Trans-Pacific Partnership Agreement?' (2016) 26(2) *Public Health Research & Practice* e2621622.

191 See, eg, Andrew D Mitchell, Tania Voon and Devon Whittle, 'Public Health and the Trans-Pacific Partnership Agreement' (2015) 5(2) *Asian Journal of International Law* 279, 291–293; Simon Lester, 'The TPP Tobacco Carveout: A Triumph of Politics Over Good Policy' (1 December 2015) *Huffington Post* (online).

192 See Mitchell and Munro, above n 23.

The amendments agreed to SAFTA in 2016 include a new use for a joint committee of the States parties. Instead of allowing the parties to issue binding interpretations of any SAFTA provision, or regarding whether a challenged measure is included in the relevant list of non-conforming measures, SAFTA provides in its financial services chapter for 'the authorities of the respondent and the Party of the claimant' to issue (on request by the respondent in an ISDS proceeding) a joint determination on whether certain exceptions in the Financial Services chapter apply to the measure.[193] Should the respondent's authorities be unable to agree with the home State of the claimant investor, the matter falls to be determined by a 'Chapter 16 arbitral tribunal',[194] that is, a tribunal set up under the procedures for resolving State-State disputes rather than ISDS. The TPP,[195] KAFTA[196] and ACIFTA[197] include similar mechanisms in their financial services chapters.

SAFTA's 2016 agreed amendments also include in Article 22 of the Investment Chapter (ch 8) a carve-out from ISDS for tobacco control, going further than the TPP carve-out, in that it does not require the host State to 'elect' to exclude ISDS, and the definition of tobacco control measure appears slightly broader (not excluding tobacco leaf):[198]

Tobacco Control Measures

> No claim may be brought under this Section in respect of a tobacco control measure[19] of a Party.
>
> [19] 'Tobacco control measure' means a measure of a Party related to tobacco products (including products made or derived from tobacco), such as for their production, consumption, distribution, labelling, packaging, advertising, marketing, promotion, sale, purchase, or use, as well as fiscal measures such as internal taxes and excise taxes, and enforcement measures, such as inspection, recordkeeping, and reporting requirements. 'Tobacco products' means products under Chapter 24 of the Harmonised System, including processed tobacco, or any product that contains tobacco, that is manufactured to be used for smoking, sucking, chewing or snuffing.

---

193 SAFTA 2016 ch 9 arts 22.2, 21.4.

194 SAFTA 2016 ch 9 arts 22.2(c), 22.3.

195 TPP art 11.22.

196 KAFTA art 8.19.

197 ACIFTA art 12.18.

198 The internal trade liberalisation between Canada's provinces and territories goes further, in excluding tobacco control measures from the agreement altogether: *Canadian Free Trade Agreement* (April 2017) art 806.

In the agreement to amend SAFTA, footnote 18 to section B (on ISDS) of ch 8 also excludes from ISDS certain Australian schemes relating to health and pharmaceuticals:

> No claim may be brought under this Section in respect of the following measures of Australia: measures comprising or related to the Pharmaceutical Benefits Scheme, Medicare Benefits Scheme, Therapeutic Goods Administration and Office of the Gene Technology Regulator. A reference to a body or program in this footnote includes any successor of that body or program.

This incremental approach to excluding matters from ISDS (which is in addition to exclusions in non-conforming measures lists) appears to have taken the place of the broader 'public welfare' exclusion in ChAFTA. The more product/program-specific approach may provide more certainty to Australia (and Singapore and other TPP countries), but it also provides less scope for protection of analogous programs, products and policies, potentially creating a risk that future developments will reduce its utility. Because of the difficulty of negotiating amendments to PTAs and other treaties—particularly those including multiple parties—if developments arise due to new technologies or new health risks, the specific carve-outs may not protect them (although the reference in the new footnote 18 of SAFTA to 'successor' programs might cover some newer developments). Unfortunately this more incremental approach appears to match the growing list of specific examples of measures directed at public health that are being added to the annex on expropriation in Australia's recent PTAs, as discussed above.

E Code of Conduct

Under the TPP, the 'TPP Commission' is to establish rules of procedure for panels resolving State-State disputes under ch 28,[199] which rules are to include a 'code of conduct' for panellists.[200] In turn, before the TPP enters into force, the TPP parties are to:

> provide guidance on the application of the Code of Conduct for Dispute Settlement Proceedings under Chapter 28 (Dispute Settlement) to arbitrators selected to serve on [ISDS] tribunals pursuant to this Article, including any necessary modifications to the Code of Conduct to conform to the context of [ISDS]. The Parties shall also provide guidance on the application of other relevant rules or guidelines on conflicts of interest in international arbitration.

---

199 TPP art 27.2.1(f).
200 TPP art 28.10.1(d).

> Arbitrators shall comply with that guidance in addition to the applicable arbitral rules regarding independence and impartiality of arbitrators.[201]

The 2016 amendments to SAFTA go further in setting out in annex 7 the relevant code of conduct applicable to both State–State dispute settlement under ch 16 and ISDS under ch 8. The obligations on arbitrators include:

- being independent and impartial; avoiding impropriety and direct and indirect conflicts of interest;[202]
- disclosing before selection as an arbitrator interests and relationships that might reasonably create the appearance of impropriety;[203]
- not being 'influenced by self-interest, outside pressure, political considerations, public clamour, loyalty to a disputing party or non-disputing Party, or fear of criticism';[204] and
- not using the 'position on the tribunal to advance any personal or private interests'.[205]

These obligations may be useful, but they do little to clarify what constitutes a conflict of interest or to reduce the likelihood of such a conflict arising. For example, a rule preventing arbitrators from acting simultaneously as counsel or preventing counsel from acting as arbitrators within a given subsequent period of years might be effective in reducing potential for conflicts and for removing the discretion from individual arbitrators to determine when they may properly sit as an arbitrator or act as counsel.

V EU'S PROPOSED INVESTMENT COURT INCLUDING APPEALS

The European Commission has proposed, in the context of negotiations with the US on the TTIP, a shift away from ad hoc arbitration as the primary means of ISDS and towards a more permanent investment court, including an appeals mechanism.[206] Initially, this approach has been

---

201 TPP art 9.22.6.
202 SAFTA 2016 annex 7 [1], [11].
203 SAFTA 2016 annex 7 [2].
204 SAFTA 2016 annex 7 [12].
205 SAFTA 2016 annex 7 [14].
206 European Commission, *Concept Paper: Investment in TTIP and beyond—the path for reform* (May 2015) 4.

incorporated in the CETA[207] and the EU–Viet Nam FTA.[208] Ultimately, the EU envisages that the new approach will allow the development of a 'multilateral investment tribunal and appellate mechanism'.[209] Ethical requirements go some way to enhancing independence and impartiality of judges in such a system. In particular, instead of acting on an ad hoc basis, judges would be appointed for a term of six years,[210] and upon appointment they would not be able to act 'as counsel or as party-appointed expert or witness in any pending or new investment protection dispute under this or any other agreement or domestic law'.[211] However, it is not clear that this latter obligation continues beyond the judge's appointment (in contrast to concrete restrictions in the WTO Appellate Body regarding continuing ethical obligations).[212] In addition, the fact that the judges' terms may be renewed once[213] creates the possibility of disputing parties attempting to influence judges' reasoning and decision-making through the reappointment process, as has happened in the WTO Appellate Body context,[214] where judges have terms of four years, also renewable once.[215]

Nevertheless, Australia's FTAs focus on less radical reforms than the EU proposal, as noted above. The more recent FTAs merely contemplate the possibility of an appellate mechanism. For example, the SAFTA amendments agreed in 2016 provide in art 28.11 of ch 8 (on investment):

> In the event that an appellate mechanism for reviewing awards rendered by investor–State dispute settlement tribunals is developed in the future under other institutional arrangements including under another Agreement to which both Parties are party, the Parties *shall consider* whether awards rendered

---

[207] CETA ch 8 arts 8.27–8.30. See also EU TTIP ch II proposal (12 November 2015) arts 9–11.

[208] EU–Viet Nam FTA ch II s 3 arts 12–15.

[209] CETA ch 8 art 8.29; EU–Viet Nam FTA ch II s 3 art 15. See also EU TTIP ch II proposal (12 November 2015) ch II s 3 art 12.

[210] EU TTIP ch II proposal (12 November 2015) ch II s 3 arts 9.5, 10.5.

[211] EU TTIP ch II proposal (12 November 2015) ch II s 3 art 11.1.

[212] WTO, *Post-Employment Guidelines: Communication from the Appellate Body*, WTO doc WT/AB/22 (16 April 2014).

[213] EU TTIP ch II proposal (12 November 2015) ch II s 3 arts 9.5, 10.5.

[214] See, eg, *Statement by the United States at the Meeting of the WTO Dispute Settlement Body* (23 May 2016); 'US Slammed at DSB For Blocking Korean Appellate Body Reappointment' (24 May 2016) *Inside US Trade* (online); Robert Howse, 'The World Trade Organization 20 Years On: Global Governance by Judiciary' (2016) 27(1) *European Journal of International Law* 9, 71.

[215] DSU art 17.2.

> under Article 33 (Awards) should be subject to that appellate mechanism. The Parties shall strive to ensure that any such appellate mechanism they consider adopting provides for transparency of proceedings similar to the transparency provisions established in Article 29 (Transparency of Arbitral Proceedings).[216]

Similar 'best endeavours' type provisions appear in the TPP[217] and KAFTA.[218] KAFTA also provides for the parties to 'consider' within three years of entry into force whether to establish a bilateral appellate mechanism for ISDS,[219] while ChAFTA states that within three years of entry into force the States parties '*shall* commence negotiations with a view to establishing an appellate mechanism', which 'would hear appeals on questions of law'.[220]

VI CONCLUSION

Australia's approach to ISDS requires re-examination, not only with respect to the consent to ISDS in BITs, but more broadly. If ISDS is not justified in Australia's relationship with New Zealand (as confirmed in the ANZCERTA Investment Protocol and in side letters to AANZFTA and the TPP), is it nevertheless justified in Australia's relationship with Canada, the United States and Japan (notwithstanding its exclusion from AUSFTA and JAEPA respectively)? The inclusion of ISDS in the TPP need not be determinative, even though the 12 negotiating parties have already signed the TPP, given that the US has now withdrawn and unless that country re-engages the TPP cannot enter into force in its current form. In any case, Australia should be pursuing an ambitious reform agenda with respect to the investment regime in general and ISDS in particular. Rather than carving out specific areas one by one (such as tobacco and the PBS), Australia has the potential to play a role in broader amelioration of the investment treaty system. Australia could undertake this role not only by supporting novel approaches such as the EU's proposed investment court system, the UNCITRAL Transparency Rules and the associated Mauritius Convention, but also by adopting individual treaty mechanisms such as the provision for States parties under ChAFTA to make joint determinations concerning public welfare measures. Australia's significance in this regard is perhaps enhanced with the

[216] Emphasis added.
[217] TPP art 9.23.11.
[218] KAFTA art 11.20.13.
[219] KAFTA annex 11–E.
[220] ChAFTA art 9.23 (emphasis added).

demise of the TPP, given the ongoing negotiations towards the RCEP, in which China is participating but where Australia may nevertheless take a lead role.

6. Environmental Protection: Moderate Safeguards and Novel Opportunities

I INTRODUCTION

The previous chapters of this book examine four important subjects covered by Australian PTAs and BITs (intellectual property, services, investment, and ISDS), considering the balance between the economic and welfare benefits of obligations in these areas and their impact on Australia's regulatory autonomy. This chapter takes a slightly different approach, by focussing on a specific area of government activity—regulating to protect the environment—and considering some of the most significant ways in which Australian PTAs and BITs affect regulatory space in this area.

The relationship between international economic obligations and the environment has been the subject of a considerable body of commentary and academic literature,[1] and the environment is often a focus of concern about the impact of PTAs and BITs on regulatory autonomy.[2] In relation

[1] See, eg, Duncan Brack, *Trade and Environment: Conflict or Compatibility* (Taylor and Francis, 2013); Erich Vranes, *Trade and the Environment: Fundamental Issues in International Law, WTO Law, and Legal Theory* (Oxford University Press, 2009); Nathalie Bernasconi-Osterwalder, John Howard Jackson and Edith Brown Weiss (eds), *Reconciling Environment and Trade* (Martinus Nijhoff Publishers/Koninklijke Brill, 2nd ed, 2008); Steve Charnovitz, 'Environment and Health under WTO Dispute Settlement' (1998) 32 *International Lawyer* 901; OECD (ed), *Environment and Regional Trade Agreements* (OECD, 2007); Thomas Waelde and Abba Kolo, 'Environmental Regulation, Investment Protection and "Regulatory Taking" in International Law' (2001) 50 *International and Comparative Law Quarterly* 811; Jorge Viñuales, *Foreign Investment and the Environment in International Law* (Cambridge University Press, 2012); Kate Miles, *The Origins of International Investment Law: Empire, Environment and the Safeguarding of Capital* (Cambridge University Press, 2013).

[2] See, eg, Peter Hannam, 'Trans-Pacific Partnership Bad for the Environment, Green Groups Say' (7 October 2015) *Sydney Morning Herald* (online); Sierra Club, 'A Dirty Deal: How the Transpacific Partnership Threatens Our

to trade obligations, several WTO cases have considered the compatibility of regulatory measures relating to the environment with obligations relating to trade in goods under the GATT 1994,[3] technical barriers to trade (for example, concerning labelling or product ingredients) under the TBT Agreement,[4] or sanitary and phytosanitary measures (for example, concerning food safety) under the SPS Agreement.[5] These disputes have addressed bans on the importation of certain products to protect human, animal, or plant life or health,[6] labelling requirements relating to environmental standards (such as 'dolphin safe' tuna),[7] and measures relating to fuel quality and the minimisation of noxious emissions.[8] Although Australia has been a respondent in only a small number of disputes that have proceeded to the stage of a Panel Report in the WTO dispute settlement system,[9] two of these disputes found Australian quarantine and import restrictions on agricultural products—ostensibly to prevent the introduction of diseases that could affect local flora and fauna—inconsistent with the SPS Agreement.[10]

These WTO disputes demonstrate the relevance of obligations relating to trade in goods—particularly those concerning non-discrimination, technical barriers to trade, or sanitary and phytosanitary measures—to environmental protection measures. However, this chapter does not focus

---

Environment' (December 2015) <https://content.sierraclub.org/creative-archive/sites/content.sierraclub.org.creative-archive/files/pdfs/1197%20Dirty%20Deals%20Report%20Web_03_low.pdf> (last visited 7 April 2017).

[3] See, eg, Appellate Body Report, *US—Gasoline*; Appellate Body Report, *US—Shrimp*; Appellate Body Report, *Brazi—Retreaded Tyres. EC—Seal Products* was also related to the environment although it was largely argued on the basis of animal welfare pursuant to the public morals exception in GATT art XX(a): Panel Reports, *EC—Seal Products*, [7.640]; Appellate Body Reports, *EC—Seal Products*, [5.290].

[4] See, eg, Appellate Body Report, *US—Tuna II (Mexico).*

[5] See, eg, Appellate Body Report, *EC—Hormones*; Panel Reports, *EC—Approval and Marketing of Biotech Products.*

[6] See, eg, Appellate Body Report, *Brazil—Retreaded Tyres.*

[7] See, eg, Appellate Body Report, *US—Tuna II (Mexico).*

[8] See, eg, Appellate Body Report, *US—Gasoline.*

[9] See generally Andrew D Mitchell, Elizabeth Sheargold and Tania Voon, 'Australia and International Trade Law' in Emily Crawford and Donald R Rothwell (eds), *International Law in Australia* (Thomson Lawbook Co, 3rd ed, 2017) 317, 322–324.

[10] Appellate Body Report, *Australia—Apples*; Appellate Body Report, *Australia—Salmon.*

on obligations relating to trade in goods. Almost all of Australia's PTAs[11] include obligations of non-discrimination with respect to trade in goods,[12] as well as more specific disciplines relating to technical barriers to trade[13] and sanitary and phytosanitary measures,[14] but all these provisions largely mirror obligations contained in the relevant WTO agreement.[15] At least at present, given the WTO's well-established dispute settlement mechanism and the limited functionality of State-to-State dispute settlement under PTAs in general (apart from NAFTA) and Australia's PTAs in particular, Australia's PTA and BIT partners are most likely to raise any disputes in these areas within the WTO dispute settlement mechanism.[16]

This chapter instead focuses on the features of Australia's PTAs and BITs that we consider most likely to shape Australia's regulatory autonomy in relation to environmental measures, in addition to the pre-existing WTO requirements: namely, the investment standards discussed in Chapter 4, and the threat of enforcement of those obligations through ISDS, discussed in Chapter 5. In part II of this chapter we consider how investment protections affect regulatory autonomy to enact environmental measures, through a detailed examination of relevant NAFTA cases. This analysis provides important insights into how investment treaty tribunals may interpret and apply the corresponding obligations of Australia's PTAs and BITs in relation to environmental measures.

---

[11] The exception is ANZCERTA, which establishes a more complete free trade area than any other Australian PTA, and which was first concluded well before the establishment of the WTO, and two decades before any other Australian PTA: see our discussion in Chapter 1 part IVA.

[12] See TAFTA ch 2; AUSFTA ch 2; ACIFTA ch 3; AANZFTA ch 2; MAFTA ch 2; KAFTA ch 2; JAEPA ch 2; ChAFTA ch 2; TPP ch 2; SAFTA 2016 ch 2.

[13] See TAFTA ch 7; AUSFTA ch 8; ACIFTA ch 7; AANZFTA ch 6; MAFTA ch 6; KAFTA ch 5; JAEPA ch 6; ChAFTA ch 6; TPP ch 8; SAFTA 2016 ch 5.

[14] See TAFTA ch 6; AUSFTA ch 7; ACIFTA ch 6; AANZFTA ch 5; MAFTA ch 5; KAFTA ch 5; JAEPA ch 5; ChAFTA ch 5; TPP ch 7; SAFTA 2016 ch 5.

[15] Of Australia's PTAs, the agreement with the most novel requirements in these areas, particularly in terms of sanitary and phytosanitary measures, is the TPP. See DFAT, *Trans-Pacific Partnership Agreement Chapter Summary: Sanitary and Phytosanitary Measures* (Fact Sheet updated 7 December 2016).

[16] For example, New Zealand (Australia's co-party to the ANZCERTA), challenged Australia's import regime relating to apples through the WTO dispute settlement mechanism, successfully alleging that Australia had breached obligations under the SPS Agreement. See Appellate Body Report, *Australia—Apples*.

Part III of the chapter then considers the provisions of Australia's PTAs and BITs that are specifically designed to protect regulatory autonomy for environmental measures, including general exceptions clauses. The theme running through parts II and III of the chapter is that substantive investment standards imposed by Australia's PTAs and BITs, and the possibility of enforcement through ISDS, may pose a threat to Australia's autonomy to regulate to protect the environment. However, in part IV of the chapter we take a different perspective, examining how PTAs and BITs could encourage or even require Australia to improve or better enforce its environmental standards. This part includes a consideration of dedicated chapters relating to the environment contained in three of Australia's PTAs,[17] as well as the potential for ISDS to be used as a means for foreign investors in Australia or Australia as a host State to enforce Australia's environmental regulations.

As a federal system of government, Australia's laws and regulations are made at both national and state/territory levels. The Australian Constitution grants no specific legislative power to the federal government to enact environmental laws.[18] However, the federal government has enacted one major piece of environmental legislation relating to 'matters of national environmental significance',[19] drawing on authority from other constitutional heads of power, such as the regulation of trade and commerce, and external affairs.[20] The limited scope for environmental regulation by the federal government in Australia means that most environmental regulation is enacted and enforced by Australian states[21] or territories or by local government. Thus, although the Australian federal government enters into obligations under PTAs and BITs, these obligations generally apply in relation to environmental laws, regulations and administrative decisions at the state or local government level in Australia.[22]

---

[17] AUSFTA ch 19; KAFTA ch 18; TPP ch 20.

[18] See Australian Constitution s 51.

[19] *Environment Protection and Biodiversity Conservation Act 1999* (Cth) ch 2 pt 3.

[20] Australian Constitution s 51(i), (xxix). See also Dr Allan Hawke, *Report of the Independent Review of the Environment Protection and Biodiversity Conservation Act 1999: Final Report* (October 2009) 3.

[21] See, eg, *Environment Protection Act 1970* (Vic); *Protection of the Environment Operations Act 1997* (NSW); *Environmental Protection Act 1994* (Qld).

[22] The responsibility of States for actions of all levels of government, whether they are central or territorial, is a well-recognised principle of international law and the default rule. See International Law Commission, *Articles on*

II DOES INVESTMENT PROTECTION UNDERMINE ENVIRONMENTAL REGULATION? ASSURANCES FROM NAFTA CH 11 DISPUTES

To date, no Australian regulations relating to environmental protection have been challenged under Australia's PTAs or BITs. However, several significant investor–State disputes have addressed environmental measures (or measures purporting to have an environmental purpose) enacted by other host States. In particular, the investment obligations of NAFTA, contained in NAFTA ch 11, have given rise to a number of significant ISDS cases concerning legislation, regulations or administrative decisions regarding environmental protection. In this part of the chapter we consider these cases in detail, to reveal how the investment standards imposed by Australia's PTAs and BITs may affect regulatory autonomy in connection with the environment.

These NAFTA cases are not the only investment disputes to date involving environmental measures,[23] but they provide a suitable case study for this book for four main reasons. First, the existence of a series of cases under a single treaty allows for more detailed consideration of the nuances of key obligations, such as fair and equitable treatment and indirect expropriation, and how these apply in the context of environmental regulation. Second, because of the influence of US drafting practice on key aspects of the investment chapters of Australian PTAs,[24] cases applying and interpreting NAFTA could be a source of reference or guidance for future tribunals interpreting and applying Australia's investment obligations. Third, in most of these NAFTA disputes, the respondent State is either Canada or the US: two countries that employ a broadly similar approach to Australia in developing and implementing regulatory

---

Responsibility of States for Internationally Wrongful Acts in UN General Assembly Resolution, *Responsibility of States for Internationally Wrongful Acts*, A/RES/56/83 (28 January 2002) annex art 4. In relation to PTAs and BITs, obligations do sometimes clarify whether they apply only to central, regional or local levels of government. See, eg, JAEPA art 9.2(e) (definition of 'measure adopted or maintained by a Party').

23 Examples of investor–State disputes assessing the consistency of environmental regulations with other BITs and PTAs include: *Tecmed v Mexico*, Award; *Al Tamimi v Oman*, Award; *Copper Mesa Mining v Ecuador*, Award; *Bear Creek Mining v Peru*, Respondent's Counter-Memorial; *Vattenfall v Germany*, Notice of Arbitration.

24 For example, in relation to the minimum standard of treatment. See Chapter 4 part IIB2.

measures. Finally, like Australia, all three NAFTA countries (Canada, Mexico and the US) have federal systems of government in which different levels of government are involved in legislative and administrative actions affecting the environment. Many of these disputes involve measures taken at the sub-national level, highlighting the relevance of this level of decision-making for Australia's potential liability to foreign investors under its PTAs and BITs.

In the following sections, we first assess the comparability of key investment obligations under NAFTA and Australian IIAs, before turning to examine seven NAFTA ch 11 disputes involving environmental measures, classified according to whether the measures were found consistent or inconsistent with the relevant NAFTA provisions. We conclude the section by identifying lessons for Australia from these seven disputes.

A Comparing Key Provisions of NAFTA Chapter 11 with Australian BITs and PTAs

As will be seen in the discussion of the cases that follows in parts IIB and IIC, three of the investment obligations contained in NAFTA ch 11 are repeatedly raised by investors challenging environmental regulations: art 1105 (minimum standard of treatment, including FET), art 1110 (expropriation), and art 1102 (national treatment). We address these in turn below in comparison to the corresponding obligations in Australian IIAs. The minimum standard of treatment and expropriation obligations contained in Australia's IIAs are discussed in detail in Chapter 4 of this volume and are revisited briefly here to compare them to the NAFTA text.

Nearly all of Australia's BITs provide a simple formulation of the minimum standard of treatment, stating that each party shall 'ensure fair and equitable treatment in its own territory to investments'.[25] The language of NAFTA art 1105 provides minimal additional guidance, by referring to FET as a part of the treatment required 'in accordance with international law'. As discussed in Chapter 4, in response to the interpretation of the FET obligation in NAFTA art 1105 by ch 11 tribunals, the NAFTA Free Trade Commission issued an interpretation of art 1105 seeking to narrow the scope of the standard.[26] The language used by the NAFTA Free Trade Commission, in particular its reference to

---

[25] Australia–China BIT art III(a).

[26] NAFTA Free Trade Commission, *Notes of Interpretation of Certain Chapter 11 Provisions* (31 July 2001) preamble.

the customary international law minimum standard of treatment as a limitation or ceiling on the standard required by the FET provision, is reflected in Australia's PTAs that contain an FET obligation.[27] In relation to Australia's FET provisions in PTAs in particular, arbitral decisions applying NAFTA art 1105 may provide useful guidance.

With regard to expropriation, the NAFTA treaty language is similar to that provided in Australia's BITs. These treaties cover indirect expropriation through regulatory measures, through references to measures that are 'equivalent'[28] or 'having a similar effect'[29] to a direct expropriation or nationalisation. NAFTA art 1110 covers measures that indirectly expropriate an investment or are otherwise 'tantamount to an expropriation'. Unlike these earlier provisions, Australian PTAs beginning with the AUSFTA tend to narrow the scope of the expropriation obligation, particularly in relation to regulatory measures.[30] Thus, NAFTA cases on indirect expropriation under art 1110 are most analogous to Australia's obligations under its BITs and its earliest PTAs;[31] the scope of indirect expropriation under many of Australia's later PTAs may be narrower, particularly with regard to measures taken for a public purpose such as environmental protection.

In Chapter 4, we did not discuss national treatment obligations relating to investors or investment in detail, as they are not included in many of Australia's BITs.[32] However, as shown below, discrimination against foreign investors was central to some of the NAFTA cases in which a respondent State failed in its defence of an environmental measure.[33] Thus, in relation to regulatory autonomy for environmental protection, the extent of national treatment obligations in Australia's BITs and PTAs is important.

NAFTA's national treatment obligation in art 1102 provides:

---

27 See Chapter 4 part IIB2.

28 See, eg, Australia–Papua New Guinea BIT art 7(1); Australia–Viet Nam BIT art 7(1).

29 See, eg, Australia–China BIT art VIII.1.

30 See Chapter 4 part IIC1.

31 See SAFTA 2003 ch 8 art 9; TAFTA art 912.

32 The BITs without national treatment obligations are: Australia–Papua New Guinea BIT; Australia–Hungary BIT; Australia–Poland BIT; Australia–Indonesia BIT; Australia–Czech Republic BIT; Australia–Egypt BIT; Australia–Lithuania BIT; Australia–Uruguay BIT; Australia–Indonesia BIT; Australia–Lao PDR BIT; Australia–Pakistan BIT; Australia–Philippines BIT; Australia–Romania BIT.

33 See, eg, *SD Myers v Canada*, Partial Award, [255].

1. Each Party shall accord to investors of another Party treatment no less favorable than that it accords, in like circumstances, to its own investors with respect to the establishment, acquisition, expansion, management, conduct, operation, and sale or other disposition of investments.
2. Each Party shall accord to investments of investors of another Party treatment no less favorable than that it accords, in like circumstances, to investments of its own investors with respect to the establishment, acquisition, expansion, management, conduct, operation, and sale or other disposition of investments.

These paragraphs are relatively simple statements of the national treatment standard, providing no substantive guidance to tribunals in defining 'like circumstances'. Similar standards are included in virtually all of Australia's PTAs and BITs that include a national treatment obligation relating to investment/investors,[34] although as noted above many of Australia's BITs contain no such obligation.

A few Australian IIAs have additional elements in their national treatment provisions, which may narrow their scope in comparison to the NAFTA provision. A small number of agreements qualify the national treatment obligation such that national treatment is owed to investors 'subject to [the host State's] laws, regulations and investment policies'.[35] This language seems almost to eviscerate the national treatment obligation.

A less dramatic narrowing of the scope of the national treatment obligation is contained in a footnote to the national treatment provision of the TPP. Footnote 14 of the TPP investment chapter (ch 9) reads:

> For greater certainty, whether treatment is accorded in 'like circumstances' under Article 9.4 (National Treatment) or Article 9.5 (Most-Favoured-Nation Treatment) depends on the totality of the circumstances, including whether the relevant treatment distinguishes between investors or investments on the basis of legitimate public welfare objectives.

Through this footnote, the TPP explicitly brings a consideration of the purpose of a measure (such as environmental protection) into the assessment of whether the measure is discriminatory for the purposes of

[34] See Australia–Hong Kong BIT art 3; Australia–Peru BIT, protocol in relation to art 4; Australia–Sri Lanka BIT art 4.1; Australia–Mexico BIT art 4.2; TAFTA art 907; AUSFTA art 11.4; ACIFTA art 10.3; AANZFTA ch 11 art 4; MAFTA art 12.4 (but see art 12.16.4); ANZCERTA Investment Protocol art 5; KAFTA art 11.3; JAEPA art 14.3; ChAFTA art 9.3; TPP art 9.4; SAFTA 2016 ch 8 art 4.

[35] Australia–Argentina BIT art 5. See also Australia–Turkey BIT art 4.2.

the national treatment or MFN treatment obligations. The same kind of footnote appears in the amendments agreed to SAFTA in 2016,[36] and in the TPP and SAFTA with respect to the non-discrimination obligations in the services chapters,[37] as discussed in Chapter 2 of this volume.

This clarification in the TPP and the SAFTA amendments is important, particularly given that the WTO Appellate Body has refused to include a consideration of regulatory purpose[38] (or the 'aims and effects')[39] of a measure in determining likeness for the purposes of the non-discrimination obligations in GATT 1994[40] and GATS.[41] As noted in Chapter 2, the WTO Appellate Body has also declined to consider regulatory purpose in identifying less favourable treatment for the purposes of the MFN obligation in GATT art I:1, the national treatment obligation in GATT art III:4,[42] and the non-discrimination obligations in GATS arts II:1 and XVII.[43] In contrast, the Appellate Body takes a different approach to the non-discrimination obligations in TBT art 2.1,[44] as noted in Chapter 2. Moreover, several NAFTA tribunals have considered the purpose of a measure in assessing its consistency with art 1102, despite the absence of a textual direction to do so.[45]

Without overlooking the important variations between investment obligations contained in Australia's BITs and PTAs, the relevant NAFTA provisions can be understood as analogous to those obligations in at least some key respects. Bearing in mind how variations in the drafting of these obligations may affect their scope, the following sections examine how NAFTA ch 11 tribunals have interpreted and applied NAFTA

---

36 SAFTA ch 7 n 8.

37 TPP ch 10 n 2; SAFTA 2016 ch 7 n 3.

38 See generally Andrew D Mitchell, David Heaton and Caroline Henckels, *Non-Discrimination and the Role of Regulatory Purpose in International Trade and Investment Law* (Edward Elgar, 2016).

39 See Robert E Hudec, 'GATT/WTO Constraints on National Regulation: Requiem for an "Aims and Effects" Test' (1998) 32 *The International Lawyer* 619; Tania Voon, *Cultural Products in the World Trade Organization* (Cambridge University Press, 2007) 82–89.

40 See, eg, Appellate Body Report, *EC—Bananas III*, [216], [241].

41 See, eg, Appellate Body Report, *EC—Bananas III*, [241].

42 Appellate Body Reports, *EC—Seal Products*, art 5.125.

43 Appellate Body Report, *Argentina—Financial Services*, [6.106], [6.111], [6.112], [6.115], [6.121] (in *obiter dicta*).

44 See, eg, Appellate Body Report, *US—Clove Cigarettes*, [215].

45 See, eg, *SD Myers v Canada*, Partial Award, [254]; *Pope & Talbot v Canada*, Merits Award Phase 2, [78]; *Clayton and Bilcon v Canada*, Award, [722]–[724].

obligations on the minimum standard of treatment (including FET), expropriation, and national treatment with respect to environmental measures.

B Environmental Measures Found Consistent with NAFTA

In the following three cases—*Methanex v US*, *Glamis Gold v US* and *Chemtura v Canada*—the respondent State successfully defended its challenged measures on the basis that they were legitimate environmental regulations rather than violations of NAFTA's investment protections.

1 *Methanex v US*

Methanex, the Canadian claimant, brought a claim against the US under NAFTA to challenge a Californian ban on the sale and use of the fuel additive MTBE.[46] The ban was effected through a 1999 executive order by the Governor of California.[47] Two years earlier, the Californian government had passed a bill requiring the University of California to conduct a study comparing the effects on the environment of MTBE with those of other fuel additives (such as ethanol).[48] The executive order stated in its recital that it was based on the results of the University of California study (including peer review by other experts and agencies), which found that, 'while MTBE has provided California with clean air benefits, because of leaking fuel storage tanks MTBE poses an environmental threat to groundwater and drinking water'.[49]

Methanex alleged that, before the ban, Governor Davis had been in contact with one of its competitors, Archer Daniels Midland Company (known as ADM),[50] a US company that produces ethanol. In addition, Methanex alleged that ADM had contributed to Governor Davis' electoral campaign.[51] Methanex produced methanol, which it alleged was interchangeable with ethanol, as both compounds' respective ethers can be used as oxygenates in fuel.[52] Although Methanex was at the time the world's largest producer of methanol (the 'feedstock' of MTBE), it never

---

[46] *Methanex v US*, Final Award, pt I, [1].

[47] California Executive Order D–5–99 (25 March 1999), appendix 2 to *Methanex v US*, Final Award.

[48] *Methanex v US*, Final Award, pt II, ch D, [10].

[49] *Methanex v US*, Final Award, pt II, ch D, [15].

[50] *Methanex v US*, Final Award, pt III, ch B, [13]–[14].

[51] *Methanex v US*, Final Award, pt III, ch B, [13]–[14].

[52] *Methanex v US*, Final Award, pt II, ch D, [6].

produced or sold MTBE itself.[53] In addition to having similar uses, Methanex alleged that methanol and ethanol have similar environmental impacts, with both substances having been detected in local groundwater.[54] In Methanex's submission, California had effectively acknowledged that the contamination of groundwater resulted from poor regulation of the underground storage tanks used for fuel.[55] Methanex claimed that MTBE was a 'safe, effective and economic component of gasoline' that it 'produce[d] significant environmental and other benefits'.[56]

Based on this view of the facts, Methanex alleged that the Californian measures had treated it less favourably than domestic ethanol producers, such as ADM, in violation of NAFTA art 1102. Methanex also alleged that this intentional discrimination against foreign investors was not fair and equitable, as required by NAFTA art 1105, and that the measures effectively expropriated a significant portion of Methanex's investment, in breach of NAFTA art 1110. The Tribunal dismissed each of these claims, largely on the basis of the Tribunal's general finding that 'Methanex's contention that the California ban was designed to transfer the oxygenate market to ethanol ... is simply unsupportable on the evidence'.[57]

The Tribunal conducted a detailed analysis of scientific evidence put forward by both parties,[58] accepting the University of California report as 'reflecting a serious, objective and scientific approach to a complex problem in California'.[59] The Tribunal held that the peer review and public consultations conducted after the study were 'the best evidence that it was not the product of a political sham engineered by California'.[60] The Tribunal found no credible evidence of any protectionist intent with respect to the US ethanol industry, nor any intent to harm foreign methanol producers.[61] Instead, the Tribunal held that California's measures relating to MTBE were 'motivated by the honest belief, held in

---

53 *Methanex v US*, Final Award, pt II, ch D, [3].
54 *Methanex v US*, Final Award, pt II, ch D, [24].
55 *Methanex v US*, Final Award, pt II, ch D, [24].
56 *Methanex v US*, Final Award, pt II, ch D, [2].
57 *Methanex v US*, Final Award, pt III, ch B, [55].
58 See generally *Methanex v US*, Final Award, Part III, Chapter A.
59 *Methanex v US*, Final Award, pt III, ch A, [101].
60 *Methanex v US*, Final Award, pt III, ch A, [101].
61 *Methanex v US*, Final Award, pt III, ch A, [102].

good faith and on reasonable scientific grounds, that MTBE contaminated groundwater and was difficult and expensive to clean up'.[62] These factual findings by the Tribunal were critical to the outcome of the case, illustrating the importance of a tribunal's assessment of whether an environmental measure has a *bona fide* public policy goal.

The Tribunal also made more specific findings relevant to each of Methanex's substantive claims. In relation to the national treatment claim, the Tribunal held that it would be 'perverse' to ignore close comparators of Methanex (that is, US methanol producers affected similarly to Methanex) and instead focus on the effects on less comparable US entities (that is, US ethanol producers such as ADM).[63] In addition, the Tribunal found that methanol and ethanol products did not compete with each another; therefore ethanol producers were not in 'like circumstances' to Methanex.[64] As Methanex was not being treated any less favourably than US methanol producers—that is, domestic entities in 'like circumstances'—the Tribunal found no breach of NAFTA art 1102.[65]

In relation to NAFTA art 1105, the *Methanex* Tribunal held that discrimination (had Methanex been able to prove that California's regulations were discriminatory) would not necessarily violate the FET standard.[66] But perhaps the most significant aspect of the *Methanex* award was its findings on indirect expropriation. Methanex framed the claim as California 'taking' Methanex's share of the Californian market and giving it to the ethanol industry. In response, the Tribunal held:

> [a]s a matter of general international law, a non-discriminatory regulation for a public purpose, which is enacted in accordance with due process and, which affects, inter alios, a foreign investor or investment is not deemed expropriatory and compensable unless specific commitments had been given by the regulating government to the then putative foreign investor contemplating investment that the government would refrain from such regulation.[67]

Because the Californian MTBE measures were non-discriminatory and for a public purpose and accorded with due process, they were a 'lawful regulation and not an expropriation'.[68] The *Methanex* Tribunal thus

---

62 *Methanex v US*, Final Award, pt III, ch A, [102].
63 *Methanex v US*, Final Award, pt IV, ch B, [17].
64 *Methanex v US*, Final Award, pt IV, ch B, [28].
65 *Methanex v US*, Final Award, pt IV, ch B, [22], [38].
66 *Methanex v US*, Final Award, pt IV, ch C, [14]–[27].
67 *Methanex v US*, Final Award, pt IV, ch D, [7].
68 *Methanex v US*, Final Award, pt IV, ch D, [15].

implied that a dichotomy exists between legitimate regulations for a public purpose and expropriatory measures. This understanding of the customary international law doctrine of police powers has been described as one of the more 'radical' formulations of that doctrine.[69] As elaborated below, the extent to which a *bona fide* public purpose exempts an environmental measure from the scope of the NAFTA expropriation obligation is highly contentious.

2 *Glamis Gold v US*

Glamis Gold, a Canadian company, undertook preliminary works for a gold mine in California, known as the Imperial Project, on federal public lands from 1994 to 2002.[70] The project received public attention for a range of reasons, including the open pit leach pad mining method that Glamis Gold intended to use, and the proximity of the mine site to Native American lands and sites of cultural importance.[71] In order to operate the proposed mine, Glamis Gold required federal and state government approvals. Glamis Gold's NAFTA claims related to both federal and state government approval processes. It alleged that the US federal government had wrongfully delayed consideration of the project and that, after this hurdle appeared to have been cleared, the Californian government imposed a legislative and regulatory framework for the mine that 'rendered the project economically infeasible'.[72] The Californian regulations related, in particular, to the remediation of mine sites after mining had ceased, including backfilling and contouring requirements to approximate the natural landscape.[73] Glamis Gold alleged that these actions

---

[69] Jonathan Bonnitcha, *Substantive Protection under Investment Treaties: A Legal and Economic Analysis* (Cambridge University Press, 2014) 242–243.

[70] *Glamis Gold v US*, Award, [10].

[71] *Glamis Gold v US*, Award, [10].

[72] *Glamis Gold v US*, Award, [11].

[73] The Californian measures were contained primarily in a number of Senate Bills (particularly SB 22) and regulations issued by the State Mining and Geology Board (SMGB). SB 22 provided that approval could not be given for a hardrock surface mining operation that was on or within one mile of a Native American sacred site in an area of special concern, unless the reclamation plan for the mine provided for backfilling of excavations that were similar to the original contours of the land, and financial assurances were provided to guarantee completion of backfilling and grading. See *Glamis Gold v US*, Award, [175]. The subsequent SMGB regulations imposed similar backfilling requirements for all hardrock mines, regardless of proximity to Native American sacred sites. See *Glamis Gold v US*, Award, [183].

violated the expropriation and minimum standard of treatment obligations under NAFTA arts 1110 and 1105, but the Tribunal rejected both claims.

The Tribunal dismissed the claimant's indirect expropriation claim under NAFTA art 1110 relatively easily, due to not meeting the 'threshold examination' of inquiry, that is, a failure to prove sufficient interference with the claimant's property rights.[74] The Tribunal found that the Californian backfilling measures did not cause a 'radical diminution' of the value of Glamis Gold's investment and therefore did not constitute an indirect expropriation or regulatory taking.[75] This finding provides important insights for host States about the extent of interference by an environmental law that will constitute an indirect expropriation. By clarifying that anything less than a 'radical diminution' of the value of an investment does not constitute expropriation, the Tribunal reserved a significant amount of policy space for governments to regulate to protect the environment notwithstanding negative impacts on investment.

In relation to FET in NAFTA art 1105, the disputing parties agreed that the relevant standard of treatment was that imposed by customary international law.[76] However, the parties differed as to the content of this standard. The Tribunal held that Glamis Gold had failed to establish the evolution of custom from the *Neer* standard,[77] therefore imposing the high threshold required by *Neer* for a violation of the international minimum standard:[78] 'a gross denial of justice or manifest arbitrariness', or 'the creation by the State of objective expectations *in order to induce investment* and the subsequent repudiation of those expectations'.[79] The Tribunal held that deficiencies in the US federal government's actions, which were largely procedural failings such as delay or lack of due process, did not meet this threshold.[80]

The Tribunal's findings in relation to the Californian measures are particularly significant for regulatory autonomy. The Tribunal began its analysis of these measures under the FET obligation in NAFTA art 1105 by noting that a measure is not in breach on the grounds of arbitrariness simply because the Tribunal disagrees with the relevant agency. Rather,

---

74 *Glamis Gold v US*, Award, [356].

75 *Glamis Gold v US*, Award, [366]. See also [534]–[536].

76 *Glamis Gold v US*, Award, [541].

77 *Glamis Gold v US*, Award, [21]–[22].

78 For further discussion of the *Neer* award, see Chapter 4 part BII2.

79 *Glamis Gold v US*, Award, [22] (emphasis in original). See also [616], [627].

80 *Glamis Gold v US*, Award, [771], [772], [776], [785]–[787].

an arbitrary measure in breach of art 1105 must 'exhibit a manifest lack of reasons'.[81] The Californian measures addressed at least some of the harm caused to Native American sites by open pit mining,[82] and 'the government had a sufficient good faith belief that there was a reasonable connection between the harm and the proposed remedy'.[83] In addition, the Tribunal noted that the measures were of general application and the project in question 'was not the subject of discriminatory targeting'.[84] In both *Methanex* and *Glamis Gold*, then, the tribunals accepted, based on the evidence before them, that the measures at issue had a legitimate goal of protecting the environment (and, in the case of *Glamis Gold*, culturally significant sites), which was key to the tribunals' conclusion that the measures were not arbitrary or discriminatory.

A final point worth noting from the *Glamis Gold* award is that the US had argued that the Tribunal, like 'domestic judiciaries', should 'favor deference' to the domestic regulatory agencies and not 'second guess' them.[85] The Tribunal rejected this argument, noting that the level of deference in national court systems does not apply to international tribunals, particularly 'where a measure of deference is already present in the standard to be applied',[86] such as the elements of 'manifest' and 'gross' arbitrariness in relation to the FET standard.[87] Thus, the *Glamis Gold* Tribunal made clear that it was not simply deferring to the judgment of US regulatory authorities; its conclusions were instead based on a full consideration of the merits of the challenged measures.

3 *Chemtura v Canada*

Chemtura v Canada concerned regulation of the pesticide lindane, which was used on canola crops and had been registered in the Canadian market since 1938[88] but was not approved for use in the US.[89] Due to its risks to human health and the environment, lindane has been subject to international regulatory efforts since the 1970s.[90] The claimant, Chemtura, was one of four registrants of lindane products in Canada in the late

---

81 *Glamis Gold v US*, Award, [803] (citations omitted).
82 *Glamis Gold v US*, Award, [804].
83 *Glamis Gold v US*, Award, [805]. See also [817]–[818].
84 *Glamis Gold v US*, Award, [828].
85 *Glamis Gold v US*, Award, [23], [617].
86 *Glamis Gold v US*, Award, [23].
87 *Glamis Gold v US*, Award, [617].
88 *Chemtura v Canada*, Award, [6].
89 *Chemtura v Canada*, Award, [7].
90 *Chemtura v Canada*, Award, [8].

1990s.[91] The US EPA announced that, from 1 June 1998, it would no longer allow US farmers to import from Canada canola seed that had been treated with lindane.[92] This announcement triggered a review by the Canadian government of its own regulation of lindane, a process culminating with the relevant regulatory agency determining in late 2001 that 'termination of lindane products was warranted', through phasing out via 'suspension of registrations or voluntary discontinuation'.[93] In February 2002, the agency informed Chemtura that its registrations for lindane products were terminated through suspension,[94] on the basis of safety concerns.[95]

The Tribunal found no breach of the FET standard under NAFTA art 1105[96] or of the expropriation obligation, among other claims.[97] The arbitrators rejected the suggestion that Canada had breached art 1105 by acting in bad faith or that its review of lindane was disingenuous,[98] instead finding 'ample evidence that the use of lindane caused genuine concerns, both in Canada and abroad'.[99] This conclusion was supported by the fact that Canada's regulation of lindane arose in part from its international obligations under the Aarhus Protocol and the Stockholm Convention.[100] Importantly, the *Chemtura* Tribunal seemed to take a more deferential approach than those in *Methanex* and *Glamis Gold*, stating: 'it is not for the Tribunal to judge the correctness or adequacy of the scientific results' of the Canadian agency's review of lindane.[101]

With regard to expropriation, the *Chemtura* Tribunal's findings were very similar to those in *Glamis Gold*. Sales of lindane comprised only a small part of Chemtura's business, representing only about 10 per cent of its business.[102] The Tribunal therefore found that the measure did not amount to the 'substantial' interference necessary to be tantamount to an expropriation.[103] The Tribunal also held that the measures 'constituted a

---

91 *Chemtura v Canada*, Award, [14].
92 *Chemtura v Canada*, Award, [13].
93 *Chemtura v Canada*, Award, [30].
94 *Chemtura v Canada*, Award, [32], [34].
95 *Chemtura v Canada*, Award, [32].
96 *Chemtura v Canada*, Award, [163], [180], [193], [225].
97 *Chemtura v Canada*, Award, [267], [237].
98 *Chemtura v Canada*, Award, [138].
99 *Chemtura v Canada*, Award, [184].
100 *Chemtura v Canada*, Award, [136]–[137].
101 *Chemtura v Canada*, Award, [153].
102 *Chemtura v Canada*, Award, [262].
103 *Chemtura v Canada*, Award, [263].

valid exercise of [Canada's] police powers'.[104] Borrowing key elements from the expropriation findings in *Methanex* and *Glamis Gold*, the Tribunal thus upheld Canada's environmental measures.

C Environmental Measures Found Inconsistent with NAFTA

The cases discussed in the previous section all found the challenged measures to be legitimate environmental regulations consistent with the respondent State's NAFTA obligations. However, several prominent NAFTA cases have concluded that measures purportedly enacted for environmental reasons breached investment protections under NAFTA. In this section we review four such cases in detail, excluding matters that were settled after initiating a NAFTA ch 11 arbitration.[105]

1 *SD Myers v Canada*

SD Myers, the claimant, was a US-based company with a range of enterprises, including remediation of PCB,[106] a fire-resistant insulating material that biodegrades slowly and remains in the environment for a considerable period of time.[107] For more than two decades before this NAFTA ch 11 dispute arose, PCBs had been recognised as 'highly toxic' and hazardous to both human and animal health.[108] The most common technique used to dispose of PCBs—high temperature incineration—creates highly toxic air pollution.[109] Unsurprisingly, given their toxicity, PCBs have been subject to 'increasingly strict regimes' of regulation both in Canada and internationally.[110] In 1990, Canada banned the export of PCBs to any country other than the US, with exports to the US permitted only with the prior approval of the US EPA.[111]

---

104 *Chemtura v Canada*, Award, [266].

105 For example, the dispute between Ethyl Corporation and Canada regarding regulation of the certain fuel additive was settled after the Tribunal handed down its decision on jurisdiction. See *Ethyl Corporation v Canada*, Decision on Jurisdiction; Government of Canada, Global Affairs Canada, *NAFTA—Chapter 11—Investment: Cases Filed Against Canada, Ethyl Corporation v Canada* <http://www.international.gc.ca/trade-agreements-accords-commerciaux/topics-domaines/disp-diff/ethyl.aspx?lang=eng> (last modified 6 January 2016).

106 *SD Myers v Canada*, Partial Award, [90].

107 *SD Myers v Canada*, Partial Award, [94].

108 *SD Myers v Canada*, Partial Award, [98].

109 *SD Myers v Canada*, Partial Award, [95]–[96].

110 *SD Myers v Canada*, Partial Award, [98].

111 *SD Myers v Canada*, Partial Award, [100].

When SD Myers began considering entering the Canadian market in the early 1990s, it faced very few local competitors.[112] SD Myers' Canadian PCB remediation business operated by obtaining waste containing PCBs from Canada, to be treated in its US-based facility.[113] The EPA authorised SD Myers to import PCB waste from Canada for remediation by letter dated October 1995,[114] when it granted similar authorisation to another nine US companies.[115] In response, the 'fledgling' Canadian PCB manufacturing sector began a 'vigorous lobbying campaign' to persuade the Canadian government to keep the border closed.[116] In November 1995, less than a month after SD Myers received the authorisation, the Canadian Minister of the Environment announced an Interim Order banning the export of PCBs from Canada.[117] The Interim Order was later confirmed by the Privy Council, and the border remained closed for 16 months, until February 1997.[118] During a brief window of time, SD Myers then was able to operate its PCB remediation service by exporting waste from Canada, but the border was once again closed in July 1997, following a decision by the US Court of Appeals for the Ninth Circuit.[119]

SD Myers alleged a breach of several provisions of NAFTA ch 11, including arts 1102, 1105 and 1110.[120] Its claim of expropriation failed because Canada's export ban curbed SD Myers' entry into the market for only a limited period, and because the measure entailed no 'transfer of property or benefit directly to others'.[121] However, the investor succeeded

---

112 *SD Myers v Canada*, Partial Award, [110]–[112].

113 *SD Myers v Canada*, Partial Award, [93].

114 This was not technically an authorisation, but rather, an 'enforcement discretion', which is a document issued by the US EPA stating that it will not enforce as against SD Myers the US regulations banning the importation of PCBs. The enforcement discretion was subject to certain conditions, eg that the PCB waste could not be sent to landfill. See *SD Myers v Canada*, Partial Award, [119]. For ease of reference, we refer to the enforcement discretion as an authorisation.

115 *SD Myers v Canada*, Partial Award, [119].

116 *SD Myers v Canada*, Partial Award, [122].

117 *SD Myers v Canada*, Partial Award, [123].

118 *SD Myers v Canada*, Partial Award, [127].

119 *SD Myers v Canada*, Partial Award, [128].

120 SD Myers also alleged that the measures at issue constituted performance requirements in violation of NAFTA art 1106, but the Tribunal found no such requirements imposed on SD Myers. *SD Myers v Canada*, Partial Award, [277]–[278].

121 *SD Myers v Canada*, Partial Award, [287].

in its claims regarding national treatment and fair and equitable treatment.[122] The core of the Tribunal's decision was its finding that the Canadian ban on PCB exports, which temporarily prevented SD Myers from undertaking remediation services, was motivated by a protectionist intent 'to ensure the strength of the Canadian industry'.[123] In *SD Myers*, the Tribunal explicitly found 'no legitimate environmental reason for introducing the ban'.[124] A briefing note prepared for the Minister by officials from the Canadian Department of Environment had concluded that allowing the export of PCBs to the US for treatment would be a 'technically and environmentally sound solution',[125] while statements by the Minister seemed to emphasise that the policy was motivated by a desire for Canadian PCB waste to be dealt with 'in Canada by Canadians'.[126] Although the Tribunal regarded creating and maintaining an ability to process PCBs within Canada as a 'legitimate goal', it considered that Canada could have achieved this goal through other legitimate means (such as sourcing all government PCB remediation services from local industry, or subsidising that industry).[127]

These factual conclusions, drawn from the evidence in the dispute, contrast distinctly with those of the *Methanex* Tribunal. Comparing these two cases highlights the importance of a tribunal's factual and evidentiary findings for its characterisation of a measure as a legitimate environmental regulation or a disguised act of protectionism to the detriment of foreign investors. The *SD Myers* Tribunal did not hold that the ban on the export of PCBs was a legitimate environmental measure that nevertheless constituted a compensable indirect expropriation; such a finding would have had significant implications for regulatory autonomy. Instead, the Tribunal found that the measure was, as a matter of fact, not a *bona fide* environmental regulation but disguised protectionism. SD Myers and Canadian operators of PCB remediation were held to be in 'like circumstances' for the purposes of the national treatment obligation in NAFTA art 1102,[128] and both the interim and final orders banning PCB exports were held to have been 'intended primarily to protect the Canadian PCB disposal industry from US competition', contrary to that

122 See *SD Myers v Canada*, Partial Award, [256], [268].
123 *SD Myers v Canada*, Partial Award, [255].
124 *SD Myers v Canada*, Partial Award, [195].
125 *SD Myers v Canada*, Partial Award, [164].
126 *SD Myers v Canada*, Partial Award, [169].
127 *SD Myers v Canada*, Partial Award, [255].
128 *SD Myers v Canada*, Partial Award, [251].

obligation.[129] The majority of the Tribunal also held that, although a breach of national treatment will not always constitute a breach of the minimum standard of treatment, 'on the facts of this particular case the breach of Article 1102 essentially establishes a breach of Article 1105 as well'.[130]

2 *Pope & Talbot v Canada*

Pope & Talbot v Canada forms part of a web of disputes involving Canada and the US (and their investors) brought under both trade and investment agreements concerning softwood lumber. This dispute is not often viewed as 'environmental' *per se*, as the challenged measure was not designed to protect the environment.[131] However, we include it here because of its significance for environmental regulations, particularly with regard to its findings on the scope of indirect expropriation. Given that the case concerns the management of a natural resource, it may also provide insights regarding environmental schemes involving permits and quota allocations.

In March 1996, Canada notified exporters of softwood lumber that, for certain provinces of manufacture, including British Columbia, exports to the US would require a permit.[132] Later that year, a regime was established for the granting of these export permits, which, in accordance with an agreement signed between Canada and the US, imposed fees for exports above a certain quota. The claimant, a US-based company, challenged several elements of Canada's regime for granting these permits and allocating quotas for softwood lumber, including particular fees and verification processes for exporters. The claimant alleged that Canada had violated NAFTA arts 1102, 1105 and 1110. The Tribunal dismissed all but one of the claimant's allegations, over the course of a protracted litigation.

The Tribunal rejected the claimant's expropriation claim in an interim award, on the basis that the challenged measures did not interfere with

---

[129] *SD Myers v Canada*, Partial Award, [194].

[130] *SD Myers v Canada*, Partial Award, [266].

[131] For example, it was not included in a detailed study of the relationship between investment arbitral awards and the environment. See Jorge E Viñuales, 'Foreign Investment and the Environment in International Law: The Current State of Play' in Kate Miles (ed), *Research Handbook on Environment and Investment Law* (Edward Elgar, forthcoming) ch 2.

[132] *Pope & Talbot v Canada*, Merits Award Phase 2, [20].

the investor's property rights significantly enough to amount to expropriation.[133] To this extent, the *Pope & Talbot* interim award is similar to the *Glamis Gold* and *Chemtura* decisions on expropriation, discussed above. Separately, the Tribunal stated that 'a blanket exception for regulatory measures would create a gaping loophole in international protections against expropriation', rejecting Canada's argument that regulatory measures are 'beyond the coverage of Article 1110'.[134]

On the minimum standard of treatment, the Tribunal held that only one small element of Canada's conduct breached NAFTA art 1105: a verification review process, which the Tribunal described as having been conducted 'more like combat than cooperative regulation'.[135] The Tribunal identified as problematic several elements of Canada's conduct during this process: denying reasonable requests for information, and subjecting the investment to threats and unnecessary expense and disruption.[136] In other respects, the Tribunal found the regime consistent with the minimum standard of treatment, as it was administered 'in an open and cooperative spirit'.[137] In relation to a 'Super Fee' applied to a few exporters from the British Columbia region, the Tribunal noted that Canada 'might have chosen another approach' to achieve its aim, which 'shared the burden more equitably across the range of BC producers'.[138] However, the Tribunal found that the Super Fee did not violate NAFTA art 1105 because 'it is not the place of this Tribunal to substitute its judgment on the choice of solutions for Canada's'.[139] In sum, notwithstanding the finding of violation, with respect to FET, the Tribunal was relatively deferential to Canada's decision-making with regard to the management of softwood lumber as a natural resource. The violation related to poor administration of the Canadian regime rather than its substance.

With regard to national treatment under NAFTA art 1102, the Tribunal had to consider only whether the Super Fee was discriminatory. It adopted a two-step approach, first considering whether the foreign investor received treatment less favourable than comparable domestic investors, and if so whether that less favourable treatment was justified

---

133 *Pope & Talbot v Canada*, Interim Award, [96], [103].

134 *Pope & Talbot v Canada*, Interim Award, [99].

135 *Pope & Talbot v Canada*, Merits Award Phase 2, [181]. See generally [156]–[181].

136 *Pope & Talbot v Canada*, Merits Award Phase 2, [181].

137 *Pope & Talbot v Canada*, Merits Award Phase 2, [180].

138 *Pope & Talbot v Canada*, Merits Award Phase 2, [155].

139 *Pope & Talbot v Canada*, Merits Award Phase 2, [155].

by a 'reasonable nexus to rational government policies'.[140] The Tribunal dismissed the national treatment claim at the first step of this analysis, noting that more than 130 companies operating in British Columbia used the softwood lumber quotas subject to the Super Fee, only one of which (the claimant) was owned by NAFTA investors.[141] Thus, the Tribunal found no basis for concluding that the Super Fee discriminated against NAFTA investors or was 'not a rational choice of solution'.[142]

3 *Metalclad v Mexico*

Metalclad was a US company that sought to develop and operate a hazardous waste landfill facility in the Guadalcazar municipality of Mexico.[143] In 1993, Metalclad purchased a Mexican entity, COTERIN, which had already received authorisations from the federal government of Mexico to construct and operate the facility.[144] Metalclad claimed that it had received the necessary support and assurances of the state government as well, and it commenced construction of the facility in May 1994.[145] In October of that year, the municipal government ordered the cessation of construction, in the absence of a municipal construction permit.[146] After negotiating with the federal government and submitting an application for a municipal permit, Metalclad completed construction of the facility in March 1995.[147] However, the landfill opening was prevented by protests, including blocking the entry of workers to the site.[148] In November 1995, the investor and the federal government of Mexico entered an agreement for the operation of the landfill, including standards for management and remediation of the site, as well as mechanisms to respond to any environmental emergencies.[149] The following month, Metalclad's application for a municipal construction permit was denied.[150] The municipality noted that it had denied COTERIN's applications for a permit in 1991 and 1992, also identifying 'impropriety'

---

140 *Pope & Talbot v Canada*, Merits Award Phase 2, [78].
141 *Pope & Talbot v Canada*, Merits Award Phase 2, [103].
142 *Pope & Talbot v Canada*, Merits Award Phase 2, [103].
143 *Metalclad v Mexico*, Award, [1].
144 *Metalclad v Mexico*, Award, [28]–[30], [33]–[35].
145 *Metalclad v Mexico*, Award, [31]–[32], [37]–[38].
146 *Metalclad v Mexico*, Award, [40].
147 *Metalclad v Mexico*, Award, [41]–[43], [45].
148 *Metalclad v Mexico*, Award, [46].
149 *Metalclad v Mexico*, Award, [48].
150 *Metalclad v Mexico*, Award, [50].

in the landfill having been constructed before a permit was issued.[151] Metalclad and the municipal government initiated various administrative and judicial review processes, and a federal authority granted Metalclad a permit to expand the facility.[152] In addition to these ongoing problems with the municipal government, a second issue arose in September 1997: the issuance of an 'Ecological Decree' by the state Governor, which Metalclad alleged 'effectively and permanently precluded the operation of the landfill'.[153]

Metalclad successfully claimed that the various actions of the state and local municipalities violated the minimum standard of treatment under NAFTA art 1105, also constituting an expropriation of the landfill in violation of NAFTA art 1110. The Tribunal found various faults in the state and municipal government decision-making processes, such as the municipality acting beyond its jurisdiction and failing to accord Metalclad due process,[154] contrary to the FET obligation.[155] The Tribunal noted that although NAFTA art 1114 allows a Party to take environmental measures with respect to investments, in this case the federal government's actions showed that the 'project was consistent with, and sensitive to, its environmental concerns'.[156] Having found a violation of NAFTA art 1105, the Tribunal went on to find a violation of art 1110 as well, because the 'denial to Metalclad of the right to operate the landfill, notwithstanding the fact that the project was fully approved and endorsed by the federal government' was tantamount to expropriation.[157]

Although it was not 'strictly necessary' for the conclusion of the case, the Tribunal also found that the Ecological Decree would have provided a further ground for its finding of indirect expropriation.[158] The Tribunal noted that it 'need not decide or consider the motivation or intent of the adoption of the Ecological Decree', implying that the measure amounted to expropriation regardless of its allegedly environmental purpose.[159] The Supreme Court of British Columbia later found that the *Metalclad* findings on the minimum standard of treatment and expropriation, as regards the conduct prior to the Ecological Decree, had improperly relied

---

151 *Metalclad v Mexico*, Award, [50].
152 *Metalclad v Mexico*, Award, [51]–[57].
153 *Metalclad v Mexico*, Award, [59].
154 *Metalclad v Mexico*, Award, [86], [91].
155 *Metalclad v Mexico*, Award, [99].
156 *Metalclad v Mexico*, Award, [98].
157 *Metalclad v Mexico*, Award, [104]–[108].
158 *Metalclad v Mexico*, Award, [109]–[111].
159 *Metalclad v Mexico*, Award, [111].

on an obligation of 'transparency',[160] and set aside the award in part, noting that Metalclad could seek to remit the case back to the arbitral tribunal for consideration of whether this conduct violated NAFTA art 1105 or 1110 (separate from any obligation of 'transparency').[161] However, because the Supreme Court of British Columbia nevertheless upheld the Tribunal's findings with regard to NAFTA art 1110 and the Ecological Decree,[162] the effect of it partially setting aside the arbitral award was minimal. The review decision set aside only a portion of the interest that had been awarded to Metalclad, relating to the period of time between the earlier misconduct and the issuance of the Ecological Decree.[163] Rather than the claimant seeking to remit the matter to the arbitral tribunal for reconsideration of the findings that were set aside, Mexico paid compensation through a settlement agreement.[164]

4 *Clayton and Bilcon v Canada*

Clayton and Bilcon v Canada is much more recent than the other cases discussed in this section involving a breach of NAFTA ch 11 involving environmental regulations. The award in *Clayton and Bilcon v Canada* was published in 2015, over a decade since *Metalclad v Mexico*.[165] The Tribunal's award in relation to FET has been particularly controversial, with one arbitrator, Professor Donald McRae, writing a forceful dissent on this issue.

The facts of the case can be stated relatively simply. The claimants, various members of the Clayton family and their company Bilcon, were US-based and operated in the building materials industry.[166] Bilcon had sought to undertake a quarry and marine terminal operation in Nova Scotia, Canada, known as the 'Whites Point' project, in order to supply the aggregate needed for its building material and concrete business.[167] In order to establish the quarry, the claimants required various approvals

---

160 *Metalclad v Mexico*, Review by Supreme Court of BC, [70]–[74].

161 *Metalclad v Mexico*, Review by Supreme Court of BC, [136].

162 *Metalclad v Mexico*, Review by Supreme Court of BC, [105].

163 *Metalclad v Mexico*, Review by Supreme Court of BC, [135].

164 See Government of Mexico, 'Metalclad Corporation c. los Estados Unidos Mexicanos Caso CIADI No. ARB(AF)/97/01' http://www.gob.mx/cms/uploads/attachment/file/42025/Ficha_tecnica_Metalclad.pdf (last visited 7 April 2017).

165 As noted above, it is also the first case to have found a breach of NAFTA art 1105 since the NAFTA Free Trade Commission issued its interpretation of the FET standard. See Chapter 4 part IIB2.

166 *Clayton and Bilcon v Canada*, Award, [6].

167 *Clayton and Bilcon v Canada*, Award, [8].

from local and federal Canadian authorities.[168] The claimants alleged that at various stages necessary approvals were refused for unjustifiable reasons. Their claim centred around one particular element of the regulatory review process for the quarry: the conduct of a Joint Review Panel, which carried out the environmental impact assessment for the planned project.

In concluding that the conduct of the Panel had violated the FET standard, the majority of the Tribunal focussed on the concept of 'core community values', which the Panel identified as a central reason for not approving the project.[169] Crucially, the Tribunal found that the notion of 'community core values' had no basis in Canadian environmental law.[170] The Tribunal contrasted this relatively subjective, socio-economic concept with the value of 'scientific information'[171] and 'evidence-based' reasoning in relation to other costs and benefits of the project.[172]

Without suggesting that impacts on the human environment have no role in an environmental assessment, the Tribunal suggested that the notion of 'community core values' was essentially synonymous with the local community's opinion about the project.[173] As mentioned in Chapter 4 of this book, the dissent took issue with this approach, noting that the majority's ruling effected 'an intrusion into the way an environmental review process is to be conducted', as well as 'an intrusion into the environmental public policy of the state'.[174] Professor McRae argued that this ruling could have far-reaching consequences for State regulatory autonomy.[175]

In addition to its findings on FET, the *Bilcon* majority found that the conduct of the Joint Review Panel violated the national treatment obligation in NAFTA art 1102, because the Whites Point project was subjected to a standard of review different from that applied to other comparable quarries and marine terminals. This finding was primarily based on the specific factual context of the case.[176] However, the Tribunal also indicated that the approach of *Pope & Talbot* regarding art 1102 provides:

---

168 See *Clayton and Bilcon v Canada*, Award, [120]–[123], [152]–[158].
169 *Clayton and Bilcon v Canada*, Award, [502]–[547].
170 *Clayton and Bilcon v Canada*, Award, [503], [591]–[594].
171 *Clayton and Bilcon v Canada*, Award, [508].
172 *Clayton and Bilcon v Canada*, Award, [530].
173 *Clayton and Bilcon v Canada*, Award, [507]–[514].
174 *Clayton and Bilcon v Canada*, Dissent [49].
175 *Clayton and Bilcon v Canada*, Dissent [44]–[55].
176 *Clayton and Bilcon v Canada*, Award, [694].

> legally appropriate latitude for host states, even in the absence of an equivalent of Article XX of the GATT, to pursue reasonable and non-discriminatory policy objectives through appropriate measures even where there is an incidental and reasonably unavoidable burden on foreign enterprises.[177]

According to the *Bilcon* majority, the burden of justifying any discriminatory treatment falls on the respondent State, and Canada had failed to 'substantiate the case ... that an apparently discriminatory measure is in fact compliant with' NAFTA art 1102:[178]

> [T]he 'community core values' approach adopted by the [Joint Review Panel] was not a 'rational government policy'; it was ... not consistent with the investment liberalizing objectives of NAFTA ...[179]

D Lessons for Australia from NAFTA Disputes Regarding Environmental Measures

The preceding examination of NAFTA ch 11 disputes involving environmental measures (or measures purportedly enacted for an environmental purpose) provides several important insights for understanding how Australia's BITs and investment chapters of PTAs may influence regulatory autonomy in the environmental arena. A range of measures have been subject to challenge through ISDS under NAFTA ch 11, including legislative and executive acts of general application, and specific administrative decisions and review processes, carried out by different levels of government. *Metalclad v Mexico* presents an example of inconsistency of action and mixed signals between national and sub-national governments giving rise to liability: an important consideration for a federal system of government such as Australia's.

As was noted in Chapter 4, expropriation is one of the main areas in which Australia has sought to update its drafting of investment obligations to protect policy space for regulatory measures.[180] Clarifying that regulations for public welfare purposes do not usually constitute indirect expropriation may provide a valuable signal to arbitrators, such as in *Pope & Talbot*, who expressed concern about creating a 'gaping loophole' in the expropriation obligation.[181] However, even in Australia's

---

177 *Clayton and Bilcon v Canada*, Award, [723].

178 *Clayton and Bilcon v Canada*, Award, [723]–[724].

179 *Clayton and Bilcon v Canada*, Award, [724].

180 See Chapter 4 part IIC6.

181 *Pope & Talbot v Canada*, Interim Award, [99].

earlier PTAs and BITs, which lack this clarification, the decision in *Methanex* provides a useful precedent for tribunals to interpret even the most basic treaty language as allowing exceptions.

Perhaps the most important lesson from these NAFTA claims of indirect expropriation via environmental regulations is that these claims are rarely successful. In the seven NAFTA disputes we have examined in detail here, only the *Metalclad* award found an expropriation. In other disputes, even where the challenged measures were found not designed to protect the environment, such as in *SD Myers v Canada*, tribunals found that the measures did not cause sufficient interference with investment for an expropriation to have occurred.[182] Only in *Metalclad*, where the investor became unable to operate its hazardous waste landfill, did environmental measures impose costs or constraints on an investor equivalent to expropriation.

Interpretations of FET by NAFTA ch 11 tribunals have evolved over time, including as a result of the NAFTA Free Trade Commission's interpretative note on NAFTA art 1105.[183] FET was the most significant obligation raised across these NAFTA disputes. In some cases, the administration rather than the substance of the measures was the main cause of violation. In *Pope & Talbot v Canada*, Canada successfully defended its export regime in most respects, failing only in relation to poor conduct of a particular regulatory process.[184] Similarly, in *Metalclad*, much of the Tribunal's concern was with inconsistencies in government action and procedural failings.[185]

Only in two cases did a finding of a violation of NAFTA art 1105 stem primarily from the substance of the measure: *Bilcon v Canada* and *SD Myers v Canada*. In these cases, the tribunals closely scrutinised the purpose of and justification for the challenged measures. The influence of the *Bilcon* majority decision on future arbitral tribunals is uncertain, given the dissenting opinion and the fact that the majority's reasoning was specific to the facts at issue. *SD Myers v Canada*, however, presents a typical example of a situation where, according to the Tribunal, the respondent sought to defend its measure by reference to an environmental purpose, but this was not the true intent of the measure. This dispute

---

182 See, eg, *Glamis Gold v US*, Award, [366]; *Chemtura v Canada*, Award, [263]; *SD Myers v Canada*, Partial Award, [287]; *Pope & Talbot v Canada*, Interim Award, [96], [103].

183 See Chapter 4 part IIB2.

184 *Pope & Talbot v Canada*, Merits Award Phase 2, [181]. See generally [156]–[181].

185 *Metalclad v Mexico*, Award, [86]–[99].

provides a contrast to cases such as *Methanex* and *Glamis Gold*, where tribunals accepted the evidence of a legitimate purpose. Another commonality of *Bilcon* and *SD Myers* is that both tribunals found that the same conduct violated the FET and national treatment standards. As noted above, the TPP (not in force) and the SAFTA amendments agreed in 2016 (also not in force) are the only Australian IIAs that direct tribunals to take account of a measure's purpose in identifying 'like circumstances' between the investor and a local competitor. However, these NAFTA cases show that tribunals examining older style investment obligations may still have regard to regulatory purpose.

Cases such as *SD Myers*, *Metalclad* and *Bilcon*, in contrast to other NAFTA cases applying the same treaty standards, show that evidence of a measure's legitimate purpose has a crucial influence on the outcome of an ISDS challenge. Where the evidence suggests that a measure has a predominant purpose unrelated to environmental protection, such as the protection of local industry or addressing domestic political concerns, tribunals are likely to find that the measure violates obligations such as national treatment or FET. In cases where NAFTA tribunals disputed the host State's identification of the challenged measure as a *bona fide* environmental regulation, government sources often indicated that the measure was not necessary to protect the environment.[186]

Community concerns often arise in Australia and elsewhere about the detrimental impact of ISDS on environmental protection. However, the NAFTA cases examined in this chapter show that this characterisation is too simple. In several cases, States have successfully defended claims against environmental measures, primarily on the basis of clear scientific evidence supporting the regulation or administrative action. In those cases where host States have failed in their defence, typically a lack of evidence was presented to support the legitimate public welfare objective of the measure, or the measure was administered in an arbitrary or inconsistent manner. Thus, with the possible exception of the recent majority decision in *Bilcon*, the NAFTA experience demonstrates that arbitral tribunals are capable of distinguishing between legitimate environmental measures and breaches of investment obligations.

---

[186] See, eg, *SD Myers v Canada*, Partial Award, [164]; *Metalclad v Mexico*, Award, [98].

III DRAFTING AUSTRALIAN PTAs AND BITs TO SAFEGUARD ENVIRONMENTAL OBJECTIVES

In light of concerns that the obligations contained in Australia's PTAs and BITs may constrain regulatory autonomy, we have seen a trend over time for these agreements to include increased safeguards for regulatory space. In this section of the chapter we focus on the use of general exceptions clauses and other provisions that may assist Australia (or its treaty partners) to defend environmental measures.

A General Exceptions: Coverage of Environmental Measures

1 GATT art XX and GATS art XIV

As discussed in Chapter 4, general exceptions provide a tool to safeguard regulatory autonomy in many Australian PTAs, but they are largely absent from Australia's BITs. Although these provisions are increasingly included in relation to investment obligations, as well as trade obligations, they have not yet been interpreted by an ISDS arbitral tribunal. Therefore, the best guidance we have on the coverage and application of these provisions for environmental measures is found in the jurisprudence of the WTO.

The original 'general exceptions' are found in art XX of the GATT 1994, which states:

> Subject to the requirement that such measures are not applied in a manner which would constitute a means of arbitrary or unjustifiable discrimination between countries where the same conditions prevail, or a disguised restriction on international trade, nothing in this Agreement shall be construed to prevent the adoption or enforcement by any Member of measures:
>
> (a) necessary to protect public morals;
> (b) necessary to protect human, animal or plant life or health;
> (c) relating to the importations or exportations of gold or silver;
> (d) necessary to secure compliance with laws or regulations which are not inconsistent with the provisions of this Agreement … ;
> (e) relating to the products of prison labour;
> (f) imposed for the protection of national treasures of artistic, historic or archaeological value;
> (g) relating to the conservation of exhaustible natural resources if such measures are made effective in conjunction with restrictions on domestic production or consumption; …

A similar provision is contained in art XIV of GATS, but without equivalents to paragraphs (c), (e), (f) or (g), given that GATS applies to trade in services rather than goods.

All of Australia's PTAs incorporate a form of GATT art XX (with respect to trade in goods)[187] and GATS art XIV (with respect to trade in services),[188] either through similar language or by reference to those provisions. As discussed in Chapter 4, many of these agreements also incorporate a form of general exception in relation to investment obligations, but these tend to have greater variations in drafting.[189]

The WTO general exceptions most likely to cover environmental measures are in paragraph (b) of GATT art XX and GATS art XIV (for measures necessary to protect human, animal or plant life or health) and paragraph (g) of GATT art XX (for measures relating to the conservation of exhaustible natural resources). The application of these exceptions is also affected by the opening paragraph of GATT art XX and GATS art XIV (the 'chapeau'), which is designed to prevent abuse of the exceptions.[190] The following sections consider the scope of these two exceptions and their adoption in Australian PTAs and BITs, with a specific focus on environmental measures.

2 Necessary for the protection of human, animal or plant life or health

By incorporating GATT art XX and GATS art XIV, Australia's PTAs safeguard regulatory space for measures necessary for the protection of human, animal or plant life or health, in relation to trade in goods and trade in services. A similar exception appears in the investment chapter of several Australian PTAs,[191] while the Australia–India BIT (recently terminated) includes a narrower exception for measures 'necessary for the prevention of diseases or pests'.[192] Many of Australia's PTAs also

---

[187] ANZCERTA art 18; TAFTA art 1601.1; AUSFTA art 22.1.1; ACIFTA art 22.1.1; AANZFTA ch 15 art 1.1; MAFTA art 18.1.1; KAFTA art 22.1.1; JAEPA art 1.9.1; ChAFTA art 16.2.1; TPP art 29.1.1; SAFTA 2016 ch 2 art 18.

[188] ANZCERTA Services Protocol art 18; TAFTA art 1601.2; AUSFTA art 22.1.2; ACIFTA art 22.1.2; AANZFTA ch 15 art 1.2; MAFTA art 18.1.2; KAFTA art 22.1.2; JAEPA art 1.9.2; ChAFTA art 16.2.2; TPP art 29.1.3; SAFTA 2016 ch 7 art 16.

[189] See Chapter 4 part IIIB.

[190] See Appellate Body Report, *US—Gasoline*, 22–23; Appellate Body Report, *Brazil—Retreaded Tyres*, [215].

[191] See Table 4.4 in Chapter 4 of this volume.

[192] Australia–India BIT art 15.

clarify that environmental measures may fall within the scope of the exception.[193] For example, the TPP states:

> The Parties understand that the measures referred to in Article XX(b) of GATT 1994 include environmental measures necessary to protect human, animal or plant life or health …[194]

In our view, although this clarification may assist in avoiding ambiguity, it does not alter the scope of the exception. The WTO Appellate Body has already interpreted measures directed at the environment as falling within the general scope of GATT art XX(b), such as a Brazilian prohibition on the importation of retreaded tyres,[195] and a US 'dolphin safe' tuna labelling scheme.[196] In the context of provisions relating to trade in goods or investment, the exceptions in paragraphs (b) and (g) may partially overlap.[197] However, as GATS and services aspects of PTAs do not generally contain an exception relating to the conservation of natural resources, the exception for human, plant or animal life or health may have a broader scope in the context of services obligations.[198] As shown in the next section, the meaning of exhaustible natural resources has changed over time. Services may also become more relevant to environmental matters than the drafters may have expected when the GATS was concluded.

3 Relating to the conservation of exhaustible natural resources

Given Australia's abundant biodiversity and prosperous mining and extractive industries, exceptions for measures relating to the conservation of natural resources are of particular significance. GATT art XX(g) has several noteworthy features. Unlike art XX(b), discussed above, the exception for measures for the conservation of exhaustible natural

---

193 See AUSFTA arts 22.1.1, 22.1.2; ACIFTA arts 22.1.1, 22.1.2; ANZCERTA Investment Protocol n 8; KAFTA arts 22.1.1, 22.1.2; JAEPA art 14.15(b); ChAFTA art 9.8.2; TPP art 29.1.2; SAFTA 2016 ch 17 art 5.2.

194 TPP art 29.1.2.

195 Panel Report, *Brazil—Retreaded Tyres*, [7.100]–[7.102] (finding not appealed).

196 Panel Report, *US—Tuna II (Mexico) (Article 21.5)*, [7.544].

197 In some cases, such as the 'dolphin safe' labelling scheme for tuna, there may be 'no meaningful difference' between the scope of the paragraph (b) and (g) exceptions: Panel Report, *US—Tuna II (Mexico) (Article 21.5)*, [7.544].

198 Thomas Cottier, Panagiotis Delimatsis and Nicolas F Diebold, 'Article XIV' in Rüdiger Wolfrum, Peter-Tobias Stoll and Clemens Feinäugle (eds), *WTO—Trade in Services* (Martinus Nijhoff, 2008) 287, 302.

resources does not stipulate that measures must be 'necessary'. Instead, it imposes a lower threshold or nexus requirement: that measures 'relat[e] to' the conservation of resources.[199] A second important feature of art XX(g) is that it requires that measures be 'made effective in conjunction with restrictions on domestic production or consumption.' As noted earlier, many Australian PTAs directly incorporate GATT art XX(g) or reproduce it without amendment, thus including this requirement of 'even-handedness'.[200]

The ANZCERTA Investment Protocol and the ChAFTA investment chapter omit the requirement for equivalent measures relating to domestic consumption and production from the exception corresponding with GATT art XX(g).[201] Such modifications in drafting when exceptions are transposed from the trade to investment context make sense, given that investment measures affect foreign persons and entities operating domestically (rather than measures that affect the movement of goods across borders). By removing this element of GATT art XX(g), while maintaining the relatively undemanding threshold that measures relate to the conservation of exhaustible natural resources, these provisions may create a particularly broad exception for environmental measures. Further, the MAFTA general exception for investment obligations simply refers to measures 'to conserve' natural resources, without stating that the measures must relate to that goal.[202] However, as noted below, environmental measures must still meet the demanding requirements of the chapeau.

As the requirement that measures relate to the conservation of natural resources is not a high threshold, the main constraint on the scope of the paragraph (g) exception is the definition of 'exhaustible natural resources'. However, WTO Panels, Members and the Appellate Body have interpreted this term in a broad and evolutionary manner, such that it extends to minerals and similar commodities,[203] clean air,[204] and

---

199 Appellate Body Report, *US—Gasoline*, 18.

200 Appellate Body Report, *US—Gasoline*, 20.

201 ANZCERTA Investment Protocol art 19; ChAFTA art 9.8.

202 MAFTA art 12.18.1(f).

203 Panel Reports, *China—Rare Earths*, [7.365] (question not contested or appealed: Appellate Body Reports, *China—Rare Earths*, [5.81]); Panel Report, *China—Raw Materials*, [7.369] (question not contested). See also Manjiao Chi, '"Exhaustible Natural Resource" in WTO Law: GATT Article XX (g) Disputes and Their Implications' (2014) 48 *Journal of World Trade* 939.

204 Panel Report, *US—Gasoline*, [6.37] (finding not appealed); Appellate Body Report, *US—Gasoline*, 13.

endangered living resources such as dolphins and turtles.[205] Again, with the apparent intention of clarifying rather than amending the scope of the paragraph (g) exception, many Australian PTAs state explicitly that this exception encompasses both living and non-living resources, whether they incorporate GATT art XX(g) by reference,[206] or reproduce it with similar language.[207]

The variations in drafting of exceptions in Australian PTAs for measures relating to the conservation of exhaustible natural resources are shown in Tables 6.1 (with respect to chapters concerning trade in goods)[208] and 6.2 (with respect to investment chapters or specific investment obligations such as regarding certain performance requirements).[209]

These tables demonstrate that exceptions relating to Australia's goods chapters in PTAs are more homogenously drafted than those applying to investment obligations. While many of these variations in drafting relate to clarifying the scope of the exception, rather than fundamentally altering it, this patchwork of different exceptions creates a risk of gaps and inconsistencies in the safeguarding of Australia's regulatory autonomy in relation to the management of natural resources. US-influenced PTAs in particular (AUSFTA, ACIFTA, TPP) have only limited exceptions regarding exhaustible natural resources in the investment chapter, with respect to certain obligations concerning performance requirements. As explained in Chapters 4 and 5, inconsistencies and deficiencies in the investment context may be particularly problematic because of the existence of ISDS in most Australian IIAs and the potential for an investor in Australia to invoke a powerful MFN obligation to obtain the better treatment accorded under another Australian IIA or to restructure its assets and subsidiaries to obtain the protection of a more favourable IIA.

---

[205] Panel Report, *US—Tuna II (Mexico) (Article 21.5)*, [7.544]; Appellate Body Report, *US—Shrimp*, [130]–[134].

[206] See, eg, TPP art 29.1.2.

[207] See, eg, ChAFTA art 9.8.

[208] SAFTA 2003 ch 2 art 12; TAFTA art 1601.1; AUSFTA art 22.1.1; ACIFTA art 22.1.1; AANZFTA ch 15 art 1.1; SAFTA 2011 ch 2 art 12; MAFTA art 18.1.1; KAFTA art 22.1.1; JAEPA art 1.9.1; ChAFTA art 16.2.1; TPP art 29.1.1; SAFTA 2016 ch 2 art 18, ch 7 art 5.

[209] SAFTA 2003 ch 8 art 19; TAFTA art 1601.3; AUSFTA art 11.9(c)(iii); ACIFTA art 10.7.3(c)(iii); SAFTA 2011 ch 8 arts 5.3(c)(iii), 21; MAFTA art 12.18.1(f); ANZCERTA Investment Protocol art 19(d); KAFTA arts 11.9.5(c), 22.1.3(d); JAEPA art 14.15(e); ChAFTA art 9.8.1(d); TPP art 9.10.3(d)(iii); SAFTA 2016 ch 8 art 19.

Table 6.1 Exceptions for Exhaustible Natural Resources in Australia's PTAs—Trade in Goods Chapters

Treaty	**Entry into force**	**Incorporation of GATT art XX(g) by reference**	**Exception with similar language**	**Removal of requirement for equivalent domestic measures**	**Clarification that resources may be 'living or non-living'**	**Clarification that exception includes environmental measures**
SAFTA original	2003	–	✔	✘	✘	✘
TAFTA	2005	✔	–	✘	✘	✘
AUSFTA	2005	✔	–	✘	✔	✘
ACIFTA	2009	✔	–	✘	✔	✘
AANZFTA	2010	✔	–	✘	✘	✘
SAFTA amended	2011	–	✔	✘	✘	✘
MAFTA	2013	✔	–	✘	✘	✘
KAFTA	2014	✔	–	✘	✔	✘
JAEPA	2015	✔	–	✘	✘	✘
ChAFTA	2015	✔	–	✘	✘	✘
TPP	–	✔	–	✘	✔	✘
SAFTA 2016 amendments[210]	–	✔	✔	✘	✔	✘

210 SAFTA 2016 ch 2 art 18 provides a general exception similar to GATT art XX(g) for the trade in goods chapter. In addition, SAFTA 2016 ch 17 art 5 incorporates GATT art XX by reference with respect to the chapters on rules of origin, TBT and SPS measures, adding in that provision the clarification about living and non-living resources.

Table 6.2 Exceptions for Exhaustible Natural Resources in Australia's PTAs—Investment Chapters

Treaty	**Entry into force**	**Incorporation of GATT art XX(g) by reference**	**Exception with similar language**	**Removal of requirement for equivalent domestic measures**	**Clarification that resources may be 'living or non-living'**	**Clarification that exception includes environmental measures**
SAFTA original	2003	–	✓	✗	✗	✗
TAFTA	2005	✓	–	✗	✗	✗
AUSFTA[211]	2006	–	✓	✓	✓	✓
ACIFTA[212]	2009	–	✓	✓	✓	✓
AANZFTA	2010	–	–	–	–	–
SAFTA amended[213]	2011	–	✓	✓	✓	✓
MAFTA	2013	–	✓	✗	✗	✗
ANZCERTA Investment Protocol	2013	–	✓	✓	✓	✗
KAFTA	2014	–	✓	✗	✓	✓
JAEPA	2015	–	✓	✗	✓	✗
ChAFTA	2015	–	✓	✓	✓	✓
TPP[214]	–	–	✓	✓	✓	✓
SAFTA 2016 amendments[215]	–	–	✓	✓	✓	✓

[211] AUSFTA art 11.9(c)(iii) provides a limited exception with respect to certain performance requirements.

[212] ACIFTA art 10.7.3(c)(iii) provides a limited exception with respect to certain performance requirements.

[213] SAFTA 2011 ch 8 art 5.3(c)(iii) provides a limited exception with respect to certain performance requirements that includes clarifications regarding living and non-living resources, as well as environmental measures, while also removing the requirement of equivalent domestic measures. However, SAFTA 2011 ch 8 art 21(e) applies to the investment chapter in general and is a more straightforward rendering of GATT art XX(g).

[214] Like AUSFTA and ACIFTA, TPP art 9.10.3(d)(iii) provides a limited exception with respect to certain performance requirements.

[215] SAFTA 2016 ch 8 art 7.3(c)(iii) corresponds with SAFTA 2011 ch 9 art 5.3(c)(iii) as just described. SAFTA 2016 ch 8 art 19(e) corresponds with SAFTA 2011 ch 8 art 21(e).

4 The 'chapeau'

The chapeau of GATT art XX and GATS art XIV is essentially an anti-abuse provision. The WTO Appellate Body has noted that compliance with the chapeau is 'a heavier task' than meeting the requirements of individual paragraphs, such as GATT art XX(g).[216] In several notable cases in which the Appellate Body has declined protection to a purportedly environmental measure under GATT art XX,[217] the measure has failed to meet the chapeau requirements.[218] In *Brazil—Retreaded Tyres*, for example, the challenged measure was provisionally justified under art XX(b) but inconsistent with the chapeau because it was applied in a discriminatory manner for reasons unrelated to and in fact undermining the environmental-related health purpose.[219] Tribunals examining general exceptions in Australia's PTAs are not bound to follow this WTO jurisprudence. Nevertheless, these cases demonstrate the stringency of the chapeau requirements and emphasise the importance of applying environmental measures in a non-discriminatory manner in order to benefit from the general exceptions.

B Other Exceptions Provisions and Non-Conforming Measures

Another form of exception in some investment chapters of Australian PTAs is a provision clarifying that States may pursue measures to ensure that investment is sensitive to certain regulatory objectives. For example:

> Nothing in this Chapter shall be construed to prevent a Party from adopting, maintaining or enforcing any measure otherwise consistent with this Chapter that it considers appropriate to ensure that investment activity in its territory is undertaken in a manner sensitive to environmental, health or other regulatory objectives.[220]

The ANZCERTA Investment Protocol includes a similar provision, but limited to environmental concerns (excluding health or other regulatory

---

216 Appellate Body Report, *US—Gasoline*, 23.

217 GATS art XIV(b) has not been raised to date in relation to environmental protection measures.

218 See, eg, Appellate Body Report, *US—Gasoline*, 29; Appellate Body Report, *Brazil—Retreaded Tyres*, [252]; Appellate Body Report, *US—Shrimp*, [186].

219 Appellate Body Report, *Brazil—Retreaded Tyres*, [252].

220 AUSFTA art 11.11; SAFTA 2016 ch 8 art 20. See also TPP art 9.16.

objectives).[221] As discussed in Chapter 4, the restriction of these provisions to measures 'otherwise consistent with [the agreement]' means that they are not strictly exceptions.[222] They may, however, be relevant in the interpretation of substantive investment obligations, as they provide context and a further understanding of the parties' object and purpose in enacting the obligations.[223] For example, the Tribunal in *Al Tamimi v Oman* viewed art 10.10 of the US–Oman FTA as a 'forceful protection of the right of either State Party to adopt, maintain or enforce any measure to ensure that investment is "undertaken in a manner sensitive to environmental concerns"'.[224] This provision was cited, *inter alia*, in finding that in interpreting the minimum standard of treatment 'the Tribunal must be guided by the forceful defence of environmental regulation and protection provided in the express language of the Treaty'.[225]

A third aspect of Australia's recent treaty practice that is relevant to regulatory autonomy for environmental measures are NCM provisions with regard to trade in services and investment obligations. The structure and content of NCM annexes in relevant Australian PTAs is discussed in greater detail in Chapter 3,[226] showing that these provisions and annexes contain little explicit reference to environmental regulation.[227] Nevertheless, some NCM provisions reserve policy space for environmental regulation in Australia in one important respect. As noted in Chapter 3, several Australian PTAs provide that pre-existing measures of regional (that is, state) levels of government are exempt from certain obligations.[228] For example, the ANZCERTA Investment Protocol states that obligations regarding national treatment, MFN treatment, performance requirements, and representation in senior management and boards of directors, do not apply to '[a]ll existing non-conforming measures at the

---

[221] ANZCERTA Investment Protocol art 24.
[222] See Chapter 4 part IIIB.
[223] *Al Tamimi v Oman*, Award, [387].
[224] *Al Tamimi v Oman*, Award, [387].
[225] *Al Tamimi v Oman*, Award, [389].
[226] See Chapter 3 part IIIC.
[227] Although Australia's treaty partners also rarely list environmental regulations within their annexes of NCMs explicitly, we note one example of a State having done so in an Australian PTA. With regard to the national treatment obligation under the ANZCERTA Investment Protocol, New Zealand reserved its right to 'adopt or maintain any measure with respect to the allocation of water rights': ANZCERTA Protocol, annex II (Schedule of New Zealand).
[228] See examples cited in Chapter 3.

regional level of government'.[229] As most environmental legislation and regulation in Australia occurs at the state level, this kind of NCM provision provides a significant safeguard for environmental laws and regulations existing upon the conclusion of the relevant PTA.

IV PTAs AND BITs AS TOOLS TO IMPROVE ENVIRONMENTAL REGULATION?

The previous sections of this chapter have focussed on how obligations contained in Australia's PTAs and BITs could constrain Australia's autonomy to enact and enforce strong levels of environmental protection. The assumption underlying much of this analysis was that these treaties could undermine Australia's goals of environmental protection. In this section, we take a different perspective, examining two ways in which Australia's PTAs and BITs may encourage higher standards of environmental regulation: through the explicit incorporation of environmental standards in PTAs; and through claims and counterclaims in ISDS to enforce environmental standards.

A Environment Chapters in Australia's PTAs

In recent years, a trend has emerged in some PTAs for the incorporation of dedicated chapters relating to the environment. The AUSFTA was the first Australian PTA to include an environment chapter,[230] reflecting US treaty practice since the conclusion of NAFTA in the mid-1990s.[231] In the US, the necessary implementing legislation for AUSFTA was enacted under the so-called 'trade promotion' or 'fast track' authority passed by both houses of Congress in 2002.[232] Fast track authority for the negotiation and conclusion of trade agreements by the US required several objectives to be met,[233] including:

---

229 ANZCERTA Investment Protocol, annex I (Schedule of Australia).

230 AUSFTA ch 19.

231 See JSCOT, *Report 61: The Australia–United States Free Trade Agreement* (June 2004) [17.2]; Lorand Bartels, 'Social Issues: Labour, Environment and Human Rights' in Simon Lester, Bryan Mercurio and Lorand Bartels (eds), *Bilateral and Regional Trade Agreements: Commentary, Analysis and Case Studies* (Cambridge University Press, 2nd ed, 2015) 385.

232 *Bipartisan Trade Promotion Authority Act of 2002*, 19 USC § 3801–3805.

233 *Bipartisan Trade Promotion Authority Act of 2002*, 19 USC § 3802–3803.

> to ensure that trade and environmental policies are mutually supportive and to seek to protect and preserve the environment and enhance the international means of doing so, while optimizing the use of the world's resources;[234] … and
>
> to seek provisions in trade agreements under which parties to those agreements strive to ensure that they do not weaken or reduce the protections afforded in domestic environmental and labor laws as an encouragement for trade;[235]

As these US negotiating objectives reveal, explicitly including environmental considerations within the auspices of international trade agreements tends to have a dual motivation: both promoting stronger environmental protection and preventing environmental regulations from unjustifiably interfering with international trade.[236] In this section, we examine the first of these interactions between trade and the environment, by considering the potential for environment chapters in Australia's PTAs to promote or require more stringent levels of environmental regulation.

Only three of Australia's PTAs contain environment chapters—the AUSFTA, KAFTA and TPP[237]—revealing that Australia is not a strong proponent of including environmental issues within PTAs. Not surprisingly, two of these agreements involve the US as a party, and the inclusion of environmental obligations was a requirement of the relevant trade promotion authority legislation.[238] DFAT representatives appearing before the JSCOT inquiry into AUSFTA explicitly stated that the US had requested an environment chapter and Australia had consented as a 'compromise'.[239] The motivation for including an environment chapter within KAFTA is less clear. The JSCOT report on KAFTA briefly mentions the chapter, in the context of criticism of the chapter as 'weak' and containing only 'low standards'.[240] Given that environment chapters were not included in any other bilateral Australian PTAs negotiated in the

---

234 *Bipartisan Trade Promotion Authority Act of 2002*, 19 USC § 3802(a)(5).

235 *Bipartisan Trade Promotion Authority Act of 2002*, 19 USC § 3802(a)(7).

236 For more detail on these different objectives, see *Bipartisan Trade Promotion Authority Act of 2002*, 19 USC § 3802(11).

237 AUSFTA ch 19; KAFTA ch 18; TPP ch 20.

238 See *Bipartisan Trade Promotion Authority Act of 2002*, 19 USC § 3802–3803; *Bipartisan Congressional Trade Priorities and Accountability Act of 2015*, 19 USC § 4201–4202.

239 JSCOT, *Report 61*, above n 231, [17.2].

240 JSCOT, *Report 142: Free Trade Agreement between the Government of Australia and the Government of the Republic of Korea* (September 2014) [4.52]–[4.53].

same period as the KAFTA (for example, MAFTA, JAEPA and ChAFTA),[241] the inclusion of the chapter may have been instigated by Korea rather than Australia.

The environment chapters in Australia's PTAs vary in their content, but with some commonalities. AUSFTA, KAFTA and the TPP all contain provisions relating to the level of environmental protection each country should maintain. These clauses start with a permissive statement, in which the parties 'recogniz[e] the right of each party to establish its own levels of environmental protection' and to adopt or modify its policies accordingly, while also stating that each party 'shall ensure ... high levels of environmental protection' and 'shall strive' for continual improvement.[242] In addition to requiring the parties to seek high levels of environmental protection, these chapters contain obligations requiring the parties not to lower their environmental standards. For example, TPP art 20.3 on 'General Commitments' includes the following paragraphs:

> 4. No Party shall fail to effectively enforce its environmental laws through a sustained or recurring course of action or inaction in a manner affecting trade or investment between the Parties, after the date of entry into force of this Agreement for that Party.[243]
>
> 6. Without prejudice to paragraph 2, the Parties recognise that it is inappropriate to encourage trade or investment by weakening or reducing the protection afforded in their respective environmental laws. Accordingly, a Party shall not waive or otherwise derogate from, or offer to waive or otherwise derogate from, its environmental laws in a manner that weakens or reduces the protection afforded in those laws in order to encourage trade or investment between the Parties.[244]

---

[241] The JAEPA does include a chapter on 'Energy and Mineral Resources': JAEPA ch 8. However, this chapter is focussed on securing a 'stable supply of energy and mineral resources goods' (art 8.3), and its provisions are primarily focused on topics such as export restrictions (art 8.4) and export licensing procedures (art 8.5). It contains some general requirements regarding 'energy and mineral resource regulatory measures' (art 8.6), which are defined as measures by a relevant energy and mineral regulatory body that 'directly affects the exploration, extraction, processing, production, transportation, distribution or sale of an energy and mineral resource good' (art 8.2(c)). Thus, JAEPA ch 8 appears more concerned with 'strengthen[ing] the relationship between Australia and Japan in these sectors' than with governing environment-related regulatory standards for extractive industries: JSCOT, *Report 144: Agreement between Australia and Japan for an Economic Partnership* (October 2014) [2.52].

[242] AUSFTA art 19.1. See also KAFTA art 18.1; TPP arts 20.3.2, 20.3.3.

[243] TPP art 20.3.4. See also KAFTA art 18.3.1; AUSFTA art 19.2.1.

[244] TPP art 20.3.6. See also KAFTA art 18.3.2; AUSFTA art 19.2.2.

These provisions, which have equivalents in both AUSFTA and KAFTA, are intended to prevent the parties from lowering or derogating from their environmental standards. In this way, they may curtail the regulatory autonomy of the parties in a way that is beneficial for the environment; they suggest that parties should not exercise their autonomy to lower their environmental standards. In response to concerns that these obligations would potentially constrain the actions of the Australian government, a DFAT representative testifying before JSCOT on AUSFTA emphasised that all Australia was required to do under these obligations was enforce its own legislation.[245]

These provisions may appear to require the parties to adopt high levels of environmental protection, but under KAFTA and AUSFTA the environmental provisions are not enforceable through any dispute settlement mechanisms.[246] Instead, cooperative mechanisms have been established to oversee their implementation.[247] Unlike KAFTA and AUSFTA, the TPP provides for dispute settlement in relation to its environment chapter, but before a Party initiates a dispute relating to certain commitments the 'Party shall consider whether it maintains environmental laws that are substantially equivalent in scope to the environmental laws that would be the subject of the dispute'.[248] This qualification applies to disputes regarding the enforcement of environmental laws required under TPP art 20.3.4, and the prohibition on lowering environmental standards as a means of attracting trade or investment under TPP art 20.3.6.

In addition to these provisions relating to domestic environmental law, another common feature of the environment chapters in Australia's PTAs is the incorporation of standards from MEAs. The AUSFTA, KAFTA and the TPP all include a general provision referring to MEAs 'to which [the treaty partners] both are party', reiterating that these agreements 'play an important role, globally and domestically, in protecting the environment and that their respective implementation of these agreements is critical to achieving the environmental objectives of these agreements'.[249] The provisions then to go on to state:

245 JSCOT, *Report 61*, above n 231, [17.2].

246 KAFTA art 18.9; AUSFTA art 19.7.5.

247 KAFTA arts 18.7, 18.8; AUSFTA arts 19.6, 19.7.

248 TPP art 20.23.3.

249 AUSFTA art 19.8. See also KAFTA art 18.2; TPP art 20.4.1.

> Accordingly, the Parties shall continue to seek means to enhance the mutual supportiveness of multilateral environmental agreements to which they are both party and international trade agreements to which they are both party.[250]

The TPP goes further than earlier agreements by incorporating or replicating substantive obligations from a range of MEAs, including the Montreal Protocol, MARPOL, and CITES.[251] These three MEAs are agreements to which all 12 TPP countries are party.[252] Further, the TPP contains a range of novel and specific environmental requirements not found in any other Australian PTA. These include disciplines on fisheries and related subsidies,[253] biodiversity,[254] and the 'transition to a low emissions and resilient economy'.[255] The extent to which these TPP provisions may become models for future Australian PTAs is doubtful, given Australia's apparent reluctance to include environment chapters in such agreements.

B ISDS as a Means of Enforcing Domestic Environmental Law

In Chapter 5, we analysed ISDS as a potential threat to regulatory autonomy. In part II of the present chapter, we examined the more specific question of how the enforcement of investment protections may give rise to liability when States engage in environmental regulation. However, two recent ISDS awards have, in different ways, raised a novel new possibility: that, in certain circumstances, host States or foreign investors could use ISDS to enforce environmental regulation. The first of these cases, *Allard v Barbados*, concerned an investor who unsuccessfully sought compensation for the host State's alleged failure to protect the environment. The second case, *Burlington Resources v Ecuador*, involved a successful counterclaim by a host State against an investor, including an award of damages for environmental harm caused by the company's operations.

In *Allard v Barbados*, the claimant was a Canadian investor who had acquired land in Barbados to establish an eco-tourism business.[256] The

---

250 AUSFTA art 19.8. See also KAFTA art 18.2; TPP art 20.4.2.

251 TPP arts 20.5, 20.6, 20.17.

252 See Howard F Chang, 'The Environment Chapter of the Trans-Pacific Partnership: An Environmental Agreement within a Trade Agreement' (2016) 47(5) *Trends* 16.

253 TPP art 20.16.

254 TPP art 20.13.

255 TPP art 20.15.

256 *Allard v Barbados*, Award, [33].

'Sanctuary' development was situated in wetlands, which included mangrove forests, ponds and lakes connected to the ocean.[257] After working with the government for the necessary approvals, the site was developed and the Sanctuary opened to visitors in 2004.[258] The following year, a nearby treatment plant discharged raw sewage into the Sanctuary wetlands.[259] In 2008, zoning changes to the area around the Sanctuary came into effect, and land previously designated for agricultural and recreational use was redefined as a residential zone and urban corridor.[260] With the exception of an onsite café that continued to operate, the Sanctuary closed in early 2009.[261]

Mr Allard contended that Barbados had failed to accord him FET and full protection and security and had indirectly expropriated his investment.[262] His allegations centred on claims that Barbados had allowed environmental degradation at the site, through improper management of a sluice gate, the sewage discharge, and zoning changes.[263] After conducting an extensive review of the scientific evidence adduced by both parties, the Tribunal concluded that the claimant had not made out his allegations that the environment of the Sanctuary had been degraded, with regard to salinity, water quality, the health of the mangroves, the diversity and health of fish or bird species, or a decline in the crab population.[264] The Tribunal went on to note that even if environmental degradation had occurred, it could not have been attributed to the actions of Barbados.[265] Despite the failure of the claims, the dispute raises the prospect of an investor harmed by environmental degradation (such as a tourism operator) establishing an investment treaty violation. Such a claim might be more likely to succeed if the host State had made specific representations to the investor or otherwise created a legitimate expectation that the State would maintain the quality of the relevant environment.[266]

---

257 *Allard v Barbados*, Award, [34].

258 *Allard v Barbados*, Award, [42].

259 *Allard v Barbados*, Award, [43].

260 *Allard v Barbados*, Award, [45]. This new zoning plan was first announced in 2003.

261 *Allard v Barbados*, Award, [46].

262 *Allard v Barbados*, Award, [51].

263 *Allard v Barbados*, Award, [50], [57].

264 *Allard v Barbados*, Award, [102], [110]–[111], [117], [126], [133], [138].

265 *Allard v Barbados*, Award, [166].

266 Cf *Allard v Barbados*, Award, [208].

Burlington Resources v Ecuador raised the contentious issue of counterclaims in ISDS. Although ISDS cases are brought by foreign investors against host States, counterclaims may arise where the State alleges that the investor has breached an applicable law. For ICSID arbitration, the ICSID Convention allows counterclaims 'arising directly out of the subject-matter of the dispute provided that they are within the scope of the consent of the parties and are otherwise within the jurisdiction of the Centre'.[267] A significant issue to arise in cases looking at counterclaims is whether or not the relevant treaty grants the tribunal jurisdiction over counterclaims,[268] but in the *Burlington Resources* case the parties agreed the Tribunal had such jurisdiction.[269]

In its counterclaim against Burlington Resources, Ecuador claimed that the company owed it damages for harm caused to the environment in the Amazon region by particular oil drilling activities. The parties agreed that these counterclaims were governed by Ecuadorian law, and Ecuador's claim was made specifically on the basis of tort law.[270] The counterclaim was resolved through a highly detailed analysis of the sites at issue and the specific context of each. The Tribunal reviewed an extensive documentary record and conducted a full site visit.[271] In the face of ambiguity in the evidence, the Tribunal applied the precautionary principle, as incorporated in Ecuadorian law.[272]

The Tribunal found that Burlington Resources had caused environmental damage for which it was liable to Ecuador, awarding Ecuador over US$39 million.[273] This outcome is significant in terms of precedent, but even this substantial sum was considerably less than the damages claimed by Ecuador. Ecuador had sought over US$2.5 billion, or in the alternative US$790 million, depending on the Tribunal's finding on applicable law.[274] The decision also coincided with the Tribunal's award on the primary ISDS claim by Burlington Resources, which was awarded nearly US$400 million in compensation from Ecuador.[275] Although this award against Ecuador far exceeds the award on the counterclaims, the

---

267 ICSID Convention art 46.

268 See, eg, *Roussalis v Romania*, Award, [869]–[872].

269 *Burlington Resources v Ecuador*, Decision on Counterclaims, [60]–[61].

270 *Burlington Resources v Ecuador*, Decision on Counterclaims, [72].

271 *Burlington Resources v Ecuador*, Decision on Counterclaims, [58].

272 *Burlington Resources v Ecuador*, Decision on Counterclaims, [343].

273 *Burlington Resources v Ecuador*, Decision on Counterclaims, [1075].

274 *Burlington Resources v Ecuador*, Decision on Counterclaims, [53].

275 *Burlington Resources v Ecuador*, Decision on Reconsideration and Award, [635].

fact that an arbitral tribunal held an investor liable for environmental damage pursuant to an enforceable damages award is a significant development in the investment law field. However, ISDS as a tool for governments to enforce environmental laws and standards is only available where the investor has initiated an arbitration, creating a forum in which the State may seek to bring a counterclaim.

Allard v Barbados and *Burlington Resources v Ecuador* raise different factual contexts and legal issues. They nevertheless represent a possible new trend: the use of ISDS to enforce or improve environmental standards. In future, foreign investors in the Australian tourism industry or other sectors may resort to ISDS if they believe that the Australian government has harmed their investment by failing to maintain environmental standards. Conversely, if an investor consented to jurisdiction over a counterclaim or such jurisdiction could be implied in the relevant IIA, Australia could make a counterclaim regarding an investor's failure to comply with domestic environmental laws. The reality of such possible future developments is reinforced by another recent award in which an ICSID tribunal accepted jurisdiction over counterclaims by Argentina concerning alleged human rights violations of the claimant investors.[276] The tribunal found that the claimants did have human rights-related obligations under international law,[277] but that they had not breached any such obligation.[278]

V CONCLUSIONS

In this chapter we have examined how Australia's PTAs and BITs affect regulatory autonomy in the area of environmental protection. Although no disputes have been raised to date under Australia's PTAs or BITs implicating environmental regulations, the experience of other countries provides useful guidance as to the likely interpretation and application of Australia's obligations in this regard. This conclusion is particularly true of NAFTA ch 11 case law, which offers insights into the application of Australia's investment obligations to environmental regulation.

Much concern has been expressed about the impact of PTAs and BITs on regulatory autonomy with respect to environmental protection, but this chapter suggests that such concerns may be overstated. Many of Australia's more recent PTAs and BITs include general exceptions and other

276 *Urbaser v Argentina*, Award, [1155].
277 *Urbaser v Argentina*, Award, [1199].
278 *Urbaser v Argentina*, Award, [1220]–[1221].

clauses that specifically seek to safeguard policy space for environmental measures. Moreover, the NAFTA experience demonstrates that investment obligations—the aspects of Australian PTAs and BITs that are most likely to influence regulatory space for environmental regulation—are generally interpreted with sufficient understanding of environmental objectives so as to avoid host State liability. The central theme to emerge from the NAFTA cases reviewed in this chapter is that the evidence supporting an environmental measure, and whether or not it was truly enacted for environmental purposes, are often determinative of the outcome of an ISDS dispute. However, whether the majority decision in *Bilcon* is an outlier or will establish a lower threshold for finding a breach of the FET standard in future remains unclear.

In this chapter we have also considered the potential for Australia's PTA and BIT obligations to encourage higher standards of environmental protection. Although Australia is not a proponent of environment chapters in economic agreements, such chapters appear in three Australian PTAs, including a range of provisions relating to the maintenance and enforcement of environmental protections. ISDS cases involving host State failure to maintain the environment or counterclaims against investors for environmental damage seem unlikely to become commonplace. Nevertheless, the possibility of such disputes demonstrates the complexity and multifaceted nature of the relationship between environmental regulation and Australia's PTAs and BITs.

We argue throughout this book that sovereign autonomy to enact measures for legitimate public welfare purposes is a good that Australia needs to safeguard. Yet we also note that regulatory autonomy is not an absolute good. A host State could invoke a legitimate regulatory objective to defend a protectionist measure, or exercise regulatory autonomy to lower environmental standards in order to attract foreign investment. Australia's PTAs and BITs need to be understood in light of these risks, which provide a more complete picture of how these agreements interact with domestic environmental measures.

7. Balancing the Benefits of Liberalisation with Policy Space

I INTRODUCTION

On 7 February 2017, the Foreign Affairs, Defence and Trade References Committee of the Australian Senate issued its report on the TPP. That report captures many of the current challenges faced by international economic law in Australia and internationally, in the specific context of PTAs. The committee detected 'in submissions to the current inquiry' 'wide acceptance of Australia's approach to trade as a vehicle for economic growth, job creation and rising living standards'.[1] The committee nevertheless expressed a range of concerns about the TPP and—particularly as regards procedure—PTAs more generally:

> Both in Australia and overseas, a key aspect of community opposition to recent trade agreements has evolved from a lack of transparency and consultation in treaty-making processes, the extension of trade agreements into broader policy areas beyond tariffs and customs arrangements and a perceived 'democratic deficit' in the treaty-making process.[2]

The JSCOT reports and hearings on Australia's PTAs, particularly in more recent years, evidence a clear understanding on the part of DFAT and the Australian government of the tensions involved in these agreements, which have resulted in continual efforts to draft provisions that will protect Australia's regulatory sovereignty while also allowing access to the economic and welfare gains associated with liberalisation of international trade and investment. These efforts extend across the areas we have examined in this book: intellectual property, trade in services, investment protection, and environmental regulation. However, the outcomes in a given PTA are naturally subject to significant influence by the

[1] Senate Foreign Affairs, Defence and Trade References Committee, *Proposed Trans-Pacific Partnership (TPP) Agreement* (7 February 2017) ('*Senate TPP 2017 Report*') [5.13].

[2] Ibid [5.14].

negotiating demands of the relevant treaty partners. The position of the US, in particular, is apparent not only in the AUSFTA and the TPP but in other Australian treaties with States that themselves have PTAs with the US, such as Chile (ACIFTA) and the Republic of Korea (KAFTA). Overlaid on the substantive negotiation with the treaty partner is the need, highlighted in the Senate Committee report just mentioned, to take into account the interests of Australian industry and other stakeholders.

In this concluding chapter, we draw together in part II the main conclusions from Chapters 2 to 6 to make a general assessment, in the fields examined, of the level of regulatory autonomy preserved by Australia's current PTAs and BITs, particularly with respect to key policy areas such as public health and environmental protection. In addition to making recommendations within each of these fields, we offer in part III some suggestions and reflections on the interaction between these fields and the relationships between different agreements. In part IV, we return to the recommendations of the Productivity Commission and various parliamentary committees on treaty processes in Australia.

We conclude that Australia has made demonstrable efforts to preserve Australia's regulatory autonomy under international economic law. However, Australia could still make a number of improvements to its current PTAs and BITs, by attempting to reduce inconsistency between them (especially in relation to investment standards and ISDS), continuing to pursue balanced and comprehensive negotiations in all sectors with a view towards progressive liberalisation (especially in relation to trade in services), and resisting any further ratcheting up of intellectual property protections in PTAs with the US or other countries. These suggestions are intended to help achieve a better balance for Australia between increasing economic liberalisation and maintaining regulatory flexibility.

II REBALANCING STANDARDS: INTELLECTUAL PROPERTY, SERVICES, INVESTMENT, ENVIRONMENT

Treaty negotiators need to pursue a delicate balance in the IP and services chapters of PTAs and in the investment provisions in PTAs and BITs. In relation to intellectual property, the most relevant balancing to date has been less about using IP provisions to liberalise trade (as they tend to go well beyond matters of trade liberalisation) and more about the balancing that occurs with intellectual property laws in general: providing sufficient IP protection to reward creators and thereby incentivise innovation, but not so much IP protection that consumers and users lose affordable access to the relevant materials. As explained in Chapter 2, reviews such as reports in 2010 and 2016 by the Productivity Commission typically conclude that Australia's IP protections in areas such as copyright and patent provide too much IP protection and that these tendencies stem in part from Australia's PTAs, and in particular the AUSFTA (which would have been reinforced by the TPP as signed in 2016). If the heightened IP protections under the AUSFTA cannot be rolled back, Australia can at least attempt not to agree to further increases in IP protections in bilateral and regional contexts in the absence of robust evidence supporting such increases and their sustainability in the future. Australia should also resist incorporating AUSFTA-type provisions in PTAs that do not include the US, even if the relevant PTA partner has itself agreed to such provisions with the US, but especially if it has not.

In the services context, Australia has used a variety of tools to preserve policy space in its PTAs, such as general exceptions, lists of exempt NCMs, and carve-outs from the scope of the services chapter. At the same time, Australia has attempted to encourage progressive liberalisation of trade in services, for example through the use of negative lists in most of its modern PTAs and through its leadership role in the TiSA negotiations. This kind of leadership, including through an openness to gradual reductions in the limitations on its own services commitments, will be important if services trade is to reach its full potential in contributing to the global economy. TiSA may be particularly significant in this regard given the failure of the TPP as originally envisaged and the inapplicability of various GATS approaches (such as the outdated GATS classification of services) to the digital age.[3]

As regards investment, treaty negotiators in Australia and elsewhere when first signing BITs may not have been fully cognisant of the need for a balance between investment protection and safeguards for regulatory autonomy, as we noted in Chapter 1 with respect to Poulsen's work. Hence:

---

[3] See, eg, Lee Tuthill and Martin Roy, 'GATS Classification Issues for Information and Communication Technology Services' in Mira Burri and Thomas Cottier (eds), *Trade Governance in the Digital Age* (Cambridge University Press, 2012) 157.

> IIAs traditionally do not aim at a balance between investor rights and the state's right and obligation to regulate economic activities. Instead, investment agreements predominantly seek to protect the investor.[4]

However, the vagueness and breadth of core investment obligations as sometimes interpreted by investment treaty arbitrators has become clearer in more recent years, along with the potential intrusiveness of ISDS as an enforcement mechanism. Furthermore, developed and developing countries now understand that they may be involved in ISDS claims either as a host State respondent or with one of their investors as a claimant. This fact increases the importance of drafting balanced treaty obligations in the investment context as well as undertaking reforms to enhance the legitimacy of ISDS as a means of international dispute settlement. While Australia has gradually added to the safeguards for policy space in its PTAs (in relation to both investment standards and ISDS), progress has sometimes wavered in particular agreements, and Australia could play a more forceful role in international efforts, for example to improve transparency through the Mauritius Convention.

Some of the major ways in which the international investment regime is being reconceptualised include through the EU proposal for a multilateral investment court as noted in Chapter 5 and through the introduction of possibilities for counterclaims by host States against claimant investors as discussed in Chapter 6 in the context of investors' compliance with environmental regulation. Moreover, as we suggest in Chapter 6, PTAs provide a new opportunity to establish international standards in areas such as environmental protection and labour rights,[5] as a means of improving domestic regulation in Australia and other countries and harmonisation at the international level. Miles argues:

> [R]eluctance within the international investment community to take adequate account of the public interest and to integrate principles from international environmental and human rights law is out of step with current trends in public international law.[6]

---

[4] Markus Krajewski, 'Balancing Legal Certainty with Regulatory Flexibility' in Aik Hoe Lim and Bart De Meester (eds), *WTO, Domestic Regulation and Services Trade: Putting Principles into Practice* (Cambridge University Press, 2014) 79, 86.

[5] See, eg, Joo-Cheong Tham and Keith D Ewing, 'Labour Clauses in the TPP and TTIP: A Comparison Without a Difference?' (2016) 17(2) *Melbourne Journal of International Law* 369.

[6] Kate Miles, 'Reconceptualising International Investment Law: Bringing the Public Interest into Private Business' in Meredith Kolsky Lewis and Susy

The IMF, World Bank and WTO have also jointly noted the connections between trade agreements, economic growth, labour and the environment, indicating that conformity with 'core ILO labor standards can be an important tool for development', while commitments to international labour and environmental standards can also 'reassure domestic workers that international competition is evenhanded' and that 'they are not disadvantaged by strong environmental standards'.[7] Australia has an opportunity to play a stronger role in these various novel developments and hence in reshaping international economic law to achieve more sustainable economic and broader welfare benefits.

III THE INTERACTION OF SECTORS, OBJECTIVES AND AGREEMENTS

This book highlights the importance of understanding the many ways in which different chapters and provisions within a PTA interact. For example, we noted in Chapter 2 how the characterisation of trade mark rights in the IP chapter may affect whether a challenged measure constitutes expropriation for the purposes of the investment chapter. We explained in Chapter 3 how lists of NCMs are often common to services and investment chapters, and how PTA negotiators must consider how to address the potential overlap between obligations regarding mode 3 services delivery (via commercial presence) in the services chapter and protections for foreign investment in the investment chapter. The increasing inclusion of investment obligations in PTAs itself increases the interactions between international trade law and international investment law, which may have implications for treaty interpretation. For example, the interpretation of a particular investment obligation is affected by the context and object and purpose of the PTA pursuant to VCLT art 31(1), whereas the same obligation in a BIT may have a narrower context, object and purpose (for example as reflected in the treaty's preamble). Some of these possible differences and interactions are yet to be fully examined in scholarly work or investment treaty arbitration.

We have identified the potential for both intellectual property and investment provisions to affect public health regulation, and for various PTA provisions—including those regarding trade in goods, trade in

---

Frankel (eds), *International Economic Law and National Autonomy* (Cambridge University Press, 2010) 295, 296.

7 IMF, World Bank and WTO, *Making Trade an Engine of Growth for All: The Case for Trade and for Policies to Facilitate Adjustment* (2017) [67].

services, TBT, SPS measures and investment—to impact domestic measures to protect the environment. General exceptions are also often contained in a separate chapter towards the end of a PTA, but may apply to obligations located throughout the agreement. Even within a given PTA chapter, close examination of a substantive obligation, such as in the services or investment context, is incomplete without an assessment of any relevant carve-outs, exemptions or NCMs. An investment obligation that is not subject to an ISDS mechanism may raise different (often fewer) concerns for public policy than one enforceable through ISDS, and an environmental obligation may not have the effect intended if it is not enforceable through a dispute settlement mechanism.

The proliferation of PTAs and BITs also complicates connections with existing and future bilateral, regional and multilateral treaties and institutions in international economic law. According to the WTO, as of 2017, 270 regional trade agreements are in force, based on notifications from WTO Members.[8] UNCTAD reports 2369 BITs in force in addition to 303 treaties with investment provisions, and 767 known treaty-based investor–State arbitrations.[9] As we explained in Chapters 2 and 3, questions arise as to the WTO-compatibility of each PTA and BIT, particularly PTAs containing TRIPS-plus provisions (which may be contrary to the WTO's TRIPS Agreement) or GATS-minus provisions (which may fall outside the exception for economic integration agreements in GATS art XIV), or BITs not listed as MFN exemptions under the relevant WTO Member's GATS schedule. The overlaps we discussed in Chapters 4 and 5 between ChAFTA and the Australia–China BIT are common, creating complex questions of treaty law that are rarely resolved clearly by the relevant VCLT rules or the provisions in the PTA/BIT in question.[10]

These intersections demonstrate the importance of both scrutinising individual treaties in international economic law in a cross-disciplinary

---

[8] *WTO: Regional Trade Agreements* (as of 10 March 2017) <https://www.wto.org/english/tratop_e/region_e/region_e.htm> (last visited 7 April 2017). See also Rohini Acharya (ed), *Regional Trade Agreements and the Multilateral Trading System* (WTO and Cambridge University Press, 2016).

[9] UNCTAD, *Investment Policy Hub* <http://investmentpolicyhub.unctad.org> (last visited 7 April 2017).

[10] See, eg, Christina Binder, 'An International Law Approach to Interactions between Preferential Trade and Investment Agreements and the BIT World' in Rainer Hofmann, Stephan Schill and Christian J Tams (eds), *Preferential Trade and Investment Agreements: From Recalibration to Reintegration* (Nomos, 2013) 71.

manner and maintaining awareness of pre-existing and proposed treaties in understanding the impact in context of a treaty under negotiation. This more holistic analysis is crucial for all countries with multiple PTAs and BITs and indeed for all 164 WTO Members, which participate in that multilateral forum while also engaging in one or more PTAs.[11] The powerful MFN rule is limited to some extent in investment chapters of most Australian PTAs, for example, through an NCM listing excluding its application to pre-existing international agreements. However, its potential use to invoke stronger protections in subsequent agreements must not be discounted. Moreover, the ability of multinational enterprises to restructure their assets and subsidiaries to take advantage of a more favourable (older-style) BIT means that countries cannot afford to seek improvement in future treaties without regard to their vulnerability as host States under treaties that may be decades old and lack more modern nuances (although, as we have discussed, such an attempt by Philip Morris against Australia failed).

As Australia and other countries learn about the practical implications of PTAs and BITs, for example as awards in ISDS disputes mount and international negotiations post-TPP/Trump continue, they naturally seek to improve standards and treaty approaches in negotiations designed to increase access to new markets around the world. However, in order to address risks posed by existing treaties, governments may need to pay greater attention to more mundane matters mentioned in this book such as: engaging in regular systematic internal reviews and comparisons of treaty obligations; investing political and diplomatic capital in joint reviews with treaty partners to agree amendments in order to modernise older treaties (such as in SAFTA in 2016) or fill gaps even in newer treaties (such as in ChAFTA in 2017); and considering more unusual approaches such as joint interpretations (similar to the NAFTA Free Trade Commission's interpretation of the FET standard) or mutual termination (for example, in conjunction with newer negotiations, as Australia did in terminating its BIT with Chile upon entry into force of ACIFTA or as it planned BIT terminations with Peru, Mexico and Viet Nam upon entry into force of the TPP).[12]

---

[11] WTO, 'WTO Members Reach Milestone on Regional Trade Agreements', News Item (2 June 2016).

[12] See, eg, David Gaukrodger, 'The Legal Framework Applicable to Joint Interpretive Agreements of Investment Treaties', OECD Working Papers on International Investment 2016/01 (OECD, 2016); Kathryn Gordon and Joachim Pohl, 'Investment Treaties Over Time—Treaty Practice and Interpretation in a

IV TREATY PROCESSES: NEGOTIATION, CONCLUSION, ENTRY INTO FORCE

Improving treaty processes in Australia and other countries provides one means of facing the continuing challenges to international trade law and international investment law and addressing the constant need for balancing economic and non-economic objectives in PTAs and BITs. The 2017 report on the TPP of the Senate Foreign Affairs, Defence and Trade References Committee discussed earlier in this chapter, the 2015 report 'Blind Agreement' of the same committee discussed in Chapter 1, and the 2010 report of the Productivity Commission on 'Bilateral and Regional Trade Agreements' also discussed in Chapter 1 all highlighted Australia's treaty processes as problematic, especially in connection with economic agreements such as PTAs.

The Australian treaty-making process presents a democratic challenge for all treaties. In the TPP negotiations, 'the Australian Government consulted 485 people and organisations'.[13] However, meetings or events in which government representatives address stakeholders while negotiations are continuing are limited by the inability to disclose drafts of treaty texts being negotiated. Only once treaty negotiations are complete is the agreed treaty text released to the public and subject to formal parliamentary scrutiny through the JSCOT (although, in the case of the TPP as mentioned below, some limited access for parliamentarians was provided before the negotiations were completed). By that stage, particularly when treaties have more than two parties, re-opening negotiations to amend the text is politically impracticable. Public input from industry and other stakeholders at this point therefore cannot have a meaningful impact. For example, JSCOT's report on the AUSFTA[14] was tabled in Parliament on 23 June 2004, and the Australian legislation to implement that treaty[15] was passed in the House of Representatives one day later, with no real opportunity for debate.[16]

Changing World', OECD Working Papers on International Investment 2015/02 (OECD, 2015).

13 JSCOT, *Report 165: Trans-Pacific Partnership Agreement* (November 2016) ('*Report 165*') [5.6].

14 JSCOT, *Report 61: The Australia–United States Free Trade Agreement* (June 2004).

15 *US Free Trade Agreement Implementation Act 2004* (Cth).

16 See Ann Capling, 'Can the Democratic Deficit in Treaty-Making Be Overcome? Parliament and the Australia United States Free Trade Agreement' in

This process poses particular problems for PTAs and BITs because of their economic impact and the potential for ISDS claims to impose heavy burdens on the public purse, or to create excessive regulatory chill. Concerns have arisen in respect of various Australian PTAs regarding processes such as the selection of PTA partners, the non-transparency of negotiations, and the sequencing of parliamentary scrutiny only after negotiations have already been completed. Attention to these various processes in the creation of Australia's PTAs may assist in improving outcomes, for example through a better understanding of the implications of PTAs for non-economic policies, which would allow for better treaty drafting.

One of the recommendations for improved treaty processes made in the reports identified above and in submissions to the underlying inquiries, as well as in evidence to JSCOT on particular PTAs, is to have an independent body such as the Productivity Commission undertake a detailed cost-benefit analysis of a proposed PTA before or soon after the commencement of negotiations,[17] rather than only a national interest analysis prepared by DFAT at the end of negotiations.[18] In addition to this eminently sensible suggestion, we suggest that further resources be put towards undertaking a detailed and independent economic analysis of the impact of Australia's existing PTAs and BITs on the Australian economy, and a legal analysis of the kind contained in this book in relation to the impact on Australian regulations and regulatory autonomy, extended to all relevant PTA matters and in consultation with government. Even for older and crucial agreements such as the AUSFTA, only limited evidence exists of the impact on Australia, and the evidence that does exist does not tend to show a clear positive impact,[19] leading to uncertainty as to whether Australia should continue pursuing such

---

Hilary Charlesworth et al (eds), *The Fluid State: International Law and National Legal Systems* (Federation Press, 2005) 57.

[17] *Report 165*, Recommendation 2; Parliament of Australia, Senate Foreign Affairs, Defence and Trade References Committee, *Blind Agreement: Reforming Australia's Treaty-Making Process* (June 2015) ('*Blind Agreement*') [5.31]; Productivity Commission, Australian Government, *Bilateral and Regional Trade Agreements: Productivity Commission Research Report* (November 2010) Recommendation 5(b).

[18] *Senate 2017 TPP Report*, [4.18], [5.10]; *Report 65*, [5.57].

[19] See, eg, Shiro Armstrong, 'Economic Impact of the *Australia-US FTA*' (2015) 69 *Australian Journal of International Affairs* 513, 520; Julian Alston et al, 'Supply and Demand for Commodity Components: Implications of Free Trade versus the AUSFTA for the US Dairy Industry' (2006) 50 *Australian Journal of Agricultural and Resource Economics* 131.

agreements. Such a study could also attempt to assess the effects of the inclusion of ISDS mechanisms in Australia's PTAs on the country's incoming and outgoing investment.

When it comes to the negotiations themselves, tensions arise as regards the level of disclosure of relevant information, parties' proposals and treaty texts to the public or relevant stakeholders. DFAT's position is that confidentiality is required and a 'standard treaty negotiation procedure'.[20] However, complete transparency and sharing of treaty text and negotiating positions with the Australian public may not be possible, for example due to agreements with negotiating partners, a desire not to reveal prematurely Australia's positions to those partners, and additional delays associated with ongoing public feedback and submissions. Furthermore, revealing details of negotiations that will involve the loss of protection for particular industries, which may have greater opportunities and incentives for participation than other stakeholders and civil society, may create a risk of such commercial interests derailing or capturing the process.

In the TPP, Australia released model letters by which the TPP parties agreed to keep material confidential until four years after the TPP's entry into force or, in the absence of entry into force, four years after the last round of negotiations.[21] Unusually for Australia, members of federal Parliament were eventually granted access to the treaty text under strict conditions,[22] and the agreement was publicly released before signature (first on 5 November 2015 subject to 'legal scrub', and then on 26 January 2016, in advance of signature on 4 February 2016). These should be standard practices rather than ad hoc concessions.[23] Nevertheless, the secrecy of negotiations aggravated community concerns about the content and effect of the TPP. The inevitable leaking of texts online also risked misunderstandings about the context, currency and status of the text. JSCOT's inquiry did not commence until February 2016: well after the point at which input could affect the negotiating outcomes.

Questions of transparency in the course of treaty negotiations apply equally to any democratic society, and approaches adopted in other countries are instructive for Australia in considering improvements to the current Australian systems. Commentators have noted similar problems

---

20 JSCOT, *Report 165*, [5.13].

21 DFAT, *Release of Confidentiality Letter* (25 February 2014).

22 See, eg, Lenore Taylor, 'Australian MPs Allowed to See Top-Secret Trade Deal Text But Can't Reveal Contents for Four Years' (2 June 2015) *The Guardian* (online).

23 See *Blind Agreement*, [3.60].

in many countries, for example with New Zealand's processes in the conclusion of the TPP.[24] The 'cleared advisor' mechanism used in the US allows industry and some NGO representatives access to negotiating documents subject to confidentiality obligations.[25] In the TPP negotiation, such access fell within the terms of the parties' confidentiality arrangement, which allowed access by 'persons outside government who participate in that government's domestic consultation process and who have a need to review or be advised of the information in these documents'.[26]

DFAT has noted that such a process would have resource implications with respect to the necessary security clearances.[27] However, the much more limited access of Australian businesses and civil society representatives to confidential negotiating documents including treaty texts puts Australian industry and other stakeholders at a disadvantage vis-à-vis their US counterparts. The introduction of a similar process in Australia should be seriously considered, as recommended by JSCOT and the Senate Foreign Affairs, Defence and Trade References Committee.[28] This approach would allow more detailed analysis by relevant experts and various interest groups, who could provide further insights into the implications of particular provisions and proposals and associated adjustment costs and mechanisms. As access would be restricted to a limited number of individuals with appropriate security clearance, the integrity and confidentiality of the negotiations in terms of broader public knowledge need not be compromised.

Another important recommendation to enhance the transparency and legitimacy of Australia's negotiation of IIAs is to introduce a model Australian BIT setting out the country's preferred provisions, as recommended by the Senate Committee.[29] Model BITs are used by several countries around the world[30] and in recent years have provided a

---

24 See Amokura Kawharu, 'Process, Politics and the Politics of Process: The Trans-Pacific Partnership in New Zealand' (2016) 17(2) *Melbourne Journal of International Law* 286.

25 See, eg, 'USTR Allows Cleared Advisers to View TPP Texts as of July 9' (10 July 2015) *Inside US Trade* (online).

26 DFAT, *Release of Confidentiality Letter* (25 February 2014).

27 Evidence to JSCOT, Canberra (7 November 2016) 20 (Elizabeth Ward, Chief Negotiator, TPP, DFAT).

28 *Report 165*, [5.28]; *Senate 2017 TPP Report*, [5.10]; *Blind Agreement*, [4.72].

29 *Blind Agreement*, [5.35].

30 See Chester Brown (ed), *Commentaries on Selected Model Investment Treaties* (Oxford University Press, 2013).

mechanism for presenting aspirational or best practice provisions (for example, the India Model BIT (2015) and the Norway Model BIT (2015)). One benefit of a publicly available Model BIT for Australia would be that it could be developed with public consultation and input, avoiding the problems of confidentiality associated with a live treaty negotiation. A Model BIT could also provide a means for Australia to show leadership in the field of international investment law and to play a more active role in building consensus on optimal treaty practices and drafting.

V CONCLUSION

> [W]e stand at the threshold of a new generation of investment treaties that will be more balanced and will safeguard a modicum of policy space, thus marking a break with the grand old tradition of asymmetric investment protection.[31]

Overall, Titi's quoted 2014 prediction of increased policy space in IIAs is borne out by this book's survey of Australian IIAs. However, the gradual improvement of substantive investment protections and procedural aspects of dispute settlement (especially in ISDS) does not alleviate concerns about Australia's regulatory autonomy in the investment context because of the many old-style BITs that remain in force for Australia and the persisting inconsistencies even among investment chapters in Australia's PTAs. These gaps and contradictions create risks for Australia in view of the MFN obligation and multinationals' disconnection from national boundaries, potentially allowing them to seek the protection of any IIA they wish.

Our examination of allowances for environmental regulation in international investment law confirms, through a review of relevant NAFTA ch 11 case law, that investment treaty tribunals are generally able to distinguish legitimate environmental measures from discrimination or disguised protectionism. The more recent case of *Clayton and Bilcon* does raise concerns about tribunals' intrusiveness into host State determinations and domestic processes in the environmental context, but the strong dissent in that case may assist in reducing its power as a precedent in international investment law. These cases also show tribunals' ability to grant appropriate levels of deference to host States even where the

---

[31] Aikaterini Titi, *The Right to Regulate in International Investment Law* (Hart, Nomos, Dike, 2014) 303.

relevant treaty obligation does not contain clarifications or exceptions. The use of such tools may provide further protection, although their interaction and implications will require further examination in the future, as jurisprudence and treaty law continue to develop.

In contrast to the increasing flexibilities seen in Australia's investment protections, intellectual property provisions in Australia's PTAs have tended to become stronger over time, particularly after the AUSFTA, without corresponding evidence or benefits. Here the 'policy space' in question relates to Australia's regulation of IP, which in turn may have fundamental impacts on access to affordable medicines and other public health objectives. In the services context, movement towards greater levels of liberalisation in terms of breadth and depth of commitments has been much slower, while Australia and other countries have routinely ensured that they may regulate in particular sectors through the use of various treaty mechanisms, such as NCMs, general exceptions, and softening of positive obligations. Such reservations may help conclude services PTAs including the ambitious TiSA, but too much policy space may lead to too little liberalisation, undermining the potentially major economic benefits from liberalising services trade.

Several of these suggestions apply equally to other countries, who also face the eternal balancing exercise required in PTAs and BITs between the economic and broader social benefits of liberalisation (which are predicated on restrictions on government action) and the need to avoid constraining governments too much in their pursuit of non-economic policy objectives such as promoting public health or the natural environment. In our view, international economic law offers a forceful tool for achieving national and international welfare gains, as well as the capacity to identify legitimate policy objectives and associated regulations and to minimise any adverse impacts of such regulations on the goals of liberalisation. The optimal treaty language and analytical approaches for carrying out this dual role may be elusive, variable over time, and dependent on context. However, useful ideas and provisions can sometimes be identified in PTAs, model treaties, WTO and NAFTA case law, or submissions to government. Pursuing a more complete understanding of PTAs and BITs in the wider international context and a deeper appreciation of the insights available from industry, academia, the legal profession and civil society may assist in ensuring that the next generation of these agreements is better than the last.

Bibliography

BOOKS

Acharya, Rohini (ed), *Regional Trade Agreements and the Multilateral Trading System* (WTO and Cambridge University Press, 2016).

Alexander, Kern and Mads Andenas, *The World Trade Organization and Trade in Services* (Martinus Nijhoff, 2008).

Alvarez, José E et al (eds), *The Evolving International Investment Regime* (Oxford University Press, 2011).

Andre, Pamela, Stephen Payton and John Mills (eds), *The Negotiation of the Australia New Zealand Closer Economic Relations Trade Agreement 1983* (DFAT and New Zealand Ministry of Foreign Affairs and Trade, 2003).

Bartels, Lorand and Federico Ortino (eds), *Regional Trade Agreements and the WTO Legal System* (Oxford University Press, 2006).

Bernasconi-Osterwalder, Nathalie, John Howard Jackson and Edith Brown Weiss (eds), *Reconciling Environment and Trade* (Martinus Nijhoff Publishers/Koninklijke Brill, 2nd ed, 2008).

Bhagwati, Jagdish and Robert Hudec (eds), *Fair Trade and Harmonization: Prerequisites for Free Trade?* (MIT Press, 1996).

Bonnitcha, Jonathan, *Substantive Protection under Investment Treaties: A Legal and Economic Analysis* (Cambridge University Press, 2014).

Bown, Chad and Joost Pauwelyn (eds), *The Law, Economics and Politics of Retaliation in WTO Dispute Settlement* (Cambridge University Press, 2010).

Brack, Duncan, *Trade and Environment: Conflict or Compatibility* (Taylor and Francis, 2013).

Broude, Tomer, Marc L Busch and Amelia Porges (eds), *The Politics of International Economic Law* (Cambridge University Press, 2011).

Brown, Chester (ed), *Commentaries on Selected Model Investment Treaties* (Oxford University Press, 2013).

Brown, Chester and Kate Miles (eds), *Evolution in Investment Treaty Law and Arbitration* (Cambridge University Press, 2011).

Bücheler, Gebhard, *Proportionality in Investor–State Arbitration* (Oxford University Press, 2015).

Buckley, Ross P, Vai Io Lo and Laurence Boulle (eds), *Challenges to Multilateral Trade: the Impact of Bilateral, Preferential and Regional Agreements* (Kluwer Law International, 2008).

Burri, Mira and Thomas Cottier (eds), *Trade Governance in the Digital Age* (Cambridge University Press, 2012).

Capling, Ann, *All the Way with the USA: Australia, the US and Free Trade* (University of New South Wales Press, 2005).

Capling, Ann, *Australia and the Global Trade System: From Havana to Seattle* (Cambridge University Press, 2001).

Chaisse, Julien and Tsai-yu Lin (eds), *International Economic Law and Governance: Essays in Honour of Mitsuo Matsushita* (Oxford University Press, 2016).

Chapman, Simon and Becky Freeman, *Removing the Emperor's Clothes: Australia and Tobacco Plain Packaging* (Sydney University Press, 2014).

Charlesworth, Hilary et al (eds), *The Fluid State: International Law and National Legal Systems* (Federation Press, 2005).

Charlesworth, Hilary et al, *No Country is an Island: Australia and International Law* (UNSW Press, 2006).

Chauffour, Jean-Pierre and Jean-Christophe Maur (eds), *Preferential Trade Agreement Policies for Development: A Handbook* (World Bank, 2011).

Crawford, Emily and Donald R Rothwell (eds), *International Law in Australia* (Thomson Lawbook Co, 3rd ed, 2017).

Crawford, John, Nancy Anderson and Margery GN Morris, *Australian Trade Policy, 1942–1966: A Documentary History* (Australian National University Press, 1968).

Daunton, Martin, Amrita Narlikar and Robert Stern, *The Oxford Handbook on the World Trade Organization* (Oxford University Press, 2012).

de Mestral, Armand and Céline Lévesque (eds), *Improving International Investment Agreements* (Routledge, 2014).

de Schutter, Olivier, et al (eds), *Foreign Direct Investment and Human Development* (Routledge, 2013).

Dee, Moreen, *Friendship and Co-operation: The 1976 Basic Treaty between Australia and Japan* (DFAT, 2006).

Dolzer, Rudolf and Christoph Schreuer, *Principles of International Investment Law* (Oxford University Press, 2nd ed, 2012).

Drahos, Peter and Susy Frankel (eds), *Indigenous Peoples' Innovation: Intellectual Property Pathways to Development* (Australian National University E Press, 2012).

Dreyfuss, Rochelle C and Justine Pila (eds), *The Oxford Handbook of Intellectual Property Law* (forthcoming, Oxford University Press).

Epps, Tracey and Michael J Trebilcock (eds), *Research Handbook on the WTO and Technical Barriers to Trade* (Edward Elgar, 2013).

Evenett, Simon and Bernard Hoekman (eds), *Economic Development and Multilateral Trade Cooperation* (World Bank, Palgrave Macmillan, 2006).

Henckels, Caroline, *Proportionality and Deference in Investor–State Arbitration: Balancing Investment Protection and Regulatory Autonomy* (Cambridge University Press, 2015).

Hepburn, Jarrod, *Domestic Law in International Investment Arbitration* (Oxford University Press, 2017).

Hofmann, Rainer, Stephan Schill and Christian J Tams (eds), *Preferential Trade and Investment Agreements: From Recalibration to Reintegration* (Nomos, 2013).

Jackson, John, *The World Trading System: Law and Policy of International Economic Relations* (2nd ed, MIT Press, 1997).

Kelsey, Jane (ed), *No Ordinary Deal: Unmasking the Trans-Pacific Partnership Free Trade Agreement* (Allen & Unwin, 2010).

Kinnear, Meg N et al (eds), *Building International Investment Law: The First 50 Years of ICSID* (Kluwer Law International, 2015).

Kulick, Andreas (ed), *Reassertion of Control over the Investment Treaty Regime* (Cambridge University Press, 2016).

Lester, Simon and Bryan Mercurio (eds), *Bilateral and Regional Trade Agreements: Case Studies* (Cambridge University Press, 2009).

Lester, Simon, Bryan Mercurio and Lorand Bartels (eds), *Bilateral and Regional Trade Agreements: Commentary and Analysis* (Cambridge University Press, 2nd ed, 2015).

Lewis, Meredith Kolsky and Susy Frankel (eds), *International Economic Law and National Autonomy* (Cambridge University Press, 2010).

Lim, Aik Hoe and Bart De Meester (eds), *WTO, Domestic Regulation and Services Trade: Putting Principles into Practice* (Cambridge University Press, 2014).

Lim, Chin and Bryan Mercurio (eds), *International Economic Law After the Global Crisis: A Tale of Fragmented Disciplines* (Cambridge University Press, 2015).

Lippoldt, Douglas (ed), *Policy Priorities for International Trade and Jobs* (OECD, 2012).

Macrory, Patrick, Michael Plummer and Arthur Appleton (eds), *The World Trade Organization* (Springer, 2005).

Mattoo, Aaditya, Robert M Stern and Gianni Zanini (eds), *A Handbook of International Trade in Services* (Oxford University Press, 2008).

Meredith, David and Barrie Dyster, *Australia in the Global Economy: Continuity and Change* (Cambridge University Press, 2nd ed, 2012).

Miles, Kate, *The Origins of International Investment Law: Empire, Environment and the Safeguarding of Capital* (Cambridge University Press, 2013).
Miles, Kate (ed), *Research Handbook on Environment and Investment Law* (Edward Elgar, forthcoming).
Mitchell, Andrew D, *Challenges and Prospects for the WTO* (Cameron May, 2005).
Mitchell, Andrew D, *Legal Principles in WTO Disputes* (Cambridge University Press, 2008).
Mitchell, Andrew D, David Heaton and Caroline Henckels, *Non-Discrimination and the Role of Regulatory Purpose in International Trade and Investment Law* (Edward Elgar, 2016).
Molinuevo, Martín, *Protecting Investment in Services: Investor–State Arbitration versus WTO Dispute Settlement* (Wolters Kluwer, 2012).
Natens, Bregt, *Regulatory Autonomy and International Trade in Services* (Edward Elgar, 2016).
Newcombe, Andrew and Lluís Paradell, *Law and Practice of Investment Treaties: Standards of Treatment* (Kluwer Law International, 2009).
Okediji, Ruth L (ed), *Copyright Law in an Age of Limitations and Exceptions* (Cambridge University Press, 2017).
Picker, Colin, Heng Wang and Weihuan Zhou (eds), *The China Australia Free Trade Agreement: A 21st Century Model* (Hart, forthcoming).
Pogge, Thomas, Matthew Rimmer and Kim Rubenstein (eds), *Incentives for Global Public Health: Patent Law and Access to Medicines* (Cambridge University Press, 2010).
Pomfret, Richard WT (ed), *Australia's Trade Policies* (Oxford University Press, 1995).
Poulsen, Lauge N Skovgaard, *Bounded Rationality and Economic Diplomacy: The Politics of Investment Treaties in Developing Countries* (Cambridge University Press, 2015).
Ricketson, Sam and Jane C Ginsburg, *International Copyright and Neighbouring Rights: The Berne Convention and Beyond* (Cambridge University Press, 2nd ed, 2006).
Rimmer, Matthew (ed), *Indigenous Intellectual Property: A Handbook of Contemporary Research* (Edward Elgar, 2015).
Roberts, Anthea et al (eds), *Comparative International Law* (Oxford University Press, forthcoming).
Sauvant, Karl and Lisa Sachs (eds), *The Effect of Treaties on Foreign Direct Investment* (Oxford University Press, 2009).
Sauvé, Pierre and Martin Roy (eds), *Research Handbook on Trade in Services* (Edward Elgar, 2016).
Sauvé, Pierre and Anirudh Shingal (eds), *The Preferential Liberalization of Trade in Services: Comparative Regionalism* (Edward Elgar, 2014).

Schill, Stephan W (ed), *International Investment Law and Comparative Public Law* (Oxford University Press, 2010).

Schill, Stephan W, *The Multilateralization of International Investment Law* (Cambridge University Press, 2009).

Scollay, Robert, Christopher C Findlay and Uwe Kaufmann, *Australia New Zealand Closer Economic Relations Trade Agreement (ANZCERTA) and Regional Integration* (Institute of Southeast Asian Studies, 2011).

Snape, Richard H, Jan Adams and David Morgan, *Regional Trade Agreements: Implications and Options for Australia* (Australian Government Printing Service, 1993).

Snape, Richard H, Lisa Gropp and Tas Luttrell, *Australian Trade Policy, 1965–1997: A Documentary History* (Allen & Unwin, 1998).

Taubman, Antony, Hannu Wager and Jayashree Watal (eds), *A Handbook on the WTO TRIPS Agreement* (Cambridge University Press, 2012).

Titi, Aikaterini, *The Right to Regulate in International Investment Law* (Hart, Nomos, Dike, 2014).

Trakman, Leon E and Nicola W Ranieri (eds), *Regionalism in International Investment Law* (Oxford University Press, 2013).

Viñuales, Jorge, *Foreign Investment and the Environment in International Law* (Cambridge University Press, 2012).

Voon, Tania, *Cultural Products in the World Trade Organization* (Cambridge University Press, 2007).

Voon, Tania (ed), *Trade Liberalisation and International Co-operation: A Legal Analysis of the Trans-Pacific Partnership Agreement* (Edward Elgar, 2013).

Voon, Tania, Andrew D Mitchell and Jonathan Liberman (eds), *Regulating Tobacco, Alcohol and Unhealthy Foods: The Legal Issues* (Routledge, 2014).

Voon, Tania, Andrew Mitchell and Jonathan Liberman with Glyn Ayres (eds), *Public Health and Plain Packaging of Cigarettes: Legal Issues* (Edward Elgar, 2012).

Vranes, Erich, *Trade and the Environment: Fundamental Issues in International Law, WTO Law and Legal Theory* (Oxford University Press, 2009).

Waibel, Michael et al (eds), *The Backlash against Investment Arbitration* (Kluwer Law International, 2010).

Watal, Jayashree, *Intellectual Property Rights in the WTO and Developing Countries* (Kluwer Law International, 2001).

Weiss, Linda, Elizabeth Thurbon and John A Mathews, *How to Kill a Country: Australia's Devastating Trade Deal with the United States* (Allen & Unwin, 2004).

Wolfrum, Rüdiger, Peter-Tobias Stoll and Clemens Feinäugle (eds), *WTO—Trade in Services* (Martinus Nijhoff, 2008).

JOURNAL ARTICLES

Abbott, Frederick, 'A New Dominant Trade Species Emerges: Is Bilateralism a Threat?' (2007) 10 *Journal of International Economic Law* 571.

Abbott, Frederick, 'The WTO Medicines Decision: World Pharmaceutical Trade and the Protection of Public Health' (2005) 99(2) *American Journal of International Law* 317.

Adlung, Rudolf, 'Export Policies and the General Agreement on Trade in Services' (2015) 18(3) *Journal of International Economic Law* 487.

Adlung, Rudolf, 'International Rules Governing Foreign Direct Investment in Services: Investment Treaties versus the GATS' (2016) 17 *Journal of World Investment & Trade* 47.

Adlung, Rudolf, 'The GATS Negotiations: Implications for Health and Social Services' (2003) 38(3) *Intereconomics* 147.

Adlung, Rudolf, 'The Trade in Services Agreement (TISA) and Its Compatibility with GATS: An Assessment Based on Current Evidence' (2015) 14(4) *World Trade Review* 617.

Adlung, Rudolf, 'Trade in Healthcare and Health Insurance Services: WTO/GATS as a Supporting Actor (?)' (2010) 45(4) *Intereconomics* 227.

Adlung, Rudolf and Hamid Mamdouh, 'How to Design Trade Agreements in Services: Top Down or Bottom–Up?' (2014) 48(2) *Journal of World Trade* 191.

Adlung, Rudolf and Sébastien Miroudot, 'Poison in the Wine? Tracing GATS-Minus Commitments in Regional Trade Agreements' (2012) 46(5) *Journal of World Trade* 1045.

Allee, Todd and Andrew Lugg, 'Who Wrote the Rules for the Trans-Pacific Partnership?' (July–September 2016) *Research and Politics* 1.

Alschner, Wolfgang and Dmitriy Skougarevskiy, 'The New Gold Standard? Empirically Situating the Trans-Pacific Partnership in the Investment Treaty Universe' (2016) 17 *Journal of World Investment and Trade* 339.

Alston, Julian et al, 'Supply and Demand for Commodity Components: Implications of Free Trade versus the AUSFTA for the US Dairy Industry' (2006) 50 *Australian Journal of Agricultural and Resource Economics* 131.

Anderson, Kym, 'Contributions of the GATT/WTO to Global Economic Welfare: Empirical Evidence' (2016) 30(1) *Journal of Economic Surveys* 56.

Anderson, Kym and Will Martin, 'Agricultural Trade Reform and the Doha Development Agenda' (2005) 28(9) *The World Economy* 1301.

Armstrong, Shrio, 'Economic Impact of the *Australia-US FTA*' (2015) 69 *Australian Journal of International Affairs* 513.

Bonnitcha, Jonathan, 'Foreign Investment, Development and Governance: What International Investment Law Can Learn from the Empirical Literature on Investment' (2016) 7 *Journal of International Dispute Settlement* 31.

Burnett, R, 'Australia's Bilateral Trade Treaties—Developments 1972–1975' (1974) 6 *Australian Yearbook of International Law* 153.

Burrell, Robert and Kimberlee Weatherall, 'Exporting Controversy? Reactions to the Copyright Provisions of the US–Australia Free Trade Agreement: Lessons for US Trade Policy' [2008] *University of Illinois Journal of Law, Technology & Policy* 259.

Campbell, Christopher, 'House of Cards: The Relevance of Legitimate Expectations under Fair and Equitable Treatment Provisions in Investment Treaty Law' (2013) 30(4) *Journal of International Arbitration* 361.

Chaisse, Julien, 'Exploring the Confines of International Investment and Domestic Health Protections—Is a General Exceptions Clause a Forced Perspective?' (2013) 39 *American Journal of Law and Medicine* 332.

Chang, Howard F, 'The Environment Chapter of the Trans-Pacific Partnership: An Environmental Agreement within a Trade Agreement' (2016) 47(5) *Trends* 16.

Charnovitz, Steve, 'Environment and Health under WTO Dispute Settlement' (1998) 32 *International Lawyer* 901.

Chi, Manjiao, '"Exhaustible Natural Resource" in WTO Law: GATT Article XX (g) Disputes and Their Implications' (2014) 48 *Journal of World Trade* 939.

Correa, Carlos and Jorge E Viñuales, 'Intellectual Property Rights as Protected Investments: How Open are the Gates?' (2016) 19 *Journal of International Economic Law* 91.

Davison, Mark and Patrick Emerton, 'Rights, Privileges, Legitimate Interests, and Justifiability: Article 20 of TRIPS and Plain Packaging of Tobacco' (2014) 29(3) *American University International Law Review* 505.

Dolzer, Rudolf, 'Fair and Equitable Treatment: Today's Contours' (2013) 12 *Santa Clara Journal of International Law* 7.

Flynn, Sean M et al, 'The US Proposal for an Intellectual Property Chapter in the Trans-Pacific Partnership Agreement' (2012) 28(1) *American University International Law Review* 105.

Garnett, Richard, 'National Court Intervention in Arbitration as an Investment Treaty Claim' (2011) 60 *International and Comparative Law Quarterly* 485.

Gathii, James and Cynthia Ho, 'Regime Shifting of IP Law Making and Enforcement from the WTO to the International Investment Regime' (2017) 18 *Minnesota Journal of Law, Science and Technology* (forthcoming).

Gleeson, Deborah and Sharon Friel, 'Emerging Threats to Public Health from Regional Trade Agreements' (2013) 381 *The Lancet* 1507.

Grosse Ruse-Khan, Henning, 'Time for a Paradigm Shift? Exploring Maximum Standards in International Intellectual Property Protection' (2009) 1(1) *Journal of Trade, Law and Development* 56.

Grosse Ruse-Khan, Henning, 'Challenging Compliance with International Intellectual Property Norms in Investor–State Dispute Settlement' (2016) 19 *Journal of International Economic Law* 241.

Hafner-Burton, Emilie M and David G Victor, 'Secrecy in International Investment Arbitration: An Empirical Analysis' (2016) 7 *Journal of International Dispute Settlement* 161.

Henckels, Caroline, 'Protecting Regulatory Autonomy through Greater Precision in Investment Treaties: The TPP, CETA, and TTIP' (2016) 19(1) *Journal of International Economic Law* 27.

Hirono, Katherine, Deborah Gleeson and Becky Freeman, 'To What Extent Does a Tobacco Carve-Out Protect Public Health in the Trans-Pacific Partnership Agreement?' (2016) 26(2) *Public Health Research & Practice* e2621622.

Howse, Robert, 'The World Trade Organization 20 Years On: Global Governance by Judiciary' (2016) 27(1) *European Journal of International Law* 9.

Hudec, Robert E, 'GATT/WTO Constraints on National Regulation: Requiem for an "Aims and Effects" Test' (1998) 32 *The International Lawyer* 619.

Islam, M Rafiqul, 'The Australian Policy and Practice of Preferential Bilateral Trade: A Benign or Malign Alternative to the WTO Multilateral Free Trading System?' (2003) 2(2) *Journal of International Trade Law & Policy* 43.

Kawharu, Amokura, 'Process, Politics and the Politics of Process: The *Trans-Pacific Partnership* in New Zealand' (2016) 17(2) *Melbourne Journal of International Law* 286.

Kohona, Palitha TB, 'Investment Protection Agreements: An Australian Perspective' (1987) 21 *Journal of World Trade* 79.

Kotlowitz, Danny and Tania Voon, 'Telecommunications Services in the Trans-Pacific Partnership: Will the Mobile Roaming Provisions Benefit Tourists and Traders?' (2016) 17(2) *Melbourne Journal of International Law* 404.

Krajewski, Markus, 'Public Services and Trade Liberalization: Mapping the Legal Framework' (2003) 6(2) *Journal of International Economic Law* 341.

Kurtz, Jürgen, 'Australia's Rejection of Investor–State Arbitration: Causation, Omission and Implication' (2012) 27(1) *ICSID Review* 65.

Kurtz, Jürgen and Luke Nottage, 'Investment Treaty Arbitration "Down Under": Policy and Politics in Australia' (2015) 30(2) *ICSID Review* 465.

Lang, Andrew, 'The GATS and Regulatory Autonomy: A Case Study of Social Regulation of the Water Industry' (2004) 7(4) *Journal of International Economic Law* 801.

Liberman, Jonathan, 'Plainly Constitutional: The Upholding of Plain Tobacco Packaging by the High Court of Australia' (2013) 39 *American Journal of Law & Medicine* 361.

Liddell, Kathleen and Michael Waibel, 'Fair and Equitable Treatment and Judicial Patent Decisions' (2016) 19 *Journal of International Economic Law* 145.

Mattoo, Aaditya and Arvind Subramanian, 'Regulatory Autonomy and Multilateral Disciplines: The Dilemma and a Possible Resolution' (1998) 1 *Journal of International Economic Law* 303.

Mercurio, Bryan, 'The Impact of the Australia–United States Free Trade Agreement on the Provision of Health Services in Australia' (2005) 26 *Whittier Law Review* 1051.

Mercurio, Bryan, 'Should Australia Continue Negotiating Bilateral Free Trade Agreements? A Practical Analysis' (2004) 27 *University of New South Wales Law Journal* 667.

Mitchell, Andrew D, 'Proportionality and Remedies in WTO Disputes' (2006) 17(5) *European Journal of International Law* 985.

Mitchell, Andrew D and James Munro, 'Someone Else's Deal: Interpreting International Investment Agreements in the Light of Third-Party Agreements' (2017) *European Journal of International Law* (forthcoming).

Mitchell, Andrew D and Constantine Salonidis, 'David's Sling: Cross-Agreement Retaliation in International Trade Disputes' (2011) 45(2) *Journal of World Trade* 457.

Mitchell, Andrew D and Tania Voon, 'Face Off: Assessing WTO Challenges to Australia's Scheme for Plain Tobacco Packaging' (2011) 22(3) *Public Law Review* 218.

Mitchell, Andrew D and Tania Voon, 'Patents and Public Health in the WTO, FTAs and Beyond: Tension and Conflict in International Law' (2009) 43(3) *Journal of World Trade* 571.

Mitchell, Andrew D and Tania Voon, 'Someone to Watch Over Me: The Use of FOI Requests by the Tobacco Industry' (2014) 22 *Australian Journal of Administrative Law* 18.

Mitchell, Andrew D, Tania Voon and Devon Whittle, 'Public Health and the Trans-Pacific Partnership Agreement' (2015) 5(2) *Asian Journal of International Law* 279.

Moir, Hazel VJ, 'The Patent Price of Market Access in the AUSFTA' (2015) 69(5) *Australian Journal of International Affairs* 559.

Nottage, Luke, 'Do Many of Australia's Bilateral Treaties Really Not Provide Full Advance Consent to Investor-State Arbitration? Analysis of Planet Mining v Indonesia and Regional Implications' (2015) 12(1) *Transnational Dispute Management* (online).

Nottage, Luke, 'The TPP Investment Chapter and Investor–State Arbitration in Asia and Oceania: Assessing Prospects for Ratification' (2016) 17(2) *Melbourne Journal of International Law* 313.

O'Brien, Paula et al, 'Marginalising Health Information: Implications of the Trans-Pacific Partnership for Alcohol Labelling' (2017) *Melbourne University Law Review* (forthcoming).

Paparinskis, Martins, 'MFN Clauses and International Dispute Settlement: Moving beyond *Maffezini* and *Plama*?' (2011) 26(2) *ICSID Review* 14.

Pomfret, Richard, 'Trade Policy in Canada and Australia in the Twentieth Century' (2000) 40 *Australian Economic History Review* 114.

Puig, Sergio, 'Tobacco Litigation in International Courts' (2016) 57(2) *Harvard International Law Journal* 383.

Ricketson, Sam, 'Plain Packaging Legislation for Tobacco Products and Trade Marks in the High Court of Australia' (2013) 3(3) *Queen Mary Journal of Intellectual Property* 224.

Rimmer, Matthew, 'The *Trans-Pacific Partnership*: Intellectual Property, Public Health, and Access to Essential Medicines' (2017) 29 *Intellectual Property Journal* 275.

Roberts, Anthea, 'State-to-State Investment Treaty Arbitration: A Hybrid Theory of Interdependent Rights and Shared Interpretive Authority' (2014) 55(1) *Harvard International Law Journal* 1.

Santana, Roy and Lee Ann Jackson, 'Identifying Non-Tariff Barriers: Evolution of Multilateral Instruments and Evidence from the Disputes (1948–2011)' (2012) 11(3) *World Trade Review* 462.

Schill, Stephan W, 'Editorial: The Mauritius Convention on Transparency' (2015) 16(2) *Journal of World Investment & Trade* 201.

Schultz, Thomas and Cédric Dupont, 'Investment Arbitration: Promoting the Rule of Law or Over-Empowering Investors? A Quantitative Empirical Study' (2014) 25 *European Journal of International Law* 1147.

Schwebel, Stephen M, 'In Defense of Bilateral Investment Treaties' (2015) 31 *Arbitration International* 181.

Sheargold, Elizabeth and Andrew D Mitchell, 'The TPP and Good Regulatory Practices: An Opportunity for Regulatory Coherence to Promote Regulatory Autonomy?' (2016) 15 *World Trade Review* 587.

Shirlow, Esmé, 'Dawn of a New Era? The UNCITRAL Rules and UN Convention on Transparency in Treaty-Based Investor–State Arbitration' (2016) 31(3) *ICSID Review* 622.

Steger, Debra P, 'Institutions for Regulatory Cooperation in "New Generation" Economic and Trade Agreements' (2012) 39 *Legal Issues of Economic Integration* 109.

Šturma, Pavel, 'Goodbye, *Maffezini*? On the Recent Developments of Most-Favoured-Nation Clause Interpretation in International Investment Law' (2016) 15 *Law and Practice of International Courts and Tribunals* 81.

Sykes, Alan, 'Comparative Advantage and the Normative Economics of International Trade Policy' (1998) 1 *Journal of International Economic Law* 49.

Tham, Joo-Cheong and Keith D Ewing, 'Labour Clauses in the TPP and TTIP: A Comparison Without a Difference?' (2016) 17(2) *Melbourne Journal of International Law* 369.

Trakman, Leon, 'Investor State Arbitration or Local Courts: Will Australia Set a New Trend?' (2012) 46(1) *Journal of World Trade* 83.

Van den Bossche, Peter, 'Looking for Proportionality in WTO Law' (2008) 35(3) *Legal Issues of Economic Integration* 283.

Vandevelde, Kenneth J, 'A Brief History of International Investment Agreements' (2005) 12 *UC Davis Journal of International Law & Policy* 157.

Voon, Tania, 'Acquisition of Intellectual Property Rights: Australia's Plain Tobacco Packaging Dispute' [2013] 2 *European Intellectual Property Review* 113.

Voon, Tania, 'Discrimination in International Mobile Roaming Regulation: Implications of WTO Law' (2013) 16(1) *Journal of International Economic Law* 91.

Voon, Tania, Introductory Note to WTO Appellate Body Report, *China – Measures Affecting Trading Rights and Distribution Services for Certain Publications and Audiovisual Entertainment Products* (2010) 49(2) *International Legal Materials* 516.

Voon, Tania, 'Philip Morris v Uruguay: Implications for Public Health' (2017) 18(2) *Journal of World Investment and Trade* 320.
Voon, Tania and Andrew D Mitchell, 'Denunciation, Termination and Survival: The Interplay of Treaty Law and International Investment Law' (2016) 31(2) *ICSID Review* 413.
Voon, Tania, Andrew D Mitchell and James Munro, 'Legal Responses to Corporate Manoeuvring in International Investment Arbitration' (2014) 5(1) *Journal of International Dispute Settlement* 41.
Voon, Tania, Andrew D Mitchell and James Munro, 'Parting Ways: The Impact of Mutual Termination of Investment Treaties on Investor Rights' (2014) *ICSID Review* 451.
Waelde, Thomas and Abba Kolo, 'Environmental Regulation, Investment Protection and "Regulatory Taking" in International Law' (2001) 50 *International and Comparative Law Quarterly* 811.
Wagner, Markus, 'Regulatory Space in International Trade Law and International Investment Law' (2014) 36(1) *University of Pennsylvania Journal of International Law* 1.
Wakefield, Melanie et al, 'Australian Adult Smokers' Responses to Plain Packaging with Larger Graphic Health Warnings 1 Year After Implementation: Results from a National Cross-Sectional Tracking Survey' (2015) 24 *Tobacco Control* ii17.
Weatherall, Kimberlee, 'Intellectual Property in the TPP: Not "The New TRIPS"' (2016) 17(2) *Melbourne Journal of International Law* 257.
Weatherall, Kimberlee, 'Of Copyright Bureaucracies and Incoherence: Stepping Back from Australia's Recent Copyright Reforms' (2007) 31 *Melbourne University Law Review* 967.
Webb Yackee, Jason, 'Do BITs "Work"? Empirical Evidence from France' (2016) 7 *Journal of International Dispute Settlement* 55.
Wehland, Hanno, 'The Regulation of Parallel Proceedings in Investor-State Disputes' (2016) 31(3) *ICSID Review* 576.

Index